Torah Through a Zionist Vision

Avraham Feder

Torah Through a Zionist Vision

Avraham Feder

Volume II

VA-YIKRA
BA-MIDBAR
DEVARIM

Layout: Marzel A.S. — Jerusalem
Cover Design: S. Kim Glassman

ISBN: 978-965-229-442-5
Edition 1 3 5 7 9 8 6 4 2

Gefen Publishing House Ltd.
6 Hatzvi St.
Jerusalem 94386, Israel
972-2-538-0247
orders@gefenpublishing.com

Gefen Books
600 Broadway
Lynbrook, NY 11563, USA
1-516-593-1234
orders@gefenpublishing.com

www.israelbooks.com

Printed in Israel

Send for our free catalogue

Contents

Volume II

VA-YIKRA

BA-MIDBAR

DEVARIM

* * * * * *

Volume I

BEREISHIT

SHEMOT

Dedicated to
Leona Posner Feder z"l
and
Tzipora Ne'eman Feder

and to
Bracha, Nehama and Tzvika, David and Maayan
and
Lielle, Batya, Etai, Hila, Lianna

ACKNOWLEDGEMENTS

In putting my signature to a book of this kind, I offer its contents as a summary of my learning and thinking over many years with many teachers and students of Torah. It has been said that a student has truly made a bit of learning his own when he has forgotten from whom he learned it. Where I could attribute insights to specific teachers of Torah, I have done so by name. Where I have spoken in my own name, it is with full appreciation for the opportunities I have had to absorb Torah and general studies from many others whom I do not name but whom I thank for their wisdom and imaginative insight.

In my years in the rabbinate as teacher, preacher, and fellow student I have been privileged to serve two congregations — Beth Tikvah in Toronto, Canada, and Moreshet Yisrael in Jerusalem, Israel. Over the years the members of these two communities have given me a forum for the vital interchange and cultivation of ideas so indispensable for producing serious discussions of Torah.

The MAOR Foundation has provided the material sustenance that has allowed me to write this book. Many individuals have supported this effort. I single out for particular thanks Philip and Nancy Turk, Shelly and Sharon Wiggins, Ben and Malka Hayeems, Morris Justein, and Joe Dubrofsky. Isaac Silverstein and Norman Stern have offered their friendship and eager support in seeing through this project as well as others over the years.

I owe a debt of gratitude to my long-term friend, colleague, and fellow student Dr. Lewis Rosen for his ongoing advice, critical suggestions, and shared visions for Torah and the Zionist future. Arlene Kaplinsky was of invaluable help in typing the manuscript and guiding me through the new world of word processing.

I appreciate the efforts of Mr. Ilan Greenfield and the staff of Gefen Publishing House in producing the book, with special thanks to Fern Seckbach for her excellent editing of the manuscript.

VA-YIKRA

Socio-Religious Dreams

In discussing aspects of the *akeidah*, we mentioned earlier a prayer recited by the *mohel* immediately following the circumcision: "Creator of the universe! May it be Your gracious will to regard and accept the performance of circumcision *as if I had offered up this infant before Your gracious throne.* And may You, in Your abundant mercy, through Your holy angels, give a pure and holy heart to this child who has just now been circumcised in honor of Your great Name. May his heart be fully open to comprehend Your holy Torah, so that he may learn and teach it, keep and fulfill it" (*Hamadrikh*, Goldin).

The infant Jewish child is thus brought into the covenant of Abraham. Furthermore, a tradition will develop of starting a Jewish child's education in Torah not with the Book of Bereishit but rather with the Book of Va-Yikra — that book which includes in great detail laws relating to sacrifices. What possible reason can there be for this pedagogic tradition except to recognize that in certain respects a Jewish child is indeed a sacrificial offering. He is to be like Isaac who was offered up and then saved so that he could go on living — not dying — but living as a *korban* ("sacrifice"), living *al kiddush Hashem* ("for the sanctification and glorification of God"). Like Isaac, like Isaac's father Abraham, and like Isaac's son Jacob-Israel, the Jewish child is meant to walk through the world with wholehearted dedication to God's covenantal purposes.

What will it mean for a child of Israel to live as a *korban*? There will be two deeply personal elements in the answer: a *need* and a *goal.*

The Psalmist says (84:2–3): "How lovely are Your Tabernacles, O Lord of hosts: My soul yearns, yes, even pines for the courts of the Lord; my heart and my flesh sing for joy unto the living God." A *korban* will be one who yearns, who *needs* to live as if he would not be embarrassed to be in God's court all the time. Rabbi Mendl of Kotzk will tell the story of the hunter — a latter-day descendant of Nimrod — whom the prophet Elijah meets in the wilderness. Elijah asks the hunter why he is living there without the Torah and without the *mitzvot.* The hunter defends himself: "I never could find the gate that leads to the presence of God." Elijah responds: "You were certainly not born a hunter; so from whom did you learn to follow this calling, the call of the hunter?" "My *need* has taught me," answers the hunter. The prophet responds: "And in your losing your way to God, if the *need* to find Him again were felt by you to be as great, do you think your *need* would fail to show you the way to Him?"

The Jewish child, in other words, is meant to learn to sense a Presence in his life beyond his immediate human environment. He is to grow into an adult who will feel the *need* to deepen his sensitivity to the Presence. He will see himself standing and walking and living before the Presence — being in God's court, as it were, all the time. This child will thereby seek to learn, to teach, to keep, and to do Torah.

It follows that the *goal* in life of this Jewish child will be to climb Jacob-Israel's ladder in order to rise above what otherwise might be his inclination to imitate Nimrod or Nimrod's "disciple" Esau. He will thereby come closer to achieving God's creative purposes in the world. He will envision the world as meant to be: God's sanctified court where His Kingship is recognized and actualized in the lives of all who enter it — individuals and nations, Jew and Gentile. For like the newly born child brought into the covenant of Abraham by way of circumcision, Israel the newborn nation will be ushered into the struggle to live a collective life as a *korban*, appreciating and actualizing God's covenant in the Promised Land.

The legislative picture that Moses draws in Leviticus for Israelite society in the Promised Land is dream-like in its aspirations. Is it utopian? The question does not call for an answer. For the Children of Israel are at the stage of embarkation into the Wilderness. They are not yet at the threshold of the Promised Land. The legislation proposed in Deuteronomy will have a greater immediacy as Israel is being prepared forty years later for imminent settlement in Canaan. Here in Leviticus instructions for ritual practice and ethical behavior are certainly meant to be taken seriously. The penumbra of holiness which suffuses the book, however, appears to be as prayerful in its aspiration as practical in its possible implementation. For the legislation is so severe in its intolerance of spiritual and moral weakness that it is difficult to imagine a group of fallible human beings conforming to every last letter of its law. This "Book of Holiness," as the Book of Va-Yikra is called, argues for the possibility of a nation, no less, building a society in the Land of Israel that can serve as a sacrificial tribute to the Creator. A utopian wish?

The covenant will argue an emphatic "No!" The question, however, will stand throughout the length and breadth of Jewish history.

Va-Yikra ויקרא

"*Vayikra el Moshe*" ("God called to Moses") is a stentorian phrase. The Rabbis are curious as to why at this time God has to issue a special call to Moses. After all, God has been speaking intimately with Moses ever since the "Burning Bush" episode. An ongoing dialogue between God and Moses has pervaded the trials in Egypt, the victory at the Sea of Reeds, the Revelation at Sinai, and the building of the Tabernacle. Why not just continue the dialogue? Why a special call?

Exploring the subtleties of the biblical text, the Rabbis suggest the following: When God first appears to Moses from the "Burning Bush," Moses hides his face, and so God calls to him, "I am sending you to Pharaoh to lead My people out of slavery; for if you do not redeem them, there is no one else." At the Sea of Reeds with the Egyptians stampeding down on the Israelites, Moses stands aside, and so God calls to him, "Lift up your rod and split the sea; for if you, Moses, do not take this action, no one else will." At the foot of Mount Sinai, with a newly emancipated people waiting for spiritual direction, Moses again stands aside, and so God calls to him, "Come up to Me; for if you do not come up, do not expect anyone else to." And finally in the Tent of Meeting, Moses also stands aside. As if in summary, after all Moses' experience in leadership — particularly of late — he still hesitates. And so God calls to him impatiently: "*Ad matai ata mashpil atzmekha*" ("How long will you keep lowering yourself")? And God continues in a tone of disquiet, if not rancor: "How long will you negate yourself in modesty. The hour, the sublime, glorious hour of worship awaits *you*, Moses, to show the way."

Moses is being scolded by God for his excessive "humility." In his defense, it must be pointed out that accompanying Moses' "humility" has always been his sacred availability. If he is destined to be described as the most humble of men, it is hardly because he has been afraid of wrestling with men and even with God. Yet in these earlier stages of his vocation as a redeemer, his way has been characterized by a degree of reticence. Moses can claim that God is the ultimate all-powerful all-knowing Redeemer; therefore, Moses must wait for the call — yes, each time. But this time the call is to supervise sacrificial worship. Moses should now serve as an example for all of Israel to witness that he is eager to legislate for such sacrificial worship. Any hesitation at this point may be misconstrued as weakened faith.

Ritual Sacrifice and *Derekh Eretz*

The Torah assumes such worship to be a universal need. At the outset of God's instructions, *every man* is being acknowledged — not just the Israelites: *"Adam ki yakriv...."* ("Every man who comes to offer a sacrifice....") There is felt to be a universal need to be close to God, to thank God for blessings, to atone for sin and wrongdoing by offering oneself or of oneself. The resonant phrase *"adam ki yakriv"* reverberates back to the primeval Adam, the Adam who in the Garden-of-Eden paradise had chosen to hide from his creaturely-creative destiny. Adam, first Adam, had sought to escape from responding to God and His *ayeka* ("where are you")! As a result, this first Adam had been driven out of the Garden of Eden.

Ever since, Adam the First has been striving to get back into Eden but finds that he cannot. "The fiery ever-turning sword guards the way to the Tree of Life" and prevents him from re-entering. Ever since Adam the First has been expelled from a situation of perfect harmony in the Garden, Man, Adam's descendant, has been trying to re-enter the harmonious bubble, to at least come close, to come near again to the Presence. Is the fiery ever-turning sword to prevent him from ever coming near? Has the disappointment with Adam the First been so crushing and the ensuing punishment so final?

Throughout the biblical account beginning with Abel and continuing with Noah and the Patriarchs, worship with animal sacrifices has been the norm. Whatever the perceived purpose of the individual offering — atonement for sin, thanksgiving, propitiation — the worshiper feels himself coming close to God, slipping through, as it were, the lethal thrusts of the "fiery ever-turning sword." Ancient Man, including the Children of Israel, will be supremely confident of the efficaciousness of this mode of worship.

But the prophets of Israel will take aim at it when the social atmosphere within Israel will be perceived by them to be totally out of tune with God's covenantal demands. Micah will excoriate his brethren: "With what shall I approach the Lord, with burnt offerings? Will the Lord be pleased with thousands of rams, with myriads of streams of oil? It has been told you, O Man, what is good, and what God wants of you — only to do justly, to love mercy, and to walk humbly with your God." Micah's protest is the most eloquent of many prophetic protests against the very idea among corrupt members of society that their animal sacrifices can compensate for their evil deeds. Sacrificial offerings may have spiritual value — but only if they are offered by ethical human beings.

The prophets will be asserting the primacy of *"derekh eretz"* — defined here as ethically appropriate behavior for this world. Their emphasis will be the inspiration for the teaching in *Va-Yikra Rabbah* that *derekh eretz* preceded the Torah by twenty-six generations — namely, that the bedrock precondition for any accompanying or subsequent religious behavior must be ethical intention and deed. The verse quoted in Genesis 3:24 describes the "fiery ever-turning sword" and its effectiveness *"lishmor et derekh etz ha-hayyim"* ("guarding the way to the Tree of Life"). The word *derekh* is understood to refer to *derekh eretz*; the phrase "tree of life" written *afterwards* is Torah. Thus, *derekh eretz* meaning ethically appropriate behavior *preceded* Torah. This means that *derekh eretz* is a constant check-and-balance on whatever a given generation of religious believers determines is a Torah-endorsed way of life.

Once it is clear that the individual worshiper cannot neglect his responsibilities to *derekh eretz*, i.e., fulfilling the injunction to love the "other" as himself, then he may consider himself worthy to approach the threshold of an intimate spiritual relationship with God. Animal sacrifices may be the mode of worship at a given historic juncture. Verbal prayers will be the mode at another. But Adam in general and the Israelite in particular are making the attempt to experience intensively "loving God with all one's heart, one's soul, one's everything." The critical question for any descendant of Adam the First — in particular this Israelite Adam — as he brings his "all" to God in a pristine moment of worship, is whether he, Adam, is "fully there." And being "fully there" demands of him an integrated heart and soul, i.e., his "all," to dedicate to *derekh eretz*. In short, his best ethical self must "be there."

The eternally probing question *"ayeka"* is addressed to Man seeking to elicit from Man an honest realization of the injunction "you shall love the

Lord your God..." The very question expresses God's search for greater intimacy with Man. The search for Man's response is an offer to him to come closer to God. But the question insists that Man must offer his own true ethical self. It can't be him with a mask hiding ill treatment of other human beings. Before daring to bring one's *korban* to God, before daring to bring oneself to God, Man must face himself, and see himself as only he knows. Would he dare to have the hauteur to say that he wishes to see God's "face" when he may as yet not have had the courage to stare at his own face "unmasked," i.e., his own behavior, his own *derekh eretz*? Jewish tradition will require that mirrors be covered in a house of mourning. Faced with thoughts of mortality and having to "meet one's Maker," one should not have to see what one looks like if there is a shade of pretense in what one looks like.

Indeed in a house of mourning, during a period of heightened vulnerability, one cannot and should not be forced into looking at oneself. But to expect that one can come before God in any but a self-consciously honest mode is to mock oneself, not to mention God Almighty. The worshiper will need, therefore, to cultivate a self-critical capacity that will cut through his self-deceptions. To conceive of oneself as *religious* will be to program oneself for regular *ethical* self-criticism. "*Adam ki yakriv*" ("Man who brings an offering") is the *nefesh ki teheta* ("the person who sins"). And the person who has sinned and is seeking *kapparah* (atonement) must begin by admitting to the sin, an admission that entails rigorous self-criticism. Within this new "circumcised" nation of Israel, no one is to be exempt from the mandatory ethical self-criticism — obliged are not only the *amei-ha-aretz* (the common people), but the leadership as well, from the *nasi* (the tribal prince) to the *kohen gadol* (the high priest).

Authenticity and the Sacrifices

Man offering a sacrifice to God, an authentic offering to God, cannot offer, as Rashi says, anything stolen. Just as Adam the First who owned everything in his world could not but offer what belonged to him, so must his descendants. These Israelite descendants — in contrast to Adam the First — will not own very much. But whatever they present it must be theirs. The Maharal will point out that all the commandments are included under the general heading of "you shall not covet." All sins, in other words, ultimately find their root in the one basic sin of covetousness, i.e., looking with envy at others, at others' possessions, at others' traits and attributes. Instead of studying ourselves, investigating, and investing in ourselves to "enrich" ourselves spiritually and ethically, we covet what is not ours. In so doing we thereby breach the trust put in us by the Creator, not to mention the significant other human being or beings whom we contemplate "violating." Would we then dare to concoct a ritual which would countenance our coming before God with that which is not ours!

We may return to the model of Moses who is the "humblest among all men" and who is, as indicated earlier, a paragon of self-effacement at the most critical moments in his life and in the early life of Israel. He is at the same time a wholly authentic person, if by authenticity we point to his wholly fulfilled self in answering the questions "*ayeka*" and "*ey Hevel ahikha.*"

Authenticity in biblical terms is not achieved unless there is an ongoing critical dialogue between one's ego and God the Ultimate Super-Ego. The in-depth examination of self untrammeled by external objective standards and demands may be the path of atheistic thinkers like Nietzche and Sartre. They will claim that out of this self-examination a subject will emerge who is free, totally responsible to self and for self, and who will thereby be authentic. For Moses and Abraham and Jacob-Israel, however, there is always God as Ultimate Super-Ego, God as constant forceful Presence, challenging the self to reconsider, to re-examine, to re-appraise. If left to one's own self-examination as exclusive determiner of degrees of authenticity, one may be relying on one's most limited dimensions. God pushes an Abraham, a Jacob-Israel, and a Moses beyond themselves. Their "*hineini,*" their "here I am," is not a posture reflecting an already achieved full activation of potential. It is admitting a readiness to grow further, to expand one's aspirations and one's spiritual and moral capacities.

The expansion is in two directions at once: (1) towards a keener sensitivity to the source of the questions "*ayeka*" and "*ey Hevel ahikha*"; and (2) towards a greater commitment to living out the implications of the two questions in the world of *derekh eretz*. Regarding the question "*ayeka,*" if Adam did not know how to respond, Noah did, and Abraham certainly did. In Noah's case, as described by Rabbi David Hoffman: "Only Noah who saw with his own eyes the destruction of the entire world of the wicked leaving only himself and family alive could appreciate his miraculous survival. Only he could feel how dependent he was for sheer life on God and that therefore an eager expression of his thankfulness was in order in the form of an animal sacrifice to this all-merciful Creator, Destroyer and Redeemer."

Whereas Noah's sacrifice is offered in thanksgiving, Abraham's "sacrifice" at the *akeidah* is readied in fearful submission. God — the God of ethical monotheism — will of course not countenance the actual slaying of an innocent child as an act of sacred worship. He will stop Abraham — but not before allowing Abraham to give in totally to what he has assumed to be his Ultimate Super-Ego's command. Abraham's submission is indeed total — like Noah's. But Abraham needs to learn that the submission need not, must not, and dare not be actualized by the willful slaying of another human being. Such a submission, such an actualization would be perverse. It will be enough to offer a lower animal in appreciation for being granted the life of his son, the extension of his own life.

The system of sacrificial offerings will be superseded by verbal prayer when the future Temples are destroyed. Whichever system becomes the ritual norm, the commitment that the system reflects at its best — that is, at its sincerest — allows for the worshiper to feel himself on the threshold of God's loving Presence. If the worshiper is prepared to give *all*, then he anticipates that God will respond — somehow — to the total commitment. Rabbi Yitzhak in the talmudic tractate *Menahot* says: Why regarding the bringing of the meal-offering does the term *"nefesh"* come in place of *"adam"*? (*Nefesh* can be translated "soul of a person" as opposed to *adam* as the external shell of that person.) Because the meal-offering is the best that a poor person can offer, God treats it, therefore, as if he has given his most authentic self in the sacrifice. Similarly, those Israelites who are higher up on the economic scale are being judged concomitantly as to their honesty, their sincerity, their unmasked authenticity.

For all the members of the community, rich and poor, powerful and meek, the most disinterested of the sacrifices is the *korban olah*. This sacrifice is wholly burnt, offered in its entirety to God. The worshiper is thus completely dedicating himself to God's purposes. It is the dutiful act of an ego who is submitting to God, who is laying himself out before God the Ultimate Super-Ego. At the same time the worshiper in covenantal reciprocity has become the Ultimate Super-Ego's minor alter-ego. In this pristine moment of offering the *olah*, this minor alter-ego of God remains a human ego happy to be in a state of reciprocal dependence.

The *korban hatat* (the sin offering), on the other hand, is given in order to compensate for a specific human shortcoming, misdeed, sin. There is no human being who is free from sin. The Bible will assert that there is no *tzaddik*, no righteous person, who is free from sin. God has learned from His experience with Adam and Eve in the Garden that sin, if it be a falling short of expectations, a violating of a standard, is not total rebellion. God has concluded that the human being, whether he sins inadvertently or intentionally, needs a way of canceling the blemish. If a crime or misdemeanor has been committed against another human being, then that other human being must receive tangible compensation before the blemish can be expiated. But a sin against God must be forgivable. There must be atonement, which at the same time will erase the blemish and restore the closeness, the possibility of renewed intimacy with the Almighty.

The *korban shlamim*, the sacrifice of peace, well-being, and harmony, unlike the *hatat*, and certainly unlike the *olah*, is focused on the worshiper's appreciation-for-life and his need for joyous expression of that appreciation. It is the meal of fraternal love and bondedness. The human being as a human being confronts life and with minimal good fortune is able to find moments of happiness, occasions of sheer blessedness. Such moments, such occasions will call for human acknowledgment of God's providential caring. The human being's giving in the case of *shlamim* is not total. The *shlamim* in fact represents a receiving and a celebration thereof. But the celebration or communal-meal in honor of the celebration is intended to be in God's Presence. It is still a divinely blessed occasion, even and especially because the recipients are the human family. The sense of fulfillment experienced by the family on the given occasion has about it the harmony of Eden, the harmony ever so fleeting, but still discoverable even in a post-Eden reality.

The Question of Animal Sacrifices

The question is asked: Must the spiritual and psychological needs of the human being be met by a system of worship that includes animal sacrifice? A corollary to the question is a reference to Rambam's disparagement of the system in his *Guide of the Perplexed*. In that work the Rambam attributes its inclusion in the worship as a necessary acquiescence on the part of Moses to a newly emancipated people accustomed to one mode of worship — animal sacrifice — despite its idolatrous purposes in Egypt. To change the mode prematurely would have been, according to Rambam, disastrous. It was enough to reject the idolatry. The mode would change eventually.

Nevertheless, the same Rambam at the end of his *Mishne Torah* (*Code of Jewish Law*), speaking of the messianic era, says: "The Messianic King is destined to restore the kingship of David, to rebuild the Temple and to gather in the dispersed of Israel. And all the laws and legal procedures from his day will be renewed. *And sacrifices will be offered.* And the seventh year and jubilee traditions will be restored according to all its specifications. He who does not believe in the coming of the Messiah or he who is not waiting for his coming, does not only deny the other prophets, but the Torah of Moses our teacher as well."

The Rambam will be known as the great rationalist. But rationalists can dream; rationalists can pray. And so Rambam's view as expressed in the *Guide* on the one hand and within the *Code* on the other hand is traditional in its integrated understanding of sociopolitical reality along with an acceptance of the mystery of Jewish being. And this integration cannot gloss over dialectical views regarding animal sacrifices. Even though the Temples will no longer exist, the debate over the relevancy of such worship will continue throughout the centuries leading up to the modern era. Whereas most modern thinkers will reject the institution of animal sacrifices as anachronistic, Franz Rosenzweig will protest against the superficialities in their thinking: "The reasons usually given for rejection of sacrifices are so weak that they obviously cannot be the true ones. For the horror at the 'slaughter of innocent animals' is comical rather than serious on the lips of confirmed non-vegetarians. Whatever is said beyond this, however, holds for every other visible and established ritual just as much as for sacrifice, which manifests the relationship between the natural necessity of taking food on the one hand and Him who gives food on the other."

Rosenzweig is reminding us of the Torah's programmatic attempt to sanctify all of human living by placing every creaturely activity of the human being in a framework of holy purpose and gesture. Human beings must eat in order to survive. They will eat fruits and vegetables and grains and animals. A range of ritual procedures commanded to be performed whether in the sanctuary or in private non-sanctified environs will require liturgy, dietary restrictions, and spiritual significances lending religious meaning to the acts of preparing and consuming food.

Biblical and rabbinic Judaism will develop a network of rules and procedures for observance at everyone's table outside the Temple. But when the Temple and its precursor, the Wilderness tabernacle, are in existence, the priestly functions related to animal sacrifices are central. They remove the immediacy of the sanctifying function from non-priestly families. This is so even though all the priestly acts are for the therapeutic benefit of non-priestly families. We have seen that this is true of the *shlamim* sacrifice wholly eaten. It is equally true of the *hatat* which is partly eaten, although the purpose in relieving the sin of the offerer renders it therapeutic as well. The *korban-olah*, the sacrifice given over totally to burning, has a clear God-centered purpose. But even as such, even as it is asserting that within His creation God is central, the worshiper looks to the *korban-olah* to impact therapeutically on all discrete elements in His creation, not the least of which is Man.

Akiva and Elijah

Wherever the subject of animal sacrifices leads, the deeper meaning involving the idea of a human being committing himself totally to God rises to the surface for awe-filled consideration. And the subject of total commitment brings us back to Abraham and the *akeidah*. God wants to test Abraham's readiness to give his all to him. God wants to tempt Abraham into revealing the limitation in his faith, except that God knows from the beginning that He has posed two questions to humankind. God knows that the question "where is the 'other'" in humankind's consideration is equally important — perhaps more important — than the *ayeka*. From the beginning of the test/temptation, therefore, God wants Abraham to struggle with his response to the point of rejecting God's command in favor of the call of his son. But Abraham surprises God by coming so close to the brink of slaying Isaac that God must intervene. God does not want Isaac to become an "*olah*-to-death," just as God seeks assurance that there will be other human beings ready to offer themselves as ultimate sacrifices — but to life.

This brings us to Rabbi Akiva's martyrdom. It is recorded in several places in the Talmud and Midrash. In the name of covenantal commitment, Akiva teaches Torah despite the risk entailed in defying the Roman occupiers and persecutors. He is imprisoned, condemned to a horrible death. In response to the astonishment of his students, summarized in *"zo Torah ve-zo sekharah"* ("this is the reward for teaching Torah"), Akiva gives the paradigmatic answer for all future Jewish martyrs.

All his life he has wondered what it would take to fulfill the injunction to love the Lord with all his soul/life. Now he knows. And he is prepared to offer himself as an *olah* with the word *ehad* on his lips as he expires. *Ehad* is the final word of the declaration of Jewish allegiance to the ultimate unity that is God. Thus Rabbi Akiva can die with serenity as he declares before all Israel: *"Shema Yisrael Adonai Elohenu Adonai* Ehad!" But Rabbi Akiva with all his homiletical sensitivity has not sought death or martyrdom a priori. His concluding homily to his disciples is clearly a *bedi'avad* (after the fact) explanation; and as such serves as an after-the-fact justification. God has not wanted Akiva as an "*olah*-to-death" as long as the world could be a place of Torah. If within the danger-filled rivers of life under the God-less Romans, however, Akiva has been caught in the nets of the Serpent-driven oppressors, God will then welcome him as an *olah* — only then.

The closest example to an a priori human *olah* in the Bible is Elijah. God calls to Elijah to conclude his ministry. He raises the prophet to the heavens by means of "fiery chariots and horsemen." It is a mysterious act whose folk explanations will satisfy generations of Jews who will be yearning for succor and hints of the ultimate redemption. The Jewish folk spirit will envision Elijah becoming the spiritual protector of Jewish children providing them with raisins and almonds on the outgoing of the Shabbat. He will be looked to in order to solve talmudic conundra. Moses will die, will be buried in a place unknown to his future descendants, and will play no role in evolving Jewish eschatology, whereas Elijah — in having become an *olah* — will be chosen to herald the coming of the Messiah.

Why Elijah? Perhaps it is because of his contest on Mount Carmel with the false prophets of Baal. It is there where Elijah dares to test/tempt God to support his sacrificial offering and not those of the others. God's positive response to Elijah's plea reflects His realization that the sincere commitment to the covenant is not just the responsibility of Man but of God Himself. The risk that Elijah is willing to take in testing/tempting God motivates God into bringing Elijah to His immediate Presence.

At the covenant-of-circumcision of every future Jewish male-child a prominent place will be given to the throne of Elijah. It will remind all present of the *olah* status of the child, even though it will be, thank God, an "as if" status. The child, each child will be looked upon as an "*olah*-to-life," a never-ending hope for ultimate redemption!

Tzav צו

The critical modern sensibility resists the idea of offering a *korban*, let alone being a *korban*. It is not a question of whether or not one believes in God. One can believe in God. One can insist that one's belief is predicated upon a faith that holds that God is Creator of the Universe including humankind; that God is the Revealer of Torah to the Children of Israel; and that in His good time God is the hoped-for Redeemer of Israel and all of humanity. In short, one can have faith in the three central attributes of the God of Israel — that He is Creator, Revealer, and Redeemer — and still be coy about concepts and rituals emanating from ideas which seem too literal, too spatial, too anthropomorphic. The biblical-rabbinic sensibility has insisted, after all, no less than the critical modern sensibility, that God is invisible and untouchable.

Yet Jewish liturgy through the ages will reflect a human yearning to be a *korban*, that is, to be near to God. The Jew will yearn to dwell in God's Sanctuary, in His courtyard, in His house which He has not built but which mortals have built, confident that if they build it in good faith, His indwelling Presence will be there. And this worshipful Jew, notwithstanding his critically educated sensibility, will not be put off by the liturgy's uninhibited references to God in terms that are often literal, spatial, and anthropomorphic.

The worshipful Jew through the ages will not hesitate to pray the biblical Psalms that echo anthropomorphic phrases like *"shiviti Adonai le-negdi tamid"* ("I have set the Lord before me always"). Such a phrase has become a liturgical-theological motto. And this Jew knows that in the liturgy even this declaration is not the most literal, the most spatial, or the most anthropomorphic allusion to Man's capacity to reach out to the Transcendent. There are other more vivid allusions which he will not hesitate to recite: "Lord of hosts, how beloved is your dwelling; My soul thirsts, it yearns for the courts of the Lord; My soul and body sing joyously unto the living God." The Jew will recite three times a day *"ashrei yoshvei veitekha"* ("happy are they who dwell in Your house"). The popular hymn *Adon Olam* will conclude with the serenely expressed: "In His hand I place my spirit, whether asleep or awake and along with my spirit my body, God is with me, I shall not fear."

Institutionalized Holiness

The biblical sensibility reinforced by the talmudic legislation of the later Rabbis will be as uninhibited in describing and prescribing for the spiritual realm in life as they must be in describing and prescribing for living in the material realm. The biblical-rabbinic mind believes that the whole earth is God's house or at least is His "footstool." And when *derekh eretz* in the valuational sense is being properly observed in the material realm, the biblical-rabbinic mind holds to the belief that the whole earth is "full of His glory." Nevertheless, this biblical-rabbinic mind beginning with Moshe Rabbenu knows that *derekh eretz* as the material way of the world is a jurisdiction that is somehow less holy, less pure than God's "immediate" Presence might ideally allow. But what are ordinary human beings to do? Israelites must labor, they must build, they must tear down, they must participate in the less holy, less pure activities of the world as God has made it in order to survive, in order to mend that world which God has made.

The Torah recognizes the problem and therefore calls for the setting up of especially designated institutions that are to be set aside as "holy," as "pure," as specifically God's "house" or "courtyard" especially hospitable to His "Presence." And there is to be no hesitation in calling these institutions literally, spatially, anthropomorphically "Houses of God." Furthermore, as a corollary to the designation-for-holiness of a special sanctuary, it will be equally necessary to appoint especially ordained individuals to serve in the sanctuary. These individuals will be endowed with a special degree of "holiness." These are the *kohanim* (priests) who are charged with maintaining in their every mode of ritual dress and behavior a vivid image or at least a vivid dream of perfect holiness and purity.

The ordination of the priests to their task is represented quintessentially by the *tzitz* or diadem worn as a crown of gold by the high priest when he officiates inside the tent of the *mishkan*. On it are engraved the words *kodesh la-Shem* (sacred to the Lord). Everything the priest does, says, wears, is to represent for ordinary Israelites — mired as they are in the profane dimensions of day-to-day living — Godly perfection. It is true that the Children of Israel have as a group been designated themselves to be a "kingdom of priests." And that designation will have its own sociomoral thrust for the day-to-day lives of people in their non-sanctified homes and market places. But the need for institutionalization of an ideal of spiritual sanctity will require the establishment of a class of religious functionaries. In themselves, they will not represent any more definitively God's transcendent Presence than will ordinary Israelites. What they are is what they will do for the communal worship. In their punctilious performance of the sacrificial ritual they will serve as a vehicle for suggesting the possibility of communication between the transcendent and the immanent and that all Israelites may share in the communication.

The priests will represent for the Children of Israel a tangible promise of access to the Transcendent. The particular air of holiness which they represent is not transferable, not "contagious" — to use Menahem Haran's term — in the way that *tum'ah* (ritual impurity) is. Later Jewish history will more and more distance itself from such modes of access to the Transcendent. The priesthood as possessing such representational power will gradually give way before the democratization of post-Temple worship. But in the Wilderness, it is the priests who are chosen to be the central pillar of the entire liturgical structure of altar, sacrifice, and propitiation.

Is there a sociomoral significance to the activities of the priests as they function day after day in the tabernacle? In the larger context of God's having instructed Moses to build the *mishkan* and to consecrate the *kohanim* for service in the *mishkan*, the spiritual purpose of the regimen of sacrifice must be seen as part of the total agenda of Torah, i.e., an agenda with high sociomoral significance. Therefore, even the most prosaic of priestly activities done daily may be perceived in an inspirational sociomoral context. To illustrate: (1) they are to remove the ashes of the sacrifices from the night before; (2) they are to put on new vestments for the coming day's service; and (3) they are to prepare fresh wood for the *olah*, the complete burnt offering, of the new day.

Each of these necessary instrumental activities may be interpreted as part of a larger sociomoral instruction to the priests and through their activity to the entire House of Israel: (1) Removing the ashes of the sacrifices from the night before reminds the simple Israelite of the indispensability of removing the sins of the past. (2) The priests putting on the vestments for the coming day's service represent the daily opportunity to work positively today and every day for the productive possibilities which present themselves today and every day. And (3) the preparation of fresh wood for the new *olah* is the daily earthly reminder of the ultimate purpose of human worship — offering oneself totally on this fresh new day to God's creative purposes.

These prosaic activities of the priests in the Wilderness, along with similar activities to be elaborated upon in the later great Temples in Jerusalem, mundane as they are, lack the drama, for example, of the later Elijah's competition on Mount Carmel with the false prophets of Baal. In fact — biblical "fact," that is — Elijah in those special circumstances will be the priest in the role of the prophet challenging the Transcendent to participate vividly — empirically — in an earthly religious confrontation. But God will not do things that way again, just as he has avoided such "interference" before. For as recorded in the Book of Va-Yikra, the sacrificial worship and its mystery must be looked upon as institutionalized, as normalized.

Later rabbinic tradition will look upon what Elijah will have done on Mount Carmel as a *hora'at sha'ah* (an emergency measure not to be repeated). Moreover, the personality of Elijah will henceforth be "relegated" to an association with the coming of the "Great Day" of messianic deliverance when history will have reached its denouement and all ritual norms, including sacrificial worship, will be superseded. The apocalyptic message of Elijah as understood by the prophet Malachi will then supersede ritual in general as it fulfills a messianic dream: "I will send the prophet Elijah to you before the coming of the awesome, fearful day of the Lord. He shall reconcile parents with children and children with parents so that, when I come, I do not strike the whole land with utter destruction." *But until that day*, until Elijah comes to herald the messianic deliverance, the ritual in its *institutionalized normalcy* will sustain the people in their day-to-day yearning for God's closeness, for God's concern.

Bringing Near

The prophet Malachi at that later time will envision the reconciliation of generations within Israel as the sine qua non to national survival. It will be an essential part of the messianic dream; yet it will offer a message for pre-messianic observance as well. For an ongoing function of the institutional priest, besides his official conduct of the sacrificial worship, will be to serve as God's vehicle for sharing with all of Israel God's three-fold blessing of *shalom* (peace). Again, the obeisance to *derekh eretz*, in this case familial respect and affection, is to be primary, notwithstanding the concern with ritual meticulousness regarding ceremonies of worship.

Beyond nuclear family considerations, Elijah will represent the theme of reconciliation within the larger House of Israel. In the tractate *Eduyyot* it is written: "Elijah will not come to pronounce unclean or to pronounce clean, to put away or to bring near, but to put away those brought near by force and to bring near those put away by force." In the first part of the Mishnah, Elijah's messianic mission will not be to abrogate duly legislated laws or to decide on who is or who is not legitimately part of the community. The exception will be those cases where violence has been used to include the illegitimate or to exclude the legitimate. In the latter part of the Mishnah, Rabbi Yehudah says "to bring near but not to put away…," but then the Sages say: "neither to put away nor to bring near, but to make peace in the world."

This Mishnah will reflect one aspect of the latent conflict between priestly concern for protecting the officially approved ritual and the severe prophetic critique of ritual when it is unaccompanied by *derekh eretz*, i.e., ethically approved behavior. As applied to the Children of Israel, what shall God's designation "kingdom of priests" imply? Shall it emphasize a distinction to be maintained on the insistence of some kind of intrinsic ritual "purity" based on biological pedigree? Or shall "kingdom of priests" be a metaphor referring to a hoped-for sense of ethical aspiration in striving to be a model of morality for all mankind?

The debate in the Mishnah with Elijah at the center is sensitive to a historic development which will always be problematic for any group seeking to define itself. How much inclusivity/exclusivity does it seek? How much can it afford? Just as the official Israelite priesthood is exclusive, i.e., only biological descendents of Aaron are eligible to belong, the hard core of Israelite national association is to be similarly biological in origins. Conversion from outside the Jewish community will be the great revolutionary addendum to the biological criterion. But by the generation following the given individual conversion the national and religious identification will return to being biological.

Such modes of identification — birth and the possibility of conversion —

will best be able to cope with the question of inclusivity/exclusivity. Anyone who wishes to enter the covenant of Israel, to become a Jew, will be able to do so. But in order to maintain the integrity of the community as well as that of the new Jew himself, the halakhic criteria for conversion will require a clear and consistent commitment on the part of the convert to become both a spiritual and a "biological" member of the Jewish people. When Ruth the Moabite insists on joining Naomi on her mother-in-law's return to Israel, she affirms: "*Amkha ami, ve-Elohayikh Elohai*" ("Your nation shall be my nation, as your God shall be my God"). In other words, the fact that one who is born a Jew is automatically a member of the "tribe" serves as an objective criterion for determining who belongs and who does not belong to the Jewish nation and the Jewish religion. At the same time, a non-Jew like Ruth will be able to join herself to the history and destiny of the Jewish people — but only by binding herself to both the soul *and the body* of that people.

Once within the fold — whether by birth or by conversion — should distinctions be made on the basis of definitions of ritual purity, degrees of overt commitment to ritual commandments and extensions of commandments, then prophetic passion and ire will be aroused. It is under such circumstances that a Rabbi Yehudah in the Mishnah quoted above expresses an inclusive purpose: "to bring near, but not to put away." The religion of Israel as Rabbi Yehudah will see it is to flesh out for everyone the maxim of bringing all those who wish to come closer to God to be welcomed. No matter how distant, the convert is not to be rejected. The Sages in our Mishnah go further by rejecting the whole discussion concerned with legitimizing and delegitimizing. Making peace in the world is to be the goal and the means-to-the-goal of the religion of Israel. All of Judaism's rituals are to aim towards that goal. Peace and harmony among people must be the purpose of all religious gesture and striving.

More pointedly, if the central purpose of the entire sacrificial worship — whether with animals or with words — is to come near to God, then, ideally speaking, there shall not be nor can there be any preoccupation with delegitimization. For every human being, without exception, in his very mortality, is equal before God. Every human being, no matter how well endowed physically, mentally, or materially, and how well reputed morally and socially, has sinned in his life. Every human being, no matter how much misfortune he has endured, has something to be thankful for — at least life itself. Everyone, therefore, has the right to try to bring himself closer to God's Presence — to be a *korban*.

Subduing the *Yeitzer ha-Ra*

The *Midrash Tanhuma* on the verse: "If he will offer a sacrifice of thanksgiving...." comments: "In the 'future' all sacrifices will be cancelled, rendered void, except for the sacrifice of thanksgiving." The *Pahad Yitzhak* commentary adds: "It may be said that even he who has had the merit of not having sinned, even inadvertently, who, in other words, has never needed to offer a sacrifice, for his merit alone, he is obligated to thank God and to bring a sacrifice of thanksgiving for his having been protected from sin."

But in truth Torah legislation is based on the proposition that all human beings sin. The *yeitzer ha-ra* (the evil drive) tempts all human beings. Therefore the capacity to appreciate, to offer thanksgiving for "having been protected from sin" is itself a "transcendent" impulse. But how can we see this "transcendent" impulse? How can we learn to appreciate it? The verse Leviticus 7:15 asserts: "And the flesh of his thanksgiving sacrifice of well-being shall be eaten on the day that it is offered...." A Hasidic master will comment that the sacrifice of thanksgiving — the *korban todah* — must be eaten in one day. The reason for the restrictive stipulation is that this particular offering is in appreciation for the miracle which has transpired *that day*; for every day has new miracles, as it is said: "for Your miracles which are daily with us." Therefore, just as each day has its miracle, each day should have its sacrifice of thanksgiving.

The human being, every human being, has been witness to situations where life-giving miracles occur in a day, in an hour, in an instant. There are emergency situations in which a life hangs in the balance; and that life, that precious life, is saved or restored or replenished. The next day, or next hour, or even the next instant, may see a new trial or new temptation of the *yeitzer ha-ra*; but a new miracle occurs. And the source of old and new miracles remains what it has been, the Supreme Creator, Revealer, and Redeemer. God the Creator has from the outset breathed into Man a special kind of breath which raises him above the *yeitzer ha-ra*, or at least energizes him to be able to combat the *yeitzer ha-ra*. God the Revealer has bestowed upon Israel the covenantally detailed structure for day-to-day living and day-to-day struggling with the *yeitzer ha-ra*. God the Redeemer has promised a day, a time, an era, a dimension of restored harmony within His creation when the *yeitzer ha-ra* will finally be defeated. That will be a day, a time, an era, a dimension of being in which all that God has commanded and demanded will be vindicated.

The human being shares much with the animals; yet, in essence, is different. This is not to say that the animals are not God's creatures; they obviously are. But because the human being has something of God's transcendent spirit breathed into him, he himself has a transcendent dimension. It is this transcendent dimension that entitles him to receive revelation and to have the potential to be redeemed — provided he can conquer this powerful, adamantine *yeitzer ha-ra*.

Abrabanel poses a question related to all the injunctions concerning the sacrifices: "Why on the one hand has God chosen to have offered on His altar the *helev* (fat) and the *dam* (blood), yet on the other hand has forbidden their being eaten by the Children of Israel?" Before answering his question he refers to a passage in the talmudic tractate *Berakhot*:

> When Rav Sheshet kept a fast, on concluding his prayer he added the following: "Sovereign of the Universe, You know full well that in the time that the Temple was standing, if a man sinned he used to bring a sacrifice, and though all that was offered of it was its fat and blood, atonement was made for him therewith. Now I have kept a fast and my fat and blood have diminished. May it be Your will to account my fat and blood which have been diminished as if I had offered them before You on the altar, and do You favor me."

Abrabanel then explains that health and beauty can themselves be the cause of sin. Blood is the source of health and fat is the source of beauty. It is known that he who allows his blood to boil is a sinner. Similarly fat as the cause of sin is confirmed by the biblical verse: "And Jeshurun (Israel) became fat and kicked in rebellion." Therefore God has enjoined Israel to burn on the altar the two physical properties within the human organism that bring on sin, reminding Man to neutralize if not cancel out his lustful tendencies.

Is Abrabanel recommending a form of asceticism? Hardly! These elements within the body represent leanings or drives each of which and both are the stimulants to sin if excess is allowed to prevail. They are to be considered metaphors, just as for Yehudah Halevi the heart is the metaphorical locus of the *inyan ha-Elohi* (the Godly or prophetic dimension). As has been pointed out earlier, for Yehudah Halevi the *inyan ha-Elohi* is that Godly or prophetic dimension which is found at the fifth and highest stage of God's creation. The four lower stages are minerals, vegetation, animals, and Homo Sapiens (cognitive man.) The *inyan ha-Elohi*, coming as it does to combat the *yeitzer ha-ra*, compels us to listen to the voice that we don't wish to hear. It is the voice of the Ultimate Super-Ego who knows our weaknesses as manifested by the *yeitzer ha-ra* only too well. Even and especially cognitive man needs the corrective power of the *inyan ha-Elohi*.

Western civilization will associate the heart with notions of romantic love. It is a notion not entirely contrary to the biblical and midrashic view that the heart — like notions of romantic love — is deceptive. The heart can mislead because it itself is divided, as the teaching has it; "You shall love the Lord your God with all your heart(s)," i.e., with both your drives, the *yeitzer tov* and the *yeitzer ra*. In other words, one has to consecrate his total self to the love of God including that part of him most prone to "kicking" out at his destiny. The question always is: When we insist we love God, or we love other human beings, or we love people in general, or we love our people in particular, are we certain that our proclaimed loves are nevertheless no more than self love! The proof is whether or not we are truly prepared to sacrifice our "heart's" selfish desires for higher altruistic purposes.

Conquering the *yeitzer ha-ra* or consecrating it to a higher purpose is the ongoing challenge of being human and reaching a spiritual level worthy of being in God's Presence. An animal doesn't have that spiritual-moral struggle. It is reminiscent of the story of the sage who wishes to teach a lesson about the difference between a human being and an animal. And so he shares with his students a parable.

The sage tells them of the man who saddled up his horse to travel to St. Petersburg in order to save the imperiled community there. Of necessity he stops periodically to give his horse rest and provender. He feeds the horse his usual diet of oats. The sage then cuts short his story-telling and asks his students, "Why are the man and his horse going to St. Petersburg?" Various answers are given but none satisfy the sage. Finally the sage himself gives the answer. He says: "The man goes to St. Petersburg in order to save lives; but the horse goes for the oats." The sage is asking his students to see the difference between a man and a "pferd" ("horse" with a contemptuous connotation). If Man as a thinker doesn't move to the level of sociomoral engagement, he'll degenerate into an animal, a dumb animal whose exclusive interest is the "oats."

This thought may be expanded further. If one doesn't aim to live his life as a *korban*, i.e., as an offering to God, representing within the world's *derekh eretz* a degree of holiness making him worthy to appear in God's court, as it were, then inevitably he will sink into being a "pferd." He will not know or care where he is going; for he will only be dreaming of the oats or other ephemeral pleasures he may meet along the way of a carefree purpose-free life.

Ezekiel and Eternal Hope

This preoccupation with holiness will be accelerated in the history of early Israel once they enter the Promised Land. They will conquer the Land and experience the travails of building a unity among the people sufficient to establishing a society. They will choose a monarchy and they will build a permanent tabernacle — the Holy Temple in Jerusalem. Tensions between priestly and prophetic tendencies, however, will become more and more exacerbated as political, social, economic, and cultural conflicts break out and subvert the lives of the people. The more corrupt life in Israel will be perceived to be, the more the priests will look to "purity" of spirit and the prophets will look to "humility" of conscience in order to bring the people "back to God" and to His and their covenant.

Ezekiel — both priest and prophet — will articulate a spiritual and ethical aspiration in one: "I will pour out on you pure water, so that you may be purified from all your impurities and from all your abominations I will purify you. And I will give you a new heart and a new spirit, which I will place within you. I will remove your heart of stone from your flesh and I will give you a heart of flesh." The prophet is surely not alluding to a prosaic bath, even a ritually ordained bath. Nor is he envisioning what medical science will achieve millennia later as part of its miraculous advances in organ transplants. When Ezekiel is examining the Jewish people as they are in the dark period of the destruction of the First Temple, he sees not only that they have failed to fulfill their mission to have a "heart" hospitable to God's indwelling

Presence, but this so-called "treasured people, kingdom of priests, holy nation" will have developed — according to Ezekiel — a heart of stone. They have plummeted to the very nadir-level of creation — the level of inanimate minerals — spiritual, social, and moral petrifaction.

Covenanted Israel will not reject the censures of prophets like Ezekiel. Their emerging liturgy will reflect the antithesis of rationalization in the face of defeat at the hands of ruthless implacable empires. No matter how strong Assyria or Babylonia may be, or later, how invincible Rome will be, Israel will blame itself for its defeats. *"U-mipnei hata'enu galinu me-artzenu"* ("because of our sins we were exiled from our land"). Israel will seek to repent — ethically and spiritually. From a situation of physical decimation and spiritual despair, they will be aroused in exile to renew their faith in God and in themselves. Ezekiel will envisage dry bones coming together in a renewal of flesh and spirit. The heart of stone will become a heart of flesh; and flesh and sinews will awaken the bones to life as God will breathe a new spirit of creativity into them. They will be ready to assume the burden of trying again.

But here in the Wilderness, they will be on the threshold of trying for the first time. Their flesh and spirit, their heart and soul, will be tuned in to covenantal purpose by means of the inspirational worship conducted by the priests in the Tabernacle. They will make the attempt to purify themselves, to be worthy of standing in God's courtyard. They will be determined to expand God's courtyard into a Promised Land — a Land so sanctified as to be worthy of welcoming God's Presence.

Shemini שמיני

Among the most resonant words in the Torah are the two words *"va-yidom Aharon"* ("and Aaron was silent"). His silence pierces the heart of anyone who has suffered to a degree so intense that tears and words cannot express his agony.

The Kotzker Rebbe has said: "He who reveals what he knows has little to say." What does the Kotzker mean? Does he mean that he who reveals *everything* he knows must have little to say or that he who reveals what he *really* knows obviously has little to say? Bialik's essay *"Gilui ve-Kissui be-Lashon"* ("Revealment and Concealment in Language") argues that not only does language *reveal*; language also *conceals*. We may expand Bialik's thesis to suggest that language reveals and conceals insight. The Kotzker Rebbe may then be arguing with the comment "he who reveals what he knows has little to say" that what we really *know* about the profundity of life is inexpressible. And if, therefore, we can reveal what we know, then what we know isn't very profound. In the case of Aaron, the newly consecrated High Priest of Israel, to have lost two children so suddenly, so shockingly, is to experience inexpressible sorrow. And so *"va-yidom Aharon"* ("Aaron is silent").

The Kotzker Rebbe has spoken much of "silence." He has spoken not merely of the silence which reflects humility, that silence recommended by *Pirkei Avot* when it states *"seyag la-hokhmah shetikah"* ("a hedge around wisdom is silence"). He speaks of the agonized silence caused by someone's certainty that he has discovered a truth about an aspect of reality that he cannot share with others. "A lock ought to hang over one's mouth," utters the Kotzker, "let your heart burst before uttering so much as a moan."

The Kotzker — and Aaron well before him — are testifying not to a shock in the face of an indigestible truth or an unbearable degree of suffering. Such a shock leads to a paralysis of thought and a silence which is empty, blank, void of feeling. The Kotzker's view of his world and Aaron's reaction to the tragedy of his sons' incineration while in the service of God bring on a silence that they *can* put into words but which — in their view — demands restraint, total self-control. God Himself will be described often as "*mi khamokha* ba'ilmim *Adonai*" ("who can be compared to You among the silent, O Lord"). For God has surely seen and empathized with the suffering of His people and must have an insight into the reason for their suffering. Yet he has chosen to be silent.

Sorrow and Silence

Abraham Joshua Heschel, a twentieth-century expositor of the Kotzker's teachings, quotes the master's comment regarding three stages involved in approaching sorrow: "The person on the lowest level cries; the person on the second level is silent; the person on the highest level knows how to turn his sorrow into song." Aaron has experienced in common with his fellow Israelites the stage of *ze'akah* (crying). At a critical point during the enslavement, the *ze'akah* has pierced the heavens sufficiently to draw God's attention and to activate God's saving power. Aaron has witnessed in Egypt much suffering among his people. As a leader of this people he has wept over the loss of human beings who were his brothers and sisters, elders and children. But now the suffering has ended. A new era has begun. And here, as a leader who is witnessing and participating in the consecration of his and his sons' conduct of Israel's worship, his mood is antithetical to the mood of sorrow and sadness. It is a moment of exquisite joy and exultation. But a catastrophe occurs. And Aaron's reaction is beyond crying; it is at the second stage — silence.

Abrabanel describes the silence as one of Aaron's heart turning into stone, unreceptive to words of consolation, even from Moses. For Aaron has been left, as it were, without a *neshamah* (soul). He has no "talk" in him nor has he any capacity for attending to other people's "talk." The *Shem Olam* commentary, on the other hand, draws a distinction between *demamah* and *shetikah*. *Shetikah* means a cessation of speech; but *demamah* refers to a quietness in the heart, a calmness in the inner recesses of one's soul. For Aaron doesn't question God's attributes. He has accepted God's judgment. Of course Aaron could express his grief by weeping, by crying out. As a father, how could he not weep, how could he not burst forth in frenzied grief! He is not an ecclesiastical robot. But Aaron knows and has accepted that he is a priest, dedicated to serving an omniscient, omnipotent God. And so whatever internal distress may be afflicting him as a distraught father, as long as he must show a resolute public face, he maintains a resonant silence.

Abrabanel's understanding of Aaron's silence limits the father-priest's capacity to ever move from the second stage of silence to the third stage of creativity. Aaron cannot recover from a silence so paralyzing that he is bereft of a *neshamah*. But he can recover — if we follow the *Shem Olam*'s understanding of Aaron's silence — from a heart which has been broken by tragedy to a heart which moves to a level of spiritual resuscitation because there *is* a soul in him. It is a soul which has been struck a blow but which still has a fundamental calmness of temperament, nurtured and disciplined by an allegiance to the Transcendent. And this calmness of temperament will yet be hospitable to creativity.

The Israelites who will come after Aaron and Moses will go through the Kotzker's three stages of suffering which will test their faith in a God who will be silent, who will be in eclipse. The prophets Isaiah, Amos, Hosea, Jeremiah, and Ezekiel will castigate Israel even as they know that cruelties will have been inflicted upon their brethren which are grossly beyond what their behavior at its worst should have elicited. After the era of the prophets, the rabbis of the talmudic era will revise theologies in the face of the martyrdom of so many Israelites who *have* had faith and who *have* tried to build a covenanted society. Some of these talmudic rabbis and their successors through the ages will challenge God to awaken from His silence and to re-assert His active rulership over Israel and the nations. How long can God maintain a silence without Himself moving up the ladder, as it were, from despair to a renewed spiritual and moral creativity?

Returning to Aaron and to his sons Nadab and Abihu, there is a puzzle. It concerns why the two young priests have been incinerated. The Torah explains the reasons clearly: "Now Aaron's sons Nadab and Abihu each took his fire pan, put fire in it, and laid incense on it; and they offered before the Lord alien fire, which He had not enjoined upon them. And fire came forth from the Lord and consumed them; thus they died at the instance of the Lord." Despite the clarity of the *peshat* (the simple meaning), there is a malaise among the commentators, a sense that Nadab and Abihu were not evil men, not wicked or even sinful men. The commentators and their sympathetic imaginations can not let go of the image of what the drama of revelation must have been for its direct witnesses. The aftermath of Sinai cannot but have continued to overwhelm the Israelites — and their leaders, including the priests. Among the young priests like Nadab and Abihu, their sense of abiding awe must have been accompanied by tension and confusion.

There are rabbis in the Talmud, therefore, who've gone to the extreme in showing compassion to these priests — despite the *peshat* of the Torah text. In tractate *Zevahim* they allude to the verses following the catastrophe that quote Moses attempting to comfort Aaron: "This is what the Lord meant when He said, '*Bi-kerovai ekadesh*' ('through those near to Me I show Myself holy'), and gain glory before all the people." And the text continues with the words "*va-yidom Aharon*" ("and Aaron was silent"). But the question is raised: When did God make these comments? When did God say: "Through those near to Me I show Myself holy?"

The answer given is before Sinai, alluding to verse Exodus 29:43 before the *mishkan* is built: "There in the *mishkan* will I meet with Israel and the Tent will be sanctified by My Glory." The word for "My Glory" is "*bi-khvodi.*" But the Talmud says: "Don't read '*bi-khevodi,*' but rather '*bi-mekhubadai*' meaning 'My honored ones.'" The Talmud says that the Holy One Blessed Be He said this to Moses, but it was not fully known or understood by him nor by Aaron until the death of the latter's sons.

Once Nadab and Abihu have died, Moses is able to say to Aaron: "My brother, your sons only died in order to sanctify the name of the Holy One Blessed Be He." And so Aaron, knowing that his sons were marked to be the favored ones of God, is silent and is summarily rewarded, as it is written "*va-yidom Aharon.*" An echo of this teaching is found in Psalms 37:7 in encouragement to a beleaguered war-weary David: "*Dom la-Shem ve-Hitholel Lo*" ("Be quiet and wait patiently for Him"). The comment is made based on the word play of *hitholel*, coming from the root *h-l-l*. Even though you may suffer many casualties in your wars "*halalim, halalim,*" (like Aaron), "be still," "*dom!*"

Lethal Spontaneity

Against the background of these opening chapters of the Book of Leviticus with their lengthy discussions of a sacrificial system to be carefully, meticulously observed, rabbis in the Talmud will have tried to rehabilitate Nadab and Abihu. They will have made of them a paradigm for all the *korbanot* (sacrifices), the human victims, the Children of Israel, who throughout the ages have been martyred as sacrifices for the sanctification of God's Name. This entire discussion has been found appropriately in the tractate *Zevahim*, the one devoted to the subject of sacrifices.

The rabbis understand the profound interplay of God's attributes in this episode of Nadab and Abihu. The *middat ha-din* (the attribute of justice) and the *middat ha-rahamim* (the attribute of mercy) are inextricably interwoven in the fate of the two priests on this unique occasion of celebration of their consecration to priestly service. All of Israel is witness to a microcosmic interface of the world-as-blessed and the world-as-cursed at the same time. In the world as in the Tabernacle — though it is totally unexpected in the Tabernacle — destruction may rain down at any time upon the innocent. But even as they suffer, the innocent are in a mysteriously transcendent sense the *mekhubadai*.

The world has already been experienced by the ancestors of Nadab and Abihu as light and darkness interlocked in a struggle for ascendancy. Descending into a golden civilization that was Egypt, the family of Joseph had enjoyed the economic fruits and sociocultural benefits of living a comfortably secure life in Goshen. All of this was turned into ashes when a new Pharaoh arose. The interweaving of blessings and curses will span the history of the Children of Israel as they travel through the Middle Ages into the post-Emancipation present. For the Jew as for all peoples in the Western World the twentieth century will exemplify more exquisitely and horrifyingly than Dickens could ever have imagined "the best of times and the worst of times." Alain Finkielkraut will note the insoluble riddle of the Shoah (the Holocaust) in which "our civilization was murdered by the very weapons of our civilization. The wound inflicted upon Western humanism and progress cannot be healed. A fracture has occurred because of modern technology, industry and bureaucracy." A century all beneficial and all homicidal!

Returning to the *peshat*, however, the question persists: Are the commentators and the rabbis in the Talmud justified in relating to Nadab and Abihu as the *yedu'im* (the beloved) and the *mekhubadim* (the honored)? Nadab and Abihu, after all, are described in the *peshat* as having offered "strange fire."

Again, it must be stressed that the commentators — as the rabbis before them — resist condemning out of hand those who have been called upon to serve God under vividly tremulous conditions. They cannot bring themselves to accept the *peshat* without homiletic resistance. Even when they are willing to follow the *peshat*, they look to acknowledge a positive dimension to the sin. In seeing a new kindling of fire offered in praise of God, Nadab and Abihu have sought perhaps to add to the love expressed in this new special ceremony of sacrifice. Adding new incense to the statutory elements in the sacrificial worship is an expression on their part of spontaneous joy. They are multiplying joy — as they see it — in the service of God. What can have been wrong with manifesting such unbounded love?

Notwithstanding this homiletic clemency on the part of the rabbis, however, one must return to the Torah. In its striving to combat the worst depravities of ancient idolatrous worship, the Torah has determined to bring to the worship of the God of ethical monotheism discipline in form as well as spiritual and moral elevation in content. Uncontrolled spontaneity is considered dangerous. And even though spontaneity may be host to a rich quality of surprise and freshness of expression, at this stage of the introduction of a new theology and a new worship to an apprehensive people, Moses is fearful and God is "anxious." Moses is trying to establish an institution that will offer a worshipful alternative to the "sacred harlotries" of the Egyptians and the Canaanites. Unbridled spontaneity is likely to defeat this purpose. Indicative of Moses' deep concern is his admonition of the surviving brothers Elazar and Itamar when they in turn are careless in not eating their share of the sin-offerings in the holy place indicated.

Granted, the confrontation between spontaneity and predictable normalization in the realm of religion in general and worship in particular will never cease. Judaism will seek to recommend a balance between *keva* (order), i.e., predictable continuity, and *kavanah* in its connotation of emotional intention suggesting a degree of existentially motivated spontaneity. The Hebrew language will not have an original Hebrew root for "spontaneous." For even *kavanah* has other dimensions of meaning which suggest — to the contrary — "direction," "purposeful intention." Nadab and Abihu have lamentably broken with the prescribed ritual and no matter what their motives, they have had to be short-circuited in their zeal. They have leaped forward to worship God with spontaneous extra passion. But the extra passion engulfs them totally as it scars Aaron permanently and marks the day of celebration as a memorial full of admonition and portent.

From Fire to the Still Small Voice

The horror of the episode serves as a warning to all of Israel as it is a warning of particular gravity to leaders, actual and potential, of this newly covenanted people. Precisely because Nadab and Abihu are recognized leaders and thereby models for all the people to observe and to emulate, their self-scrutiny should have been particularly acute. Rabbi Naftali Herz Weisel says: "What they did was unauthorized by Moses, but was a product of their own initiative...." Indeed, considering the punctiliousness applied to the construction of the Tabernacle, the dressing of the priests, and the prescriptions regarding the sacrificial offerings, how could Nadab and Abihu, notwithstanding their "sincerity," fail to appreciate the risk they were taking. Weisel criticizes them for an absence of humility: "It was seemly for those who had been sanctified by God (no less) to be humble, fulfilling the injunction to 'walk humbly with your God' and to fear approaching the sanctuary with anything less than moral rectitude."

As leaders, Nadab and Abihu should have represented a disciplined respect for pattern, for standards, for a concept of ceremonial correctness and appropriateness. Instead they offered an exhibition of ecstatic transport. Such Dionysiac displays are always suspect of reflecting self-indulgence and self-adulation rather than reverence for the Transcendent. And so the young priests are "sacrificed" in the most horrifying manner.

But is there not a counterargument that, after all, hadn't Elijah on Mount Carmel been as spontaneous as Nadab and Abihu? In terms of biblical fact, hadn't Elijah been outrageous in assuming that God would send down fire from heaven as "empirical" evidence to support the prophet's claims against the false prophets of Baal! The Rashbam is aware of the possible comparison and responds with a yes-and-no interpretation. *Yes*, in both cases God sends down fire from heaven in order to affirm the sanctity of His concern for humankind. But *no*, in the case of Elijah it is in response to the prophet's prayer which will call upon God to send down fire from heaven. The *peshat* and the Rashbam emphasize that it will be fire initiated by God himself. And therefore any comparison between Elijah's initiative and that of the priests is invidious.

For it is precisely because Elijah is waging a critical battle with idolatrous "prophets" on God's behalf, God Himself wants to *send down* fire for all to see. But God does not wish to see "earthly" fire stoked spontaneously by pretentious human beings *sent up* to Heaven as in the case of Nadab and Abihu. Moreover, according to the verses describing the catastrophe, the two priests offer their fire within the blaze which has already "come forth from before the Lord." It is as if they seek to "enrich" God's fire with strange ingredients of their own. In their malfeasance, in their "playing with such fire," they will certainly risk incineration.

In any case, Elijah's zealous act, as described earlier, is considered an act inspired by an emergency from which a precedent cannot be learned — not even for Elijah himself. As has been underscored by Andre Neher in his *L'Exile de la Parole*, within the biblical text itself there is a clear rejection of the melodramatic nature of the scene on Mount Carmel as efficacious for any other time. Emil Fackenheim has described Elijah as manifesting a "staggering recklessness in putting, for the sake of the covenant, the God of the covenant to a single, decisive, win-all-or-lose-all test." Neher points out that the chapter immediately following the contest on Mount Carmel is meant to prove that such "staggering recklessness" dare not be considered a precedent. Chapter 19 of I Kings is intended as a direct antidote to the potential "poison" of chapter 18's zealousness.

First, Elijah discovers that his victory on Mount Carmel is short-lived. Jezebel and Ahab regroup and recoup "their losses" by slaying many of God's prophets. Secondly, in hot pursuit of Elijah they force the prophet to flee to the Wilderness. In utter dejection, if not despair, Elijah returns to Horeb-Sinai seeking a reaffirmation of his faith. And what is he told? He is instructed to stand on the mountain before God where according to the biblical account God will pass before him. "There was a great and mighty wind, splitting mountains and shattering rocks by the power of the Lord; *but the Lord was not in the wind.* After the wind an earthquake; *but the Lord was not in the earthquake.* After the earthquake — fire; *but the Lord was not in the fire.* And after the fire *a still small voice*...then a voice addressed him...." Neher is arguing that Elijah dare not ever again risk any empirical manifestation of God's concern — let alone a hyperdramatic conflagration, i.e., a fire-to-order — just because he, a human being, albeit covenanted, wills it, wishes it, pleads for it.

God will sooner respond in the interstices which lie between the thoughts and images, intuitions and perceptions, of a human being than in spectacular natural upheavals. Not that God cannot, if He wishes, bring on a cyclone or an earthquake or a conflagration! But perhaps Sinai is meant to be the final *revelatory* cataclysm. There will be lightning and thunder and rain and all the natural phenomena to be feared and celebrated by poets and meteorologists. But as for prophets and teachers, thinkers and moralists, ordinary and extraordinary human beings, they will henceforth have to listen for the still small voice inspiring and legislating norms for luminous living.

The Still Small Voice of Holy Legislation

It is the "still small voice" that inspires and legislates the complex system of dietary laws for a people which is mandated to be holy. There is no activity more creaturely than consuming food, and there is no concern more urgent for all creatures than the acquiring of food. Of primary concern when Israel ventures forth into the Wilderness is food, including water which is also "food." If sexual appetite, like food, is also a natural appetite, then, like the providing of food and the digesting of food, it will also come under the close scrutiny of the "still small voice" of divine inspiration and legislation. In order for individual Israelites and the entire House of Israel to be holy, in order for Jews and the Jewish people to represent an image of holiness, it has been revealed that dietary laws are to be enacted and respected, that standards of sexual behavior be likewise promulgated and publicized.

In essence the entire Book of Leviticus is commanded legislation for holiness — holiness of the body and mind and spirit. God's mysterious Presence hovers over the Book — not as a God of apocalypse, although the threat of punishment for sin is there — but in the intimate details of bodily functions, mental cogitations, and spiritual yearnings. Moses instructs the people on what to do so that *"va-yeira alekhem kevod Adonai"* ("the Glory of God appears to the entire people").

Rashi, sensitive to the difficulties of comprehending the phenomenon of "the Glory of God appearing to the people," quotes Psalm 90: "May the favor of our Lord be upon us; affirm the work of our hands for us, indeed affirm it."

Rashi is suggesting that the appearance of God's Glory is reflected somehow in our sensing His favor or grace and in our prayerful anticipation of our efforts being worthy enough to be affirmed by Him. The Psalmist consistently stands before God with a touch of Elijah's audacity — if not his recklessness. The Psalmist is not putting God to an immediate empirical public test. But for the Psalmist, even an affirmation by the "still small voice" will energize his faith and enable him to continue with his covenantal striving.

Not that there will not be historically verifiable public affirmations of God's glory active in the destiny of Israel! As pointed out previously, Ezekiel will articulate the vivid description of national resurrection in his vision of the valley of the dry bones. He will have witnessed the destruction of the First Jewish Commonwealth, and the total dismay, political and theological, of a people vomited out of the Promised Land, their Promised Land. Their expectations as a nation will have now been shrunken into anorexic despair. And it is at this juncture that God issues a direct challenge to Ezekiel the prophet's faith: "*Ha-tihyenah ha-atzamoth ha-eleh*" ("Shall these bones live")? And Ezekiel's response is less than enthusiastic: "O Lord God, *Ata yadata*" ("You know")! In short, even Ezekiel isn't sure!

But God in a restorative epiphany announces: "These bones are the entire House of Israel. Behold I am opening up their graves in order to raise them up to Me, and I will bring them back to the very earth of Israel." In other words, God's favor has not been removed from Israel permanently. And the "proof" of the appearance again of God's glory will be a highly *empirical* going up again of Jews to the Land in order to begin the building of a Second Jewish Commonwealth.

This restoration, while envisaged by Ezekiel as an overwhelming miraculous deliverance, will herald in truth a new era where the divinely detailed legislation of Leviticus will be reintroduced to the people by Ezra and Nehemiah. As underscored earlier, the dreams and covenantal expectations of Leviticus will be reawakened and a new contract, an *amanah*, will be announced. It will be an *amanah* effected and signed while God is now in eclipse, while official prophecy has now ceased. Yet the people of the first *Shivat Tziyon* (return to Zion) will dare to visualize a covenanted society living without apocalyptic proofs of God's glory vividly present before them. They will now understand that the "still small voice" is the more than sufficient herald of God's redemptive Glory.

Their understanding will have itself been hinted at long before with the death of Aaron's Nadav and Abihu. They will recover from their own conflagration, i.e., the burning of the Temple and the loss of sovereignty. They will have wept by the rivers of Babylon, been struck dumb by the mournful silence of God, but will have climbed the ladder of stubborn survival in order to sing again the songs of a Zion reborn. They will continue throughout their history to learn the three-stage pattern of mourning: weeping, silence — but always creative resurrection.

Tazri'a תזריע

The Bible scholar Baruch Levine has indicated that in ancient times concern for the welfare of the mother and her newborn child is often expressed in fear of "destructive, demonic or anti-life forces." Anyone who has lived with a sense of history and a modicum of sensitivity to the reality into which children are born, knows that these children — despite their innocence — are indeed not immune to the impact of destructive, demonic, or anti-life forces.

Moses has just shepherded a people out of a major civilization that in order to "calm" a totalitarian ruler's "anxieties" fostered a planned program of infanticide. Moses as an infant has himself been saved from death miraculously. According to the Midrash, his very conception had been under duress because of the legitimate fears of Israelite parents that their newborn children were sentenced to be slain a priori. Why have more children if only to have them led to the slaughter! For Moses then, as for his Israelite flock, there are genuine traumas plaguing every new birth. This is the case even before delving into the mysteries of physiological conception and birth, menstrual flows, intimations of life-and-death struggles within the body of the conceiving mother herself.

As to this mother, her struggle to bring life into the world is framed within two borders of ritual impurity. Blood represents life; the shedding of blood and all forms of death represent obviously the antithesis of life. At one border of the reproductive process is the menstrual cycle with its blood flow signifying that there has been no conception. The blood flow represents if not death, then certainly the physiologically emphatic denial of life. During this period of menstruation the woman is considered ritually impure because death itself — or denial of life — is held to be the realm of the impure. At the other border of the reproductive process is successful birth which is nevertheless accompanied by some bleeding. According to biblical understanding, therefore, the new mother — even though not a menstruant — is also considered ritually impure; or as Baruch Levine has described it, she is "susceptible" to impurity for a limited period.

Life, Death, and Purity

At first look, this ritual impurity appears to have no ethical overtones unless there is associated with it some injury to another human being. The distinction made between *tahor* and *tamei* (pure and impure, respectively) touches the *religious* attempt to distinguish between organismic vitality and disintegration. At the same time, Moses and the God of *ethical* monotheism will be seeking to raise generations of Israelites who will be keenly attuned to noting the distinctions between ritual purity and impurity in order to have them promote life-giving forces around them and eschew their opposite. The priests will publicly be forbidden — except in particularly unusual circumstances — to have any association with death. Their task will be: (1) to provide ritual procedures for removing "impurities" from the camp; (2) to supervise the ritual purification of those judged to be temporarily impure; and (3) to superintend the public cult whose principle purpose is to represent the worship of the God of Purity and Life. It is clear then that at second look there *are* ethical overtones associated with this priestly responsibility.

In their prescribed task of lubricating within the living camp the machinery for purity and purification, the priests are serving a people who are themselves designated a "kingdom of priests." Israel itself as a lay-group is charged with maintaining themselves "in purity." Such maintenance is difficult because as human beings they cannot avoid death. Nor can they avoid those forces around them which in various ways subvert their ability to sustain in their individual and communal selves life-building dispositions, drives, and impulses.

The religion which Moses is presenting to these Children of Israel offers a comprehensive agenda intended to train and to educate them towards the cultivation of life as intrinsically good and therefore the principal goal for human striving. That which promotes life — individual, communal, national, universal — is good; that which in any way denies life to the individual, to the community, to the nation, to universal humankind is evil. And this covenantal religion of life begins with the life of the newborn babe.

It must start with the beginning of life itself. According to the Midrash, it begins even before birth! Quoted earlier was part of the passage from the talmudic tractate of *Niddah* where there is recorded the following in its entirety: "What does an embryo resemble when it is inside its mother? Folded writing tablets! Its hands rest on its two temples respectively, its two elbows on its two legs, and its two heels against its buttocks. Its head lies between its knees, its mouth is closed and its navel is open, and it eats what its mother eats and drinks what its mother drinks. As soon as it goes out to the air space of the world, the closed organ — the mouth — opens; and the open organ — the navel — closes. For if this wouldn't happen the embryo could not live even one single hour. A light burns above its head and it looks and sees from one end of the world to the other. It is also taught all the Torah from beginning to end. As soon as it sees the light, an angel approaches, slaps it on its mouth and causes it to forget all the Torah completely."

The pre-natal nurturing of this potential life is a pure act of grace, as is the giving of life itself. The infant does not choose to be born; it is gifted with life. As such, if there is a pristine moral basis to life, it begins with the act of pure giving, total sustenance. And on top of the biological factuality of total sustenance there is added, in the view of the Midrash, another act of grace, the infant's intuitive grasp of the whole world. There is bestowed upon the infant a pre-scientific pre-analytical curiosity — reverie — in the face of all reality. The Midrash places into the imagination of the infant an innocently comprehensive vision of the world; and like the Psalmist in Psalm 19 connects this vision of nature with an intuitive "knowledge" of the beauties of Torah, its capacity to "renew life, to make the simple wise, to rejoice the heart, to light up the eyes...."

But then the angel "approaches, slaps it on its mouth and causes it to forget all the Torah completely." The angel appreciates that the Torah that the embryo has "learned" in the ideally safe world of the mother's womb, a pure uncontaminated world experienced by the embryo as Eden, cannot be a workable Torah for this future inhabitant of the real world. For that real world is a postpartum, post-Eden world of destructive, demonic, and anti-life threats to love, nurtured warmth, and safety. But even though the infant is slapped into forgetting Eden, it never does forget it totally. It carries with it the spark of pristine purity upon which will be added the elements of a this-worldly post-Eden Torah, so that it can then grow to cope more confidently with worldly impurities.

Thus Moses has placed before this newly born people of Israel the image of a newborn babe who will never be able to blot out the "innocence" of its origins. Similarly, during all its trials, past, present, and future, this *newly born child Israel* — called by God His firstborn — will find comfort in the words of Job who will anticipate the *midrash*: "O that I were as in months gone by. In the days when God watched over me, when His lamp shone over my head, when I walked in the dark by its light..." The House of Israel in its journey through the wilderness of history will find that the world is no longer innocent, but that it can and must be reconstructed through a Torah which at least has a memory of innocence and purity. Secure in its memory, the House of Israel will thereby never cease cultivating a dream and vision of innocence and purity for the future.

The original purity of the soul is underscored in a prayer that Jews will recite every morning expressing both personal and collective thanksgiving: "My God, the soul You have given me is pure. You created it and You formed it. You breathed it into me and You keep it within me. A time will come when You will take it from me, but You will return it to me in the life to come. So long as the soul is within me I acknowledge You, O Lord my God and God of my fathers, Master of all creation, Lord of all souls. Praised are You, O Lord, who restores the soul to the dead."

The Holiness of Healing

This original purity is meant to provide the human being while on earth with the transcendent light of holiness that will guide this "holy nation" of Israel in its pursuit of *tikkun olam* (mending the world). As indicated, ritual impurity is associated with death and processes leading to or reminding us of death. Samson Raphael Hirsch has explained *tum'ah* (ritual impurity) on the basis of the conclusion of the Torah portion of *Shemini* where the *tum'ah* is caused by contact with the carcass of a dead reptile.

Among the most distinguishing features of the human being and his purity of soul is that he is to a significant degree free to act, to move, to decide, to live, to plan, to actualize plans, to dream, to hope, to envision. This is certainly true in spiritual and ethical matters. The Torah is contingent upon the human being's spiritual and ethical freedom — his freedom to obey as well as his freedom to initiate and to implement. But coming into contact with dead bodies, even those of animals, brings home to the human being an antithetical message. It reminds us of the reality that with all our freedom we are nevertheless subject to physical necessity. Moreover, we inevitably succumb to physical necessity. We are born against our will and whether we will it or not, we die.

The mother giving birth is described first as *"isha ki tazri'a"* and then for a set period of time she is *"ve-tam'ah"* (impure). Why? She has brought forth life! At the same time, however, there is an acknowledgment that her producing of progeny has also been part of a physiological process. In common with the plants and the animals, this process has granted her the seed-forming capacity for the continuation of her species. But the child — once conceived — has been born out of physical necessity. And this physical necessity brings with it the recognition that nature not only brings forth life but harbors within its processes death. Acknowledgment of *tum'ah*, therefore, must make up part of the period following birth. But what then separates the human species from the lower orders of nature? It is the process of *tohorah* (purification) which removes the *tum'ah* and thereby transports the human species to the state of spiritual and ethical freedom that God has "breathed" into human beings through the soul.

As long as the body as host to the soul maintains a degree of normal health in the face of physical necessity, it is mandated to be dedicated to the ongoing purification process. Moses is emphasizing to the people through this legislation regarding bodily functions that the God who has taken them out of sociopolitical bondage is equally interested in their ongoing biophysical health. God is concerned to help raise human beings who are physically circumscribed, whether healthy or less than healthy, to a level beyond the animal-vegetative state to a state of *tohorah*, which in turn is a precondition for *kedushah* (holiness).

It follows that for Israel the development of medicine as a healing process endorsed by God and in which the human being imitates God the Healer is to be of the same spiritual and moral order as the redemption from Egypt. The emerging attitude of the Torah towards healing, i.e., avoiding the *tum'ah* of death, will insist that human beings are charged by God with responsibility for their lives. Along with that responsibility, human beings are given permission — nay, they are commanded — to seek mastery and control over their environment. And it is God Himself the ultimate Healer who is to be imitated by human beings as they commit themselves to the healing process.

Granted, God as Creator has created the entire cycle of life and death for all His creatures; and there is a certain ordered pattern to the universe which is to be summarized as *"olam ke-minhago noheig"* ("the world proceeds according to its custom or regime"). Nevertheless, the breath of the soul within the human being is a sign by God that He wishes the human being the longest possible life. *Tikkun olam* (mending the world) applies to each individual human ill — spiritual, moral, social, and physical. In the phrase *"ve-rapo yerapei,"* included in the earliest legislation in Exodus, the doubling of the verb "to heal," lies the injunction to Man to do all that he can to bring healing to human beings who are afflicted and in pain.

Mortality has been ordained for human beings from the moment of the primordial exile from Eden. For if mortality were not the fate of all creatures, then idolatry would prevail; and rebellion against the Creator would bring on the apocalypse. At the same time, the human being has been chosen to subdue the rest of nature in order to bring out nature's latent blessings. Among these latent blessings are those that can bring succor and healing to human beings and to the higher animals. And so the discipline of healing is an integral part of the covenant and will become a specialty for the treasured "kingdom of priests."

As such, this discipline will have to combat various ancient misreadings and superstitions regarding disease. This discipline will have to confront, for example, the proposition that disease not only among the ancients but throughout human history has been considered by many as a curse. It is a curse not just understood metaphorically, but literally, as if the affliction emerges out of a premeditated satanic plot aimed at the victim. It will manifest itself in folk mythologies of Jewish and Gentile communities through the ages. The *ayin ha-ra* (evil eye) cast upon someone by someone in order to bring a blatant curse of illness upon someone by someone will be endemic to those believing in a mysterious theurgic power which cannot be neutralized. The discipline of healing will be charged with the task of defeating such superstitions in the name of the Ultimate Healer Himself.

A major strand within the evolving tradition of biblical-rabbinic Judaism will look upon disease as a symptom of punishment. It will have rejected the idea inspired by a belief in magic, that disease comes from a theurgic curse. Yet a tradition within "biblical-rabbinic" thought will hold to the proposition that *yisurin shel onesh* (the torments of punishment) are meant to contribute to the expiation of sin, assuming that appropriate worldly compensation has taken place. Another minor strand within the tradition will accept and adopt as explanations for certain conditions of disease the phenomenon of *yisurin shel ahavah* (torments of love). God is seen as tolerating the afflicting of the innocent with disease out of a sense that in an imperfect world the innocent are the most vulnerable to suffering. And in their suffering, like sacrificial offerings, they are perceived as closest to God.

Such attitudes — in finding their way into Jewish tradition as well as other world cultures — will have held back the positive evolution of medical healing. At best, *yisurin shel onesh* and *yisurin shel ahavah* will have served *after* the fact of suffering as therapeutic rationalizations, as constructive value-concepts explaining (justifying?) the affliction. *Yisurin shel onesh* as an explanation will reflect the power of guilt to motivate moral correction. *Yisurin shel ahavah* will generate in the rare sensibility greater sensitivity to the faults within creation and within human nature, and thus better enable one to endure one's suffering or the suffering of one's loved ones.

But what Judaism will principally contribute to the progressive attitude towards medical healing will be the original and fundamental idea that every human creature is created *be-tzelem Elohim* (in the image of God). "In the image of God" will mean that the human body as well as the human spirit is to be treated with love and caring. This does not and cannot mean that the human body is to be worshiped when it is at its strongest and abandoned when it shows illness, infirmity, and advanced age. However old, however lame, however diseased the person, he is to be respected for his Godly purity. He and his body are holy; for his soul is holy.

Sociomoral Leprosy

The Shulhan Arukh, the Code of Jewish Law of Joseph Karo, will summarize the traditional attitude towards healing: "The Torah has given permission to the physician to tend to the sick — and to cure the sick. It is a commandment; it is saving a human life. And if he prevents himself from tending to the sick, it's as if he has shed blood." But the burden for tending to the sick does not fall exclusively on the professional. The primary care-giver is the patient himself; for, as Hillel has said, treating one's own body and soul is caring for God's image.

It may be argued that one does not necessarily have to put one's faith in a superior being in order to respect fully the human being's body — to treat with loving care one's own self. There is a pristine instinct for self-caring even among dumb animals. One does not have to consider himself a "believer," therefore, to treat himself with respect enough to want to live and to keep living. Sartre has said: "Man is nothing else than the ensemble of his acts, nothing else than his life." Sartre has no use for dreams, expectations, hopes — for if those are all a person has without attempting to actualize them, then such a person may legitimately be defined in pathetic terms as one with failed dreams, vain expectations, miscarried hopes. Dreams, expectations, hopes aside, the human being is nothing else but his life lived fully, vitally — and that cannot be done unless the human being keeps his body healthy for as long as he has control over his body.

In Sartre's atheistic model of the free human being, however, there is a limitation if not a self-idolatrous illusion. The limitation is the choice which atheistic Man arrogates to himself — to live or to commit suicide, to end his life whenever he chooses. Atheistic existentialists like Sartre and Camus will argue that because the free human being has the choice to commit suicide but desists from it, then he in effect has chosen to live. Once he chooses to live, then he has accepted full responsibility for that life. These existentialists are arguing the case for full moral responsibility conditioned on full choice. This focused choice is the equivalent of the absolute choice of an absolute ruler deciding between life and death for the human being, any and every human being under his charge. For the believer, such autocracy — even over one's own life — is morally dangerous and potentially disastrous.

For the human body sooner or later must face disease and deterioration and disintegration. And once this process begins, only the purity of the soul transcending the gradual surrender of the body to "necessity" maintains the integrity of the moral conscience. The "image of God" continues to characterize the human being even as he lies increasingly helpless in the face of biological necessity. The "image of God" elicits from others the ongoing concern for tending to the sick even though there is less and less utilitarian justification for it.

Convention may define the human body at its highest level of vitality as "healthy," as "beautiful." But the Bible recognizes that there are conditions which affect the human body in a way that causes sores, scabs, scales, general repulsiveness. All variations of *tzara'at* are seen by the Torah to bring *tum'ah*.

And all human beings afflicted with *tzara'at* are judged to be *teme'im* (impure). These afflicted ones are "removed" from society for the duration of their impurity — not because of the danger of possible contagion — but because of the perceived repulsiveness of their condition. Nevertheless, the *tzara'at*, the impurity, must be treated, must be cured, if possible. For repulsiveness is not a condition for which one should be removed permanently from society any more than the diseased person warrants less concern and treatment than the healthy person.

The first time *tzara'at* or "leprosy" is spoken of in the Torah is in the portentous dialogue between God and Moses in Exodus 4:1–7. At this stage of the dialogue Moses is protesting against the awesome task that God has imposed upon him — taking the Israelites out of slavery. Moses says, "What if they don't believe me and do not listen to me, but say that the Lord did not appear to you?" God responds in several ways including the instruction to Moses: "Put your hand into your bosom." Moses obeys and when he takes it out it is "encrusted with snowy scales." Such a symptom is described in Leviticus 13:2–3 as leprous. Why then does God use this form of "miracle" to respond to Moses' doubts and hesitation?

The most common response to the question is that Moses is implying in his words that Israel may not be worthy of the message and the blessing of the coming redemption. As such he is indulging in *lashon ha-ra* (evil talk) regarding Israel. And God punishes him by afflicting him briefly with the disease interpreted by the Rabbis as most appropriate to slandering. Moses is guilty of being a *motzi shem ra* (one who gives someone a bad name). (The Hebrew word for leper — *metzora* — is seen homiletically to be associated with the words *motzi shem ra*.)

But the appropriateness of this brief punishment with which God afflicts Moses goes deeper. The enslavement of Israel is a gross sociomoral and political evil. An entire people suffers from the combined threat of permanent bondage and extermination. And the day-to-day moment-to-moment conditions under which the enslaved endure their fate are insufferably diseased and appallingly ugly. They are in a collective "leprous" state, as slaves within the Empire of Egypt are condemned to be. The ten plagues that God brings on the Egyptians are to retaliate in kind on behalf of the slaves against their masters.

The plagues in their combined impact bring total disease and ugliness into every master's house so that there is no immunity from pain and suffering. Moses at the "burning bush" is a reluctant candidate for "redeemer." He must, therefore, be struck vividly, emphatically, unforgettably, with the sense of death-at-the-gate awaiting helpless Israelite victims as well as their Egyptian victimizers. Moses dare not run away from his call to step into the breach to help heal these Israelite victims. In any case God won't permit him to stand aside. The victimizers will be left to their own fate. But Israel deserves to be healed, to be purified in order to face a new day, a better, healthier day.

The *tzara'at*, in other words, is meant to refer to a general socio-moral-aesthetic repulsiveness which can affect any and all the accoutrements of human beings as well as all parts of their individual bodies. It may be seen in any "sick society" in the clothes people wear, in the houses in which they live. As the Ramban will put it in describing an Israelite society that struggles to build a nation which is healthy from a sociomoral, political, and spiritual point of view: "When Israel is fully in harmony with God's covenant, when the spirit of God, as it were, hovers over their efforts, then their very clothing and houses will 'look good'! But when there is sin and crime, then the ugliness will manifest itself — in the clothing, in the houses, in the flesh."

The Goal of National Health

Moses and the Children of Israel are embarked on a journey to national health. And the health being programmed is meant to be comprehensive. It is to bring beauty not just to things but to the relationships which are engendered when people attempt to live in sociomoral harmony with one another. Physical death cannot be eliminated. But in the face of life — life lived with aspirations for communal security and felicity — death can be relegated to the domain of impurity.

Such relegation will serve to underscore and highlight the blessings of purity, holiness, and a vision of illusive but palpably imagined innocence. The vision of innocence will be experienced and vividly enforced every time a new child is born. Such a fact — the newborn child — will promise again and again that visions of human innocence are not vain imaginings. The newborn child emerges into a world of *tum'ah* and *tohorah*. But this same newborn child offers a renewed overriding hope to an unredeemed world that redemptive purification of human effort is possible.

Metzora מצורע

Among the various kinds of leprosy described in the Book of Leviticus, the most curious is the plague of leprosy attached to a house. The priest inspects the house after all who live in it have removed themselves, and then proceeds to cleanse it. If, however, the leprosy returns, the house is judged to be "malignant" and must be demolished. Moreover, all its stones, timber, and mortar must be carried out of the city into an unclean area.

In and of itself, such a passage can be seen as a straightforward prescription for sanitary care. But Rashi offers a strange comment on the passage: God informs Israel that He Himself is responsible for the "malignancy" in the houses as a consequence of the idolatrous Amorites having buried treasure in the walls of these houses during the forty years of the Israelite sojourn in the Wilderness. When Israel destroys the civilization that is represented by this Amorite idolatry, i.e., demolishing the stones, timber, and mortar of these houses, they will be rewarded by discovering the hidden treasure.

Promise and Threat

The question to be asked is "Why should Israel have to go through the entire process of enduring the 'leprosy' of the houses and their demolition before the treasure can be discovered?" An answer can be found in the biblical verse *"Esa de'i le-mei-rahok u-le-fo'ali etein tzedek"* ("I shall lift up my mind to those who come from afar, and to my Maker I shall attribute righteousness"). This verse may be seen to refer to Abraham who when called upon to perform the *akeidah* was described as looking and seeing the appointed place *mei-rahok* (from a distance). And Rabbi Haninah understands the "place" — *ha-Makom* — to refer to God to Whom we are distant, but who in His largesse draws us near to Him. Abraham proved to himself and even more emphatically to God that he was ready to surrender the most precious thing in his life — his beloved son — without being promised immediate results, i.e., without fully understanding. God is distant. To approach Him requires herculean effort, angst, even suffering.

In other words, the essence of faith is to hold firm to a belief system whether or not the actualization of the belief system can be seen near or far, whether immediately confirmable or distant. As described earlier, Moses is scolded by God when doubting Israel's readiness to believe in the long-term agenda of redemption. God smites Moses with momentary *tzara'at* (leprosy) in order to give him a "virtual" punishment, a sign of death, so as to awaken him from his own timidity, his own lameness of spirit. And with regard to this "mini-plague" with which God afflicts Moses, the commentator Sforno says: "....the second part of the 'mini-plague,' i.e., the return of the afflicted limb to normalcy, will have even greater impact in that it stretches credibility further." The *tzara'at* whose snowy whiteness is as death to the limb that has been affected has now disappeared. To have the given limb *shava ki-vesaro* (return to its natural flesh-colored health) is indeed a greater miracle. For Sforno the wonder of this double sign — moving from life to death and then the resurrection of the limb from death to life — convinces Moses that his view-of-reality needs to be grounded in unremitting long-term hope.

Is this Rashi's direction in his understanding of the *tzara'at* of houses? Rashi's Torah commentary normally focuses wherever possible on simple literal meanings. What is he looking for here in his reference to Amorite treasures? Is he saying something about the importance of long-term faith? Undoubtedly, but there's more! Rashi's comments are wedded consistently to the value-concept of *ahavat Yisrael* (the love for Israel). It has shown itself in his criticism of Moses for questioning Israel's faith at the "Burning Bush" and the resulting personal "mini-plague." Now it appears again in his refusal to indulge the thought that the plague of houses could come as a result of Israel's independent sinning. Instead, Rashi underscores the sins of the Amorites. He reminds us that Israel is coming into a land that has previous occupiers who have been steeped in idolatry and moral disease. Such spiritual and moral decay will require extirpation. The people chosen for such a purpose, in doing God's will, will be rewarded. But at the same time they will be reminded that the fate of the Amorites will be their fate should they behave like them.

What is to be the reward according to Rashi? The many years of spoils hidden in the walls by the Amorites! But will they truly be a reward if at the same time they are a warning! Moses has oscillated in his rhetoric in describing the various "leprous" conditions that can affect parts of the body from limbs to hair, to clothing, and to houses. The warning which will be thundered forth at the conclusion of the Book of Leviticus will concern the Land itself. Spiritual, moral, and social pollution can bring on a massive all-pervasive *tzara'at* which will infect every crevice of society and which will hide whatever "treasures" have been acquired, manufactured, and built by that society. However "great" such a society, whatever achievements will be celebrated in its name, it will surely meet its latter end — whether by war, by pestilence, or by other "acts of men" or "acts of God."

The so-called "great society" will leave behind majestic edifices as evidence of its former greatness. The treasures will serve later generations of students of archaeology and anthropology who will vie with each other in reconstructing the memories of this "great" ancient civilization. But Moses and Israel must learn the truth now by the example of the Amorites. They must be taught and retaught the deeper purpose of the Exodus and what must be the correct motivation in conquering the land of the Amorites. Long-term faith must be grounded in long-term admonition.

In the "Covenant of the Pieces" between God and Abram, it is recorded that the Amorites inhabit the land of Canaan and that *"lo shalem avon ha-Amori ad heina"* ("the iniquity of the Amorite is not yet full"). God is informing Abram that his descendants, the Children of Israel, will spend a lengthy period of enslavement in Egypt *because* the Amorites have not as yet forfeited their opportunities in the Promised Land. The implication is that they have been given the opportunity, just as Israel will be given the opportunity, to build a society in which God's Presence can dwell. As part of the Amorites' opportunity, according to Rashi, as part of its alleged achievement, there has been an accumulation of material treasures. But these treasures will not immunize the Amorites against Godly retribution once their "iniquities are full."

Therefore the reward promised to Israel is given as a veiled threat. Israel will be charged with an awesome moral challenge. They will be commanded to wage a *milhemet mitzvah* (a war commanded by God) to punish the Amorites and the other idolatrous peoples of Canaan. Israel will be God's "rod of anger" against the Amorites. Such wars, as recorded in the Bible, will never again be perceived as commanded by God. Their genocidal actualization will be too horrible to contemplate no matter what the justification or rationale — even as alleged punishment of the indigenous population for sins against God. In other words, only certain wars recorded in the Bible will be defined as *milhamot mitzvah* because only the Bible will claim for itself, in Jewish terms, a revelatory origin.

Once the Bible will be sealed, there will be no further revelation as a source and authority for military conquest. The Torah has been given as the detailed concretization of the covenant. And only the keeping of the sociomoral norms of the Torah by an Israel living faithfully and committedly in its Promised Land will assure its long-term security in that Land. No further revelation will be necessary once the Torah has not only been given but has been accepted and actualized by Israel.

Whether or not Rashi's particular interpretation of the leprous houses is exaggerated or even far-fetched, its homiletic thrust is clear. Israel will be tested, as always, as to how it perceives its authentic self as a nation. The same will be true for every individual man and woman within Israel. The detailed review which Moses presents in Leviticus of the *tzara'at* as representing disease and impurity — physical and spiritual at the same time — must leave and will leave its "captive" audience of newly freed awe-struck Israelites overwhelmed with promise and foreboding. A double-edged preachment of long-term faith and long-term admonition!

The Leprosy of Slander

The Children of Israel as a collective, and each individual Israelite among them, have to be brought to the threshold of appreciating the sharpness of the double-edged sword of the covenant. The Children of Israel have been taken out of Egypt and then to Sinai. They will then be taken to Canaan and settled there in order to discover their sense of authentic being as God's treasured people. To be a *treasured* people will entail discovering the true treasures of human existence; not the false "gold" of human perverseness and exploitation. But their encounter with the relentless temptation of materialistic growth and power will give them no respite. Such materialistic achievement will not only *appear* beautiful. It will in large measure *be* beautiful. But when will such beauty turn leprous — and will Israel discover the symptoms in time? Will it diagnose the disease before it becomes terminal?

The verbal association made by the Rabbis between the word for leper *"metzora"* and the slanderer, "the *motzi shem ra*" has been noted. And the first appearance of the word *metzora* in connection with Moses' "slanderous" allusion to Israel's hesitancy has similarly been noted. But the connection is deeper than a fortuitous sharing of Hebrew letters. To slander someone is to point the finger of "death" at him. It is obviously not murder, legally speaking. There must be a distinction made between the act of physically taking someone's life and "merely" making verbal remarks aimed at slighting or destroying someone's name and reputation. But nevertheless, one's name and reputation begin with an aura of innocence and optimistic expectation. There is a sense of buoyancy, of an optimistic fragrance characterizing the new life of a given person or people. If and when slander begins to be hurled at this innocent new life, the optimistic images begin to collapse, to become stale, and then moribund. Thus slander is tantamount — morally if not legally — to shedding blood.

Why will Miriam, the early faithful guardian of the babe Moses, be stricken later with leprosy when, amongst the tension-riddled Israelites in the Wilderness, she falls prey to gossiping about her brother? Is Miriam the leader of the women's song at the triumph of the Sea of Reeds to be so severely condemned when what she shares with Aaron about Moses' less than optimal domestic life is probably true? Yet even a Miriam is casting at Moses the arrows of "bad talk," is tearing him down, is "shedding his blood," as it were. In her weakness she is communicating moral disease and must be quarantined. For she has made herself impure, and the impurity of slander is ugly and contagious.

The Psalmist (Psalm 120:4) proclaims *"hitzei gibor shenunim"* referring to the sharp arrows of mighty slanderers. Nehama Leibowitz notes Jeremiah's use of a similar metaphor: *"Hetz shahut leshonam"* ("their tongue is a sharpened arrow"). In what way is the tongue likened to an arrow? The Midrash answers: "If one draws his sword in order to slay his fellow and the intended victim prays for mercy so that the potential slayer is sufficiently moved to change his mind, he may return his sword to the scabbard — without having done irreparable harm. With the arrow, however, once he has drawn the bow and shot it, even should he wish to call it back, he can't." It is gone to do its damage. The damage done by leprous talk is not only irreparable; it destroys from a distance with greater callousness than with the sword.

In other words, God has needed to upbraid even Moses for his slander at the "Burning Bush." There, Moses had doubted Israel's readiness to believe in God's redemptive power. But God decides to punish Miriam with more than the momentary *tzara'at* which Moses had suffered. At the point of Miriam's sin in the Wilderness, as Israel is being mobilized under Moses' leadership for the journey, her slander will be considered severe enough to warrant quarantine. Her "bad talk" is tantamount to the poisonous weapon of the Serpent transformed into conventional tools of gossipy communication among conventionally-decent people. God insists that the sociopolitical disease which can destroy a nation from within must be understood particularly at the beginning of the journey. In essence, the entire agenda of Leviticus is a covenantally inspired prescription for sociopolitical health as it purports to guide ordinary Israelites through the mysteries of disease, health, and spiritual well-being.

Sanctity of Land, House, and Body

There is no question but that the Rabbis of the talmudic era are not comfortable with the laws concerning the leprous house. The leprous house is considered by them to be in the same conceptual category as the *sorer u-moreh* (the disobedient and rebellious son) and the *ir ha-nidahat* (the city condemned to destruction). Just as these latter two conditions are determined by the Rabbis to be virtually inconceivable, the *bayit ha-menuga* (the leprous house) is considered as "never was" and "never will be." Why then, the Talmud asks, has the Torah mentioned it and discussed it? *"Derosh ve-kabeil sakhar"* ("Learn and be rewarded").

The Rabbis will never directly contradict the written words of the Torah. Halakhically, however, they interpret, they legislate, they qualify, and do whatever they determine must be done in order to neutralize those Torah strictures which are considered to be too sharp, too extreme, too cruel, to be applied with reason and with grace. And so the Rabbis "limit" each of the three institutions — the *sorer u-moreh*, the *ir ha-nidahat* and the *bayit ha-menuga*. They so limit the qualifications necessary for defining respectively the son as rebellious, the city as condemned, or the house as leprous, that it is determined that there never could be nor can be such a son, such a city, such a house.

If such is the case, and the Rabbis freely acknowledge the logical question, "Why are these institutions mentioned in the Torah," then closer examination of their answer is called for. What is meant by their instruction: "Learn about these institutions which never were and never will be and be rewarded"? The Children of Israel are mandated to enter the Promised Land, to conquer and to settle it as an ideal society living according to the terms of the covenant. There are three pillars, the health of each indispensable to the successful fulfillment of the task. These pillars are the individual, the family, and the larger community made up of individuals and families. If any one of these pillars is diseased the nation disintegrates.

The *Torah she-bi-Khetav* (the Written Torah) examines with God's attribute of justice each of these pillars and argues for appropriate legislation that will preclude the appearance, the growth, and the potentially poisonous influence on the nation as a whole of the *sorer u-moreh*, the *bayit ha-menuga*, and the *ir ha-nidahat:* (1) The nation cannot tolerate an individual who lacks the minimal sensitivity to the presumed constructive guidance and instruction of his parents and by extension his elders. (2) The nation cannot tolerate a family-household which is blatantly dysfunctional, spiritually, morally, psychologically, and socially. (3) The nation cannot afford to absorb into its midst a community which has surrendered minimal social standards, aspirations, and behavior patterns. Therefore, God's attribute of justice as articulated in the *Torah she-bi-Khetav* must deal with aberrations that are judged to have emerged from any or all three of these institutions. And so we have the *sorer u-moreh* and the *bayit ha-menuga* and the *ir ha-nidahat* all facing destruction in the name of the covenant.

The Rabbis, on the other hand, whose wisdom constitutes the *Torah she-be-al peh* (the Oral Torah), consider themselves charged with interpreting and legislating a Torah which is to be alive to a nation's real needs in the face of human temptations. The new Israelite society will have to learn not just to think about applying high spiritual, moral, and social standards while they are in the Wilderness. They will have to flesh out idealistic sociomoral theories in the Sturm-und-Drang reality of building a civil society out of the "wilderness" of human day-to-day struggle. These Rabbis will carry the extra burden of knowing that the First Jewish Commonwealth in Israel has risen

and fallen; and that the Second Jewish Commonwealth in Israel has risen and fallen with even a shorter and more fragile period of sovereignty than the first.

The traditional liturgy will reflect Israel's collective sense of guilt in having failed the covenant. The liturgy will also express Israel's collective appeal for mercy in the face of standards that have demanded perhaps too much. And so the Rabbis, viewing the three pillars of continuity, lean towards God's attribute of mercy in liberating the *peshat* from its overly severe strictures: (1) It will be deemed impossible to determine that a young individual shall be sentenced to execution because he may have stepped over an arbitrary line which defines intolerable gluttony. (2) It will be deemed impossible to determine that a family's dysfunction is so final, unalterable, and irredeemable that new chances cannot be offered for rehabilitation and recovery. (3) It will be deemed impossible to determine that a community be destroyed because of general idolatry, when it is always possible that even in such a degenerate community there are on some Israelite houses *mezuzot* representing monotheistic hope.

The concern for the health of these three pillars which make up the state of the nation will justify through the integrated use of both the attribute of justice and the attribute of mercy collective concern for all aspects of human living and intercourse. Even the most intimate secretions of the human body are subjects of concern to the legislation of Leviticus. Because these secretions are connected with semen for the man and menstrual blood for the woman, they are identified with ultimate considerations of life and death, birth and denial of birth. Whether or not legislating for such intimate areas of an individual's life is the community's responsibility will be the subject of continuous debate until and including especially the modern era. The Torah's *peshat* position will argue that male and female discharges are not just private "issues" — pun intended — but sooner or later, directly or indirectly, they become questions of public concern.

The coming chapters in Leviticus will be discussing and legislating appropriate sexual behavior for the Israelite covenanted community. But here, before the specific sanctions and prohibitions are listed, there is a review of various physical discharges to be treated, including the source for what will become in Jewish tradition the cycle of woman's pure and impure days. The spiritual foundation of these concerns is the foundation for all the legislation

— ritual, moral, social — in the Book of Leviticus. It is holiness; a holiness indissolubly connected to health, physical, mental, and spiritual. When Isaiah in his scalding attack on the Jewish community of his day will look for an appropriate rhetoric he will choose the medical: "Every head is ailing, and every heart is sick. From head to foot no spot is sound: All bruises and welts, and festering sores — not pressed out, not bound up, not softened with oil." All this by way of describing a land which is now *shemamah* (a wasteland)!

Isaiah's rebuke is climaxed in the comparison of Jerusalem with Sodom. The echoes of such a comparison cannot but recall Rashi's allusion to the treasures of the Amorites, left behind in the leprous houses which will have had to be destroyed. But Isaiah's picture of the wasteland is not a tragic remembrance of the rise and fall of the Amorite empire. This time it is a horrific description of the rise and fall of the *Israelite* empire. The sickness is all pervasive. The sanctity has been irretrievably defiled.

In contrast, Moses has seen Egypt from both sides of the master/slave divide. He owed his early nurturing not only to his own mother assisted by his sister but to Batya the daughter of Pharaoh who had qualities of gentleness in her — enough to succor a slave child and to raise him to be an Egyptian prince. As such, Moses knows that the masters of Egypt had enough nobility of intellect and spirit to build an empire. But in seeing and mixing with the Hebrew slaves, Moses had seen the decay undergirding that empire. Unlike the later Isaiah, Moses at this early stage in the history of Israel has the opportunity to "enjoy" the optimism of a new venture along with the revelatory inspiration of a God who really expects a new evolutionary step in the upward progress of the human spirit.

For Moses then, as recorded in Leviticus, it will be an uncompromised attempt to preach sanctity as the goal of this evolutionary process. Through an understanding of God's Torah, Moses is convinced that only a fully committed reaching-out towards sanctity of soul and body can enable the individual, the family, the community, and thereby the nation to become a "treasured people, kingdom of priests, and holy nation." Moses is offering the new Israel a new agenda, a sweeping comprehensive program of personal, familial, and communal purification. The very idea, the very aspiration to achieve a level of spiritual awareness that will seek to legislate attitudes and behavioral patterns towards the most mysterious aspects of human physiology bespeaks the spiritual ambition of the Torah. The Rabbis will refer to the Torah as no less than the *sam ha-hayyim* (the elixir of life).

Both Moses, and Isaiah after him, will know, however, that the factor complicating the sanctification of this new human being, this new family, and communities of families is that the process is to take place as the Children of Israel live out their destiny not in a sequestered "holy" environment artificially protected from the world. On the contrary, it is to be in the secular "way of the world" environment where the test will be monitored. It must be this way, for God has created the "secular" world. It is there where the enterprise must succeed — or fail to succeed.

From National Sickness to Health

Israel will fail to succeed — twice. It will go into exile and suffer the anguish of dependency, traumatic insecurity, national degradation. What will "save it" spiritually will be a heightened commitment to sanctification of the individual, familial, and communal soul and body. Desperate to maintain its national or at least its communal élan, the Jewish people in exile will prescribe for itself a regimen of observances — ritual, ethical, and social — that it will insist is the way to sanctify the Name. It will exhaust itself as it will fight to survive poverty and powerlessness. It will never lose the dream, however, of returning to the original format-opportunity of building a sovereign society in sanctity. In the meantime it will have created a model for *galut* living in sanctity which will provide soul-filled dignity to a people otherwise deprived.

And then there will come the Emancipation — sooner or later in all parts of the world to which Jews will have been exiled. The call for redemption — more accurately, self-redemption or auto-emancipation — will accelerate. The "health-sickness" metaphor will be turned in on itself by a Leo Pinsker, a physician by profession, who will be decrying the tragic state of his Jewish people: "In a sick man, the absence of desire for food and drink is a very serious symptom. It is not always possible to cure him of this ominous loss of appetite. And even if his appetite can be restored, it is still a question whether he will be able to digest food, even though he desires it. The Jews are in the unhappy condition of such a patient."

Will Pinsker and his fellow "rebels" be considered slanderers, looking to defame with leprous talk a holy people brought to lofty heights of spirituality precisely because they have been in exile? Or in an ironic turn of history and destiny determined by both realpolitik and transcendent agendas, are Pinsker and the others preaching at least half of Moses' levitical message — that if there is ever to be a chance of implementing any program of human betterment, cultural, social, ethical, spiritual, it must be in a comprehensive situation of sovereign independence. A Sephardic rabbi from Sarajevo, Yehudah Alkalai, will legitimize the "rebels" by insisting that "redemption will come *naturally*, not miraculously, for even according to the way of the world the redemption will be wondrous; for the wonder will be that it will come from the *nation itself*."

Moses in the Wilderness, speaking of leprosy and purification, bodily intimacies and spiritual portents, is wagering that his nation is listening and preparing itself. He believes that his investment in the detailed lessons of Leviticus will bear sanctified fruit. The question will always be whether or not the nation believes it, too.

Aharei Mot אחרי מות

Moses is now possessed with the task of concretizing for his people the dream of the covenant, so he piles ritualistic detail upon ritualistic detail, all somehow having to do with holiness and purification. Israel must be taught to resist the blandishments of spiritual pollution and moral profaneness. It is not enough for them to recall the Exodus; they must translate the memory into an active agenda which maintains their clan as a chosen people for a chosen destiny.

They will tell and retell the story of their emancipation from slavery. They will make the telling an essential part of their annual celebration of the event. But throughout the telling they must remind themselves of the temptations which from the beginning have sought to sway them from their holy purpose. Future liturgists of the people will recognize the backslidings in Jewish history. They will not hesitate to quote that most vitriolic of prophets, Ezekiel, in their preoccupation with teaching the importance of holiness, with emphasis upon its blessings. At the same time they will realize the pedagogic necessity of periodic warnings and chastisement.

The Reality of Evil

Ezekiel the priest-prophet will choose to lament the faithlessness of the people, their ungratefulness, in stark withering terms: "By origin and birth your father was an Amorite and your mother a Hittite. As for your birth, when you were born your navel cord was not cut, and you were not bathed in water to 'clean you.' No one pitied you enough to do any of these things for you; there was no compassion for you; on the day you were born, you were left lying, rejected in the open field. When I passed by you (says the Lord) and saw you wallowing in your blood, I said to you, out of your blood come alive, out of your blood come alive!" Rabbi Eliezer will ask why does the prophetic text have to say the phrase "and I said to you, out of your blood come alive" twice? His answer will be that by the merit of the *dam Pesah* (the blood of the Paschal Lamb) and the merit of *dam brit milah* (the blood of the covenant of circumcision) God will have redeemed Israel from Egypt and will redeem Israel again in the future.

For Israel, any ingestion of blood will be considered an abomination. But as dedicatory reminders, the two "blood" symbols separately and together will represent the two contrary gestures which will define Israel. The blood of the Paschal Lamb on the doorpost of each Israelite household in the eyes of all the Egyptians will constitute a proclamation of auto-emancipation from the idolatrous conformism of the larger totalitarian society. And the blood of the circumcision will continue from the time of Abraham to be the positive sign of the covenant — the sign of positive self-identification as God's witnesses. As long as Israel is prepared to accept the burden of the two-sided "blood" commitment, it will receive God's favor. But Ezekiel will prophesy in an age when Israel will have forgotten God's original largesse in having "nursed," as it were, Israel as a newborn babe. They will have rejected the Torah; they will have denied God and violated His covenant.

The same Ezekiel — like Moses — will never reach a point of such despair that he will reject Israel. On the contrary, it will be the same Ezekiel who will envision the resurrective capacity of Israel in the supremely vivid miracle of dry bones coming together and growing anew sinews and flesh. But Ezekiel and the other prophets including Moses himself will take pains to understand the causes of Israel's backsliding.

Will it be a matter so fundamental to the origins of humankind that to expect Israel to transcend the machinations of the Serpent will be naïve if not dangerously irresponsible? For Moses is ready to accept the proposition that evil is not just an absence of good. The elaborate ceremony of casting lots on goats, one goat for God and one for Azazel, cannot be merely a vestige of pagan myth which, for populist reasons, Moses feels he has to integrate into his agenda of ceremonials. Granted, the monotheistic ground on which the Bible is based will insist that Azazel — or the Serpent — is not and cannot be an independent source of evil, that God is the source of everything. Nevertheless, it is clear that the biblical mentality is preoccupied with the reality of evil, the potency of it. The Bible holds that the world that humanity inhabits may be initially good and ultimately good; but in the interim, there is a relentless battle being waged between supremely powerful forces — Good and Evil. Not to respect the power of evil is to already expose oneself to lethal consequences.

What is Azazel? Within the literature there is a fanciful explanation in the Book of Enoch (and other places) that explains that during the corrupt generation of the Flood, God is, to say the least, dejected. Two angels named Shamhazai and Azazel (or Aza'el) step forward to address God in His melancholy state: "Lord of the Universe, didn't we tell you when You created Your world that Man cannot be relied upon." God protests: "But what then would happen to the world? Who would serve as My caretaker in the world?" They answer: "We would!" God says: "It is clear to me that if you two were attending to the world, the evil impulse would so dominate you that you would be no more resistant to temptation than Man." Shamhazai and Azazel plead for the opportunity to live among the creaturely beings in order to prove God wrong. They promise to sanctify God's Name in the world. God agrees.

Their mission, as anticipated, is a disaster. They fail almost immediately. As God predicted, the two angels — not being able to control their *yeitzer hara* — fall into fornicating with the daughters they find on earth. The legend continues with Shamhazai repenting, suspending himself upside down between heaven and earth and continuing indefinitely in a state of repentant suspension. Azazel does not repent. Without pause he continues to corrupt his way on earth as a clear and present model and temptation to any vulnerable human being. Therefore "Israel offers on Yom Kippur a sacrifice to Azazel so that he should suffer the sins of all Israel."

That the legend has emerged from this mysterious ceremony in the Book of Leviticus reinforces the emphasis of the book on *kedushah* (holiness). For the striving after holiness is intended to be the only possible antidote to the venomous power of evil. Human beings have a need to deny that evil is this powerful. And so human beings have cultivated a natural capacity for cathartic repression and neutralized the stark truth regarding this power of evil. Through art, through discussion and analysis, through reasoning and rationalization, human beings will soften, dull, blunt the sharpness of evil's threats and destructive manifestations. But these same human beings will discover that simplistic, humanly initiated, and actualized definitions of morality and Man's moral predicament are weak, unpredictable, and plainly inadequate in the face of unadulterated evil.

The history of Israel will mark periodically the attempts of various forces for good — and for minimal survival — to combat contrary forces for evil. The marking will reach a nadir in the twentieth century with the Shoah. Post-Shoah explanations for the unspeakable sociomoral catastrophe will range from seeing the Holocaust as a vast collective madness to viewing it as a result of a series of political, social, economic, and technological circumstances all converging to bring about for the exposed and defenseless victims total disaster, nay almost total extinction. But the most fundamental explanation — the "simplest," albeit the starkest — will rarely be enunciated: the appearance and reign of Evil Incarnate, supported by actively willing and passively accepting hordes of millions of otherwise "civilized" human beings.

Moses is prepared to accept the reality of Evil Incarnate in his legislating ritually for the sacrifice to Azazel. His descendants of a much later "more tolerant" age will becloud the issue and will thus leave themselves more vulnerable than otherwise might need be. For self-deception in the name of an anticipated "perfectibility" of humankind will lead these descendants to accept political emancipation as messianic. Instead it will turn out to be a chimera concealing anti-Semitic hatred ready to be ignited at the first opportunity.

Moses is arguing that if there is a strategic-pedagogic antidote to the power of evil, it must entail going beyond conventional morality. It must have as an indispensable ingredient reverence for the human being qua human being created in the image of God. The realm of *kedushah* postulates a therapeutic mystery to the intrinsic condition and ultimate value of every human being. Within that mystery, no human being's life may be violated. Until and unless Israel absorbs that message, until and unless humankind as a whole can be educated to absorb that message, they will all resemble Shamhazai, the angel suspended upside down in the world with no possible means of setting the world straight and therefore helplessly subject to the wiles and wishes of Azazel.

Rabbi Joseph Hertz's modern commentary on the Torah, for example, will reject the notion held by the medieval Ramban and others that Azazel is a wilderness demon. His claim will be that the Torah condemns the offering of sacrifices to satyrs. But a serious look at the Ramban will in no way suggest that worship of Azazel is to be commanded or encouraged; but that precisely on Yom Kippur, the Day of Atonement, the goat to be sent into the

Wilderness is being sent to the demonic force in nature which is represented by "wilderness," i.e., *hurban* ("destruction"). It is sent there to acknowledge that there is a power that is associated with "the sword, wars, quarrels, wounds, plagues, division and destruction." Whether or not the Ramban's world-view or cosmology will satisfy later theologians, philosophers, or even common-folk, his major thrust is that evil when uncontained has an independent lethal force and must be reckoned with as such, confronted, and defeated, as such.

Holiness versus Evil

The confrontation with evil must be done nationally, communally, and individually. In his ongoing legislative instruction to Israel, Moses moves back and forth from considerations of public policy to private morality. It is all to be orchestrated and modified by Torah. A review of a series of propositions which guide the legislation is in order: (1) the goal of the Torah is not merely to create a *morally sensitive* individual, society, and nation; (2) it is to create a *holy* individual, society, and nation; (3) if the earth and its social organisms are vulnerable to the machinations of evil, conventional morality will not be sufficient to counteract the stratagems of Azazel; (4) therefore, there must be a stronger transcendent force brought to bear in the battle for ultimate good, ultimate justice, and ultimate harmony.

Holiness — a socially engaged holiness — will have a keener insight into the evil reality in all its starkness. The world may be described as an arena where a cosmic battle is being waged between cosmically potent forces. Conventional morality keeps a tenuous balance between the two, leaning slightly to the good so that bare existence is possible; and as such, maintaining standards of conventional morality is necessary. But it is not sufficient! It will not lift that existence to a new level of humane potential. A higher truth and a more dynamic spiritual thrust is needed. And the higher truth lies in the beauty and sublimity of holiness, a relevant this-worldly holiness!

Relevancy begins with the family. A listing of all forbidden sexual liaisons, underlining every sexual sin and perversion, is to mandate a sense of pervasive purity in that most intimate psycho-physical theater of human relationships. To many the admonition will seem severe. But the two overriding guidelines are clear: (1) Negatively speaking, the worlds of Egypt whence

Israel has emerged and Canaan into which Israel is to enter are to be rejected along with their debased sexual mores. And (2) in order for the rejection to be efficacious, Israelite sexual standards must be clear and "severe"; there can be no compromise, or Azazel will subtly intrude, lead astray, subvert, and pervert.

The standard of "holiness" which will include conventional standards of morality but which at the same time will transcend them is intended to keep Israel from being lost among the nations, lost among the "Egyptians" and the "Canaanites" of any given generation or of any given locale. Even if the conventional standards of the particular nations are not debased to the level of ancient Egypt and Canaan, Israel is intended to live among them but at the same time to be *distinguished* from them. Yaakov Herzog summarizes it in his book *Hen Am Levadad Yishkon (It Is A People Which Dwells Alone):* "There is no nation in the world which has only one religion, and there is no religion in the world which is restricted to one nation. There is no nation in the world which in order to define and maintain its existence has to plan strategies not only in wartime but in peace time as well." Except Israel, that is, argues Herzog! Dwelling alone, yet among the nations, requires a profound defining of identity and purpose. The identity and purpose have been articulated at Sinai and are here being detailed in the Holiness Code of Leviticus.

Moses' defining instructions become the foundation for endless later variations, interpretations, and commentaries. Among the most comprehensive, for example, is a definition given by Rabbi Yehudah the Prince in a debate with the Rabbis over the question of the power of Yom Kippur to bring atonement to Jews who have been sinful as individuals and as a people. The debate begins with the well-known majority assertion that the observance of Yom Kippur brings with it atonement provided the observance is accompanied by *teshuvah* (repentance). But Rabbi Yehudah the Prince appears to disagree. He says: "Yom Kippur atones for all the sins of the Torah regardless of whether or not there is *teshuvah* — except for three sins: And they are (1) *'porek ol'* ('breaking the yoke of God's kingship'), (2) *'megaleh panim ba-Torah'* ('revealing arrogance to the Torah'), and (3) *'meifir brit basar'* ('violating the flesh-covenant')."

The question arises: what sins can Rabbi Yehudah be referring to when he asserts that whether or not the sinner does *teshuvah*, Yom Kippur provides the atonement? Surely, the Torah covenant's concern for morality cannot countenance a ritual cleansing, i.e., that effected by Yom Kippur, without requiring a concomitant moral cleansing. Unless we consider those sins done inadvertently without knowing one has committed them! Or perhaps hurting people indirectly without being aware that one has done it! A human being may seem to be "permitting" evil, when in truth one was helpless to prevent the occurrence. In all such cases. Rabbi Yehudah appears to be saying: "Let the mysterious blessed process of Yom Kippur with its fasting and confession provide the atonement — even without *teshuvah*." After all, how could there have been *teshuvah* in such cases? The sinner didn't know that he had sinned. God's love for Israel lets the Jew atone for these sorts of sins by means of Yom Kippur alone.

But then Rabbi Yehudah excludes three cardinal sins which are unforgivable without the fullest and sincerest repentance. In these three cases the observance of Yom Kippur alone is ineffective: (1) breaking the yoke of God's kingship, i.e., abandoning the God of Israel; (2) revealing arrogance to the Torah or, in other words, rejecting the detailed prescriptions of the Torah of Israel; and (3) violating the flesh covenant, more specifically, cutting oneself off from one's flesh-and-blood relationship with the Children of Israel. These three cardinal sins cannot be atoned for by the mere fasting of Yom Kippur.

In reviewing these three sins, however, one is struck by the realization that, taken together, these sins are so comprehensive that Rabbi Yehudah's whole argument appears deceptive. These three sins include everything contained in the covenant! But no! A Jew — as cited above — may not know that he is committing a given sin. Or he may know, but for him the sin may seem trivial enough so that the non-observance of the given *mitzvah* or the violation of the given trivial norm may not seem critical to him. He may genuinely believe that he has faith in the God of Israel, that he has respect for the Torah tradition, and that he is sincerely loyal to the Jewish people. And so, such a Jew really believes that he has not violated Rabbi Yehudah's conditions.

But here Rabbi Yehudah's argument turns out not to be deceptive at all — nor transparent. His argument is severe in its insistence that without realizing what may be happening, the Jew, the Israelite, living out his daily life without a constantly renewed commitment to the covenant and its prescriptions for holiness, may be letting three things happen: (1) his faith in God may be slipping; (2) he may be neglecting his attention to the legislation of the Torah; and (3) he may be losing his association with his flesh-and-blood people.

And Rabbi Yehudah is insisting that such slippage, such neglect, and such loss of connection is inexcusable, unforgivable, and unatonable.

Moses is dispensing to Israel a Torah of life. A human being may be able to live out his life without God, without Torah, and outside the reality and destiny of the Children of Israel. But for Moses and, it is felt, for the God who redeemed Israel out of Egyptian bondage, a Jew removing himself (1) from concern with the fulfillment of God's kingship, (2) from the daily life of Torah, and (3) from the living association with the House of Israel is committing the supreme violation of the terms of the emancipation from slavery. It is obvious that when God says: "You shall keep My laws and My rules, by the pursuit of which Man shall live," He means a life to be lived *in a special way* in order that there be *a special quality to that life — call it "holy"!*

The Life to Be Lived

Again, what is this life to be? Rashi considers that the "life" to be lived ideally is one which cannot be achieved in this world. Here, sooner or later everyone dies. The ideal "life" promised, therefore, must be reserved for *olam ha-ba* (the next world). Nevertheless, in order to earn that "life" in the next world one must live the life of the covenant here and now in this world. For Rashi this means the fulfillment of a spiritual-religious mandate. The Ramban, contrary to Rashi, interprets the "life" intended as life on this earth. It is to be a life assured and protected by the laws of society and for the peace and well-being of individual members of that society so that injury and mayhem are avoided and public order is maintained. Hundreds of years after Rashi and the Ramban, the Netziv of Volozhin sees in the verse a prescription for an all-encompassing vision of a human being on earth who is different from an animal. The life of an animal is fully described and circumscribed by his creaturely instincts. A human being, on the other hand, has not fully achieved his "life" potential unless he has reached intellectual, moral, and spiritual fulfillment.

Moses, in this sense, sees a fully alive Jewish people in its own land as having the task of aiming to achieve national fulfillment by expanding its intellectual, moral, and spiritual horizons. Thus the ongoing struggle that Israel will face will be precisely over every aspect of human endeavor legislated in anticipation by the Torah. A wise man will someday describe such a struggle as "the turbulence of earthly things in the presence of God." Moses' message may be summarized as follows with the help of all three interpreters respectively. The Ramban offers at the most basic primitive human level a scheme for minimal social survival with the Torah's laws offering the details of that scheme. The Netziv presents the Torah legislation as a scheme for particular human self-development in order to reach maximal humane potential. Finally Rashi affirms that the keeping of the detailed scheme will connect one with eternal spiritual forces — transcending human limitations, extending beyond individual mortality.

The message of "*ve*-hai *bahem*" ("you shall *live* by them") will be the guiding force propelling the Children of Israel throughout their history. It will motivate the lives of communities well through the middle ages and into modernity. With the coming of the Emancipation, an A.D. Gordon will translate the biblical injunction "*ve-hai bahem*" superimposed on the command to be a "holy nation because I am holy, (says God)" into his idea of an *am-adam* (a specially endowed humane people). He will see this *am-adam* as a this-worldly realization of the original "wilderness" dream of *goy kadosh*. What Gordon intends is for an old/new nation to see itself as bearing a special mandate to reflect humaneness. And the humaneness, even in Gordon's "secular" terms, bears the imprint of the transcendent, of the holy.

Is It Possible? The Zionist Response

The post-Emancipation State of Israel will look upon itself — echoing the Ramban's interpretation of "*ve-hai bahem*" — as the bearers of civilization. The builders of the State will recognize an ancient truth that there is nothing ennobling about poverty and disease; that there is a positive human value to prosperity and to democracy as the least humanly destructive form of government. Churchill in 1939, embroiled in the White Paper controversy with Prime Minister Chamberlain, will remind the latter of his statements in 1919: "A great responsibility will rest upon the Zionists who, before long, will be proceeding, with joy in their hearts, to the ancient seat of their people. Theirs will be the task to build up a new prosperity and a new civilization in old Palestine, so long neglected and misruled."

The post-Emancipation State of Israel — the third Jewish Commonwealth — will struggle to bestow a new definition of covenantal commitment upon its Jewish citizens. As the Children of Israel will have done twice before in Jewish history, the modern State of Israel will serve as an arena for humane interaction among its variety of populations. A Gentile writer, John Le Carre, will describe the polyglot aggregate of people as "the most colorful carnival of human variety that I have ever seen in my life." He will note the "process of self-molding based on the shards of its past, one moment Eastern, one moment Western, one moment secular, one moment religious, but always admonishing itself, and testing its morality, criticizing itself… a nation bursting with debate, constantly revealing its past at the same time that it fights for its future." The Netziv's interpretation of *"ve-hai bahem"* — in addition to the Ramban's — will thus not be alien to Le Carre's vivid description of a living actualizing Jewish state.

As to Rashi's dream of spiritual transcendence as process and ultimate reward for living the life of holiness, the post-Emancipation State of Israel will for Joseph Klausner be its concretization — even in its secular form. Following the Shoah and before the official establishment of the State, Klausner will proclaim without a shred of inhibition: "This nation whose abilities are greater than other nations, and whose sufferings are proportionately greater… ultimately its future cannot be anything but great and good! Messianic days must come provided humanity doesn't destroy itself completely. But those days will come to Israel first, and only through Israel will they come to other nations. Ours has been the Messianic idea and ours will be its realization; and in Zion in which the Messianic idea was born, will be its center and its zenith."

Will such an encomium seem prideful to the point of arrogance? On the contrary, against the background of Moses' admonitions in Leviticus, which will be endorsed and exceeded in passion in Deuteronomy, and against the background of an endless *galut* (exile) following previous failure at sovereignty, let alone Messianic fulfillment, Klausner's statements will be "humbilifying." To become a holy nation and/or a humane nation will not only be daunting. It may be, in the final prognosis, impossible. But the goal will always be claimed as achievable. The goal will never be seen as inhibiting the covenantal effort. Faith in God will command the effort. The real and lethal presence of Azazel in the world will demand it.

Kedoshim 

And so Moses and the Torah and the later Jewish tradition argue that against the power of evil conventional morality is insufficient and inadequate. One must bring to bear in the battle against evil other forces cultivated by the power of *kedushah* or holiness. The command of Leviticus 19:2 "You shall be holy, for I, the Lord your God, am holy" appears as an absolute command with no additional explanation, condition, or qualification. It is to be considered a goal with no further justification needed. In Israel's quest to understand the Torah from an anthropocentric point of view, however, the *need* for "holiness" is justified as the need to develop those resources capable of combating evil. So be it! But whether "holiness" is a goal or a means, it is *the* relevant religious category that conditions everything else Israel does or is supposed to do.

Crystallizing Holiness

For this reason, *"kedoshim tihyu"* ("you shall be holy") must be interpreted in the broadest, deepest, and most comprehensively unlimited sense. One must be careful not to restrict the observance and maintenance of "holiness" to certain specified areas of Torah legislation under the pretext that everything not dealt with in the Torah is permissible. The Ramban's critique of Rashi underscores the demand for unlimited creative legislation in all areas of human life. Rashi explains *"kedoshim tihyu"* as directed principally at sexual improprieties. "Separate yourselves from sexual sins," he says, and emphasizes in the word *perushim* the importance of removing oneself, segregating oneself, as it were, from the temptation to fall into the net of sexual licentiousness, i.e., *averah*.

But the Ramban disagrees: "In my opinion, this recommended '*prishut*' ('withdrawal') is precisely *not* to be restricted to sexual 'felonies' and 'misdemeanors.' There is to be no limitation to the recommended *perishut.* It is meant to refer to all areas discussed in the Talmud by those authorities who are known as *perushim* or Pharisees. The Torah is certainly warning against sexual libertinism — as it warns against consumption of forbidden foods. But even in those areas which are permitted, such as sexual intercourse between man and wife, the eating of kosher meat, the drinking of permissible wine," the Ramban cautions against overindulgence of one's appetite. One should not claim that since these acts are permitted by Torah legislation, therefore "anything goes," e.g., a man may fornicate with his wife, be gluttonous with kosher meat and wine, and speak loosely and lecherously. In other words, "let no one excuse himself by citing that if certain activities or modes of activities are not mentioned in the Torah, they are therefore approved. On the contrary, such an argument is the argument of a *'naval bi-rshut ha-Torah'* ('a scoundrel with the permission of the Torah')."

The bitter sarcasm in the phrase *"naval bi-rshut ha-Torah"* echoes all the acerbity in the prophetic critique of Israelite society with particular venom aimed at religious hypocrisy. Even with all the halakhic detail given in the Written Torah, let alone the Oral Torah, not every conceivable circumstance can be covered by a positive or negative command. The person who considers himself religious and moral must cultivate a religious and moral character, a religious and moral intuition, which he can rely upon to inform his behavior even when specific injunctions — positive or negative — are not given in writing. That the injunctions in the portion of *Kedoshim* in Leviticus as in similar portions in Deuteronomy seem to lack a particular order only emphasizes the purpose of Torah legislation: *all* areas of human conduct are to be "justiciable." He who would hide behind the excuse that his "preferred" area of licentiousness hasn't received legislative attention is no less than a *"naval,"* indeed a scoundrel!

There are two major errors regarding the definition and function of *kedushah* in the world. The first is that to be holy is to remove oneself from the world. Granted, the word *perushim* might suggest principled separation. If it does, the separation is only for the purpose of constantly returning to life in order to raise life to higher levels of sanctity. For sanctity is that dimension intended to refine the human being so that he may climb the ladder to more and more creative levels of humaneness vis-à-vis the world and the humanity dwelling therein.

Corollary to the first error is the second: that the world is meant to be compartmentalized, that is, divided permanently between sectors which are to be pre-determined as respectively holy and profane. The Torah opposes any such compartmentalization, even though the movement towards holiness within the profane or secular world is always unsteady and unpredictable. In the Torah's stipulation that Israel is to be a holy nation it places before them not just an ecclesiastical regimen, but a life's regimen as lived in the secular world. The "ecclesiastical" regimen itself is to include a range of instructions that overlap into the "secular" realm, where moral standards are expected to be maintained. Not only is care with respect to the sacrificial cult to be meticulous! Not only must all semblances of divination be rejected! Each of these standards applies to the ecclesiastical realm. But offering up children to Molech is to be condemned as *both religiously and morally* abhorrent.

There is further overlapping of the "religious" and the "socioethical" in laws such as: the prohibition against cutting of the flesh, the prohibition against sacred harlotry, and the rules regarding *orlah*, i.e., holding the fruit of trees to be uncircumcised for the first three years, sanctified for the fourth year, and only available for food thereafter (when they are presumed to be fully ripe).

In order to maintain a dynamic push towards creative application of holiness in society-as-lived, each member of society is to be considered responsible for everyone else. Among the further commands given by Moses in this portion of *Kedoshim*, therefore, is the summary verse *"hokhei'ah tokhi'ah et amitekha ve-lo tisa alav het"* ("reprove your kinsman so that you incur no guilt because of him"). As a more pointedly severe extension of this command there comes the talmudic assertion in *Shabbat* 54b: "Anyone who can protest to the members of his household regarding their wrongdoing and does not is liable for their wrongdoing. Similarly, anyone who has the capacity to protest to the citizens of his community regarding their sins and does not is in turn himself liable for their sins. And similarly regarding the whole sinful world, he who might consider himself innocent is not at all innocent if the rest of humanity is failing spiritually and morally." In short, this "innocent" human being is liable for the shortcomings of everyone else, if he could have somehow influenced others and did not.

Further to this teaching, the Rabbis tell a homiletic tale in which God is described as One who has never retracted His favorable word on behalf of someone once He has given it — except in the following drastic situation: God is on the verge of destroying Jerusalem which has become corrupt. He instructs His messenger Gabriel to go through the midst of Jerusalem and to set a mark of ink upon the foreheads of the righteous ones in the city so that the destroying angels will not have power over them. Gabriel is further instructed to continue on his inspection tour of Jerusalem in order to set a mark of blood upon the foreheads of the wicked so that the destroying angels *will* have power over them.

The *Middat ha-Din* ("the Attribute of Justice") protests to the Holy One Blessed Be He saying: In what way are these different from these? God says the obvious — that one group are *tzaddikim* (righteous) while the other group are *resha'im* (wicked). But the *Middat ha-Din* continues to challenge the Holy One Blessed Be He with the claim that the righteous have had the capacity to protest, to demonstrate their active opposition to the wicked ways of the *resha'im*, but didn't! God answers in turn that any such protest, any such manifestation of corrective opposition would have been in vain since the wicked would in any case not have heeded any warnings from the righteous. Nevertheless the *Middat ha-Din* persists in his prosecution of the *tzaddikim*, arguing: "Lord of the Universe, perhaps it was revealed to You, who are omniscient, that the wicked would not listen to any moral admonitions; but the mortal *tzaddikim* certainly didn't know that!" And so, the story concludes, God begins the destruction of Jerusalem with the righteous, the so-called righteous, who could have and should have been in the forefront of the battle to have the wicked, the so-called wicked, repent in time to save Jerusalem!

The Jewish liturgical tradition will encapsulate this idea of collective guilt in confessionals like *"ashamnu, bagadnu, gazalnu...rashanu, shihatnu, hamasnu"* ("we have trespassed, we have dealt treacherously, we have robbed...we have been wicked, we have corrupted, we have been iniquitous"). Such collective self-incrimination precedes the litany of *"al het shehatanu"* ("for the sins which we have committed"), knowing full well that we couldn't possibly have been directly guilty of all the sins listed. Yet, if we as potential *tzaddikim* could have prevented others from perpetrating the sins, the crimes, the misdemeanors, and we didn't, then we — if not criminally responsible — are certainly spiritually and morally responsible for not having borne more of the burden of collective spiritual and moral effort within society.

Many centuries later, atheistic existentialism will seem to be imitating the Torah in placing total responsibility for the fate of the world upon the shoulders of the single individual human being. Jean Paul Sartre will claim: "Man being condemned to be free carries the weight of the whole world on his shoulders; he is responsible for the world and for himself." The weakness, however, in the atheistic existentialist position is in its naïve lack of concern for moral content, value content, aimed at establishing and maintaining humane relationships in a world too prone to interpreting freedom as license to descend to moral depravity. For Israel, the Torah places a value-laden burden on its shoulders, not spelling out every conceivable sociomoral application, but giving enough detailed instruction so as to leave no doubt as to the Torah's all-embracing covenantal purpose.

The Place of Criticism

If the fundamental concern for building a covenantally inspired humane society rests on each individual being prepared to correct himself and others, how prepared are individual human beings for the necessary criticism which must precede correction? The Rabbis debate the issue in terms of the readiness to criticize, the readiness to accept criticism, and the method for giving criticism. Rabbi Tarphon would be astonished to find anyone in his generation capable of *giving* reproof. Rabbi Elazar ben Azariah would be astonished to find anyone in his generation capable of *accepting* reproof. And Rabbi Akiva would be astonished if anyone in his generation knew *how* to reprove.

Rabbi Tarphon's concern is that in his generation any objective standards for measuring appropriate behavior seem to have been lost. Under such circumstances who then can be looked to as the spiritual-moral "paragon of virtue," respected enough by most to rearticulate acceptable normative spiritual and moral standards. Rabbi Elazar ben Azariah is asking a psychologically grounded question: "Is there anyone so secure in his own spiritual-moral self-esteem as to be capable of receiving reproof?" Such a person must accept and suffer the fact that he is less than perfect. Furthermore he must be open to the goal of self-improvement and desirous of working towards it.

When Rabbi Akiva's contribution to the discussion focuses on the *way* to give reproof, he is not avoiding the question of whether there are in his generation worthy-enough people to give and receive reproof. On the contrary, the Talmud tells the story of Rabban Gamliel inflicting blows on Rabbi Akiva when the latter would err. Rabbi Akiva cannot have been delighted with the corporal punishment. Yet not only does he not object; but Rabbi Yohanan ben Nuri reports that "Akiva was often punished through me because it was I who would report his errors to Rabban Gamliel, but all the more did Akiva shower love upon me (despite my tattling)." In the initial and final analysis, Rabbi Akiva represents the verse from Proverbs: "Do not rebuke a scoffer, for he will hate you; reprove a wise man, and he will love you."

Akiva, notwithstanding his beginnings as an ignorant man, will rise to become a leading sage among his people. It will be Akiva who will be representing Torah learning in generations long after Moses. And following in the footsteps of Moses' humility, Akiva is ready to accept reproof — no matter how "brutally" it may be given by a Rabban Gamliel. The summary conclusion is that the injunction *"hokhe'ah tokhi'ah"* is aimed at *amitekha* (your fellow), the Accadian root *emutu* meaning family or community. Unless there is ongoing reproof there are no standards. Without standards there can be no stability within family and within community. Conversely, only in a true family or community is there honest and well-intentioned reproof. For without reproof, i.e., self-correction, re-optimization of means and ends, there can be no long-term survival.

If then the continuity and durability of the family and the community are dependent upon the capacity for constructive critical interaction among its members, then the key determinant for character development of the individual is precisely his interaction with others. It is not simply defining an individual member of society as holy or moral; it is his actions vis-à-vis others that determine whether he is an agent who acts in an ethically holy manner.

The Kotzker Rebbe has a well-known epigram: "If I am I because I am I and you are you because you are you, then I am I and you are you; but if I am I because you are you and you are you because I am I then I am not I and you are not you." The contemporary search for existential authenticity of the individual finds such an epigram supportive. But the epigram is only half-true. The legislation of the Torah assumes that our spiritual and moral identity is forged in the crucible of societal interaction. We seek social relationships in order to fulfill a basic part of our character. The authentic "I" is an elusive shadow waiting to be "fleshed out" in the hurly-burly of interlocking relationships, so that in at least a partial sense "I am I *only* because you are you and you are you *only* because I am I."

The long list of miscellaneous sociomoral instructions that dominate the portion significantly entitled *Kedoshim* reinforce the determination of moral agency as resting upon interpersonal relationships. Parents are to be feared. The institution of the Shabbat is a communal responsibility. And then there is a list of miscellaneous sociomoral *mitzvot*: leaving crops for the poor; condemning all manner of theft, cheating, and lying; not standing aloof when witnessing injustice to others; respect for the elderly; maintaining fair weights and measures; absolute abhorrence of adultery, incest, bestiality, and all forms of abnormal sexual liaisons.

Between "I" and the "Other"

This does not mean that the "I" as a subjective kernel of personality does not exist. The Torah prescribes for a terrain of activity in which the "I" as subject is struggling to measure up to the spiritual demands made upon him by ritual. On this terrain, the person trying to be holy struggles to be a *korban* (sacrifice) in the sense of being worthy of standing before God's Presence. What may prevent him from doing so is the so-called *se'or she-ba-isa* (the leaven in the dough), otherwise known as the *yeitzer ha-ra* or "evil drive" — the drive that prevents us from transcending our animal nature and thus limits our capacity for spiritual attachment to God.

But eventually whatever spiritual heights "I" perceive myself to have attained as a result of meticulous observance of the rituals, I cannot pretend to be a representative member of a holy nation, a nation commanded to be holy, unless I am fulfilling the sociomoral injunction *"ve-ahavta le-re'akha kamokha."* I am mandated to fulfill in my behavior the injunction "to love the other as myself." Is it possible? Yes, respond mothers and martyrs. Yes, respond fathers and spouses. But even if it were not psychologically possible, the command is there — and it is there in the name of God: *"Ani Adonai."* The tradition understands and accepts the difficulty. Rabbi Akiva states that *"ve-ahavta le-re'akha kamokha"* is a great general principle in the Torah. At the same time, he articulates the normative principle that *"hayekha kodmim le-hayei haverkha"* ("saving your life pre-empts saving the other's").

Akiva's latter principle is exemplified in the oft-taught story of the two men stranded in the desert with A in possession of enough water to save his own life but not the life of B, the "Other." B has no water. Ben Petura concludes that both must share the limited supply of water even though as a result they will both die. Akiva disagrees, but not because he does not feel the tragedy of both B and A. Akiva knows that in A saving his own life — a legitimate decision — he will never be entirely free of the guilt-ridden responsibility for the decision. But this story is meant to be taken as an abstraction with none of the real-life emotional, psychological, and ethical dimensions of the decision to be considered in each specific case. As an abstraction, it poses the question: Individual cases aside, how is one to make a decision under such radically urgent circumstances? Of course, both lives are equally precious. But shall they therefore both die when one can live? Then how is one to decide who shall live? There must be an objective method for deciding. The flask of water objectively resting in the possession of A decides the matter — in the abstract.

The Torah from the beginning, in its insistence that each human being is created in the image of God, has established an objective criterion for measuring the value of each human being. A different aspect of this objectivity is recommended in Hillel's turning the injunction "to love one's fellow as oneself" into his negative application: "That which is hateful to you do not do unto your fellow!" The positive formulation of "Do unto others…" may be too subjectively "creative" and may lead to the imposition — well-meaning or otherwise — of one's subjective tastes on one's fellow. Hillel's negative formulation recognizes the common objectively real factor of feeling pain and injury to one's body, mind, and spirit. Such pain and injury are universally felt. Thus the content of Hillel's principle can serve as a powerful objective formulation of a lofty moral injunction.

The verb "love" in the Torah injunction "to love your fellow as yourself" is less challenging than the objective "as yourself." You are to be reminded that your fellow is like yourself. As such he deserves to be treated with justice and fairness. It is impossible to love everyone, let alone with the concern one has for oneself. But the degree of love in terms of emotional arousal, empathy, and affection cannot be relied upon in the way that the objective fact can;

namely, that he is another human being, whether you love him or not, and must be treated justly and fairly. In the dilemma that A faces abstractly in the talmudic example, Akiva's decision is excruciatingly painful because he may love B as he does himself. The decision, therefore, is taken out of A's hands and placed in the realm of objective value: each life is equal to another; if one life can be saved, let that which is closer to yours — your own — have priority. Put another way, that the Torah leans on objective criteria for determining obligation to all human beings cannot gainsay the fact that at times it is impossible for "I" to do right to everyone or to be fair to everyone.

On the national level as well, the Torah recognizes the legitimate ethnocentric preferences and priorities of Israel — not because Israel considers itself "the chosen people," but because ethnocentric concern is natural. Who else is there — objectively speaking — to give priority to Israel's welfare if not Israel? Israel is reminded constantly that it must treat the stranger justly and fairly, that it must never forget that it too was "a stranger in Egypt." But this does not and cannot mean that Israel must deny its own right to national survival because of an abstract universalism which is inapplicable in the maelstrom of realpolitik.

As a nation, Israel has come onto the world scene and has settled in an area which will geographically always find itself astride greater powers than she. As such, Israel will have to ascertain how best to survive as an independent national entity, considering her relative weakness. If the conquest of Canaan — less than complete under Joshua and the Judges and King Saul — reaches its apogee under David and Solomon, there is no assurance that Israel will maintain its independence forever. Indeed, Israel's own imperial achievements will bear with them the seeds of future socioreligious, political, and military decline and disintegration. But Israel's unbroken historic loyalty to the covenant, notwithstanding the falling away of many individual Israelites and Jews from its terms, requires at the heart of its sociopolitical existence an obsessive concern for surviving as a nation. It has an objective right to survive as all other nations do. It has a natural instinct to do so — as all other nations do — and needs no further moral justification to do so.

The covenant and the Torah have added a further condition: Israel's history will appear to its faithful as a Sisyphean effort destined to go through periods of cultural and political efflorescence only to find itself thrust into the calamity of foreign occupation, exile, and dispersion. The faithful will consider that surviving as a nation for no other purpose but some minimal sort of national distinction is in the eyes of most peoples adequate. But Israel — or at least the faithful within Israel — will insist upon adding to its natural instinct for survival the burden of the covenant. Not only will this entail an additional concern beyond mere national survival for national survival's sake! The faithful will dare to insist that if the covenanted Israel disappears, the God of Israel will "disappear"! In other words, for the faithful within the nation of Israel, national survival is a cosmic necessity as long as such survival is in tune with the terms of the covenant!

The Eternal Covenant

Israel's history will always be marked by periods of national vulnerability. And this sense of vulnerability will contribute significantly to the molding of the collective Jewish psyche, a psyche perennially expecting apocalypse and at various crossroads in its history having to suffer it. Ezekiel the prophet will live out his service to God and Israel in the eye of one such apocalypse, the loss of Jewish sovereignty in Israel to Babylonia, the destruction of the Holy Temple, and the first exile.

For the covenanted Israel, the loss of sovereignty will entail not only national defeat and humiliation. It will involve, according to Israel's understanding, either a total loss of prestige for the God of Israel, or, worse, God's rejection of Israel and the breaking of His covenant with them. According to the forebodings mentioned in Leviticus and later in Deuteronomy, what will have been threatened will have come to pass. And so it will be a fully plausible conclusion for Israel to believe that just as the Amorites had been sentenced to destruction and extinction once its "sin had been full," so will Israel. Indeed, defeat and destruction do come; and most of Israel is sent into exile.

Ezekiel is one of those who has witnessed the catastrophe and gone into exile with his compatriots. Ezekiel, among all the prophets of Israel, may be considered the most wrathful in his attitudes towards his people. In his eyes, they have become impure in their violation of the laws of the covenant. Their rebelliousness against God's will has been manifest from the beginning. It is their sin which has brought on the apocalypse. It is they — not God — who have broken the covenant because of their heart of stone.

Everything has been foretold; everything has come to pass. But Ezekiel in

Babylon — like Moses in the Wilderness — will never abandon his people! He will inspire their recovery from despair by having them readjust to a new theological perspective. Ezekiel in Babylonia will never stop his prophetic daydreaming. We have stressed several times Ezekiel's universally known daydream. He will envision a reborn Israel, a resurrected organism coming to life in its own land. The House of Israel will not have been abandoned to perdition and ultimate extinction. The covenant will not have been abrogated — at least not as long as Israel will refuse to believe that it has.

Ezekiel will envision a valley of dry bones: the classic biblical vision of hopelessness. For at first, everyone, and especially the prophets, and most especially the angriest of the prophets, Ezekiel, will be unable to cope with the military, political, sociomoral, and theological disaster. Is this the end? As quoted earlier, the *Yalkut Shimoni* reflects this despair even in the prophet's response to God's first question to him "Shall these bones live?" More pointedly, God asks Ezekiel: "Do I have the power to make them live or not?" Ezekiel gives a brief response, but one which is fully reflective of the mood of the people: "O Lord God, You know!" More to the point — the *"ata yadata"* means, "*You* must know, because we mortal, sinful House of Israel surely do not know!" To this response, the *Yalkut* comments categorically *"U-le-fi shelo he'emin, lo nikberu atzmotav be-eretz tehorah"* ("because Ezekiel didn't believe, his bones were not buried in the pure land of Israel").

The question to Ezekiel is *the* serious question — one in two parts: a national one, i.e., will the nation of Israel continue to live or come alive again? And a spiritual or theological one, i.e., will the God of Israel continue to "live," that is, to function in reality as the covenanted God of Israel? God's message in the vision is revelatory in an emphatically pristine sense: "O mortal, these bones are the whole House of Israel. They say, 'Our bones are dried up, our hope is gone; we are doomed.' Prophesy, therefore, and say to them: Thus said the Lord God: I am going to open your graves… and bring you to the land of Israel…I will put My breath into you and you shall live again as I will set you upon your own soil." Moreover as Amos will have predicted before Ezekiel, the God of Israel will rebuild the fallen *sukkah* (house) of David. God will "mend the breaches, set up its ruins anew, and build it firm as in the days of old." The sovereignty of the Children of Israel over the Land of Israel will be restored! In short, the covenant will never be broken, it cannot be!

Granted, the Israelites will from time to time fail to fulfill the mandate of the covenantal injunction "*kedoshim tihyu.*" And the consequences of such failure will bring disaster — but never total rejection and abandonment. What Israel will learn in Babylonia, during the first exile, namely, to survive as a people in exile while waiting and planning for a return to the soil of Israel, will inspire them to endure when the long exile comes following the loss of the Second Jewish Commonwealth at the hands of the Romans.

Israel has been "condemned" to keep hoping and struggling to be *kedoshim*. The comfort will be that even in falling short — and suffering for it — they will continue to walk in the light of the Creator, Revealer of Covenants, and unfailing Redeemer — an often tragically disappointed Redeemer, but Redeemer nevertheless, first of Israel, then of the world.

Emor אמור

The Book of Leviticus in its legislation for holiness is not always easy to digest. According to its own internal logic, because the spiritual, moral, and social stakes are so high, i.e., walking covenantally with God, the punishments are concomitantly severe. The beginning and the end of *Parshat Emor*, for example, record two punishments which according to modern sensibilities are barbaric. The first concerns the daughter of a priest who has played the harlot. *"Ba-esh tisaref"* ("She shall be burnt"). The second refers to the blasphemer whom God instructs Moses to have stoned. The Rabbis in the Talmud will mitigate the priestess' punishment somewhat by arguing that the Torah is not referring to the more "innocent" harlotry of an unmarried priestess. It speaks of one who is already married or betrothed to be married and who has committed adultery. In the case of the blasphemer the Rabbis justify the punishment by associating the sin with the insidious attempt of the sinner to influence the entire House of Israel to sink into apostasy.

To the post-Enlightenment sensibility the punishments are plainly unacceptable no matter how much one may abhor the sins committed. For Moses, however, living millennia ago, the issues are clear and the punishments appropriate to their time. The Israelites are preparing to enter the Promised Land where the practice of institutionalized sacred harlotry is prevalent. The covenant which Israel has agreed to preaches the message of sexual and moral purity for the entire people who are to be a "kingdom of priests." All the more so for the officially designated priestly families! The daughter of a priest, therefore, must be particularly careful to protect her reputation.

As to the severity of the blasphemer's punishment, the general commitment of Israel to the One true God of the Universe who is pre-eminently the God of Israel demands a general humility on the part of all. The blasphemer has sinned — not just in cursing the Almighty, a patently serious offense under the terms of the covenant, but in denying any humble impulse, the blasphemer in effect has proclaimed in public that God is not the ultimate authority. If such is the case, then the entire covenant is a charade. In the "eyes" of God, therefore, Who instructs Moses accordingly, the blasphemer is indeed guilty of a capital crime and must be punished accordingly.

Eternal Values Reinterpreted

Descending into the realm of apologetics seems pathetic when referring to a value system which has been revealed ostensibly by God. Nevertheless it must be admitted that it is difficult not to associate punishments such as burning at the stake and stoning for blasphemy with theocracy at its worst. That the world has witnessed the iniquity of religious institutions justifying inquisitions and autos-da-fé is an irrefutable historic fact. This historic fact must be confessed and confronted straightforwardly.

In the face of moral difficulties emanating from a sacred text, Professor Moshe Greenberg's approach is therapeutic. Regarding the cruelties of such biblical punishments as well as other morally "difficult" passages, Professor Greenberg speaks unapologetically. He argues instead for the necessity of understanding the phenomenon of *hityashnut hagshamat arakhim* (the obsolescence of given concretizations of values).

Greenberg's thesis rests on three assumptions: (1) that the Bible's legislation is not a listing of external instructions aimed at robot-like obedience, but that there are worthy universally timeless values underlying its laws, its statutes, and its recommended norms; (2) that these values are concretized in the Bible in specific time-bound *halakhot* ("norms") — time-bound and custom-bound to given contemporary biblical modes of thought and behavior; and as such, (3) some of these concretizations may become morally obsolete with the passage of time without impugning the relevancy and ongoing vitality of the values underlying these concretizations.

Reviewing the case of the harlot, we remind ourselves that the Bible maintains its pristine insistence on respect for human beings. This respect suggests specific attitudes towards sexual modesty and dignity. These values are held to be eternally valid, notwithstanding the possible desirable *modification of punishments* for violations of sexual modesty and dignity that future generations may determine are necessary.

With regard to the case of the blasphemer, we again review fundamental value concerns. Why does the Bible insist on respect for human beings? Because they are *God's* creatures who are charged with superintending *God's* creation. In recognition and thanksgiving for the gift of life which has been bestowed upon human beings, humility is the value most critical to be absorbed by that species of created "animals" who have been charged with superintending the world. Humankind, because it has so much responsibility and has been blessed with so much capacity for good, must constantly be aware of the lurking threat of hubris. Humility — as opposed to hubris — is taken to be an eternal immutable value. Later generations will decide not to stone someone for blaspheming God; but humility as a value still stands firm and inviolate.

Once it is understood and internalized sufficiently that the values undergirding the covenantal structure of Torah legislation are clear, firm, and inviolate, then the Oral Torah will see to it that various concretizations of these values will be reexamined and, if and when necessary, changed. Such a strategy cannot be suspected of antinomianism. The injunction — repeated in similar form in many places — "You shall keep My commandments and do them, I am the Lord" is an uncompromising charge. And it is explained in unequivocal terms in the following verses in Leviticus 22:32-33: "You shall not profane My holy name, that I may be sanctified in the midst of the Israelite people — I the Lord who sanctify you, I who brought you out of the land of Egypt to be your God, I the Lord."

The covenant assumes that the values which it is propagating are eternal. These values are held to be the indispensable ethical pillars of the world. The Israelite individual and the House of Israel as a collective are charged with the responsibility of "*tikkun olam*" ("mending that world"). And the *tikkun* is not intended to be "merely" spiritual — vaguely and comfortably antinomian. An intense particularization of Torah concern is meant to be the charge and responsibility of a vital committed society. In other words, intense particularization of Torah concern means a constantly renewable Torah — and when necessary a changeable Torah — concretizations upon concretizations of values in order to "mend the world."

To be concerned about the threat of antinomianism, however, is not to denigrate the indispensability of the spiritual dimension in the life of the individual Israelite. For God to be "sanctified in the midst of the Israelite people," He must somehow be in the "soul-consciousness" of every individual

Israelite. How can God's Presence within the soul or soul-consciousness be ascertained? In an objectively verifiable way, it cannot be. But at the same time, it must not be denied, for the unique dimension of consciousness that we call the "soul" insists that God's Presence not be denied.

Abraham Joshua Heschel has referred to the urgency of watching over the soul as *"piku'ah neshamah."* In the spirit of the traditional early morning prayer the Jew thanks the Lord for creating the *neshamah* ("soul"), for molding it, for breathing it into him, and for protecting it within him. But the task of cultivating the soul's receptiveness to the finely-tuned demands of mending the world, of bringing it to higher levels of *kedushah* (holiness), is left to the individual. Does the individual find such a task too intangible? Is the intangibility of *kedushah* too elusive for the individual to grasp? But then again, are there not other intangibles, Heschel asks, that are so vividly real that they not only become institutionalized but are among the most powerful grounds for social living.

The institution of the "promise," for example, is among the most common intangibles without which society could not function. As long as my word is in me, says Heschel, "it is mine, but once I have opened my mouth and uttered my word (my promise), then I cannot take the word back, I cannot profane my word...for my word has become a sanctified force which rules me, which lurks at my door compelling me to fulfill it!" And so the vast majority of people will keep their word, their promise. They will desist from violating their word, their promise. For they accept intuitively that "promise" is one of the recognized indispensable institutions of committed communication. Yet, the institution of "promise" is built on an intangible. Furthermore, it is an intangible real enough and strong enough to make it possible for human beings to grow together, to help one another, to mend, as it were, God's creation. Why then should the intangible which is *kedushah* be any less powerful in mending God's creation!

Within the realm of faith, God Himself is considered *kadosh* (holy). For Israel to be charged with aiming towards *kedushah* is to enjoin all Israelites to be committed to imitatio Dei. Moreover, as Samuel Hugo Bergman has underscored, aiming towards *kedushah* is a process by which Israel performs *yihud*, or joining oneself to the enterprise of proclaiming God's unity and uniqueness to the world. When the Children of Israel participate fully in the enterprise, they become witnesses to God's Existence and Presence. As

Shimon bar Yohai has put it: "If you are My witnesses, then I am first and after Me there will be no other; but if you are not My witnesses, then, so to speak, I am not God."

The Holy Days

Aside from the behavioral particulars which Jewish tradition has associated with *kedushah*, its intangible penumbra should preclude its ever being associated with idolatry. God himself is *kadosh*; as such, the human being experiences God as dynamically intangible, but with a special numinous quality. God does not have the static quality of a permanently felt Other. He is much too free and all-powerful for any static association. Whereas various worship rituals draw their strength and predictability by appearing to be static in their demand for order, the intention of the Torah is far different. Just as the pillars of cloud and fire in the Wilderness are to represent God's *dynamic* Presence, all ritual from prayer to holiday observance must similarly evoke — despite their repetitiveness — a creatively dynamic sensitivity to God's gifts of life and its mutability appreciated by Torah.

Holiday observance is another mode of reifying the intangible quality of *kedushah* and using time and the marking of time as a vehicle for sanctification. In Thomas Mann's *The Magic Mountain* the comment is made: "Time has no divisions to mark its passage, there is never a thunderstorm or blare of trumpets to announce the beginning of a new month or year. Even when a new century begins it is only we mortals who ring bells and fire off pistols." In other words, marking off time in order to recognize significant events is a humanizing phenomenon. But the Torah is moving beyond the humanizing dimension. At the very outset of creation as envisioned by the Torah there is a marking off of time. The creative force which brings the world into being in six segments of time sets aside a seventh segment of time for a cessation of creative effort with no loss, however, of numinous power. God resting from work is a silence which is thunderous.

This first cosmic marking of time is a precursor of a whole series of other countings: seven weeks between the holy days of *Pesah* and *Shavuot*; a seventh year of land-rest and debt-release; seven seven-year cycles leading up to the Jubilee year of emancipation and restoration. The marking is a distinguishing. The marking is itself a celebration of awareness of blessing, an appreciation of self-awareness. It is a way of structuring one's experiencing of life — past, present, and future. In the Torah itself, Israel superimposes upon the cycle of natural time-celebrations narrative-markings, i.e., the history of its birth as a people and specially endowed occasions marking other historic events in the life of Israel. The spring planting becomes the celebration of the Exodus. The fall ingathering becomes the celebration of Israel's sojourn in the Wilderness under God's protecting clouds of glory.

The significance of the counting and the marking of days is most vividly illustrated by the evolution of the holiday of *Hag ha-Shavuot*. Of the three later-to-be-known pilgrimage festivals, *Hag ha-Shavuot* is not given a historical significance in the Torah. It has already been given at least an implied significance by associating it with the Revelation at Mount Sinai. But it has not been connected to a historic occasion by explicit reference. Why is *Shavuot* treated differently than *Pesah* and *Sukkot*? The answer is clear. At the time that the Torah is given, the chief "value" connection for the holiday is *bikkurim* (bringing the first fruits to the sanctuary), and this hasn't happened yet, nor will it happen before Israel enters the Promised Land. There is a double message here having to do respectively with place and time.

Pesah and *Sukkot* are originally connected valuationally with the *golah* (the exile). *Pesah* represents emancipation from slavery with God bringing Israel into its incubation period of forty years in the Wilderness. The incubation will be provided by a caring God in this Wilderness; and the caring is represented practically and spiritually by *Sukkot* and its huts in which Israel will be protected by God's clouds of glory. *Shavuot* has no connection with the *golah*. The revelatory event at Mount Sinai will be celebrated on *Shavuot*. And the Sinai event will certainly have valuational implications for later Judaism wherever Jews will live. Nevertheless, these implications cannot be fully realized until Israel enters the Promised Land. For among the many covenantal mitzvot which Israel will then perform, the bringing of *bikkurim* will be most representative of an entire collective and personal attitude of thanksgiving for God's largesse.

So it is assumed that an essential part of Israel's opportunity and capacity to realize the values commanded by the Torah is the *place* in which realization will take place. But this place will also provide *time-frames* for the *mitzvot*. Rashi comments on the incidental phrase "*ha-yom ha-zeh*" (this day): "Each day shall the '*mitzvot*' appear new to you in your eyes as if you have been commanded regarding them on this day — and every day in the future." In other words, the possibilities for the realization of the *mitzvot* in the new land will be an everyday challenge.

Heightening the importance of every day as a freshly given opportunity for affirming the covenant is the seven-week ceremony of counting the *omer* (the measure of barley) each day between *Pesah* and *Shavuot*. Counting day after day the valuational movement from physical emancipation to covenantal dedication is itself a religious value. The *Sefer ha-Hinukh* summarizes the pedagogic purpose of the "counting": "The whole purpose of the creation of Israel is the Torah; as indeed similarly the whole purpose of the creation of heaven and earth is Torah... Israel has been redeemed from Egypt so that it should receive the Torah at Sinai and proceed to fulfilling it. It is the principal good for which they've been redeemed, more important substantively than freedom from bondage... The counting everyday from *Pesah* to *Shavuot*, to the giving of the Torah, is to show — by the counting — the great desire for that yearned-for day. The counting, repeated day after day, is indicative of the longing to reach that day." The Psalmist will speak of the therapeutic importance of counting days for the individual qua individual: "Teach us to number our days, so that we may get us a heart of wisdom."

The process of counting days in order to mark given days as special, as holy days, as festivals, as reminders of historic events and their accompanying blessings and challenges, assures a particular mode of celebration. Unlike idolatrous rites which are often accompanied by *holelut* ("riotous revelry"), the very purpose of the major Torah-endorsed holy days — Shabbat, *Pesah*, *Shavuot*, *Sukkot*, Rosh Hashanah, and Yom Kippur — is to emphasize *yirah* (reverie) and *ahavah* (love). Assuming that the observance is in tune with these lofty value-concepts, then joyousness — not lightheadedness — will be the prevailing mood. For expressing *yirah* and *ahavah* seriousness of purpose is required. Shabbat, after all, celebrates creation, on the one hand, and the emancipation from bondage on the other. Reverential appreciation is the order of the day, not *holelut* which aims to distract, to intoxicate by distracting from seriousness. And while the other holy days have slightly fewer halakhic restrictions as to observance, the tone for all of them is set by Shabbat.

Two Modes of Work

The covenant, the Torah, and Judaism will take their stand against various kinds of hedonism by arguing for the joy which comes from celebrating seriousness of purpose, or, put another way, celebrating the *bearable heaviness of being*. It will not trust, for example, the concept of "leisure" and its accompanying institutions. For, as Northrop Frye has noted in an essay entitled "The Instruments of Mental Production": "In a society devoted wholly to labor, leisure would be thought of as merely rest or spare time: if there is continuous leisure, it becomes idleness or distraction. Idleness and distraction are reactions against the unpleasantness or dullness of labor: they make up for the time wasted on work by wasting time in other ways. A life divided only between dull work and distracted play is not life but essentially waiting for death, and war comes to such a society as deliverance, because it relieves the strain of waiting."

The covenant, the Torah, and Judaism demand a fully conscious concentrated effort at living. The recommended living is not to be so unrelievedly intense that one can never pause to celebrate. On the contrary, the holy days come along precisely as a commanded opportunity to celebrate. To celebrate what? To celebrate Israel's record of mending the world, and to celebrate the ongoing blessing of covenanted responsibility for that world. If the parameters of an individual's world are seen to embrace in concentric circles one's family, one's community, one's nation, and all of humanity, and the work that one does is perceived as serving one or more or all four of these communities, then the work, even when tedious, will be considered by serious men and women as contributing to life and therefore not predicated on necessary boredom "waiting for death."

Moses is a leader of a people that has just emerged from slavery. Slavery by definition means, on the one hand, no leisure time and, on the other hand, no constructive purposeful work for the benefit of the slaves. Moses has seen and lived in both worlds — the world of the enslaver and the world of the enslaved. He knows the leisure world of the hedonistic aristocracy. Yet similarly he has seen the endless, meaningless *be-farekh* (oppressive and cruel) labor of the slaves. He knows that only a sense of covenantal purpose can energize the people into offering their labor in dedicated service to their own independent communities and thereby forestalling the torpor of "waiting for death."

The rhythm of meaningful work interrupted regularly by celebrated cessation from work is the pristine message of the Creation story in Genesis. The six-day period of *avodah* (work) is as much *avodah* (worship) as the Shabbat. For *avodah* is mending God's world and Man's world. Time and the filling of time with the "work-worship" of mending the world is then a guiding measure of the rhythm of sanctified human existence. Moses projects this rhythm-in-time to his people. It will serve this people not only in their attempts to build viable societies in their own sovereign state; even in exile it will help them endure the poverty, unpredictability, political vulnerability, and often hopeless labors forced upon them by the constant struggle to survive.

Exile, Emancipation, and Zionist "Work"

Enduring the exile, however, will lead eventually to a blunted sensibility to the ravages of time, to life's vicissitudes within historic time. Following the destruction of the Second Temple and the loss of the Second Jewish Commonwealth, the Children of Israel will have endured the long exile. They will have become so accustomed to the exile that they will fail to sense radical changes occurring within time-frames of national and international upheaval. They will have been maintaining in exile their observance of the Shabbat and Holy Days; but they will have neglected to emphasize the this-worldly national implications of the celebratory message of these days, i.e., that Israel is meant to be redeemed from national bondage in order to build a sovereign state which can exercise its independent right to mend the world according to Torah.

Modern European emancipation will suddenly shine forth illuminating a whole new world of seemingly open vistas to Jews in exile to join humanity in an ethnically undifferentiated search for liberty, equality, and fraternity. Many Jews will rush blindly forth. Others will have very clear visions of opportunity to achieve personal material success, fulfilling personal dreams of human dignity, and cultural participation with non-Jews in building a new reason-based universalistic civilization.

Still others, primarily in Eastern Europe, will cling to the old ways as if deep in an endless *galut* slumber unaware of the storms of change. A Yiddish poet, Alexander Krein, will adapt an old talmudic *midrash* on a phrase from Isaiah *"ata boker ve-gam layla"* ("morning has come and also night") which speaks of conditions for future Messianic deliverance. But Krein will be speaking of lost opportunity. He will write of Ya'akov the eternal wandering peddler starting out on *motza'ei Shabbat* (Saturday night) after *havdalah* to begin a work week. He will ride his horse and wagon filled with merchandise until he falls asleep leaving the sleigh to pull the lonely figure Ya'akov along. Through storms and cataclysms he is pulled up and down hills and valleys. Fierce winds engulf him and yet he sleeps and sleeps and sleeps. When he finally wakes up and realizes that major upheavals have passed him by, he calls out to God: "How long would you have let me sleep!" And God answers sardonically: "Morning has come and night has come — but alas, you have slept through it all!"

Indeed, the rhythm of time in exile has so dulled Ya'akov-Israel that he may have missed not only what his brethren in the West have experienced, even if that particular emancipation will have its own mixed consequences, positive and negative. He will have missed as well the opportunity to react with initiative as a relative "master of his own fate." Instead, he will be caught and eventually trapped by circumstances over which he will have no control. Moreover, he will not quite know what has brought him to the gulf of personal and near-national extinction.

A small group will wake up — but not to blandishments from the West. They will seek emancipation — both from the tempting new universalistic invitations which they will not trust and from traditional "*galut*-rooted" religious interpretations of Jewish nationalism. They will be the secular Zionists realizing a covenantal dream encompassing time and place. They will be lending — in traditional biblical fashion — historical significance to their work on the land. They will have a sense of mission, of heavy seriousness of purpose even as they will suffer the vicissitudes of an unsympathetic nature, hostile Arabs, disappointment, discouragement, and occasional despair. But these pioneers will embody a new/old dream calling to their brethren all over the world to join a contemporary enterprise hoping to resurrect their entire people. Rachel in her poem "Here on Earth" (translated by Ruth Finer Mintz) will call out:

Here on the earth — not high in the clouds —
On this mother earth that is close:
To sorrow in her sadness, exult in her meager joy
That knows, so well, how to console.
Not nebulous tomorrow but today: solid, warm, mighty,
Today materialized in the hand;
Of this single, short day to drink deep
Here in our own land.
Before night falls — come, oh come all!
A unified stubborn effort, awake
With a thousand arms. Is it impossible to roll
The stone from the mouth of the well?

The thousand arms of Jacob-Israel's descendants are being called by a latter-day poetic namesake of his beloved Rachel to roll the stone from the mouth of the well of living waters. These waters will make the land bloom again. These same waters will revive to this-worldly covenantal service a new "levitical" class — workers of land for a new/old people and, though they will never admit it, workers of land for a new/old God.

Be-Har בהר

As Moses moves towards his peroration in Leviticus he relates to the issue of personal enslavement. This is not surprising. He has lived his life as a prophet egged on by a double obsession: shepherding an enslaved people out of their enslavement and assuring that the commonly accepted institution of slavery is neutralized or in some way mitigated within the new covenantally inspired Israelite state.

Moses is not naïve. He knows that the institution cannot be eliminated entirely. He knows that foreign slaves will continue to be a necessary source of manpower and that it will remain for future generations to soften the stringencies regarding these foreign or "Canaanite" slaves. Indeed the later Rabbis will be pressuring for the conversion of these foreign slaves to Judaism and in the process thereby freeing them.

As already indicated in the legislation found in *Parshat Mishpatim* the Israelite indentured servant who has fallen to his low estate because of debt or theft is assuredly not a "slave." He is working essentially as a protected employee while he "pays" his debt. The assumption is that he will conclude his service in six years. Should he decide at that time that he prefers his situation as an indentured servant, he is made to suffer the ignominy of having his ear pierced and remaining in service, other things being equal, until the Jubilee when he must go free.

Slave, Servant, and *"Eved Hashem"*

Rabbinic tradition dictates that on Yom Kippur of the Jubilee year, the *eved ivri*, that is, the Israelite servant-employee returns to his family and to his inheritance. But he is released from his servitude on Rosh Hashanah, ten days before. This is to fulfill the injunction "to sanctify publicly the beginning of the fiftieth year in declaring liberty for all the land's inhabitants." Why the need for a hiatus of ten days between his release and his return home? Rabbi Yishmael explains: "From Rosh Hashanah until Yom Kippur the *avadim* ('servants') do *not* go home, but at the same time are no longer indentured to their masters. They are enjoined to eat, drink, and be merry with crowns on their heads. When Yom Kippur arrives, the court blows the *shofar*, and the *avadim* then return to their homes and the fields return to their original owners."

The question is asked: "Why eat, drink, and be merry with crowns on their heads?" And Rashi answers: "To show that he has gone out in freedom." It is not at all odd for the rabbinic tradition to recognize that there is a psychological need for a slave to try on the trappings of creaturely "hedonistic" freedom — to eat, drink, and be merry, with a garland on his head — all in the house of his erstwhile master. What *is* odd, nevertheless, is that this particular transitional phase is to take place between Rosh Hashanah and Yom Kippur, the period which will become known as the "Ten Days of *Teshuvah*" — the period of repentance, of spiritual and moral turning.

The Ten Days of Repentance for the *eved* is indeed a time of turning. The *eved* needs ten days of turning from his old "slave" mentality. But a turning to what? To himself as "king," i.e., as relative sovereign over his own future, with his former master still in front of him reminding him of his former subjugation. Is this the best mode for throwing off the yoke of his subjugation — by eating, drinking, and being merry? The tradition may be showing here a mature understanding of human nature in endorsing a clearly hedonistic indulgence. At the same time the coming of Yom Kippur will represent the very opposite mood as it enunciates a completely different message. On Yom Kippur there is no eating, no drinking, no merrymaking, and absolutely no acknowledgment of a human sovereign. Not "I" as sovereign nor any other human being as sovereign — not the master, not the erstwhile slave! Only God is recognized as King; and when the *eved* is fully able to recognize only God as King, he is then ready to return home a truly free man.

Perhaps in allowing "the Ten Days of Turning" to serve the indentured servants as a time of sensuous release, the Rabbis are more tolerant than Moses was in viewing the "merrymaking" surrounding the "golden calf." Perhaps not! For the real message of the Rabbis is essentially the same as that of Moses: Individual Israelites and the House of Israel in general who are given their freedom may choose to devote their lives to eating, drinking, and merrymaking. But then they will have forfeited the humanizing purpose of their freedom, let alone the sanctifying purpose. Only when they look up from their creaturely "play" in order to face God, and to walk with Him, will their freedom be harnessed to noble purpose. In later Jewish history, opportunities for emancipation will always offer erstwhile "slaves" the options of living lives dedicated either to merrymaking or to covenantal mending. The world itself and its plethora of human civilizations will all face the same choice as they free themselves from the pressures of minimal creaturely sustenance.

Moses' concern with the issue of slavery has been energized from his days as a prince in Egypt. He has brought the enslaved Children of Israel out of bondage to face a new sociopolitical situation and challenge. Among the strongest teachings of his Torah, the following statement will summarize God's view of enslavement: "The earth can never be sold to any human being permanently; for the earth is Mine and therefore all mankind are resident aliens on it." Since all human beings are only resident-aliens on earth, there can never be any justification for one human being or set of human beings ruling permanently over other human beings. Furthermore, the common situation of all humankind — resident aliens all — should inspire degrees of empathy emanating, at the very least, from a clear awareness of "there but for the grace of God go I."

Since all human beings are equal in their relationship with their Creator, i.e., they are all *avadim*, they cannot be eternal servants of other servants. In this sense, every worker in the human marketplace — employer as well as employee — is a servant! Granted, the relationship between employee as servant and his employer may appear from a theological and moral point of view to be intrinsically problematic. This would be so, however, only until both understand that their functions and responsibilities may differ, but that as human beings before God they are equal.

Hermann Cohen has pointed out that in the Torah every worker is called an *eved*. There is no term to distinguish between a worker and a slave. Furthermore, he who fears God and worships God is also called an *eved*. The Messiah is called *eved Hashem*. Therefore, an *eved* can never be considered irredeemable property. He always remains an individual personality, a human being. It is for this reason that the phrase in Leviticus 25:40, "he shall be with you," is explicated in the Midrash *Sifra* as "with you in food, in drink, in clean raiment." As stressed earlier, it is understood that the master must treat the servant with care and consideration to the extent that the proverb is coined: "He who acquires a Hebrew servant has acquired for himself a master."

Utopian Dreams versus Reality

Moses places before Israel God's idealistic dream of social and economic equilibrium. The question may be asked, however: Ideas such as *shmittat karka* (Sabbatical land release), *yovel* (the jubilee year) in which there is a general return to original land holdings, and as will be cited in Deuteronomy, *shmittat kesafim* (Sabbatical cancellation of loans) — are these not utterly impractical? And if they are not practical, of what benefit are they? Moses, it is true, is a great idealist. That he has permitted God to convince him of the covenantal purposes motivating the drive to bring Israel out of Egypt and into the Promised Land is proof of his idealism. And as an idealist, there are at least three in-depth theological sociomoral propositions with economic implications to which Moses is committed: (1) that the earth is the Lord's; (2) that each human being has been created in God's image; and (3) that all men are brothers, as it is written, "*ve-hai ahikha imakh*" ("may your brother *live* with you").

At the same time, Moses is a short-term and middle-term pragmatist. But even as a pragmatist, Moses holds to the proposition that if a society is not built on the above three idealistic principles, it will go under through sociomoral decay. The seventh-year release, the jubilee, etc., may have been impractical even in its biblical day, all the more so in modern times; but Moses is looking to create an overall attitude of benevolence in society.

And the Torah is not at all "impractical." Moses' intention is to break through the pattern of slavery. How? With a number of "impractical" principles; but there are practical specifics as well. The indentured servant is emphatically not to be treated as if he were a slave but as a resident employee-for-hire. The overriding injunction is to be "*lo tirdeh bo be-farekh ve-yareita me-elohekha*" ("You shall not lord it over him oppressively and cruelly; for you must fear God in your treatment of him"). From this injunction is derived a series of obligations to the employee beyond the obvious one of honesty and fairness in the payment of wages. "*Be-farekh*" is the word associated with the grossest aspect of the Egyptian enslavement of the Israelites. Rashi interprets the word to mean *melakhah she-lo le-tzorekh* (work which is unnecessary), and because unnecessary, it is work in order to degrade and to dehumanize. The employee is to be treated as an equal because "*ve-yareta me-elohekha*" ("you shall fear the Lord"). Just as you have been created in God's image, so has the employee.

A tradition of rightful treatment of employees will serve as the precedent for much later generations of Jews becoming leading figures in socialist movements, moderate and revolutionary. Not that Judaism and Jewish law would be oblivious to the obligations of *employees*: to produce honestly and creatively! But what would be crucial for the *employer* would be the development of the moral dimensions of his own personality. He would be charged with developing righteous traits in himself. It would be mandatory for the employer — not just gracious — to treat his employees fairly. An example of this moral-educational goal would be reflected in the evolving tradition regarding severance pay: Anyone who would hire an employee, whether for long-term or even short-term service, would be obliged to give him a parting-amount when he left, above and beyond that which had been his contracted salary. Why? So that "we may acquire for ourselves noble traits, precious and sweet qualities."

The social dimension of being human, in other words, is seen by the Torah to be of equal therapeutic and moral importance to both dispenser and beneficiary. It is in everyone's interest that all human beings within society live with dignity and economic self-respect. Rashi summarizes the view: "To begin with, do not permit your fellow to fall so that it will then be difficult to lift him up; rather strengthen him as soon as you see him in tough straits. To what is it like? To a burden on a pack-animal — as long as it rests on the animal, one person is sufficient to hold it in place. Once the burden falls, then five are not sufficient to lift him and the burden."

The idea then of *shemittah*, as of *yovel*, is a dramatic extension of the idea of "the human being representing the image of God." In a profound spiritual, moral, and aesthetic sense, the entire portion of *Behar* is a reflection of Eden. It is a dream of a "return to Eden" in that God and Moses are preparing for a newly born people fresh out of bondage to settle a covenanted land. In that land, Israel the people is to build an idyllic social organism where the answers to the questions at the heart of early Genesis — *ayeka* and *ey Hevel ahikha* — will be "Here I am, O Lord, ready to serve you and indeed ready to be my brother's keeper."

Historically speaking, the institution of *shemittah* seems to have worked for a while, at least regarding *shemittat karka'ot* (Sabbatical land release). By the time of Hillel, *shemittat kesafim* (Sabbatical cancellation of loans) had to be circumvented by the *prozbol* legal fiction. The institution of *yovel* probably never worked. Nor could it ever work without social engineering of bewildering, possibly horrific Maoist dimensions! Yet, these institutions of intended serious socioeconomic consequence are legislated by Moses in detail. May it be concluded, therefore, that the Bible is in fact utopian? That it contains ideas and institutions which cannot work — like the Garden of Eden?

Utopia is a Greek word meaning "no place." Is then a covenanted Israel commanded to build and to cultivate an Eden-like society, a "no place," an impossible dream? It may be argued that there are a number of utopian dreams in the Bible — visions that can never work in the real world. Even if such were the case, Moses is even then performing an ethical service in representing at least *visionary aspirations* that have the power to inspire and to arouse the ethical imagination. But Moses is presenting much more than illusory visions. If anything, the Bible offers a program with which to concretize dreams, recognizing that Man and society will fall short of fulfilling these dreams — but will not necessarily meet abject failure. And in the face of falling short, one tries again and again.

In other words, *shemittat karka'ot*, *shemittat kesafim*, and *yovel* are weighted with aspects which are utopian, which cannot "work" — for they beg for a return to a primal state which may not only be impossible, but may be undesirable as an enduring condition. If, then, they can only be instituted at best temporarily, of what value are they? The answer is found in a consideration of the importance of the Shabbat. For undergirding these utopian "never-never-land" institutions is the institution of the Shabbat. Will the Shabbat as a human institution prove itself to be similarly temporary? Hardly, for can anyone seriously question the value of the Shabbat? As the history of civilization will prove soon enough following the biblical idea, the value of the Shabbat will lie not in some liturgical dream of a final day-of-rest which will be eternal; for that could be mistakenly interpreted as a negation of everything on earth and a holding of all technical and technological advances as evil. On the contrary, the biblical Shabbat will become an indispensable staple of all future technologically advanced societies that will persist in proclaiming their respect for the rights of humankind — all human beings, masters and servants alike.

The Influence of Utopia

Shabbat has not been introduced as a pillar of the covenant — theologically and sociologically speaking — in order to deny the importance of work and the beneficial effects of technological advances on humankind. The Shabbat as it is introduced in the Creation story is intended to serve as a dialectical pole juxtaposed to the work week to remind laborers of the higher purpose of their labor. It is to free humankind from the inevitable drudgery of their labor in order to prevent human beings from becoming slaves to their labor.

The dream of expanding the institution of the Shabbat into the idea of a Sabbatical year of release from bondage to the soil or bondage to the oppressiveness of debt is therefore not a fruitless sociomoral daydream. It anticipates technological progress in which Man may perceive himself mistakenly to be master over the earth and may exude thereby arrogance over his achievements. The Shabbat, the Sabbatical year, and the Jubilee are there to remind him that he is only a custodian of God's gift of creation, that he has been given charge of God's "earth and the fullness thereof." As such, he is to be held responsible for the well-being of the "earth and the fullness thereof."

Gershom Scholem reports of a legend with a variation of the Golem story. The prophet Jeremiah studies the mystical *Sefer Yetzirah* (the Book of Creation) and through the manipulation of letters makes a humanoid by means of the words *Adonai Elohim Emet* (The Lord God is Truth). But this newly created "man" in his technological arrogance takes a knife and with it erases the letter *alef* from the word *emet* (truth). Without the *alef* in the word *emet*, however, we're left with the two-letter word *met* which means "dead." Thus, in effect, this "man" of the Golem legend has blasphemed in the most appalling manner, determining, as it were, through his erasure that God is dead!

Let us grant that an institution like the *yovel* is a utopian dream that can never be realized. Man in his acquisitiveness and arrogance based on his awareness of his special intelligence will never agree on his own to radical redistribution of wealth which he has earned. This does not mean, however, that the concept of *yovel* does not influence the sociomoral evolution of society. The concept of *yovel* addresses itself to what the socioeconomic reality is and takes cognizance of economic needs, property needs, and sociopsychological proclivities. For society's leadership to apply intelligent decision-making to the contemporary socioeconomic reality is obviously a prodigious task. But part of the orientation to decision-making is to imagine what can yet be done to "mend" society and to permit the imagined "utopian" solution to at least serve as an inspiration if not a literal directive to further improvement. In short, Torah — even at its most utopian — provides the impulse to sociomoral civic and national betterment.

The Torah in Moses' legislative world of Leviticus is seeking to counteract the lust for physical violence, for harlotry, for gluttony, for the exploitation of wealth and land. The Torah's way is not to forbid the exercise of physical power, loving sexual relationships, the eating of food in joy, the gaining of wealth, and the ownership of land. It legislates for their constructive humane use. The Torah recognizes that accompanying these activities of human beings in the socioethical, socioeconomic, and sociopolitical arenas will be human travail. This will happen in the best of societies. The Torah offers idealistic solutions to these aspects of the human predicament. In practical terms, however, its view of *derekh eretz* (the way of the world) is to legislate towards a *moderation* of human effort, towards a control over lustful human appetites in all arenas of human concern — not the *utopian elimination* of these appetites.

If the *yovel* ever worked, it couldn't have endured for very long; nor could any other utopias. For, as said earlier, utopias by definition cannot be actualized in detail. But in the face of technological developments which may dehumanize, the *yovel* is a reminder of a transcendent alternative to dehumanization and desocialization. The Torah's operative focus is building a community of human beings with ethical and soulful sensibilities. The community that Torah envisions cannot and dare not be what Buber will say of a collectivity: "Collectivity is not a binding but a bundling together: individuals packed together, armed and equipped in common, with only as much life from man to man as will inflame the marching step. But community, growing community is the human being no longer walking side by side but *with* one another of a multitude of persons. Collectivity is based on an organized atrophy of personal existence; community is based on an increase of personal existence and a confirmation-in-life of life lived with one another."

A prime example of a principle indispensable to the building of a caring community is the biblical instruction and its legislative applications in the Talmud regarding *ona'ah*, translated as "fraud," "deception," e.g., in business transactions "overcharging and undercharging." Particularly sensitive to the demands of community integrity is the caution regarding *ona'at devarim*, i.e., misleading in speech, hurting with words, etc. As has been stressed earlier, the Torah, the Bible, and historic Judaism have accepted the proposition that whatever "redemption" or "salvation" means or inspires in its believers, it is a communal "redemption" or "salvation." It cannot come for the individual alone. In an authentic biblical sense there is no meaning to the term "holy man"; for only as one man relates to another man in honesty and dignity can community come alive. Only a community then can become holy. In the same biblical sense a single Israelite can contribute to his nation becoming holy only by participating fully in the building of such a nation. His nation is meant to be holy — but as a nation.

It follows then that only the holiness of a *nation*, i.e., a large community, can serve as an example for other nations. Rabbi A.I. Kook sees the purpose and function of this *goy kadosh* (holy nation) of Israel to be its model spiritual and ethical self. "Its way of life and the purity of its traits should serve as a living book." Israel according to Kook is not charged with teaching and preaching morality to the nations. Teaching and preaching do not make a nation holy. Only by virtue of its fulfillment of the mandate to build an authentic biblically inspired communal existence in its own land, under its own sovereignty, will Israel fulfill its destiny as a "holy nation."

Bar Yohai's Option

Thus, the attempt to offer Israel the broadest possible canvas for establishing a model for holiness — a covenanted Land — has for its goal the fulfillment of Israel's covenant with God. And the fulfillment of this covenant in the covenanted Land will impact, it is expected, on God's entire human creation. The classic talmudic debate between Rabbi Yishmael and Rabbi Shimon bar Yohai on the subject of Torah and *derekh eretz* takes on an extra intensity in the light of Israel's destiny within the world of nations.

Rabbi Yishmael sees Torah and *derekh eretz* as insisting that the Israelites, the Jewish people, must study Torah, but must also provide sustenance for themselves. To obligate themselves to the sanctified activity of ascertaining

God's will for the world requires living and moving within the world. Part of living and moving within the world is seeking sufficient autonomy to provide material well-being for themselves.

Rabbi Shimon bar Yohai, on the other hand, arrives at a diametrically opposite conclusion which reflects a totally pessimistic view of the world of nations. Rabbi Shimon — irrevocably opposed to Roman rule — is convinced that the failure on Israel's part to keep the Torah has brought about the catastrophe. Only by a total — absolutely total — commitment to Torah study is there a possibility of redemption. Rabbi Shimon's extremism is represented by his literal interpretation of the verse from Joshua, chapter 1, "may the Torah not leave your mouth day or night." If one is a farmer, there is no way that his chores will permit him the time to study even a limited amount of Torah, let alone occupying himself with Torah "day and night." For Shimon bar Yohai the answer is clear: Devote oneself exclusively to Torah! How then will the endless chores of the farmer — the work of the world — be done? The answer, according to Bar Yohai, is that if Israel is worthy, the work of the world will be done by the Gentile nations with Israel serving as the priestly representative of God's holiness-on-earth.

There is good reason for Bar Yohai's extremism. He has witnessed the victory of what he considers the Evil Empire over his people and the occupation of the Holy Land by an ungodly force. The *aggadah* has him escaping from the Romans into a cave where he dwells with his son for twelve years. Upon exiting the cave and seeing his fellow Jews indulging in agriculture, he "incinerates the crops" and returns to the cave. The legendary melodramatic aspects of the story underscore Bar Yohai's utter rejection of the world as it is. Until and unless the world changes and becomes hospitable again to Torah, Bar Yohai will have none of it and will want none of it for his people.

But what this means for the God of Israel is the end to covenantal optimism. Rabbi Shimon bar Yohai has decided that the destruction of the Second Temple and the loss of the Second Commonwealth is the end of any possibility of *tikkun olam* (mending the world). Certainly, human beings by themselves are incapable of mending the world. If God wants to bring on an apocalypse, so be it; Bar Yohai will remain in the cave until after it comes to pass. To think in terms of agriculture in a world which is doomed to apocalypse is for Bar Yohai an abomination. For him, *derekh eretz* has lost its meaning.

There is a postscript to the *aggadah*, however. After another twelve years, Bar Yohai along with his son emerge again from the cave. The son is again ready to incinerate the crops; but Bar Yohai espies a Jew carrying two torches for the Shabbat. Seeing that there is a Jew ready to remember and keep the Shabbat — *in the world* — is enough to make Rabbi Shimon bar Yohai hesitate before "destroying the world." Perhaps there *can* be redemption for this world.

But how does Rabbi Shimon bar Yohai expect it to happen if not through some effort on the part of Man? The problem with Rabbi Shimon bar Yohai's position is its post-utopian despair. As such, his position is unacceptable to the biblical sensibility. The biblical covenant in its post-Eden incarnation is not meant to be unachievable. It recognizes human failure or *falling short*. Its understanding of human nature is dedicated to allowing for new beginnings on this earth — always new beginnings.

Be-Hukotai 

In Emile Durkheim's work *Sociology and Philosophy* he says: "The more we advance in time, the more complex and immense does our civilization become and, consequently, the more does it transcend the individual consciousness, and the smaller does the individual feel in relation to it...but however small (we may feel) and however small our part may be, we do nevertheless always integrate in ourselves a part, and thus while society transcends us, it is immanent in us, and we feel it as such. While it surpasses us, it is within us, since it can only exist by and through us." Durkheim has caught and explained the dialectical interplay between society and the individual. The portion of *Be-Hukotai* catches the interplay as well. It begins with a concern for the collective social and national destiny of Israel: *"Im be-hukotai teleikhu"* ("If you — the new Israelite society — will walk in My ways"); and it ends with *"erekh nefashot"* ("the worth of individual Israelites") related to voluntary donations to the Lord's service.

Throughout the Bible the dialectical interplay between society and the individual, between the individual and society, is the crucible of concern for covenantal possibility. If Genesis begins with the creation of the individual human being, it is to prepare for the coming reproductive process which will lead to the building of families, tribes, and nations. If the Children of Israel are taken out of Egypt as a collective, as a nation, it is to be taken to Sinai where the Torah will be given to them as a collective, as a nation, but equally as an agenda for all the individuals who make up the Israelite collective, the nation of Israel.

The Terms of "If"

The destiny of the collective is to be based on two simple "if" propositions: (1) *If* Israel will follow God's laws they will be blessed with those material benefits which any human appraiser will agree make life joyful. On the other hand, (2) *if* Israel will rebel against God's laws they will be cursed with those misfortunes that the same human appraiser will agree make of life a horror.

What can the individual do to assure that his society will be worthy of blessings and not curses? In the talmudic tractate *Kiddushin* a formula is given for an individual's spiritual and sociomoral training: "He who is schooled in *Mikra* (Bible), *Mishnah* (Rabbinics), and *Derekh Eretz* (Way of the World) will not quickly sin; whereas he who is not schooled in '*Mikra, Mishnah*, and *Derekh Eretz*' is not considered civilized." We have here a recommended combination of (1) directly received revelatory legislation — as Harold Kushner has said: "God's first word but not His last" (*Mikra*); (2) ongoing detailed interpretation of legislation in tune with day-to-day life's processes (*Mishnah*); and (3) the constant application of these two — the *Mikra* and *Mishnah* — to the way of the world and vice versa (*Derekh Eretz*).

The combination of all three is mandatory. For if the conditions for blessings and curses, reward and punishment, are seen as exclusively resting on the *Mikra* or *Torah she-bi-Khetav* (the Written Torah), i.e., the received revelatory legislation, then the concerns will be directed exclusively at the collective. All reward and all punishment will be collective. If Israel as a collective obeys, there is peace, security, and economic prosperity. If Israel as a collective does not obey, then there is national defeat, destruction, and exile. Implied in the written Torah's descriptions and prescriptions is that everyone, whatever his personal character, positive or negative, every member of society celebrates victory or suffers defeat. But is such a forecast true-to-life?

In war, for example, if the collective experiences victory then all who have participated in the campaign have won. At the same time there are casualties in war, even on the victorious side. Those who have fallen are not present to celebrate the victory. In the same way, not everyone suffers equally in military or political defeat. Even in the era of Auschwitz, there will be European Jews who will escape the onslaught, let alone Jews of the West who will not be touched at all by the partially "successful" Nazi campaign against the Jewish people. In other words, even on the collective level, not every military defeat or economic failure is unrelievedly catastrophic for every individual within the collective. The Rabbis of the talmudic era thereupon make a theological and social adjustment with regard to interpreting the *Mikra* or *Torah she-bi-*

Khetav, testifying to an inventive strategy for survival under extreme collective duress. What is this strategy?

The rabbinic-talmudic period represents accommodation on the part of the House of Israel to a ruthless subjugation by Rome. The well-known summary motto of Rabbi Yohanan ben Zakkai, "*Ten li Yavne va-hakhameha....*" ("Give me a school for Torah at the little town of Yavne...."), for which he was prepared to acknowledge the surrender of Israel's sovereign capital Jerusalem, underscores the accommodation. What specifically is it?

The grand vision of holy sovereignty on which the *Mikra* or Written Torah is predicated has been severely compromised by the defeat of Israel at the hands of the Romans. Yet, the *Mishnah* and its talmudic *halakhah* continue to legislate for the daily lives of individual practicing Jews in meticulous detail. The Rabbis know that they are not facing the same extreme theological crisis that Ezekiel and his generation had had to cope with a half-millennium previously. At that time the shock of exile was unprecedented and raised the possibility that God was abandoning Israel by abrogating the covenant. Such is not the case here. The Rabbis of the period of the "destruction of the Second Temple" never entertain the notion that God is abandoning them or that the observance of the Torah is a fruitless exercise. On the contrary, the Rabbis trace the loss of sovereignty precisely to the lack of individual observance of the laws of the Torah. They conclude, therefore, that the only chance for a new redemption from the Roman enslavement is a renewed commitment to every detail explicit and implicit in the Written Torah. But these details must be brought out in the *Mishnah* and the developing "Oral Torah."

And how will the Rabbis be able to measure the degree of interpretation necessary for the implementation of Torah in daily life for new post-biblical generations? By living out the *derekh eretz* of the day, by participating critically in the "way of the world," in order to uncover the points within that way of the world which will elicit from Torah appropriate modes of sanctification.

The Rabbis refer often to *olam ha-ba* (the future world). But their legislation is very much for this world. Even in their national "degradation" they are committed to the application of their Torah covenant in the lives of individual Jews and their individual communities. They struggle with the cruel reality of the Roman occupation. Part of their collective consciousness cannot understand "God's silence" in the face of Roman control of His world in general and His Holy Land in particular. But except for men like Shimon bar

Yohai, they never surrender the programmatic demand for them as a chosen people to mend God's world by sanctification no matter what the real circumstances prevailing in that world.

The medieval commentator Yitzhak Arama in his *Akedat Yitzhak* will cite a verse from Deuteronomy: "*Ve-atem ha-dvekim ba-Adonai Eloheikhem* hayyim kulkhem ha-yom" ("You who cleave to the Lord your God are *all alive today*"). In this verse, Arama sees Israel's determined cleaving to God today — *in this world* — as the prerequisite for any spiritual reward conjured up by dreams and promises of *olam ha-ba*. Even when *olam ha-zeh* (this world) appears to be a travesty of God's original purpose in creation, Israel clings to the covenantal dream by realizing it in its maximization of detail *as if* the biblical collective promise was being fulfilled.

The Rabbis are continuing the traditional line that will extend from Moses to Ahad Ha'am — that there is no absolute bifurcation in Jewish destiny and purpose between *basar ve-ru'ah* (flesh and blood reality and things of the spirit). There are twin heresies to be rejected by Israel and the Jewish people: (1) becoming like those nations that have no spiritual moorings; or (2) looking at its own covenantal uniqueness as purely spiritual. At a much later time, in considering the modern resurrection of the Jewish nation on its own soil, Ahad Ha'am will remark: "The flesh must not rule over the spirit; nor dare the flesh ever be 'slain' in the name of the spirit; but the flesh must be lifted up by the spirit." With unbroken continuity, the sanctification of the "flesh," i.e., *olam ha-zeh*, will assure the coming of the spiritual redemption, i.e., *olam ha-ba*.

Melding together the flesh and the spirit is to be a religious and ethical exercise for each individual within the House of Israel. The collective redemption of the nation of Israel comes as a result of the summing up of all individual efforts.

The Eretz Yisrael of Rav Nahman

The land as "flesh" is indispensable to the flowering of the spiritual dimension of any people. A broadened articulation of this view is found in Martin Buber's short volume *Bein Am le-Artzo* (Between a People and Its Land). Buber focuses on the homiletical relationship between Rav Nahman of Bratzlav and the Land of Israel. It may be summarized in Rav Nahman's bon-mot: "Wherever I am going, I am headed to the Land of Israel." Rav Nahman further elaborates: "Eretz Yisrael is the highest of all the lands: it is also the lowest. The name 'Canaan' in Hebrew signifies 'submission,' reminiscent of the biblical comment 'the humble shall inherit the land.' The highest of the lands must submit in humility so that paradoxically the 'lowness' of the land (being highest and lowest at the same time) may represent ideal humility. As such, the Land of Israel must be the center of redemptive and resurrective forces."

Several questions arise from Rav Nahman's teaching: (1) How can Israel be the highest and lowest of the lands at the same time? (2) How does its dust teach humility or submission? (3) What does it mean to say that there — in Eretz Yisrael — will be the center of the resurrection?

The question "How can Israel be the highest and lowest of the lands at the same time" is a question not looking for an answer in objective empirical terms. It reflects the "height" and "depth" of the questioner. It is similar in spirit to the thought of the Psalmist in Psalm 8: "What is Man that you take note of him...yet he lacks but a little of God, so that you have crowned him with glory and pride." Rav Nahman is adding an even more dramatic dimension to the admittedly subjective concern for Eretz Yisrael. Whatever one is or whatever one perceives oneself to be, in Eretz Yisrael he lives at the most extreme manifestations of his personhood, at the level of his most pronounced sensitivities. As an Israelite, as a Jew, when he is in the Land of Israel, he is most true to himself — positive or negative. He lives at his most heightened level of intensity — emotionally, intellectually, spiritually, good and bad.

How does the dust of Israel teach humility? Submission? Rav Nahman's answer is that the dust of Eretz Yisrael differs from the rest of the world. Dust or earth can do two things, or more homiletically, it can influence Man in two directions. One direction is towards the goal of sanctification. One recognizes that the dust or earth is God's creation. As long as one's goal is to sanctify, i.e., to participate in God's creative purpose, any working of the earth is for the aim of making visible a spiritual purpose to labor no matter how mundane it be. Alternatively, one's directive goal vis-à-vis the earth may lead to desanctification. One may look at the earth as fulfilling exclusively Man's utilitarian needs and lusts without ever looking upwards to high purpose.

As already indicated, the very name "Canaan" comes from the root "submission." The desideratum is for the Children of Israel to relate to the "dust" of Canaan as an opportunity to show submission to God's purposes. They must relate to the natural resources of the "dust," no matter how abundant these resources may be, as if they were meager. Such an attitude will cultivate the ability to do with less and to appreciate God's largesse for every blessing that is given. Ya'akov's name-change to Israel forecasts Canaan's name-change to Israel. It is hoped that the name-change will reflect the Children of Israel having learned to limp through its early history as a lesson in thanksgiving for the opportunity to receive God's gift of the covenant.

Finally, what does it mean to say that specifically in Eretz Yisrael will be the center of *tehiyat ha-meitim* (resurrection of the dead)? Rav Nahman sees as inherent in *galut* (exile) the misleading, deceptive influence of the *yeitzer ha-ra* (the evil drive). The serpentine *yeitzer ha-ra*, which has insinuated itself into us and has caused us to sin, is only removed when we die and are buried in Eretz Yisrael. Only in Eretz Yisrael can the *yeitzer ha-ra* be removed and in purity the soul and body will rise again, cleansed of its deceptive "exileness" or "*galut*-keit." How do we know this? Eretz Yisrael is where *emunah* (faith) was born with Abraham. Among his many faith-filled acts was to buy burial ground for his family in the earth, the dust, of Eretz Yisrael after the celebration of his victory in Shalem or Jerusalem.

While it is true that Rav Nahman's particular kabbalistic bent reconstructs a perfect world in which Eretz Yisrael is the central life-giving force for all of Israel, normative Judaism and certainly the modern revolution within the Jewish people called Zionism will see Eretz Yisrael as the necessary place, the spot earmarked for national renewal. Because a human being as an earthly creature needs a piece of earth which he can claim is his — even if he is only a tenant with God as the ultimate landlord — the Israelite, later the Jew, must have this particular place. It must be his place. He'll be laid to rest in its dust; its dust will give him and his people the hope for eternal life beyond the dust. It will remain for a latter-day Rabbi A.I. Kook to maintain that Eretz Yisrael is a "part of the very essence of our nationhood; it is bound organically to its very life and inner being."

This adulation of Eretz Yisrael and its rebuilding is underscored in one of the bleakest passages in the whole Torah. Yet the Ramban finds comfort even and especially in the verses from Leviticus 26:32–33: "I will make the land desolate so that your enemies who settle in it shall be appalled by it…Your land shall become a desolation and your cities a ruin." The Ramban comments: "The phrase 'and your enemies shall be appalled by it' bears a favorable message for every Jewish community in exile. Our land, it states, will not receive our enemies. It is a promise and proof that this land, which is naturally goodly and spacious, and which was always inhabited, will remain desolate. Since we left it, not one nation nor tongue has been able to take over the land and cultivate it successfully."

The Ramban's "comforting" insight is not mindless chauvinism. It can't be when the larger portion on which it is based is a brutally frightening *tokhehah* (accusation). It is as lacking in chauvinistic arrogance as is the central liturgical admission of the festive Holy Days' *"u-mipnei hata'einu galinu me-artzeinu"* ("because of our sins we were exiled from our land"). Nevertheless, the idea that the Land, should it be lost to Israel for a time, perhaps for a long time, won't produce for anyone else, is an assurance that Israel will return. As a piece of God's creation the Land of Israel calls for cultivation. Only the Children of Israel can answer the call productively. Thus the full responsibility for getting back to Eretz Yisrael falls on the descendants of the House of Israel whose ancestors have lost it through their spiritual and sociomoral negligence. These descendants must never accept Diaspora living as anything but "exile."

Exile: Fear and Hope

The exile described in the *tokhehah* is one which is most succinctly described as entailing unremitting "fear." God will inject fear into the hearts of the Children of Israel in the lands of their enemies. It will be the kind of terror that will put them into an emotional state where even the sound of a driven leaf will cause them to flee, when in fact they are not even being pursued. Whether or not a sword actually hangs over them in a particular situation will be almost irrelevant. They will be frightened not only by the "thousand natural shocks that flesh is heir to" but by the calms between the shocks.

The particular fear described here is *morakh-lev* — as opposed to the Hebrew words *pahad* or *yirah*. *Pahad* is legitimate fear of real threats, real enemies. *Yirah* is the hoped-for "fear of God" or reverence. *Morakh-lev* is fear of anything and everything. *Galut* (exile) by its very nature of utter dependence, entailing thereby utter insecurity, utter unpredictability, is characterized by *morakh-lev* even when a given local Diaspora situation appears to be "good." For if the given situation is good, it is because of the fortuitous largesse of the national host. But at any moment this same national host may make a policy judgment and decision which will turn the "good" situation into a Pharaonic prison, or a Spanish edict of expulsion, or following the Nazi precedent, a "final solution."

National sovereignty as opposed to exile does not eliminate *pahad*. But *pahad* on a personal level can and should contribute to constructive acts such as showing extra care in the face of danger. Similarly, *pahad* on a national level can and should lead to constructive concerns with national defense, military security, counter-intelligence, not to mention the building of social, economic, and civic infrastructures for the protection of the population. Exile and its *morakh-lev*, on the other hand, breed paralysis of initiative and action. The paralysis is the result of fundamental misperceptions based on a colossal self-deception: that *galut* is not *galut*!

National sovereignty will burden Israel with problems — not the least of which is defense against predatory enemies. And most of the Rabbis who will suffer because of the absence of national sovereignty will develop an antipathy to the responsibilities of the "sword." To them, the "sword" will be a punishment — an affliction to be borne when as a result of their not having kept the teachings of the "book," they will become vulnerable to their powerful adversaries. But the Bible — more specifically, Moses' Torah — legislates for national sovereignty with its dependence when necessary on the "sword." Canaan and its neighbors the Midianites, the Amalekites, and others will have to be defeated in war. There is no alternative.

To avoid such conflicts means national quietism and *galut*, the worst of all the threats in the "accusation." The emphasis on *galut* as the worst of the national and individual punishments is that God will not walk with them in their situation of exile. This will not mean that God has abandoned them. The covenant will hold. But in exile there is for Israel no "walking with…"; there is only wandering. In exile Israel will feel not only that God is in eclipse but that she herself is hidden from God's Presence.

The Torah and the Bible have their own built-in corrective to the dark sides of national sovereignty. Moses himself as the first and the greatest of the prophets will herald a long line of severe critics of national spiritual apostasies, moral perversities, and social decadence. But the post-Eden reality which God Himself has taught Himself to accept is assuredly not Utopia. It is a place where nations in general and Israel in particular are to work to build a spiritually secure and socially fair polity.

One works, one makes the effort, and if one falls short, one begins again, not having lost one's spiritual and ethical aspirations. One tries harder. This is meant to be true of an individual Jew and especially true of the Jewish people. In a play by Arthur Miller entitled *After the Fall* the protagonist has failed in various aspects of his life. But he comes to an understanding of life, of the world, and of the human condition and its sober possibilities for mending that world. He concludes: "I could love the world again! To know that we meet not in some garden of wax fruit and painted trees, that lie of Eden, but after, after the Fall...it does seem feasible...not to be afraid."

Millennia after the first Exodus, the Jewish people will be brought to the absolute nadir of their national existence in the Holocaust. And out of the absolute nullity to human effort which Auschwitz will represent, there will arise for a third time a Jewish Commonwealth in the Land of Israel. Auschwitz will be the horrifying reminder that the warnings given by God in Leviticus — and later in Deuteronomy — are more than realizable in a post-Eden world. At the same time rebuilding Israel after a cataclysm like the Shoah is also realizable.

Future pedagogic emphasis on *either* Auschwitz or Jerusalem, without giving equal attention to the other will be a truncation of Jewish history that will falsify the entire saga. It will be mandatory to stress that just as one doesn't learn his entire Bible from studying the *tokhehah*, one cannot learn about Jews, Jewish history and destiny, merely from visiting Auschwitz — unless one continues on to Jerusalem. For Jerusalem will always represent the redemptive, the creative, and fulfilling dimensions of the Jewish saga while Auschwitz will represent only the nullity of exile, enslavement, and destruction. There will be no inspiration to be gained from the Shoah itself without its Zionist implications. The moral obscenity of the Shoah following upon the promise of opulence with the Emancipation in Europe is only hinted at by Moses in Leviticus and Deuteronomy. But Moses does understand "exile" as representing a spiritual, social, moral, and cultural void. It is from this void that Israel must inevitably emerge ready to move into a new state of communal being — sovereignty!

The Zionist Dream and the Individual

Following the destruction of the Second Temple and the loss of sovereignty, the Rabbis will "make do" with the "four cubits of the *halakhah*." But the long exile will place into suspension the most important pre-conditions for full exercise of the terms of the covenant: national independence and sovereignty. Granted, the Jews will have learned through the agonies of the exile that there is a price to be paid for sovereignty. In the case of Israel the price is a heavy one indeed because it is a price determined by a covenantal commitment. But without the hope of a restoration of sovereignty, there can be no serious renewal of covenantal commitment.

Modern Zionism will thus become the attempt to reaffirm a message and mission of biblical faith and aspiration. Gershom Scholem, scion of an assimilated German-Jewish family, will devote years to returning to Judaism and the Jewish people; and then, according to his own testimony, he will not need more than a half-hour to decide not only to become a Zionist in theory but to decide to make *aliyah*. He will explain: "Without Zionism, i.e., the return to homeland and the striving to sovereignty, there is no existence for the people of Israel." At the same time he will recognize that fulfilling the Zionist dream will be full of problems. But as A.D. Gordon will have said before him, "They will be *our* problems!"

And so the Book of Leviticus with its attempt at comprehensive legislation for a holy community comes to an end. It ends its concern with the collective destiny of the people at large by discussing a particular issue concerned with vows made in support of the worship-service in the Sanctuary. The donations committed by the vows are to be based on Torah-prescribed valuations of individuals.

Yehezkel Kaufmann has seen the Bible as focused on individuals even as it emphasizes the role of the community. Kaufmann says: "In the beginning there was no tribe nor nation but only the individual. The first Adam is created as his own intrinsic purpose and goal, not just as father of the human race. God's relationship to him is personal." The expression "created *'betzelem Elohim'*" ("created 'in the image of God'") is an expression meant to underscore, as the well-known Mishnah in Sanhedrin will put it, the independent inviolable nature of being an individual human being. Moses has attempted to build an agenda for a post-Eden community, but a community which by definition must be conditioned on the ongoing communion in spirit and deed of individual Israelites. Moses thus concludes this Levitical portion with the reminder that even in post-Eden Israel it is the Jewish "Adam" whose covenanted destiny as an integral part of his people's destiny is still to be considered the beginning!

BA-MIDBAR

Wilderness of Doubt

The word *ba-midbar* (in the wilderness) captures the mood of the entire book and, as such, promises a mood of despondency. Not that the last portion of Leviticus — *Be-Hukotai* — hasn't itself been full of foreboding!

It is ironic that the calendrical order of readings has *Be-Hukotai* read on the threshold of the joyous festival of *Shavuot*. *Shavuot* celebrates the revelation of Torah, an occasion for untrammeled optimism. Yet calendrically, it is preceded by the horrific threats of the end of Leviticus and followed by the narrative of national backsliding recorded in the Book of Numbers (Book of Ba-Midbar). Sensitive to this sandwiching of the joy of *Shavuot* between Torah readings that bespeak national depression, there is a liturgical tradition that has one Shabbat intervening between the public reading of the curses proclaimed in *Be-Hukotai* and the Festival of *Shavuot*. Why?

The *Sefat Emet* commentary suggests that the Shabbat — not the mood of curses — is the eminently appropriate occasion for preparing oneself to receive the Torah. The Shabbat was given to humankind before the Torah, before the joining of the covenant and its terms promising blessings and threatening curses. The Shabbat itself is a preparation for revelation — for the first mention of Shabbat comes as an integral part of creation, as part of the very grounding of human existence and human destiny. The human being is a creature who is charged to work, to build, to create, then to rest; but to rest means to reflect and to listen. The human being is to listen not to curses, but to the terms for redemptive human creativity. Revelation can only be transmitted to a people that has the heightened reflective sensibility made possible by the spirit of Shabbat.

The Book of Ba-Midbar is not unrelievedly depressing. The beginning and the end of the book exude optimism. It begins with the census ordered to ascertain the physical and military capacities of the Children of Israel. It concludes with a review of the stations reached throughout the march during the forty-year sojourn in the Wilderness. Thus the beginning and the end of the book reflect a sense of dedicated common purpose. It is the material recorded "in-between" which reflects a *midbar*, a wilderness, a wasteland of weakness, insecurity, and purposelessness.

The Book of Jeremiah records a nostalgic reminiscence on the part of God of the experience of Israel following Him into the Wilderness. God imagines Himself as the lover who in His love has betrothed the love of His youth. His beloved has agreed to the nuptial contract. And the relationship in the Wilderness is recalled as a time of relative purity of spirit and intention. As opposed to the inevitable spiritual and sociomoral compromises which will tarnish the naïve covenantal expectations once Israel has settled the Land, the experience of the Wilderness is the ideal vehicle for remembering the "good times" — at least according to Jeremiah. But the *peshat* (the simple meaning) of the Book of Ba-Midbar belies the romantic reminiscence of the Book of Jeremiah.

The Book of Ba-Midbar records the emerging despair — first of Israel, then of Moses, then of God Himself. Israel complains, quarrels, rebels. As it has from the moment of the Exodus, it complains about the lack of water. It complains about the diet of "manna," reaching a nadir of self-deception in recalling the "preferred" diet of leeks and cucumbers and other delicacies in Egypt during their enslavement, obviously repressing the memory of the harshness and cruelties of that enslavement. Israel quarrels incessantly with Moses. Eventually it rebels against his rule and against the source of his rule — against God Himself!

Israel in the Wilderness is intended to undergo an apprenticeship in preparing itself to become a holy nation — God's witnesses, God's people (*am Hashem*). Instead of becoming an *am Hashem*, however, the Children of Israel act as if they are determined to become, to use Eldad's term, an *am midbar* (a wilderness nation). This *am midbar* seems to lack the motivation to become, to use A.D. Gordon's term, even an *am adam* (a humane nation), let alone an *am Hashem*. They are too bound to their immediate instinctual cravings and anxieties. They know that they cannot return to Egypt. Yet in despair they will seek to reject the covenant that calls for the conquest and settlement of a new land. What is left for them? To remain in the Wilderness? To become petrified there?

Ba-Midbar 

The fourth book of the Torah is popularly titled "Numbers" in English and "*Ba-Midbar*" in Hebrew. Taken together, these two words reflect an ambivalence towards the subject matter. "Numbers" refers to the census of Israel marching to the Promised Land eliciting from observers, readers, and worshipers a sense of pride and *nahat* in appreciating God's love for Israel and the Jewish people. But, as noted earlier, it is Ba-Midbar which characterizes unfortunately the mood of more of the book than "Numbers." Ba-Midbar is indeed a record of "wilderness" — a wilderness of conflict and disappointment at frustrated hopes and aborted agendas.

Is Israel Ready for the Covenant?

What is it that turns the parade-like atmosphere of "Numbers" into the dark foreboding of Ba-Midbar? It is appropriate to recall the contrast that Martin Buber draws between groups of people *bundling* together as a collectivity or *binding* together as a community. Israel has escaped from Egypt. It has witnessed the fall of its enemies. It has been brought to Sinai where an epiphany has occurred, corroborating the vision and promise of their leader Moses that they are part of a redemptive apocalyptic event superintended by God Himself. And as the march begins, the march which will take them to the Promised Land, they are inflamed with enthusiasm.

But Moses wants more. He has indicated how much more he wants from them in Leviticus. Ultimately he wants a community, not a collectivity — no matter how much enthusiasm they may be exuding in their march. He wants there to be within the marching Israel a sense of *being* with one another. Among the multitude of persons, each marching individual is to be recognized as a person. Moses knows that the spiritual and moral glue needed to turn a collectivity into a community is a vision and an agenda of high purpose, an energizing aspiration, perhaps unattainable. But the goal is to fulfill a covenanted destiny which must be attainable or else God's act of liberation will have been a sham.

Is Israel prepared to undertake the required discipline and fellow-feeling required for becoming a community — a covenanted community? Apparently not quite yet! The Midrash says: "He who is not prepared to make of himself as one divested of property — as a *wilderness*, so to speak — cannot learn the wisdom of Torah." To hear the Voice, the all-commanding, all-enveloping Voice — one cannot have any pretenses, any vested interests to protect. One must be like the newborn babe listening ingenuously to everything. The story is told of how God came to give Israel the Torah while they were still in Egypt during the years of plenty following Joseph's ascent to the premiership. The story has God pleading with Israel to accept the yoke of the commandments. But Israel at that time was rich and possessed all things in abundance. God asks Israel: "Will you honor Me? Will you be holy as I am holy? Will you study My Torah? Will you live by My teachings? Will you teach them to your children? Will you sanctify My name in all your ways?" Israel answers: "There is no time, there is no need, for we have everything."

The story tells of how God weeps and says: "Now they shall become enslaved. They will lose all; they will become a 'wilderness'! Then they will seek Me, they will cry out for Me, they will listen for Me! And I will then show mercy to Israel. I will bring her into the Wilderness where I will reveal Myself to her!"

The story will repeat itself in paradigmatic fashion once Israel settles the Promised Land and begins to build an empire. They will fail to solve the dilemma-like problem of how to infuse an economically advanced society with elevating spiritual and sociomoral values. By the time they will reach the zenith of imperial opulence under Solomon, the rot of social disintegration will have set in. And the decree of exile and its accompanying suffering will have been prepared on high for issuance at the critical moment.

The very first verse of the Book of Bamidbar has the juxtaposed words "*be-midbar Sinai.*" God speaks to Moses in the "Wilderness of Sinai." Israel will learn that the message of Sinai can only be heard in the Wilderness, metaphorically understood. Only when the message of Sinai has been received in the "wilderness" of human pain, contention, and exertion, can it then be applied within "civilization." "Civilization" is built up out of the "wildernesses" of human striving. And unless the key to applying sanctity to civilization is discovered in time and actualized, then civilization is destined to disintegrate into a wasteland.

Rabbinic Judaism will argue that even on a personal level, a human being can be lifted to a higher plane of spiritual and ethical sensitivity only from within a situation of social and political affliction. The Midrash speaks of a king having four sons, each of whom is afflicted — more literally, beaten or whipped. The reactions of the four vary: the first keeps silent in the face of the beating; the second kicks back; the third begs for respite from the beating; and the fourth confronts his father with the challenge: "Beat me more!" He who is silent is Abraham who obeys God's command to offer up his son without protest, without comment. He who kicks back is Job who cannot understand why he, a decent person, is suffering. He who begs God for respite is Hezekiah who has been informed by the prophet Isaiah that he faces imminent death. And he who is ready to be "beaten more," if that is what life has decreed for him, is David or Rabbi Akiva, the latter quoted as saying "let a human being be happy over his trials more than the good with which he may be blessed." David and Akiva may be described as anticipating the bon mot of Nietzche: "That which fails to kill me will make me stronger."

When afflicted, the human being is most likely to behave like Abraham the silent, Job the protester, or Hezekiah the entreater. Shall one, can one, be expected to behave like Rabbi Akiva who, certainly in the drama surrounding his martyrdom, is described as one who welcomes *yisurin shel ahavah* (afflictions of love)? Granted, the model of Rabbi Akiva's reaction to suffering, to the "wilderness" of life, is extreme. It is certainly not normal. Nevertheless, future generations of Israel will learn from Rabbi Akiva that they dare not become immobilized by sociopolitical pain or sorrow or suffering. On the contrary, sociopolitical pain, sorrow, and suffering are to be seen as representing the imperfections of the universe waiting for correction. They are the symptoms of the uncultivated "wilderness" of collective human existence.

Israel will wander through a wilderness of sociopolitical pain, sorrow, and suffering. But unlike Abraham, Job, Hezekiah, and Akiva who have not *rebelled* against God, Israel in the Wilderness will fall into the sin that — worse than the sin of the Golden Calf — will bring God to the very brink of rejecting them totally. And notwithstanding Moses' successful intervention, God will not relent regarding *this* generation. He will give in to Moses' entreaties regarding the permanency of the covenant with future generations of Israelites. But this generation — this *dor ha-midbar* (Wilderness generation) must be punished, must die in the Wilderness. For this generation in their march towards the Promised Land could have conquered their psychic "wilderness." Instead they chose to retreat!

The Census

The *dor ha-midbar* will be forever marked by the stain of having closed themselves off from the beginnings of the redemption — if redemption means transcending the sociopolitical pain, sorrow, and suffering of the "wilderness." They have been offered the opportunity and they will reject it. They will shut out the call of Sinai in return for petrifying themselves in the "wilderness." The tragedy befalls this *dor ha-midbar*, notwithstanding the fact that their beginnings in the Wilderness have been so auspicious.

God commands Moses to take a census of His people — to count heads! Rashi explains that the census is ordered out of God's affection for His people. God loves them so much that He delights in counting His treasure every hour. The Ramban sees the counting as a positive reminder of the personal providence that God exercises over His people. This personal providence is to strengthen the faith in each individual Israelite soul that God will indeed fulfill His promises. The Ramban adds another reason — a negative one — for God's ordering Moses to conduct the census. It is to get across to Moses that he, Moses, is never to count them on his own initiative. Each Israelite is to give the specific half-shekel poll tax and by *them* the people will be numbered — not by Moses. In other words, it is forbidden to number people as if they were "things," mere objects. It is preferred that each person who is to be counted will give an amount voluntarily, so to speak, as a sign of involvement. From the collection of these amounts the total number of committed people will be ascertained.

This very note raises a question or series of questions regarding the biblical attitude to the taking of censuses in general. The most tragic census occurs during the reign of King David. It is written in II Samuel 24: "The anger of the Lord again flared up against Israel; and He incited David against them, saying, 'Go and number Israel and Judah.' The king said to Joab, his army commander, 'Make the rounds of all the tribes of Israel, from Dan to

Beer-Sheba, and take a census of the people, so that I may know the size of the population.'" The order does not meet with the approval of David's army commander. But David insists and the census is taken. It is taken, however, against the procedure described in "Ba-Midbar" according to Ramban's description and interpretation of the collection of the half-shekels. Such a procedure is not mentioned in David's census at all. Indeed, after David's census, it says explicitly in the name of the king: "I have sinned grievously in what I have done." In the continuation of the story, as punishment for what David has done, a severe pestilence breaks out throughout Israel and causes the death of seventy thousand people.

A number of questions arise from the story in II Samuel which illuminate the circumstances that Moses and Israel face in the Wilderness: (1) It is written that God incites David into conducting the census. If so, why is David guilty of sin? (2) If, on the other hand, the incitement itself is a punishment, what was David's previous sin that engendered such a decree, which in turn would lead to the plague and mass destruction among the people? And (3) if David did sin, what was the nation's guilt — that they should have had to pay such a heavy price as the loss of seventy thousand souls?

The author of I Chronicles 21 has given a response to the first question with a different version of the story stating: "*Satan* arose against Israel and incited David to number Israel." It is obvious that the author of I Chronicles is troubled by the theological-moral question: "How could God be the force which would incite anyone to do wrong, let alone David the King of Israel?" The author of I Chronicles finds his solution by positing Satan as the inciter!

But the second question arises: Why was David the King so vulnerable to the wiles of Satan? What had been David's sin, which led to his punishment, i.e., the incitement to count the people? A hint at the answer may be found in Rashi's interpretation of the rationale for the census in "Ba-Midbar." It is an answer which is tied to the classic predicament in which David the King, qua king of flesh and blood, finds himself. What does Rashi say in "Ba-Midbar," if not that God counts Israel because of His affection for them. God's love for His covenanted people is such that He delights in "real-izing" His presence with each and every member of the House of Israel at every moment, at every turn. It is a realization on God's part of the Psalmist's phrase "I have set the Lord before me always," except that from God's point of view it is "I have set

Israel before Me always." And "Israel" in God's consciousness refers both to the collective and the individuals who make up the collective.

Here lies the unavoidable moral problem that faces every king of flesh and blood like David. The Mishnah in the talmudic tractate *Sanhedrin* distinguishes between mortal Man who engraves a number of coins with one seal and they all come out alike and the Holy One Blessed Be, the King of Kings, who is able to stamp each human being with the original seal of Adam the First and yet not one comes out looking like another. A human king, in other words, in relating to his people, to the stormy volatile masses of humanity who struggle under his rule, cannot possibly relate to each individual according to the latter's subjective uniqueness. And this is the inevitable sin of the human king, of every mortal leader. A human king who is confronted by enemies and must fight wars against these enemies must mobilize his people into an army. He must turn his people into one integral unit. There is thus no escaping his fatal human need to overlook individual differences and concentrate on the general, on the *collectivity* which may be "inflamed by the marching step," but which cannot be treated as discrete members of a *community.*

The King of Kings, however, to the contrary, *is* capable of relating to His people in both I-It and I-Thou fashion at the same time. For the king of flesh and blood this is impossible, and here, therefore, is his sin. David the King's interest in conducting a census is principally to appraise the power of his army — a national necessity. But all the individuals within that army are subjectively unique. This David forgets or overlooks or can't help but overlook!

Why then must the entire nation bear the punishment of the plague? The answer is simple though painful. When Louis XIV of France will say "I am the state," he will be expressing a truth not only reflective of a monarchy — an absolute monarchy, a dictatorial monarchy. For every leader, even in a democratic state, at the moment when he makes decisions of state, and then orders the execution of decisions of state, *is* the *state.* He is the nation. The fate of the nation, for better and for worse, is tied to the decisions of its leader. If David the leader or Moses the leader sins or errs, the nation will suffer the consequences.

There are times when each member of a society must march as part of a disciplined group inflamed by the marching steps of the national collectivity. At such a time each such member must control or repress his own individuality despite the price — provided that at the same time, each such member never forgets that in the eyes of God, he has never lost or has had suspended his subjective self. In the eyes of God, every member of the House of Israel is special, beloved, and "counted." Moses in his census understands this; David in his census does not. Eventually he will — but at a great cost.

Later human history will testify to the biblical origins of the preference for democracy among politically and morally enlightened nations. "Democracy," Thomas Cahill will argue, "grows directly out of the Israelite vision of *individuals*, subjects of value because they are images of God, each with a unique and personal destiny." Not that "democracy" can ever be enough to undergird the values of a society! "Unbridled individualism," to use Fukayama's term, will abort any potential for societal growth. In the collective sensibility of historic Israel, the juxtaposition of two kinds of census, one endorsed and one condemned, emphasizes, therefore, the indispensability of a permanent dialectical concern for the individual as well as the national community.

Maximalist Dreams and Minimalist Reality

The march to the Promised Land begins in earnest. Once they reach their destination, how large is the conquest to be? How large is the Promised Land to be? How extensive must the sanctification in God's name be? God's vision for Israel's conquest is what later generations will call "maximalist." God has revealed His will to Moses — as He has done to the Patriarchs before him.

The "maximalist" vision entails the conquest, settlement, and covenanted sanctification of all of the Land of Canaan. Joshua will orchestrate what God has ordered. It is for all the tribes of Israel to have as their common mission the carrying out of the purposes of the Exodus: to establish full sovereignty over the Promised Land of Israel. At the same time the revelation at Sinai has declared that all of Israel shares the common goal of becoming under its own national sovereignty a holy nation. Therefore, all of the Sinai commandments, those associated with the Land qua land, and those not connected to the Land qua land are to be observed in good faith. In short, God's dream of ongoing creation is to see if His potential "kingship of heaven" can be realized specifically within this tiny new sovereign polity.

Israel will learn throughout its history, however, to adjust its dreams — and God's dreams — to reality. Joshua will not be able to complete the conquest. Nevertheless, according to Israel's later understanding of its history and halakhic implications of its history, Joshua's conquest and settlement will be considered the "first sanctification"; and this first sanctification will be considered a maximalist one. All the *mitzvot ha-teluyot ba-aretz* (the commandments associated with the Land qua land) will be observed as part of the covenantal agreement. These *mitzvot* are *terumah* (the share for the priests), *ma'aser* (the shares for the Levites), *bikkurim* (the first fruits), *shemittah* (seventh year rest for the land and cancellation of debts), and the *yovel* (the jubilee restoration of all inhabitants to original homesteads). All these *mitzvot* are part of the process of sanctification incumbent upon Israel in their maximally achieved conquest.

To what degree maximalist visions will have to be compromised by reality will be understood by the Rabbis of the talmudic era who will be forced to cope with the historic facts that Israelite sovereignty will have been forfeited. Will the dream of covenant be forfeited as well? Certainly not! As foretold by Jeremiah and Ezekiel and as realized by Ezra and Nehemiah, Israel will return. But Israel will not re-conquer. It will re-settle — but it will not resettle all the land conquered by Joshua. And so the dream of sanctification will be modified by the Rabbis who distinguish halakhically between *kedushah rishonah* (the first sanctification) and *kedushah sheniyyah* (second sanctification).

The *kedushah sheniyyah* will be characterized by a much smaller settlement of the Promised Land, and this will be achieved not by conquest commanded through revelation but by permission of a Gentile mortal king of Imperial Persia. God will be in eclipse. The settlement will not be by allotment to all the tribes of Israel. Only the tribe of Judah will have survived — along with some Levites — and a majority of Judaeans will remain in exile in Babylonia. Israel will not have political sovereignty over any part of the Land of Israel. Instead they will have relative religious and cultural autonomy over the area of its settlement. The *mitzvot ha-teluyot ba-aretz* will continue to be in force, but over the smaller area of settlement. Furthermore, with the majority of Jews remaining in exile, a process will begin of conceptualizing a system of commandments to be observed by the individual Jewish person no matter where he lives — in Israel or outside of Israel. And as far as the realization of God's kingship on earth, it will be put off to a future, more propitious time when Jewish sovereignty over Israel will again be made possible.

The Maccabean victories of the second and first centuries B.C.E. will awaken the possibility of a return to maximalist visions of sanctification of the Land. But the vision will be compromised almost simultaneously by disasters of internal corruption and the soon-to-emerge supreme earthly power of Rome. All through the following eighteen-hundred years of exile, the House of Israel will hold on to its maximalist vision of Messianic ingathering. The Zionist movement will bring together maximalist and minimalist visions, i.e., Herzl's political maximalism together with Hibbat Zion's minimalist-gradualist settlement policies. The dream will then continue to energize the Jewish people until a sovereign state will be established in a new eon of time. The new state will have a secular base, but fragments of the dream of sanctification will continue to beckon sensitive Jews to reaffirm an age-old biblical covenant.

Collectivity and Community

How many covenantally sensitive Jews will there be at that time? How many among the Children of Israel will be sensitive to the cosmic dimensions of the story of historic Israel played out in an arena where creation, revelation, and redemption are the central pillars of a God-human/God-Israel encounter? How many Israelites were covenantally sensitive at Sinai and throughout the sojourn in the Wilderness? One of the many *midrashim* on revelation found in the *Midrash Tanhuma* says: "When Israel went out of Egypt, there were many among them who were maimed from the oppressive work they had been forced to do with mortar and bricks where stones would fall on them breaking and severing limbs. The Holy One Blessed Be He, refusing to countenance the possibility that He would give the Torah to a 'maimed' people, signaled to His angelic servants to go down and to cure all of them immediately of whatever blemishes they had."

The proof texts for this passage are respectively the nation all *seeing* the sounds of Sinai, *hearing* the commandments, vowing *to do* the commandments, and *standing* all at the foot of Sinai, thus proving that there were no blind, no deaf, no severed limbs. Similarly as Israel begins its march through the Wilderness with God counting His people in love, one has the optimistic sense that all who are being counted *see* the blessings of creation in all their hues and colors and limitless human variations; that they *hear* beyond the normal sensibility to sound and are, therefore, attuned to committing themselves beyond the conventional given; that they are ready to learn in order to *do*, i.e., to act in full awareness that behavior is the measure of intentions; and to *stand* eternally before God as partner in the covenantal enterprise.

They are all marching, mobilized in perfect symmetrical order with the Ark of God's covenant protecting the tribes of Israel, who in turn are guarding their tablets of Providential purpose. But the question will persist: Does Israel have the will, the persistence, to move from being a marching collectivity to becoming a covenanted community?

Naso נשוא

There is a strange mixture of topics touched upon in this portion. It is a potpourri of topics ranging from the numbering of the Levites as they march with the people to a reference to guilt offerings; from the ordeal of jealousy imposed upon the suspected wife to the rules of the Nazirite. A climax of sorts is reached with the *Birkat Kohanim* (the Blessings of the Priests). Perhaps Moses is underscoring in microcosm the movement back and forth among concerns for the community, the family, and the individual, for any possible harmonization in society as represented by the sublime transporting vision of the priestly blessings must be conditioned by spiritual and moral health in all three social units — the community, the family, and the individual.

The medieval commentator the Ralbag sees a coherence in the flow from topic to topic: "The reference to the guilt offerings is to remind Israel to remove the evils from the camp which bring on quarrels and strife (the community). The ordeal of jealousy cites the need to remove enmity from the family home because *shelom bayit* (harmony within the home) is a precondition for *shelom ha-am* (peace within the nation) (the family). And the discussion regarding the Nazirite is to quiet the self-destructive temperament of the individual nourished by the physical drives within him which lead to sin (the individual)." In other words, the prescription to be offered by Torah is a three-part continuum — community to family to self and at the same time self to family to community. Such a continuum, it is hoped, will bring the hoped-for harmony, fulfillment, and peace to the nation.

Values and Concretizations

In order to implement the prescription, each individual must take upon himself the burden of responsibility. In mirror-image fashion, the individual must carry on his own individual shoulders the responsibility of the covenant much as the Levites are charged with the transport of the tabernacle and its accoutrements. The charge to the Kahathite clan among the Levites is particularly suggestive. As opposed to the Gershonites and Merarites to whom Moses gives carts and oxen for transporting, the Kahathites must carry their objects on their shoulders — *"bakatef yisa'u."* The message is clear: What one cares about, really cares about, one will assume responsibility for totally. One will carry the entire burden on one's own shoulders.

Many generations later, the Kotzker Rebbe will re-emphasize the sustained personal effort required for any truly holy work or worship. "One doesn't merit a single spark of holiness *easily*." Moses has already learned this lesson from his brief but intense period of service in God's "holy" work. What awaits him in the Wilderness will be a burden so heavy that even he will not be able to bear it for long without help. The final decree regarding his own personal destiny — that he will himself not enter the Promised Land — will be a judgment noting his all too-human inadequacy, even in the face of an unparalleled human achievement.

Indeed, how will Moses be able to carry the burden of individual, familial, and communal commitments required to fulfill the covenant? Is Moses to be held responsible for the inadequacies of individuals, individual families, individual communities within the larger corpus of Israel? As an ordinary individual, he is not responsible, nor can he be held responsible for the sins of others. But as a leader of a covenanted people, a chosen people, he does bear the burden of spiritual and moral responsibility along with the social and political. The experience of the Wilderness will teach him just how impossibly heavy the burden is.

Shelom bayit (harmony in the home), for example, is critical to social, communal, and national well-being. Moses knows that one of the chief sources of friction in the family is lack of trust. Suspicions of infidelity may plague a household. The society to which Moses has to minister is relatively unenlightened vis-à-vis latter-day standards of respect for women. The *peshat* (simple meaning) of the trial by ordeal which the suspected wife must undergo, therefore, is nothing less than sadistic. But as has been pointed out earlier, Moshe Greenberg has recommended a strategy for understanding the presence of such cruel practices appearing in what is considered a revelatory text. The strategy entails admitting to what is a *hityashnut gilum arakhim* (the obsolescence of certain concretizations of values).

It has been noted and explained that this phrase refers to certain practices in the Bible which according to the ethical standards of later generations will be considered outdated. They will be rejected by the House of Israel because at a certain point in Jewish history it will be felt that such practices are demeaning and cannot possibly represent God's long-term will. Earlier these practices may have been felt to be appropriate legal embodiments or concretizations of values held to be precious to the family and to the community, e.g., sexual modesty and marital loyalty. But before too long a practice such as the trial by ordeal imposed on the suspected wife will be felt to be ethically gross, and, therefore, to be consigned to obsolescence. In other words, values such as sexual modesty and marital loyalty are timeless. The legal embodiments or concretizations of these values, however, may be time-bound and prone to obsolescence.

And so with regard to the issue of the *sotah* (the suspected wife), the talmudic Rabbis will legislate a process of increasingly demanding pre-conditions for allowing the incrimination of the helpless wife. They will seek to eliminate, in effect, the possibility of the kind of public humiliation "mandated" by the Written Torah. Ultimately the entire practice of trial by ordeal will be eliminated. The principle stated in *Sotah* (47b) that only when the husband is himself utterly innocent will the waters of purgation test the wife's chastity will already serve as somewhat of an equalizer of moral responsibility vis-à-vis men and women.

Moses is intent upon teaching the timeless values of the Torah. He can only embody these values in the socio-legal concretizations that his contemporary community of former slaves are capable of comprehending. But built in to the Torah legislation is the understanding that there will be ongoing interpretation and development of *Torat Eretz Yisrael*. What else will the Midrash mean when later it will say that the Oral Torah was also given at Sinai along with the Written Torah!

Moses knows that ongoing interpretation of a sacred text will not be a simple matter; that, moreover, those who would try to make it a simple matter would have to be rejected. Who would such interpreters be? It would be any future "elite" group who would try to make the House of Israel believe that they — this particular "elite" group or "elite" generation — "own" the Torah exclusively. This group would be against change. They would refuse to acknowledge that new generations might conclude on the need for moderate or even radical change *le-shem Shamayim* (for the sake of Heaven). And that these new generations — in their own understanding of God's will — would have the right to demand recognition of the legitimacy of their interpretations of the Written Torah for their day.

A healthy future for *Torat Eretz Yisrael* would have to reject a reactionary mind-set of another sort that many centuries later would refuse to admit that modern Jewish history will have been witness to a three-fold apocalypse: the Emancipation, the Holocaust, and the re-establishment of a modern Jewish state in Israel after centuries of *galut*. This apocalypse would demand no less than a *revolutionary* new look at Torah in order to make of it again a new source of living waters for the Jewish people.

There would be reactionaries of still another sort who would seek to undermine any creative continuity of Torah interpretation seeking to adapt Torah to new times and to new needs. These reactionaries would argue self-righteously and hypocritically in favor of leaving the Written Torah alone — in a state of petrified irrelevancy. They would seek to relegate the traditional Torah heritage to museum-like permanent obsolescence. In effect, they would be looking for the Torah to be given a respectable burial.

Moshe Greenberg's phrase "the obsolescence of certain concretizations of values" helps the religious searcher to understand two propositions about a living Torah: (1) For enlightened spiritual and moral values to remain relevant, their concrete embodiments must be subject to constant examination, and, if and when necessary, to change; and (2) *living* Torah is relevant to any age — especially in a post-apocalyptic age, whether it be after the earlier Exodus or after the later Emancipation, the Holocaust, and the re-establishment of the State of Israel.

A further note regarding the lesson of the *sotah*: Notwithstanding the obsolescence of the trial by ordeal and the gross inequity involved in the husband's public shaming of his wife, the *sotah* serves as a powerful metaphor for the marital bond between God the husband and Israel the wife which from time to time may be called into doubt. Israel will always be tested as to its faithfulness. It will always be "drinking water," so to speak. The water will either be the *mayim hayyim* (the living water) of Torah or the *mei marim* (the bitter water) of the suspected wife. Whenever Israel will fail in its commitment to the covenant it will be made to drink the bitter waters of self-delusion and self-recrimination. It cannot be any other way in the face of the many temptations in the world to remove oneself as a people from the unremitting responsibility of the covenant.

The Nazirite

There will be those within the House of Israel who will be so hypersensitive to the demands of the covenant that they will impose upon themselves extra duties in order to ascend to what in their eyes will be higher levels of "sanctity." By so doing they will hope to assure themselves a modicum of anticipatory "redemption." Perhaps they may feel that their exercises in self-mortification will serve as a vicarious atonement for others less "sanctified."

The subject of the *nazir* is first mentioned well before this juncture in the Wilderness. It is alluded to at the end of the Book of Genesis as part of the blessing which Jacob gives to his son Joseph: "The blessings of your father are mighty beyond the blessings of my parents unto the utmost bound of the everlasting hills; they shall be on the head of Joseph and on the crown of the head of the '*nazir* among his brethren.'" The Targum translates the phrase "*nazir* among his brethren" as "apart from his brethren." Indeed, Joseph was apart from his entire family physically for twenty-two years and apart from them emotionally from the time of his youth until the reconciliation.

But the "naziriteship" of Joseph vis-à-vis his brothers was not what it became in Torah legislation. In the Bible there are two cases of distinguished people consecrated for naziriteship — Samson and Samuel. The ascetic characteristics of naziriteship, e.g., abstaining from wine, from cutting the hair, and observing extra degrees of sexual purity, are looked upon by the Torah with approval, but not with enthusiasm. In fact, the stories of Samson and Samuel belie the importance of naziriteship. In the case of Samson it can be argued that his abstinence proved to be strictly theoretical. For his behavior was often dissolute, leading eventually to his downfall. And the biblical story of Samuel clearly emphasizes that he became a prophet, a teacher, a king-maker in the Sturm-und-Drang of politics — the antithesis of an abstemious spiritual "holy man."

Why then does biblical legislation include "naziriteship" in its agenda for making Israel a holy nation? Because the concept of *hinazrut* is very much a part of religion as most of the world into which Israel enters understands religion. There is hardly a religion which doesn't laud asceticism. Restraining oneself in the face of ordinary passions and readying oneself to reach an ostensibly higher plane of holiness serves as a tempting image for individuals who regard themselves as especially hungry for spiritual elevation. But the religion of Israel comes on the scene of world history with a redemptive message that is aimed not only at the individual qua individual — no matter how "holy" he thinks he is or strives to be — but at the individual as he involves himself with the collective, i.e., his family, his tribe, and his people.

Samson's downfall is caused not only by his libido. Samson does everything alone. He apparently doesn't need an army, fellow Israelites, supporters of any kind. He lacks wholesome relationships with women or with men. In the final analysis all he does is destroy. Granted, he is a menace to his enemies who happen to be the enemies of Israel. But he is prone to self-destruction as well. And he succeeds! His story is recorded principally because, in his self-destruction that has begun long before the denouement in Gaza, he is considered a hero in Israel. But if his "judgeship" in Israel is recorded favorably in the Bible, it is only because through his exploits, adventures, and misadventures he has helped defeat the hated Philistines.

Samuel's story is recorded immediately after the Book of Judges which ends with the blatantly ironic critique of individualism — "*ish ha-yashar be-einav ya'aseh*" ("each one did what was right in his own eyes"). Samuel's naziriteship, in other words, reinforced by his novitiate with Eli the priest, fails to isolate him from the true need of Israel: sociopolitical leadership. Samuel's office is to become more "spiritually" influential not by ascetic self-purification and self-removal from affairs of state, but by putting a king on the throne (with mixed feelings) in order to build a nation which will finally defeat the Philistines.

As indicated earlier, however, religion and its universal yearning for expressions of sanctification looks to naziriteship to somehow actualize the yearning. And so the debate continues among the Rabbis. Rabbi Elazar cites the *nazir* being referred to as *kadosh* (holy). The reference is to his letting his hair grow to which Rabbi Elazar says: "If he is called '*kadosh*' even after mortifying himself in *one* way, how much more so should he be considered *kadosh* when keeping himself from additional pleasures." But his talmudic colleague Samuel notes the Torah's labeling of the *nazir* as a *hotei* (sinner). For just as anyone who *imposes* upon himself a fast should be considered a sinner, similarly anyone who will keep himself from the enjoyment of one of God's blessings, e.g., wine, or anyone who will *seek* additional self-impositions of "suffering" should be considered a sinner who must thereby seek atonement.

The Torah is sensitive to the spiritual-psychological reality that the individual — and community — is caught in a titanic struggle between self-indulgence and self-mortification. According to the Torah, both are wrong. *Kashrut* (dietary laws) and Shabbat do not deny respectively the acceptability, nay, the desirability of food and work. These institutions attempt to balance the temptations to overindulge in eating and working. But the Rambam addresses the *nazir* with the sharpest sardonic "bite": "It's not enough that the Torah has forbidden many things; but you impose upon yourself additional prohibitions! This is why they who are constantly fasting do not walk the right path. Koheleth has articulated a relevant insight: 'Do not be too righteous nor too wise, for you will become a desolate human being!'" Among modern commentators, Israel Eldad has said: "All the commandments related to *kedushah* touch the relationship which the individual has or is to have with the general community, with his elders and relatives, with the impoverished in his society, with his fellow citizens. Of what value is it to the general public if an individual becomes a nazirite merely to sanctify himself?"

The *Yeitzer ha-Ra* and God's Priestly Blessings

It may be argued that despite the negative aspects of the institution of the *nazir*, the Torah needs for its covenantal purpose reminders within the community of the importance of self-control, of standards, of discipline. Why the extreme? It is to counteract the *yeitzer ha-ra* which is stronger than Israel can imagine. Ideally the Torah system should provide the normative self-control, standards, and discipline. But what if the system as is will show tendencies to disintegrate in the face of tempting alternative life-styles?

Moses is envisioning a cultural conflict as fierce as the political-military conflict with the Canaanite-Hittite civilization into which Israel is settling. The strategy, commanded by God, is to destroy the indigenous culture. But that will not happen. Vestiges of that culture will remain. And the temptation to fall into the web of licentiousness represented by Canaan on top of the Egyptian influence that has already conditioned Israel to "golden-calf" behavior will be overwhelming. Moses knows that the Serpent's sting is ruthless and omnipresent. Its power to seduce Israel — and humanity in general — will apply throughout Jewish and human history.

Shai Agnon's short story *"Ha-Adonit ve-ha-Rokhel"* ("The Lady and the Peddler") will be written to describe the post-Emancipation Jew taken in by the seductive modern world. The peddler is the wandering Jew who has allowed himself to be taken in by the ostensibly kind "lady" and is delighted to be "wined and dined" by her. But she exposes herself soon enough as a vampire who has sucked the blood out of a number of previous paramours. The Jew manages to escape in time, but it is inevitable that the *yeitzer ha-ra* will work on the Jew time and time again leading him to lust after what is forbidden. That the lethal intentions of the erstwhile welcoming civilization will reveal themselves sooner or later will only exacerbate the predicament which the Jew's own *yeitzer ha-ra* will have evoked. The relentless combat with the *yeitzer ra*, therefore, may need the extra dimension of nazarite abstemiousness to remind the people of Israel that conventional spiritual and moral commitments to the covenant may not be enough.

In any case both Moses and Israel come to appreciate that the challenge which has been placed before them is one that will tax their human capacities to their spiritual-moral limits. Will they be up to the task? The potpourri of issues presented by Moses to the people throughout Leviticus, Numbers, and Deuteronomy underscores why in the midst of it all there shines through the *Birkat Kohanim* (the Blessing of the Priests). The *Akedat Yitzhak* commentary asks: "Of what value are these blessings coming as they do from mortal men — priests, yes, but mortal men nevertheless — when God Himself is the source of all blessing?" Can these priests really "assist" *Him*?

His answer quotes from the tractate *Shabbat*: "When Moses ascended to find the Holy One Blessed Be He placing crowns on the letters of the Torah, God said to him, 'Moses, do people not greet one another in your city upon meeting, do they not say *"shalom"* to one another?' Moses responded: 'Lord of the Universe, would a mere servant be presumptuous enough to initiate a greeting such as *"shalom"* to his Master?' God retorted: 'In any case you should have assisted Me!'" What is the meaning of God's retort? God uses Himself as a recommended model for human behavior, teaching a lesson in *derekh eretz* (the proper manners for human interaction). God knows that the blessings of *shalom* are initially and ultimately His to give; but He does not wish to denigrate the role of the human priests in sharing the giving of the blessings. The extended lesson here is that even though initially and ultimately all of creation is God's, the human share, the Israelite share, every Israelite's share in partnering creation, is encouraged — more than encouraged; it is demanded!

And because every Israelite, every human being, is needed to help mend the world, to bring harmony and completeness to the world, each of them is to be shown enough *derekh eretz* not to be utterly and finally condemned to perdition without some opportunity for repentance. In this sense, the legislation regarding the *sotah*, on the one hand, and the *nazir*, on the other, is meant to acknowledge that God knows of the *yeitzer ha-ra* and its power to lead human beings astray. God shows empathy for the human being in recognizing that because the latter can sink at times below conventional moral norms of marital fidelity, he needs, therefore, constant modes of sanctification — at times even modes of hypersanctification. In short, God wants the human being to have a stake in perfecting human civilization. God must show the way by involving Himself through His blessings in the human effort.

Fraternity and the Gifts of the Princes

The partnership between God and Israel to bring *shalom*, i.e., harmony, fulfillment, and peace to the world, is a partnership fated to suffer frustration and disappointment. Notwithstanding God's "maturation" following the exile of humankind from Eden and the equally crushing blow to God's vision with the wholesale corruption of the antedeluvians, Moses knows that it hasn't become any easier to bring about peace between brothers — especially between brothers in Israel. In the *aggadah* and the *halakhah*, the dilemma-like intensity of the problem of fraternal empathy or enmity pervades rabbinic discussions. In the *aggadah* Jacob is afraid of his brother Esau lest he be killed at Esau's hand. Jacob is equally distressed that he himself may be driven to killing Esau. That Jacob and Esau do not slay each other is not so much a matter of moral evolution as distance and elapsed time — mostly distance.

In the *halakhah* the institution of Shabbat is to represent an idyllic possibility of peace-on-earth and a promise of messianic perfection. But the Mishnah records a strange but relevant discussion regarding the wearing of weapons on the special holy day: "A man should not go out of his house on

Shabbat wearing a sword or bow or shield or staff or spear. And if he does, he is obligated to bring a sin offering. Rabbi Eliezer says that they are mere adornments and therefore may be worn. The Sages, on the other hand, say that they are degrading, as it says in the Prophets: 'they shall beat their swords into plowshares and their spears into pruning hooks; nation shall not lift up sword against nation nor shall they learn war anymore!'" The debate reflects the enmity that will exist between brothers and nations and that will need to be controlled, sublimated, tolerated if need be, as one tries to bring the world closer to the prophetic desideratum. Is it God who has the exclusive power to bring it closer to prophetic fruition? Or is God determined *not* to bring it closer until human beings have begun to share the burden of bringing it closer?

That each human being must share in the "bringing it closer" is underscored at the end of the portion *Naso* with the gifts of the twelve princes. The perennial question is asked regarding the recording of the gifts in twelve portions all saying the same thing except for the change of name of the individual prince. Why couldn't the Torah have reported all twelve lists of repeated specifics in one general statement? Ramban gives the answer: "God wishes to bestow honor on all those who revere Him…behold all the princes have agreed together to offer the same offerings and it is impossible for one not to be chosen as the first…were the other eleven to be mentioned only in general it would dishonor them in comparison. Therefore each one has his day…and just as all are equal in their intentions, so shall they be equal in merit."

Just as the portion has begun with a march of equals — at least in the sight of God, if not before kings of flesh and blood — it ends with the model of the twelve princes. There has been a lesson bound up with the primary religio-human slogan found early in Genesis *"be-tzelem Elohim bara otam"* ("in the image of God He created them"). The lesson pervades the whole Torah in many ways, some direct and obvious, others more subtle. It is the lesson of the princes and their proud individual offerings. It is the lesson of the priestly blessings bestowed upon all of Israel: that God's name is to be placed over each and every Israelite, worthy and unworthy. How worthy or unworthy the House of Israel is and how worthy or unworthy every Israelite within the House of Israel is will now be tested as Israel begins its journey through the Wilderness.

Be-Ha'alotekha בהעלותך

As the Israelites begin their journey through the wilderness, their doubts and hesitations intensify. Moses himself will be seen to lose confidence in his capacity to carry through the mission which has been placed upon his shoulders. The medieval commentator Yitzhak Arama underscores two basic manifestations of Moses' insecurity. First he will give in to his anger at the Children of Israel by appealing to God to remove him from office. He will plead with God to recognize that he, Moses, can no longer be a total provider, literally a nursemaid, to this people. Secondly, in referring to *himself* as the inadequate provider, he will be exhibiting doubt regarding *God's* ongoing capacity to provide the miracles necessary for sustenance in the Wilderness.

One can understand the weariness and frustration that can afflict someone who has undertaken a long-term commitment to a vast human experiment. In the case of Moses, he will recover from his spells of despondency — but not fully. Within and because of the Wilderness period, he will retire gradually from being the ubiquitous leader with total responsibility for every aspect of the community's welfare. He will continue, however, to be Israel's preeminent teacher, Moshe Rabbenu, who will instruct a new generation (and all generations thereafter) in the terms of the covenant.

Trials of Leadership

Moses must "fail" as a leader. For all leaders ultimately fail in providing for the dull-normal needs of a polyglot people. Moses finds that it is easier to shepherd a people through its period of dramatic revolution than to cater to the everyday problems of prosaic survival following the revolution. Moses faces the enervating task of seeing to it that day after day, every day, there is food and water. It is he who must provide answers to the endless stresses of normal day-to-day living, not to mention the uniquely prodigious challenges of surviving the special rigors of the Wilderness. Moses has been warned earlier by his father-in-law Yitro that he cannot carry all by himself the burdens of the judiciary. He now realizes that he cannot continue to assume all the executive and legislative aspects of leadership as well. Moses knows it; he must convince God of it.

This does not mean that Moses is prepared to resign his mission entirely. But he can note increasingly his own inadequacies. True, he has had the courage and intractability to challenge Pharaoh and even God Himself when necessary. But handling on a relentlessly demanding basis a large people and their daily individual necessities is too much for any human being. Moses protests to God that no human being should be asked to have exclusive responsibility for such a task.

The Children of Israel all along have continued to embody the less than complimentary epithet *am keshei oref* (a stiff-necked people). This "stiff-necked" quality has not led to outright rebellion against the covenant — at least not yet. The stiff-neckedness appears to God and by extension to Moses in the day-to-day complaints of the people in the face of shortages, disappointments, and frustrations. In his socio-spiritual biography of Moses, Buber sees the stiff-neckedness born out of the lust-for-success that Israel has seen fulfilled in its victories over Egypt and Amalek. Their faith will have to be tested, however, outside the euphoric mood of victory. How does Israel cope with loss, with defeat, with unfulfilled promises? And again, how does Israel maintain its morale inspired by transcendent promises in the face of humdrum daily vexations?

As an example of such vexations, Abrabanel asks: "Why were the Children of Israel punished now for their demand for meat in their diet when they hadn't been punished for the same demand earlier upon leaving Egypt?" The *Akedat Yitzhak*'s response is that at the earlier period, Israel's doubts, uncertainties, and general lack of faith were kept to themselves. They didn't express these deep internal concerns publicly. But now they are verbalizing their discontent publicly in the form of a *to'anah* or pretext. They must have meat! In God's eyes as well as Moses', this pretext is particularly heinous because in the interim between their demands for meat they have experienced wonders. That their lust after immediate sensuous gratification should be so uncontrollable is held to be particularly odious.

God's frustration with Israel, along with Moses' bending under the crushing responsibilities of shepherding this stiff-necked people, is reflected in a textual anomaly. There are brackets surrounding two verses that appear in the middle of the portion. These verses celebrate God's unswerving support of Israel whether they are in movement or in encampment. Why are these verses bracketed? Rabbi Shimon ben Gamliel says: "This bracketed section will be removed from here and placed where it should have been. And why has it been placed here? In order to provide a break between one trouble and another!" What is the latter trouble if not the nation's complaining and complaining. What then is the former trouble which has been recorded and not forgotten? The Torah reports: *"Va-yis'u me-har Hashem"* ("And they left the mountain of the Lord"); and Rabbi Hama ben Haninah interprets the phrase as their having "left" God. They have abandoned Him. Where then is the proper place for this bracketed passage? "It belongs in the citation concerning the ensigns of the various tribes as they align themselves for movement."

We recall that the Book of Numbers has opened with optimistic expectations that the tribes are ready and eager for movement, for movement to the goal. The two verses are an invocation to the Lord "to scatter our enemies and Yours" along with the entreaty to "return to us, to Your people Israel." It is a double "charge" to God that is meant to sustain a people that is on the march. It is clear then that the bracketed "upbeat" verses belong here with the ensigns.

Instead, the people has become a people of *mit'onenim*. The meaning is taken literally to be "complainers." The *Sifre* notes a four-stage description implicit in the word indicating self-defeat, a defeat that is all inner-generated and inner-directed: (1) The word is associated with the Hebrew word for pretext — *to'anah*. From the beginning the Children of Israel have lacked faith and at various signs of trouble or even mild discomfiture, they have looked for a pretext to question the entire enterprise. (2) Being described as *mit'onenim* is associated with a more insidious characterization. They are *ke-mitlahamim*, reminding us of the thought expressed in Proverbs 26:22, "Words of a slanderer are swallowed greedily," that is, words of slander are eagerly gulped down by a person (or a people) disposed to listen to them. (3) This leads to depression — another suggested aspect of the word *ke-mit'onenim*, i.e., *onen*, from the root "mourning." The depression is fed by every new instance of difficulty, deprivation, and anticipated defeat.

(4) Finally, and most decisively from God's point of view, they are described by the term *ke-mit'onenim ra* (as complainers of *evil*). And *ra* (evil) can only refer to idolatry, that is, a rejection of covenantal purpose and destiny.

God's tragic disappointment will be matched by that of Moses. The bracketed text begins with the confident injunction that Israel's movement to the Promised Land will be accompanied by the scattering of its enemies: "As the Ark of the Covenant moves, '*va-yafutzu oyevekha ve-yanusu mesan'ekha mi-panekha*' ('Your enemies will be scattered, those who hate You will flee from before You')." The *Sifre* underscores what Israel should feel in order to maintain its morale: It is difficult to imagine mortal nations or individuals focusing their hatred on an abstract *Force* — even if it is a *Force* that created the universe! The bracketed text, therefore, warns those who would deign to hate Israel that they are in truth showing hatred for the *Living God* and such hatred will be punished.

In other words, the covenant, in addition to its adjurations and threats in case Israel should fail to fulfill its terms, does have morale-building features. Its strongest feature is the identification of God with Israel's existential situation in the world. An enemy of Israel is an enemy of God! Is there a more inspiring epithet! It is meant to infuse spiritual energy along with an enthusiasm of righteous purpose. How can Israel not respond to it!

Yet, they don't! Not only do they complain about wants and deficiencies! They resort to selective memory. They prefer to remember their diet in Egypt which, assuming they are not fantasizing entirely, is held up against the miraculous but spare fare provided by the Almighty. One might find a cause for sympathizing with them in the light of their meager Wilderness existence; but to resort to nostalgic evocations of their erstwhile House of Slavery — Egypt! Egypt where they were not even given straw with which to fulfill their quota within their slave-labor conditions!

In essence they are taunting Moses and by extension God who have offered them freedom and national independence while they are proclaiming their yearning for a return to dependence. They have been challenged into becoming partners in a transcendently ordered covenant when they seem to prefer existentially mandated disorder and aimlessness.

Israel does have legitimate anxieties. But to attempt to face these anxieties by bursting forth in lustful yearning for a past that never was! They are misreading their past in Egypt, perversely misreading it. Yet in the face of the challenges which lie ahead of them as a sovereign independent nation, they are at this point permitting their childish self-indulgent spirit to overtake them with imagined "comforts" of their enslaved situation in Egypt. How can they be so mistaken! The power of self-delusion! And so the will of the people, weak as it has been all along, has now de-energized Moses himself. He himself is now suffering from a weariness of body and spirit.

As mentioned earlier, Yitzhak Arama summarizes Moses' state-of-being at this juncture in severe moral terms. From the pinnacle of Moses' moral righteousness and readiness for self-sacrifice, he has been brought down to virtual despair. At the episode of the "golden calf," Moses had confronted God. He had challenged the Almighty to forgive Israel's sin or erase him, Moses, their leader, God's chosen deputy, from God's chronicle of redemption. But now, as suggested earlier, his despair and anger bring him to sin in two respects: First, he pleads to be relieved of his deputyship, his appointment by God to shepherd God's people on their appointed journey. He dares to throw off his moral responsibility to the Almighty, to the Creator. Secondly, in protesting that he, Moses, can no longer provide the food and sustenance to this people as he has been doing since the Exodus from Egypt, he is showing arrogance. Has it ever been he, Moses, who was the provider and not God? And has God lost the capacity to continue providing?

As a result of Moses' confession of inadequacy, God will now command assistance for him; but in truth it will be much more. It will serve as a precursor for a new legislative process in Israel. It will herald a future move from prophetic-autocratic leadership to a parliamentary model. It will prescribe that God-directed *prophecy* must give way eventually to God-inspired *wisdom*. This process will take centuries. But it begins here. And it begins not with a revolution against a human autocrat; but with the approval, the weary acquiescence of their erstwhile miraculously endowed leader, who has now been brought low by the weight of daily burdens.

At this juncture in its history, however, Israel will continue to need autocratic leadership. It will continue to need leaders who are felt to have prophetic charisma. As a formerly enslaved rabble, there is too much demanded of them for them to be able to judge for themselves appropriate ways and means for continuing the journey to the Promised Land. If left to a populist will, they have already indicated their preference: to return to slavery!

Eldad, Medad, and Ambition

And so the seventy are chosen to assist Moses whose charismatic spirit will be shared with them. They will be taken out of the camp temporarily to assume appropriate distance from the people. Leadership demands such distance, certainly at the commencement of their service. But two prophetically gifted individuals, Eldad and Medad, remain in the camp and are seen and heard to be prophesying there. Joshua finds this intolerable. Yet Moses is proud of them. He notes that what they are doing is a positive development for the community.

Rabbi Shimon's explanation for their remaining in the camp is their humility: "When the Holy One Blessed Be He said to Moses to gather seventy men, Eldad and Medad felt themselves inadequate for such aristocratic office. As a reward for their humility, God said: 'Because you have diminished yourselves, I will add greatness to you.' And what was the greatness? That whereas with all the other prophets, they prophesied and then ceased to prophesy, Eldad and Medad would never cease to prophesy." What was the content of their prophecy? They noted that Moses will die but that Joshua will lead Israel into the Land.

In other words, Eldad and Medad have seen that Moses needs help. Unlike other influential voices among the people, they themselves will not countenance a return to Egypt. They want to fulfill the mission and destiny of Israel — to enter, to conquer, and to settle Eretz Yisrael! Their prophecy contains a personal commitment which allows them to see further even than Joshua. They realize that Moses will eventually be gone from the scene. At such time, they will follow Joshua — as long as it is to the Promised Land.

In their prophesying they are not seeking advancement for themselves. Just as Moses has been *anav mi-kol adam* (the most humble of men), so are they. If they — and Moses — have ambition, it is not of the narcissistic kind that looks at the world as if it is meant to be no more than a mirror of their own selfish passions. Theirs is a responsible ambition that looks at the world and responds to it by giving themselves over to the work of redeeming that world in a covenantal image. Both types of ambition — the narcissistic and the responsible — provide satisfaction for the ego. But narcissistic ambition ends in disaster with nothing socially constructive to show for the effort. Responsible ambition leaves something behind which is immortal because the people who have been inspired and served by that ambition have benefited, have been "saved" and "redeemed."

A great literary example of narcissistic ambition is Macbeth who wants to be King of Scotland — but not for the purpose of responding to Scotland's needs! He wants to be king for the sole purpose of self-aggrandizement! With such a goal, he feels compelled to murder the incumbent. And he himself knows how narrowly focused is his purpose: "I have no spur to prick the sides of my intent, but only vaulting ambition, which o'erleaps itself and falls on the other." All Macbeth sees is a mirror of himself. He certainly doesn't see Duncan the king except as an obstacle to his narcissistic ambition. His perception doesn't include Scotland either except as a vehicle for his own self-adulation. In the end he must fail. His end will be for him a final end — nullity!

Moses on the other hand always sees before him the community and the nation. As a prophet he has a critical understanding of his people's readiness or lack of it to assume the burdens of covenant. He has said to them: *"Kedoshim tihyu"* ("Be you holy"). They have responded: "We want the flesh-pots of Egypt." He has said to them: "You are an *'am segulah'* ("a treasured people')." They have preferred to be stiff-necked in their pursuit of anarchy. But because Moses' ambition is outer-directed in its commitment to the welfare of the nation, he will leave something enduring for them, despite their weakness, once his service ends. In this sense Moses' prophecy never ceases.

And Eldad and Medad's prophecy similarly does not cease. They look confidently and commitedly to the future — in their case to Joshua's leadership and beyond. Their commitment to the future is echoed in the prophetic words of Joel 3:1: "In the future I will pour out My spirit on all flesh; Your sons and daughters shall prophesy; Your old men shall dream dreams, and your young men shall see visions…"

A Renewal of Faith

Eldad and Medad's prophesying in the camp has a therapeutic effect upon Moses himself. When Joshua comes running to his master with the urgent plea to imprison these two upstarts, Moses responds to the contrary: "Are you wrought up on my account? Would that all the Lord's people were prophets that the Lord put His spirit upon them!" In this comment, Moses is not only exhibiting again his own matchless humility. From a different perspective he is also urging the further democratization of God's revelatory insight, i.e., the Torah. Just as God will share His spirit and Moses' acquired providential spirit with the seventy elders, the aspiration is to have all Israel have an active share in Torah insight.

And so out of the doldrums of Moses' depression which has led God to call for the seventy, and as yet unaware of the coming catastrophic mission of the spies, Moses' spirit has been revived by Eldad and Medad. Moses' dream that everyone has the potential to become a vehicle for prophetic insight will restore the entire House of Israel to the threshold of covenantal promise. His renewed spiritual energy will inspire him to intercede with God when his sister Miriam is afflicted with leprosy as a punishment for her non-sisterly backbiting.

The optimistic turn in Moses' thinking is heralded in the interpretation of a particular verse earlier in the portion (8:19): "and from among the *Israelites* I formally assign the Levites to Aaron and his sons, to perform the service for the *Israelites* in the Tent of Meeting and to make expiation for the *Israelites*, so that no plague may afflict the *Israelites* should the *Israelites* come too near the sanctuary." Rashi notes a syntactic peculiarity in the verse in that the term "Israelites" is mentioned no less than five times where pronouns would ordinarily suit the major part of the sentence after the first mention of the antecedent. Rashi's own interpretation is that we are meant to notice the affection which has been manifested in this multiple recording of the name "Israel." "Israel" is mentioned five times in order to equate its importance with the Five Books of the Torah.

Centuries later the Kotzker Rebbe will see the House of Israel divided into groups just as ancient Israel was divided into groups of priests, Levites, and Israelites. And just as each *humash* ("book") of the Torah is an independent unit by itself, each joins together with the other books of the Torah to produce and constitute one Torah. Analogously, every individual Israelite or Jew is a complex unit, but a unit nevertheless organically unified in a mind-soul-body complex. Joined to every other Israelite or Jew, we multiply the infinite varieties of personality, orientation, and aspiration indigenous to the exponentially larger group. But the total organic quality of the people — at least in the ideal sense — should never, must never, be fractured. All of Jewish history will then be witness to the Children of Israel proclaiming that the covenant has been signed and sealed with an entire people, organically unified, despite its openness to a variety of personal and sectional interests and capacities. The covenant will have inspired the people to settle a land in order to build a society comprehensively oriented to qualifying that society by standards of sanctity and humaneness.

Despite his increasing periods of despondency and anger, Moses never loses his faith that somehow the people will be brought to the Promised Land and will succeed in moving to the stage of settlement and incipient sanctification. Much later in Jewish history, a spokesman for Jewish and Zionist purpose and destiny, Martin Buber, will write a letter to a world-renowned moral exemplar, Mahatma Gandhi, explaining the transcendent purpose of modern Jewish nationalism:

> The Bible tells us, and our inmost knowledge testifies to it, that once, more than 3,000 years ago, our entry into this land took place with the consciousness of a mission from above to set up a just way of life through the generations of our people, a way of life that cannot be realized by individuals in the sphere of their private existence, but only by a nation in the establishment of its society... No other nation has ever been faced at the beginning of its career with such a mission. Here is something which there is no forgetting and from which there is no release. At that time we did not carry out that which was imposed upon us; we went into exile with our task unperformed; but the command remained with us, and it has become more urgent than ever.

The urgency with which Buber will speak will be induced by the horrific events of the Holocaust which will have begun six years earlier and, in a real sense, decades and centuries before because of the essential toxicity of the exile. Buber will be pleading his case before Gandhi, an allegedly superior moral sensibility, whose openness to all human beings will be strangely closed, however, to the national cry of the Jewish people. Nevertheless, Buber will not choose to argue his case on the basis of an instinctual creaturely cry for *mercy*. He will frame his argument in spiritual-moral terms which would hope to appeal to any reasonable human being's *sense of right*.

Buber will not hesitate to acknowledge the earlier failures of the Children of Israel to build a society in which the conditions specified in the spiritual-moral covenant were to be realized. At the same time, without hesitancy, he places before his co-respondent the right and obligation which has been imposed upon Israel at the outset of its existence. In an unabashed evocation of transcendent right joined to the Children of Israel's self-imposition of covenantal commitment, Buber will make his claim for Israel's place as a nation in its land — the Land of Israel.

The Challenge to Moses

Moses had undoubtedly been made aware of the original *Brit bein ha-Betarim* (the Covenant of the Pieces). He knows that God has applied certain similar "covenantal" conditions to the pre-Israelite inhabitants of the Land. God had indicated to Abraham that his descendants would have to wait four hundred years to begin to experience redemption because "the iniquity of the Amorites is not yet complete." The spiritual-moral standard may not be applicable to all lands on earth; but it is held to prevail with regard to the land of the Amorites, eventually to become the Land of the Israelites.

It is the mood of Abraham who had a long-term faith in the working-out of God's promise which similarly conditions Moses' oscillation between moods of discouragement and certainty regarding the destiny of his flock. He knows that his days of shepherding this flock are numbered. He will someday surrender his herculean task to others. But, in spite of his deep concerns for the future, reflected in his speeches recorded in Deuteronomy, he has confidence in his closest disciple Joshua and the future parliamentary leadership who together will be charged with applying prophetic insights to the challenges of daily living. Beyond Joshua and the future Elders, Moses also anticipates a legion of future young Eldads and Medads, whose humility and enthusiasm taken together will guarantee a commitment to the covenant.

In the meantime Moses still leads. Yet greater trials than Moses could ever have imagined await him.

Shlah Lekha שלח לך

God had had a vision — a maximalist vision. Adam and Eve in their garden would constitute a whole world of primordial bliss. The joy of innocence! These two human beings were molded biologically to propagate the entire human race. Their partnership was to be a model of future joy and happiness for that human race. The Garden of Eden was to be a living metaphor for an ideal society that would cover the whole earth. But Adam and Eve failed; the "garden" became a "wilderness" that God destroyed with the Flood; and with the destruction God surrendered His maximalist vision.

But God did not surrender His *capacity* to dream and to envision. He altered the dimensions of His dream, turning it into what for Him would be a minimalist vision. He would select an Abraham. He would isolate a particular tract of land in order to reserve it for Abraham's descendants, the Children of Israel. And He would orchestrate historic events in such a way as to place before the Children of Israel paths leading first to enslavement in a strange land but ultimately to covenantal redemption in the Promised Land. The Book of Ba-Midbar — significantly titled "in the wilderness" — documents Israel's wrestling with the terms of this covenantal redemption, the terms which will dictate Israel's progress as it moves ahead to its land of destiny.

The Sin of the Spies

There is good reason for Israel to be awestruck by the challenge of moving ahead in the Wilderness to the so-called Promised Land. A central theme of the discouraging report of the ten spies is that the Land is an *"eretz okhelet yoshveha"* (a land which devours its inhabitants). Furthermore the current inhabitants are described as "of great stature."

At the same time it can be argued that the spies are blind to the inner contradiction in their report: If the land consumes its inhabitants, how is it that it produces men of great stature? Sforno tries to resolve the contradiction by noting that because it is a tough country only the fittest can survive. But Arama underscores the contradiction as an intended falsification on the spies' part of the situation in the Land. They do not give a coherently sound report because, in truth, their fundamental purpose is to reject the Land of Israel as a destined settlement point for the Children of Israel.

Arama will articulate the future heartbreak which collective generations of Israelites will feel when the "treason" of the spies is fully grasped. "It is this rejection of Eretz Yisrael which is responsible for our tribulations and exile, for our being a reproach to our neighbors and a scorn and derision unto them that are round about us. We shall never recover our spiritual and physical equilibrium until we return to the Land."

Did it have to be that way? Was it a certainty that the majority of the spies would reject the Zionist enterprise? From the beginning of the mission Caleb is concerned about the spies' intentions. The Talmud records Caleb's detour to Hebron in order to lay himself down on the graves of his ancestors. He says to them: "Ancestors, plead for mercy for me that I may be spared from the evil counsel of the spies." Joshua has already had the prescient support of Moses indicated in the latter's change of the former's name from Hoshea to Yehoshua. The change of name is essentially a prayer: "May the Lord — Yah — save you — Hoshea — from the evil counsel of the spies." Caleb's prayer in Hebron is answered positively in that he — like Joshua — is given a "contrary spirit" regarding the mission and its tragic aftermath.

What specifically is Caleb seeking in returning to the graves of Abraham, Isaac, and Jacob — if not the covenantal spirit that inspired the Patriarchs well before the Children of Israel's descent into Egyptian servitude. He is seeking the covenantal roots of his people so that he may be strengthened as he looks ahead. Joshua's name-change testifies to his newly acquired *transcendent* spirit. Caleb wants a spirit emanating from previous *human commitments* to that transcendent spirit. Caleb's generation, and Joshua's, need to be reminded of their human antecedents, real people who stood alone when necessary in order to prepare the covenanted legacy which contemporary Israel now has the opportunity to adopt and to embody.

But to Caleb's chagrin, this generation will become known as the *dor ha-midbar* (the Wilderness generation). It will be the Wilderness that will have "hosted" and then buried slaves who came out of Egypt but who preferred going back to Egypt rather than going on to Israel! They could have been known as *dor ha-aliyah* (the generation that went up). They couldn't have been known as *dor ha-yeridah* (the generation of the descent). For they had never had the merit of "going up," of attempting to settle in the Promised Land. They would be associated with Cain the eternal wanderer in a "wilderness" of chaotic despair. Yet what in essence was the source of their sin?

Was the source of the sin of the spies fear of the future campaign, the necessary wars, the later occupation with its sundry internal problems? The sin would be summarized in the words "let us get a leader and head back to Egypt." In effect they were saying, "Let us abandon the goal!" The source of the sin was an ironic faintheartedness on the part of the spies. For with their eyes open they overlooked certain data which, from a calmly objective point of view, should have made them consider seriously the Promised Land as more than a reasonable goal:

(1) Under no circumstances could they go back to Egypt, their erstwhile oppressor, which, following the plagues and the debacle at the Sea of Reeds, would certainly now be an irreconcilable enemy.

(2) The degeneracy of the Canaanites' internal mores suggested fundamental weaknesses in their military prowess; the resistance of these Canaanites, therefore, would be less than formidable.

(3) God had helped Israel previously against Egypt; why wouldn't He want to see His redemptive agenda fulfilled by helping Israel again! But against these supportive arguments that should have strengthened the resolve of the spies, they permitted the slogan "let us head back to Egypt" to be determinative. Against such a retrogressive "goal," all that destiny could offer such a generation was indeed "wilderness."

Put another way: the failure of the Wilderness generation was not that they *couldn't*; it was that they *wouldn't*. It was not a question of objective facts. Moses, Joshua, and Caleb weren't blind. God certainly wasn't blind. They knew as well as the spies the objective data regarding the challenges inherent in conquering the Land. But they couldn't guess, they couldn't anticipate the people's lack of will. This lack of will was observable in the way first the spies and then the misguided people interpreted the data. What was truly lamentable — and in God's eyes despicable — was that the spies and the people wanted to hide their lack of will by arguing that the facts made things impossible.

The Ramban underscores the power of a neutralizing "but" — *efes* in Hebrew — in explaining the perversity of the spies' report. At first they appeared to be fulfilling their mandate in answering the questions that they had been assigned to answer. They were told to see whether the Land was fat or lean, to which they responded that it was not only fat but it was flowing with milk and honey. As to the question was there wood or not, they brought back fruit of trees. In other words, in all this they answered truthfully. The Ramban then argues that with reference to the other questions concerning whether the people were strong and whether the cities were fortified they had the obligation to tell the truth. And their telling the truth would not have been their undoing. It was that they insisted on emphasizing the word, the deafening word *efes* meaning "but," or "however," but also meaning "nothingness"!

The "but" or "however" is not just a functional conjunction, syntactically speaking, in an otherwise dry prosaic recitation. It has a resonance which Ramban describes as evil. It is evil because it leads to nullification of will. The Hebrew word *efes* meaning "nothingness" was an articulation of the spies' nullifying intention. What could have been and should have been an encouraging positive report in which the spies summarized their mission with the glowing "it is a land flowing with milk and honey and here is its fruit," instead turns into a nullification: *"Efes!"* And this summary *efes* expands into a dejected "but the people who dwell there are strong and their cities are exceedingly fortified — and in truth there are giants there..."

Caleb recognizes what is transpiring in the spies' nullifying report. He knows that the will of the people which has been shown all along to be capricious is being worn down to the level of *efes*. His exhortation is simple, eloquent, and desperate: *"Aloh na'aleh ve-yarashnu otah, ki yakhol nukhal lah"* ("Let us go up and possess the Land, for we can do it")! We have the capacity to fulfill this task for which we have been chosen... Are we *efes*? Are we nothing? Is the plan which took us from Egypt to Sinai and now onward to the Land nothing? Is God nothing?

Caleb, Joshua, and Moses all know how devastating this report is to morale-building, particularly in the light of what has already been achieved.

To have come out of slavery has itself been the fulfillment of an "impossible" dream for a slave people. The challenge which leadership realizes it must face is that the demands of the enterprise of emancipation never ends. More and more is to be required of this people and the worst "word" to invade their consciousness is the word *efes*. The successful beginning of Israel's emancipation does not mean that the aroused people can achieve anything it wishes. Wishing or willing cannot make all things come true. But the wishing and the willing have to reflect an utterly centralized passion that, modulated by sober analysis of what is possible, propels one forward to "go up!"

Other Sins

The plaintive cry of Caleb to his people "to go up because we can…" is lost in the people's paroxysms of fear born of faithlessness. And so the people decree on themselves the fate of homelessness!

This sin of the "spies" dominates the portion. But there are two additional sins mentioned in the portion which will add to the characterization of this generation as the *dor ha-midbar* (the Wilderness generation). The sins which are described explicitly as such are respectively the gathering of wood on the Shabbat and the self-initiated battle of the Israelites against the Canaanites and Amalekites at Hormah leading to an ignominious Israelite defeat.

More than a millenium later there will be recorded in the Talmud, in the tractate *Shabbat*, a debate concerning Zelafhad relevant to these two sins. Who is Zelafhad? He is the father of the five daughters who will later appeal to Moses to be given the right to inherit the property of their father Zelafhad who has died. The daughters report incidentally, though significantly, according to the Rabbis, that "our father died in the Wilderness, not as one who belonged to Korah's faction which banded together against the Lord, but as one who died *for his own sin…*" The Rabbis explore what Zelafhad's sin was. Rabbi Akiva concludes that he must have been the *mekoshesh etzim* (the wood-gatherer) on the Shabbat. Rabbi Yehudah ben Betera concludes that he was among those who were the *ma'apilim* (those who initiated, who went up presumptuously) to do battle with the enemies of Israel, only to meet military and moral defeat.

This debate will be conducted by two rabbis who will be living in Israel in the days of the Second Temple and beyond. They and their people will be struggling to survive under the yoke of Imperial Rome and will be reflecting a particularly dark dimension of this later period in Jewish history with retrospective significance for the Wilderness generation. Rabbi Akiva imagines Zelafhad to be the wood-gatherer on Shabbat, the violator of one of the cardinal religious principles of the covenant. Akiva wishes to underscore the indispensability of the Torah and its *mitzvot* (commandments) in defining a Jewish commonwealth. Under Rome, he concludes, such observance, religiously and culturally speaking, is impossible. And so Rabbi Akiva will become one of the staunchest supporters of Bar-Kokhba and the general revolt against Imperial Rome which after three years of limited success will be suppressed and finally crushed.

Retrospectively applied to the Wilderness situation, the spies' rejection of the Promised Land is seen not only as a rejection of God's more recent providential act of redemption, i.e., taking His chosen people out of enslavement, but also the frustration as well of God's dream of having His entire creation appreciated by humanity by means of the fullest and sincerest respect for the Shabbat day on which God Himself rested from His labors.

Rabbi Yehudah ben Betera agrees with Rabbi Akiva as to the indispensability of Torah and the observance of its *mitzvot* defining the Jewish commonwealth. But his choice is to leave Israel during the Hadrianic persecutions. Unlike Akiva, he will not support an attempt to overthrow Rome. He assumes that his people cannot succeed in such an effort. He will settle, therefore, in Babylonia. The *Midrash Sifre* records his departure from Israel as follows: "He and others left the Land of Israel and reached Paltam where they stopped in order to remember what they were leaving. They lifted their eyes as their tears flowed. They tore their clothing as they read the Torah text 'ye shall possess the Land and dwell on it and keep all My statutes.' They then proclaimed that settling in the Land of Israel is equal to all the *mitzvot* of the Torah." But they left the Land of Israel nevertheless.

Retrospectively applied, the Wilderness generation would be seen as having rejected an opportunity to lay claim to a Land that God had promised and was now ready to be taken with God's enthusiastic approval. For the settlement of this Land was meant to reflect the Godly dimension of the enterprise. But the report of the spies had nullified God's intentions. Israel's later attempt to "go up presumptuously" *on their own* — without God's approval — was as ill-fated as it would be to challenge Imperial Rome.

The debate between Rabbi Akiva and Rabbi Yehudah ben Betera would have a value-message for the future as well, particularly in the light of the modern Zionist revolt against what was perceived as a petrified religious tradition. Akiva felt that the Torah and its practical application could be developed in Eretz Yisrael, e.g., the keeping of Shabbat, etc., but not as long as the Jewish people could not be sovereign in their own Land. He believed that Rome — even Rome — could be defeated. He was ready to risk his life for Torah. Indeed, he gave his life for Torah. Yehudah ben Betera felt that Eretz Yisrael could be a place for Torah learning and Torahitic realization in the market place; but that Rome could not be defeated. In seeing Rome ensconced in Israel, therefore, he left to build Torah in Babylonia. Both Akiva and Yehudah saw Judaism as indispensable to Zionism and to any serious concept of Jewish nationalism. Akiva and his people went down fighting for Judaism in Israel. Ben Betera saw a flowering of Judaism as impossible to achieve in Israel in his contemporary period and so he left for exile — but he and those accompanying him wept and would continue weeping for almost two millenia.

The Dead of the Wilderness

In the modern era, however, everything would be turned upside down in that Yehudah ben Betera's policy of waiting and weeping in exile would prove to be disastrous in the face of Russian pogroms auguring the Shoah. For in a new world of competing nationalisms there would be no place for vulnerable, if not utterly powerless, national minorities. But the *galut* community, strongly influenced by a long-term religious policy of political quietism, would be afraid of Akiva's activist policy. They felt justified because Akiva's policy, after all, had led to disaster. It likely would again. The result for the Jewish Diaspora would be political paralysis. But out of a contemporary despair, born of an endless prognosis of defenselessness and persecution, it would require a modern Zionist movement of rebels — *ma'apilim* — to galvanize the Jewish nation into renewing a movement towards the Promised Land.

It would require, in other words, a modern defiance of organized Jewish religious authority to break through to a new *ha'apalah* (going up) to the Land of Israel. Eventually a form of religious Zionism would arouse itself and join the secular rebels in their pioneering renewal of Jewish settlement in the Land. In a religio-historical stroke of irony, religious Zionism would legitimize a pre-messianic *ha'apalah* — that *ha'apalah* which had been so vociferously condemned by God and Moses in the Wilderness for its fickleness, its precipitousness, its rashness.

Rashi had seen in the root of *ha'apalah* — impudence; Radak had added the traits of arrogance and malice. For in a quotation from the prophet Habakkuk, the contrast was drawn between a faulty quality of spirit in a collective national personality that could find no personal or collective serenity — as opposed to the righteous person or persons who would live by his or their faith. This contrasting principle *"ve-tzaddik be-emunato yihye"* (the righteous shall live by his faith) would become for many an overriding religio-national principle with two emphases: (1) the righteous were those who were determined to live by their faith-commitment; and (2) the righteous would be those who would discover and rediscover the ways and means to live and compete on earth by their faith. But helplessness within the Czar's hopelessly degenerate empire couldn't cultivate, let alone nourish, Habakkuk's model of the righteous. The ideational implosion had to come.

But then, if a later generation of *ma'apilim* would be perceived by its generation as fulfilling a sublime mandate of resurrecting the House of Israel by bringing it back to its homeland, how reprehensible could the original *ma'apilim* have been? It would be Chaim Nachman Bialik who would have a keen enough sympathy for the Wilderness generation, the Dead of the Wilderness, in order to connect their memory with a contemporary yearning and determination to achieve redemption. Maurice Samuel's translation of Bialik's epic poem *"Metei Midbar"* presents the original stubborn stiff-necked generation who were condemned to death in the desert lying petrified in a secret nook somewhere in the Sinai Peninsula:

> "Strong are their faces and burnished and darkened to bronze are their eyelids,
> Targets to arrows of sunlight and rocks to the fury of tempests.
> Hard are their foreheads and grim and changeless upturned to the heavens.
> Cast as lava upthrown from volcanoes and hardened their breasts are.
> Lifted like anvils of iron that wait for the blow of the hammer,
> Yet though the hammer of time beats long and unceasing upon them
> Like to the stone that enfolds it the strength of their hearts sleep forever."

The poet brings on three representatives of God's creaturely kingdom to view the dead: The eagle, about to sweep down upon his prey, halts in midair, subdued by the peace and strength expressed in their faces. The great desert serpent, writhing its coils in the hot sun, slowly glides towards the army of his ancient enemy — Man — and is ready to strike with his venomous fangs, but terrified he recoils and passes on hissing. In the moonlit night the prowling lion then comes with risen mane and tail preparing to spring, but he too pauses and retraces his steps.

Why is Bialik interested in the "*Metei Midbar*"? They — the punished, the rejected, the doomed by God? For Bialik, the Dead of the Wilderness had a certain strength and pride; they *had* escaped from Egypt, they *had* defeated Amalek, and now, after being condemned by God, and against the appeals of Moses, they *do* go up and fight the Amalekites and Canaanites of the hill country; they are defeated, but they *will* be worthy of resurrection. And Bialik the poet *does* resurrect the dead army. The time chosen is the moment when a storm breaks out in the wide expanse of the sand. Then the dead awaken and roar along with the storm their battle cry, their willfulness, their passion for freedom, their protest against the decree of God: "We are the mighty, the last generation of slaves and first generation of free men! Only our hand is to be our hand of strength, torn from the pride of our shoulders is the yoke of bondage. And who is Lord of us? Even now, though the God of vengeance has shut the desert upon us, a song of strength and revolt has reached us, and we rise. To arms! To arms! Form ranks! Forward!"

Bialik will span the centuries in joining the tragic "Dead of the Wilderness" and their abysmal failure at *ha'apalah* with the rebellious success of a much later generation that *will* go up for the purpose of restoring Israel to its place of possible redemption. To the extent that the later generation of *gibborim* (heroes) initiate and realize their *ha'apalah*, they bring vicarious redemption to the earlier "heroes" who failed.

The Wilderness and *Kol Nidre*

The Yom Kippur liturgy will permanently echo the voice of Moses pleading for mercy for those who are to become the *metei midbar*. It will draw every Jew into the vortex of regret over aspirations unfulfilled, vows unkept with an accompanying legal formula — *Kol Nidrei* — to absolve the sinner individually and the sinning people as a whole. The legal formula will anticipate the year in which should we fall short in our commitments we know we can be absolved and we can thus be permitted to begin again on the road to fulfilling covenantal destiny. What right will the later worshiper have to expect that such a process has moral or theological coherence? The verses immediately following the *Kol Nidrei* will quote Moses' plea on behalf of the *metei midbar*: "May all the congregation of the people of Israel be forgiven, as well as the stranger who dwells among them, for all the people Israel only acted in error.... In Your boundless lovingkindness, please pardon the sin of this people. Forgive us as You have forgiven our people from Egypt through all times." And did not the Lord comply at that time saying to Moses: "I have pardoned them, as you have asked."

This plea and reminder of God's forgiveness is then able to open the portals of joy for all Israel who are able to recite in thanksgiving the blessing of *she-heheyanu*. Israel thanks God that we have survived another day. But the obverse side of the memory of the *metei midbar* and their forgiveness is the repeated and repeated self-relegation of Israel to the "wilderness of exile." Jewish history will not be able to conceal a certain neurotic appeal which "Egypt" and all its *galut* successors will hold for Israel and the Jewish people. It will seem as though the Children of Israel will have to fight perennially against the temptation to prefer wandering to settling, to being dependent rather than sovereign. And to this neurosis all the annual *Kol Nidre*'s will have a hollow ring — a ring of inauthenticity because it will be hiding an apparent collective hesitation, a reluctance, a fear — the same fear which paralyzed the spies — a fear of redemption.

Korah 

Is there a more poignant appeal on behalf of Judaism, holiness, and democracy than the appeal of Korah and his band? In Numbers 16:3 they argue: "You have gone too far, Moses; for all the community are holy, all of them, and the Lord is in their midst. Why then do you raise yourselves above the Lord's congregation?"

What is wrong with Korah's complaint — enough to arouse Moses and God to condemn him and his band to destruction? Rabbi Obadiah Bertinoro gives us part of an answer in his comment that Korah's populist appeal is bankrupt in purpose. How do we know that? From careful reading we realize that Korah's appeal is demagogic — without serious covenantal intentions. Korah's initial appeal — ostensibly on behalf of democratic sharing — contrasts with that of Moses who is a monarch. We should not forget, however, that Moses is a *constitutional* monarch. More importantly, Moses has a plan, a program, a goal, a sense of noble destiny for his people who are mandated to build a model community in the Promised Land. Korah and his band, on the other hand, have not only rejected the plan, they have neither an alternative plan nor an alternative vision of Israel's destiny. They militate for nothing less than a return to the straits of servitude that is Egypt. In effect they are pushing for a return to the pit of Sheol or Hell. At least for themselves, they will get their wish!

The Rebellion of the Sophist

In Jewish tradition Korah has represented rebellion out of conceit. The Torah, it should be remembered, is not against rebellion in principle. After all, the Exodus from Egypt, notwithstanding its transcendent stimulus and inspiration, is basically a rebellion. But it is not a rebellion out of conceit. It is a rebellion against the genocidal imperial throne of Pharaoh and *his* idolatrous conceit. The clearly stated purpose of the rebellion is to achieve emancipation for an otherwise doomed Children of Israel.

In other words, what the Torah opposes in Korah's rebellion is the human conceit reflected in his demagogic appeal for "equality." Korah appears to be demanding recognition for all of the people, certainly for all of the Levites. But he is really jealous of the power that he sees as centralized in the hands of Moses. He refuses to recognize that Moses' right to govern has been granted to him by God and by his record as leader of the people in their fight for freedom. The demagoguery of Korah and his "gang" is aimed at winning power for themselves. They are prepared to have all of Israel swallowed up by the civil war that would be certain to follow any success that they might have. Instead, Korah and his "gang" will be swallowed up in the bowels of their own vanity.

In Israel Eldad's *Hegyonot Mikra* he makes the case that it is inevitable for some of the Israelites to have rebelled against Moses at this point in the story. For Moses — and Israel — have been left with three choices following God's decree upon the *dor ha-midbar*: (1) to go back to Egypt, which many of the Israelites may want but is clearly impossible; (2) to move on to Canaan, which as punishment for the hopeless advice of the ten spies God has now declared forbidden to this generation; or (3) to obey the decree and accept the fate which God and Moses have now left for this generation of Israelites — that they are doomed to die in the Wilderness! Moreover, the example of the severity with which the *mekoshesh eitzim* (the wood-gatherer) on the Shabbat has been punished, i.e., *execution*, has terrified the Israelites in that they now face the prospect of an uncompromisingly severe regime ruling over them indefinitely in the Wilderness. What else is left for them to do but to rebel!

Nevertheless, a contrary argument has to be made. Even though this generation has been doomed to die in the Wilderness, they have been told that their children will have the privilege to enter the Promised Land. In other words, the generation of the Wilderness can still perform a function that can mitigate their own personal tragedy born out of a sense of rejection. They can help prepare their children and grandchildren for the fulfillment of the larger destiny proclaimed for Israel; and thereby they can earn a share in that destiny. This compensatory task Korah and his band refuse to see, and so they prefer condemning themselves and all who will follow them literally to hell!

The sin is not only the rebellion itself. The sin is compounded by the tactics of the rebels — tactics which are meant to undermine God's Torah as taught by Moses and the later Rabbis. The Midrash elaborates. Korah is seen to ask a question regarding the necessity for a *mezuzah*, i.e., a Torah-excerpt on the doorpost of an Israelite home. Korah argues against the requirement of such a *mezuzah* for a home that already may have books in abundance. Among the books, it may be presumed, are "Torah books." "Now how can it be," argues Korah, "that a home which already has a Torah of three hundred seventy-eight portions not obviate the need for a *mezuzah* whose chief claim to honor is that it has two portions?"

The Midrash gives a further example: Korah asks another "sincere" halakhic question regarding a *tallit* or prayer shawl. If an entire prayer shawl were blue, why would it require *tzitzit* (fringes) which must include a blue thread? Wouldn't the entire "blueness" of the *tallit* obviate the necessity for *tzitzit* that are there primarily for the purpose of the blue thread?

Moses and the later Rabbis see in Korah a sophistry that the latter must use to support and justify his rebellious thrust for power. It is a sophistry that can easily seduce and then arouse the beleaguered people. It underscores, however, the difference between illegitimate rebellion against accepted social, political, and religious institutions and justifiable revolt against tyranny such as Pharaoh's Egypt.

Sophistry has the capacity to reduce any respectable institution to an absurdity, particularly a religious institution which has ceremonial ritual. This is so even though there are many ceremonial minutiae associated with the full range of other institutions necessary to the healthy functioning of society: from medicine to law, from education to commerce. Yet every ceremony, every procedure, or every ritual has an explanation which under sincere scrutiny usually provides a reasonable and constructive justification. Korah who is a Levite and has been schooled in the rituals and ceremonies associated with the tabernacle surely knows that the commandments of *mezuzah* and *tzizit* are intended to be independently valid. And so his clever questioning is clearly sophistry.

Sophistry feeds on the attractiveness of the so-called sincere individual fighting the callous impersonal establishment. Establishments — particularly religious ones — do tend to be overbearing. By their collective nature, they always risk falling prey to overweaning pride in their current exercise of power based upon previous achievement and legitimation. They often fail to appreciate individual genius; certainly not when such individual geniuses attack their established bases of power. The establishment will lean towards neutralizing or snuffing out entirely these extreme individualists. Occasionally, they may make the effort to seek an accommodation with the individualists. At the same time, however, the establishment — in this case, Moses and Aaron — have an obligation to save this newly covenanted society from being misled by cynical self-serving misfits.

Moses is building a community, a nation, with a purportedly strong religious loyalty to a covenant. And the covenant requires from Israel full attention to meticulous detail. It may be that individual feelings are not always sufficiently noted and responded to as the communal effort proceeds. Legislating for recommended behavioral patterns which are to be universalized as much as possible may overlook the area of individual religious "feelings." The law does not seek to dictate feelings; but out of necessity it does seek to regulate people's expression of feelings when these are perceived to endanger communal well-being. The sophist that is Korah chooses to criticize the demanded discipline, self-control, directed emotion, even though they are intended to suggest the aesthetic beauty of "holiness." For Korah knows that there will be certain individuals who will be receptive to his protest-arguments. Yet, lack of discipline, lack of self-control, undirected passion can incinerate a society, particularly a newly developing one. Korah is either oblivious to the danger or, sophist that he is, is callously exploiting it for his own nefarious purposes.

Furthermore, the sophist exploits his own knowledge to fund his cleverness. When the biblical epigram insists that the "beginning of wisdom is the fear of the Lord," it is cautioning precisely against those disciples of the "Serpent" who in their pristine rebelliousness against the primary source of their being set themselves up as surrogates for God Himself. Power for power's sake is the sophist's aim. And the achievement of power justifies, in his mind, all his machinations. Essentially and ultimately, Korah isn't just undermining Moses. Korah is aiming much higher. His model is Nimrod and the builders of the primordial Tower. He, therefore, must be brought down even lower than ordinary villains. He must be sentenced literally to the depths of Sheol (Hell)!

The League of Conspirators

Is Korah the only rebel — or more accurately — is he the only leader among the rebels? Korah is one of a group of interested parties, each one with his own dark motives. Korah as a Levite is ostensibly resentful at not having been given equal status with his cousins, the Levites Moses and Aaron. He is joined, however, by Dathan and Abiram of the tribe of Reuben, who have been chafing at the rejection by God of their firstborn tribe in favor of the Levites following the sin of the "Golden Calf." In addition, they complain to Moses "Isn't it enough that you brought us up out of a land of milk and honey in order to slay us in the wilderness!" And they punctuate their complaint with the words *"ki tistareir alenu gam histareir"* ("and you lord it over us as well") which echo an earlier crisis in Moses' career. When Moses had tried to intervene in the quarrel between two Hebrew slaves back in Egypt, it was the same Dathan and Abiram — according to midrashic tradition — who rejected him with the same taunt "who made you *sar* (lord) over us?"

Korah and Dathan and Abiram are joined by another group — the tragically naïve two hundred fifty princes. As recorded in the Torah, these are specially endowed men of reknown. The Natziv of Volozhin describes them as follows: "These censer bearers are truly the great ones of Israel, even with regard to their fear of the Lord. Their exclusion from priestly functions is burning in them like fire, as it denies them loving adherence to God. Theirs is not a lust for power or greed for vainglory, but a sublime passion for saintliness that can only be attained through this worshipful service. They certainly acknowledge the truth and validity of the Divine word as conveyed through Moses; without reservation they confirm it in their mind. But in their heart they can not resign themselves to the will of God."

These "great ones" are the most to be pitied among the rebels because their motives are high-minded. As opposed to Korah's lust for personal aggrandizement and Dathan and Abiram's unabashed intention to undermine if not destroy with malice the mission of Israel, these "great ones" are well-meaning. But they lack the double trait of humility and resignation. They are also representative of all the "good innocent people" through the ages who are swept along in their naïve well-meaningness by revolutionary forces cynically led by evil men.

Are these leaders all equally evil? Is Korah not of a more aristocratic bent than the obsessively devious figures of Dathan and Abiram? Korah may be seen as a Brutus-like figure in not being able to resist his own passion for greatness. The tradition will recognize that Korah will leave respectable descendants who will serve as Psalmists, no less, despite their ancestor's own ignominious end. God Himself is ready to give all the rebels a chance to withdraw from their evil machinations on the eve of the dramatic test. The Shadal commentary points to an alternative interpretation of the verse: "Come morning, the Lord will make known who is His and who is holy, and will grant him access to Himself. He will grant access to the one He has chosen." The Shadal translates the verse as "not that the Lord will *make known* tomorrow, but that the Lord will *know* tomorrow...he will grant access to the *one who will choose* Him." In other words, God and Moses are hereby giving the rebels a chance until tomorrow to "come around" to the truth, to the right path, as in their evil plans they hover over the pit.

But the rebels refuse the offer! Their controversy with Moses and with God becomes in Jewish tradition the quintessential controversy that is "not for the sake of Heaven" and therefore pre-determined to fail. As the tractate *Avot* 5:20 will put it: "Any controversy which is in the name of Heaven is destined to result in something enduring; any controversy which is not in the name of Heaven will never result in anything enduring. Which controversy was in the name of Heaven? The one between Hillel and Shammai. And which was not in the name of Heaven? The one instigated by Korah and his band."

Controversy for the Sake of Heaven

As noted earlier, Rabbi Obadiah Bertinoro describes a controversy which is in the name of Heaven as one in which the goal of the adversaries is to achieve the truth or out of the ensuing debate to clarify the truth. A controversy which is not in the name of Heaven, on the other hand, has the adversaries merely seeking lordship for its own sake and the "glory" attached thereto.

The talmudic statement in juxtaposing Korah and his band with Hillel and Shammai reveals a powerful truth about the biblical revelatory reality as opposed to the rabbinic dependence on human wisdom. One may ask a technical pedagogic question: If one were a teacher wanting to offer a contrasting example to something undesirable such as Korah's controversy, why choose an example from a different historic period? Can one really make a fair comparison between the Tannaitic period of Hillel and Shammai and the period of the *dor ha-midbar* (Wilderness generation)? The question may be put more sharply: Let us assume that an excellent example in the Torah of a controversy *not* for the sake of Heaven is the controversy initiated by Korah and his band. In truth, is there anywhere in the Torah a controversy which *is* for the sake of Heaven? Between whom? Between Abraham and God over the fate of Sodom? Between Moses and Aaron over the "Golden Calf" episode?

Neither the Sodom episode nor the "Golden Calf" episode is appropriate. For neither episode is a controversy. In Abraham's appeal to God he questions the facts — that is, whether indeed everyone in Sodom is wicked. Once Abraham is convinced that there are not even ten righteous individuals in the doomed city, we may assume that he accepts God's decree. In the case of the "Golden Calf" episode, Aaron gives in to the demands of the people while Moses is on the mountain. Once Moses returns, Aaron in no way protests when his brother condemns the act. The talmudic tractate *Sanhedrin* may use Aaron as an archetypal figure recommending the course of arbitration or compromise as opposed to Moses whose word "cuts through a mountain." But even there the brothers are not perceived as arguing with one another. Compromise, Aaron claims, regarding the pressure applied to him at the foot of Sinai, was a necessity in order to prevent mayhem and murder. In retrospect, Aaron is considered to have erred, and Moses follows through ordering a punitive execution of three thousand Israelites.

One cannot consider the several occasions when Moses pleads with God not to abandon or to destroy Israel as *mahlokot* (controversies). Moses does not deny Israel's sins nor that they deserve punishment. He begs for mercy and uses a number of different arguments to justify his pleas. If there is one controversy in the entire Bible which appears — at least initially — as one for the sake of Heaven it is that recorded in the Book of Jeremiah between the prophets Jeremiah and Hananiah ben Azur. The latter is supporting and encouraging the insurrection of Israel against the occupation of Babylonia. He predicts success for the Children of Israel. Jeremiah risks his life as he has done all along in preaching the "unpatriotic" message of accepting the occupation, of enduring the subjugation. But Jeremiah doesn't just debate Hananiah. Jeremiah, whose prophecy will turn out to be true, condemns Hananiah, whose prophecy will turn out to be false. As such, the latter will not only be perceived as a false prophet. He will also die, presumably as a punishment!

We conclude that in the Bible — in the *Torah she-bi-Khetav* (the Written Torah) — there are no *mahlokot le-shem Shamayim* (controversies for the sake of Heaven). This does not mean that there are no ethical conflicts within Israel. But from God's and His prophet's perspective, the conflict, if unresolved, has one side representing God's will while the other side becomes a rebellion against God's will, a heresy! For in God's immediate Presence or in the presence of God's prophet, the truth and ensuing path are clear. The Torah — since Sinai — may not be in Heaven, and throughout the biblical period it has been placed in human hands to interpret; and in human hands there will be differences in interpretation. But the attitude of the Bible is that there is a fundamental truth and applied path which must not be eschewed or it is rebellion!

Once Jewish history has moved into the era of Hillel and Shammai, however — the period of the *Torah she-be'al Peh* (the Oral Torah) — God is considered to be in eclipse. He is "there" or "here," but He is silent and He is no longer perceived as having prophets to officially represent His word. The Torah is certainly not in Heaven. But now it means that most truths emanating from the Torah are harder to realize in a new world with new challenges. At this point, without God's or His prophets' guidance, there will be human controversy even in the name of Heaven. There *must* be controversy. And whoever wins a particular point has not delegitimized his adversary's position. For, if the controversy has truly been for the sake of Heaven, there is a unified will regarding larger purpose and destiny guiding all parties involved. For this reason, Hillel and Shammai's controversies are appropriately characterized as *"elu ve'elu divrei Elohim hayyim"* ("these and these are the words of the Living God").

And if in the corpus of the Oral Torah Hillel's position prevails most of the time, there is a tradition which argues that in *olam ha-ba* (the future world) the legislated *halakhah* will be according to Shammai. In any case, out of a mutual recognition that there must and will be controversy, the schools of Hillel and Shammai will respect each other. Such respect is reflected in the teaching in *Tosefta Yevamot*: "Even though the schools of Shammai and Hillel disagreed on issues concerning rival wives, sisters and doubtful marriages, they did not prevent intermarriages between disciples of their schools. For they believed and behaved according to principles of truth and peace" — quoting Zechariah that we should love truth and peace. Similarly, even though one school would forbid and the other permit in the areas associated with purity and impurity, they did not desist from each other's resulting determinations, fulfilling the verse in Proverbs: "All the ways of a man seem right to him, but the Lord probes the mind."

The contrast between the terms of reference for Hillel and Shammai's generation and that of Korah becomes more and more vivid. If Hillel and Shammai's arguments are genuinely seeking to discover and implement Torah truth, Korah's motives are entirely different. He has no ideas or ideals to implement. His motives are purely personal and selfish, and ultimately false in their very essence and aim — the aim being to uproot the covenant, to deny the prophetic leadership of Moses and Divine Providence.

The Double-Hell of Korah

As indicated earlier, that Korah's descendants survive and will serve the House of Israel in later generations in important capacities leaves us with certain moderate sentiments towards this misguided heretic. Samuel is considered in the Book of Chronicles to be a direct descendant of Korah. And other descendants become psalmists and gate-keepers. But the apocalyptic denouement to Korah's scheme dominates our vision — his being swallowed up in Sheol (Hell). The verse (16:33) which summarizes this denouement has three parts: (1) they went down alive into Sheol with all that belonged to them; (2) the earth closed over them; and (3) they vanished from the midst of the congregation.

The image of descending into Sheol conjures up a liturgical image in Psalm 30 which thanks God "for bringing me up from Sheol." Rabbi Kook derives from the root of Sheol the verb *sha'al* (to ask, to seek, to yearn). He then suggests that when one is left with no more than vague asking, seeking, yearning, when one cannot specify what it is one wants in life, one is in a kind of hell. Korah and his band lack precisely a positive direction in their pursuit of grandeur. There is no way that they can overturn God's plan and His messenger's leadership. They have left Egypt; there is no going back; yet they refuse to recognize or accept the way of the world as it is to be newly constructed for them and by them, provided that they are ready to submit to the conditions of the covenant.

But the world of covenant is too much for them. They are trapped in their own tomb-like "avarice of power." It is indeed as if the earth is closing over them, covering them over hermetically. And so they vanish from the House of Israel. It is a liquidation promised to the wicked in Psalm One which speaks of God knowing intimately the way of the righteous but the way of the wicked *toved* (will be lost) — utterly, finally!

According to Rabbi Akiva in the tractate *Sanhedrin*, the verse which speaks of the earth closing over them is seen to refer to their losing *olam ha-zeh* (this world). Their vanishing from the midst of the congregation he interprets as their forfeiting *olam ha-ba* (the future world). Rabbi Eliezer and Rabbi Yehudah ben Betera each moderate Rabbi Akiva's stark position. Rabbi Eliezer reminds Rabbi Akiva that God slays, but also gives life, that God may bring Korah and his like down to Hell, but He also has the power to raise up anew even the formerly wicked. Rabbi Yehudah ben Betera is even softer in his understanding as he puts in a defensive claim for the "loss" or the "vanishing" of the wicked. For him the "loss" or "vanishing" is meant to suggest an image of a sheep having gone astray — not permanently lost nor permanently forgetful of the covenant and its terms.

In other words, the oscillation within the tradition between outright condemnation of Korah and the more moderate attempt to blunt the severity of the decrees against him bespeaks an understanding of the critical struggle within the human predicament to find God and yet to rebel against Him, to discover one's fellow man and family-community, and yet to separate oneself from that community. Korah goes through a double-hell in that he is not only misled by permitting his vanity to lead him to reject God and Moses. He and his band are never reconciled to each other's motives, which vary as they plot and initiate the insurrection. With them there is a double-hell of unspecified yearning, or yearning to achieve something as elusive as honor and self-love. Honor and self-love cannot be goals: They are occasionally felt as bi-products of other efforts and other goals. But for a group to wander about apparently together but in truth separated by their subjective motives and aims can only be a hell exponentially compounded.

For Moses, the rebellion initiated by Korah is clear evidence of a further deterioration in the already precarious situation in which all of Israel finds itself. The unity intended by the forging of the covenant is seen to be as elusive as ever. It is tragic enough for an individual to be vegetative of spirit, to lack not only single-minded purpose, but any purpose at all beyond the satisfaction of personal conceit. The double-hell or compounded-hell presaged by the Korah insurrection threatens to overwhelm and swallow up the entire House of Israel if they persist in being an *erev-rav* or *asafsuf*, i.e., a mixed multitude of slaves, a rabble that continually turns away from the single possibility of lifting themselves out of Sheol — by fulfilling a new communal and national potential.

Hukkat 

It is in this portion that the Torah skips over thirty-eight years in the record of the experiences of Israel in the Wilderness. Speculation as to why this time period is omitted includes the possibility that the alienation between Moses and the rebellious *dor ha-midbar* had become so acute that there was a loss of communication on the serious "value" level, and therefore there was nothing meaningful to report. Moses and the Children of Israel had lost a common language.

A language embodies commonly held values, distinctions, standards, and aspirations. It also represents articulated as well as subconsciously felt goals and agendas. Once the rebellious split occurred — that split foreshadowed by the spies' betrayal and Korah's insurrection — Moses and the people may have continued to speak on trivial every-day matters. The outer structure of their Hebrew language was still alive, so to speak. But sublime purposes regarding their holy destiny had been besmirched. What good then was the soul-less structure of every-day language?

Moses had always had a problem with language — or at least with speech. Early in his prophetic career he had described himself as a *kevad peh* and *aral sefatayim* (heavy of speech and uncircumcised of lips). But obviously he had overcome these "defects." He had held discourse more than adequately with Pharaoh, with the likes of Korah, and with God Himself. His thirty-eight year "silence" does not mean, therefore, that he was suffering from a form of aphasia. The reason for the thirty-eight year gap was that Moses had little to say that was "meaningful" to the Children of Israel. With little to say, there was little to record. Now when Moses was ordered to "speak to the rock," he couldn't.

A Loss of Communication

Rashi explains Moses' sin at the rock by having God say as follows: "If you had spoken to the rock and brought forth water, I would have truly been sanctified in the eyes of the people. For they would have noted that if a rock which does not speak nor hear and does not need a living sustenance, nevertheless fulfills My command, how much more so should we!" Yet it must be remembered that earlier in the sojourn in the Wilderness — specifically at Rephidim — God had commanded Moses to *strike* the rock in order to bring forth water. What is the difference between then and now?

The difference is that now using the right words is crucial. After a hiatus of thirty-eight years of "meaningful" communication, Moses is now facing a new generation which is moving forward to conquer and to settle the Land. The previous *dor ha-midbar* — the generation of the "golden calf" and the treasonous spies — had gone after their *eyes* even though they had shared at Sinai a "*hearing*" experience that would forever after be remembered as God's Revelation. This "post-Wilderness" generation would have to learn to hear again, to truly hear. Shadal argues that speaking to the rock and bringing forth water is no greater miracle per se than beating the hitherto arid rock and bringing forth water. But in the eyes of the people, effecting results by *speaking* would be ever so much more astonishing. And the wonder among the people would sanctify God's Providential care ever so much more. It would make for a reinforcement of their awareness of their special destiny. The seeing and the hearing combined would recharge their sensibilities and awaken in them — in this new generation — the therapeutic need to talk and to be talked to in revelatory terms.

The previous generation had experienced the colossal events of the Exodus, of the victory at the Sea of Reeds, of the revelation at Sinai. For continuity to be assured, thirty-eight years of pedagogic silence could not be tolerated. There had to be a normative way of living up to these events in one's everyday life; of talking in relation to these events and to their consequential demands of the people as they prepared themselves for the exacting future. The *dor ha-midbar* may have forfeited its right to an ongoing revelatory experience of talking, teaching, and learning. But it was now a new time and a new opportunity for a new generation.

The twentieth-century literary critic F.R. Leavis defines language as "the heuristic conquest won out of representative experience, the upshot or precipitate of immemorial human living." Moses is charged with enabling a new generation of Israelites to discover who they are, where they have come from, and where they are going. To do this their sense of being alive must encompass more than the immediate pulsations of sensuous existence. They must have a collective memory which is seen to have propelled them to their present moment and towards their future — short term and long term. The language which they have not invented but which they have received "embodies values, distinctions, identifications, conclusions, promptings — cartographical hints and tested potentialities." The cartographical hints are the signposts inherited from the past. The tested potentialities are the felt capacities for achievement in the future based on the old signposts.

The continuity which is indispensable will have to recognize that the necessary growth of the new generation will have to accept change as a vital ingredient of growth. But the overriding signpost pointing to a covenant that has conditioned all that has come before is looked to as the illuminating lodestar for the future. Will Moses be capable of transmitting this language of continuity to this new generation? The incident at the rock serves as a disturbingly vivid symptom of Moses' emerging debility for certain of the tasks ahead.

Again, what is the sin of Moses — that sin whose severity is such that it will keep the great redeemer from entering the Promised Land? According to the Rambam, it is the anger he has showed in using the expression, "Listen, you rebels." A man of his stature should never have given vent to such negative feelings before the whole community of Israel. God Himself is not *that* angry with Israel at this point. The Ramban disagrees. God *is* angry with Israel for their disbelief. The proof may be found in the summary verse of Psalms 106:32: "They angered Him also at the waters of Meribah, and it went ill with Moses because of them." What is Moses' sin, therefore, according to the Ramban? It is in saying, "Shall *we* get water for you out of this rock (we, and not God)!" In other words, Moses' own legitimate anger with Israel may be justified. What is inexcusable, nevertheless, is Moses arrogating to himself — and to Aaron — the power to perform the miracle.

Ramban's interpretation receives endorsement in the verse from Deuteronomy 32:51: "For you both broke faith with Me among the Israelite people, at the waters of Meribath-Kadesh in the wilderness of Zin, by failing to uphold My sanctity among the Israelite people." According to the Ramban, Moses (and Aaron along with him in this case) are guilty of *me'ilah*, i.e., benefiting or seeking to benefit from that which is sanctified. Their guilt comes from their ascribing to themselves the power to bring forth the desired water instead of proclaiming through word and deed that it is God's doing. They thereby forfeit an opportunity to sanctify God's essence in public. As punishment they will forfeit their own opportunity to share the sanctified task of dwelling in the Land: "You may view the Land from a distance, but you shall not enter it — the Land that I am giving to the Israelite people."

Moses has been given a Sisyphian task in leading this people. He has had to emancipate them against the will of an all-powerful enemy, Pharaoh, emperor of Imperial Egypt. He has had to emancipate them against their *own* will. Granted, as slaves, by definition they had had sterile visions of the future. They might not have been expected to answer the call to "freedom" with enthusiasm. They hadn't known what "freedom" entails. But once they were out of Egypt and setting forth under their own ensigns and with the vision of their own sovereignty being cast before them daily by their leader, Moses expected vigorous support or at least an absence of rancor and second-guessing. Instead, he has been the target of constant complaint, resentment, and rebellion. Moses had already shown evidence of enervation. He had demanded help from God, but the help had not been enough to quell thirty-eight years of an increasingly jaded ministry.

The Lingering Disease of Idolatry

At the end of his life, Moses will be described as one whose "eyes were undimmed and vigor unabated." Even if such a description is not a mere reflection of eulogistic hyperbole, it is referring to his sociomoral insight and mental and spiritual strength, manifested as they are in the prophetic speeches which make up Deuteronomy. The eulogy cannot refer to the political leadership of his later years — as described in the Book of Ba-Midbar (the Book of the Wilderness). Moses himself has been dragged down into a vortex of anger, impatience, and — according to the Ramban — reprehensible manifestations of egotism. The rock episode serves as the catalyst for Moses' near breakdown of religious spirit.

And so Moses, who has not been speaking "significant words" to Israel for thirty-eight years while continuing to lead them, will have to surrender the function, the obligation, and "reward" of political leadership. But he will be "punished" in a very special way, in a blessedly ironic way. For he will be "condemned" to spend the final year of his life in talking, talking, talking ceaselessly to his people. He will prepare his disciple Joshua to take over the political-social-military leadership. For he, Moses, cannot exercise such power any longer. But he, Moses, will become forever after the pre-eminent teacher of his people — Moshe Rabbenu.

Evidence of Moses' political and military debility is his failure to negotiate passage for his people through the territory of Edom. Sooner or later, the Children of Israel will have to go out to do battle with their enemies as they show against Sihon the king of the Amorites and Og the king of Bashan. When Edom refuses Israel passage and Moses accepts the refusal docilely it does not bode well for Israel's future campaigns to conquer and settle the Land. Not that there aren't situations in which the military option is to be rejected — for ethical reasons or strategic reasons! But against Edom, Moses has miscalculated. His weakness and hesitancy return to haunt him with the attack of the Canaanite king of Arad.

As the text records, the Canaanite king of Arad has heard of the Israelites' "peaceful" acceptance of Edom's refusal. For him it is the signal to attack! Ibn Ezra plays with the difficult phrase *"derekh ha-Atarim"* in the descriptive report: "When the Canaanite king of Arad who dwelt in the Negev heard that Israel was coming by the way of the Atarim, he engaged Israel in battle and took some of them captive." For Ibn Ezra, the first letter of *Atarim* is superfluous. Thus we are to interpret the phrase *"derekh* ha-tarim*"* as the "way of the spies who *'turned aside'* from the right way." Why would Arad dare to attack Israel, if not because Israel appeared to be negotiating with Edom in the spirit of the spies. They were manifesting an absence of faith in themselves and their overall destiny. Such faithlessness would bring immediate disastrous consequences.

Israel's new generation is not the generation dragged down by the faithlessness of the spies. Moses should have known it in his negotiations with Edom. The Midrash offers a telling comment on the importance of leadership when it quotes an imagined dialogue in the talmudic era between Hadrian and Rabbi Joshua. Hadrian postulates that the lamb which can survive among the seventy wolves is a great lamb. But Rabbi Joshua corrects him by asserting that it is the saving shepherd which protects and succors the lamb in the face of the seventy wolves. The question for this new generation of Israelites is whether or not Moses can continue to be their most effective shepherd in the task confronting them against the world's nations.

Because the political — and military — leadership of Moses is in effect rejected in the Book of Numbers, there is a pervasive somberness throughout the major portion of the book. It cannot be avoided. The despondency isn't relieved by two mysterious passages found in this particular portion of *Hukkat* — the passage concerning the red heifer and the passage concerning the brazen serpent. That both passages are situated in close proximity to the episode of the rock and Moses' failure is indicative of an overriding concern — as always — with the vexing subject of idolatry.

Returning once again to the episode of the "rock," Professor Jacob Milgrom has summarized all the commentaries regarding the sin of Moses. There are those who focus on Moses' action in *striking* the rock as the basic malfeasance. There are those who question his *character* because he has here manifested a loss of temper; and the loss of temper has been a consequence of increasing callousness towards the people, impatience with their human shortcomings. And then there are those who call our attention to the specific words that he uses as evidence of a range of sins from doubting God to doubting Israel. Milgrom's own contribution suggests that for Moses to accompany his speaking to the rock with the physical act of striking the rock would give an impression to the people that he was articulating an idolatrous incantation. The sin of all sins!

All these criticisms of the great emancipator underscore an overriding concern which dominates the whole Torah — human leadership bringing on idolatry. The Bible highlights repeatedly the human tendency to raise heroes, leaders — but eventually to deify them and to worship them. Therefore, at the same time, the Bible records God's efforts through His messengers the Prophets and through events themselves to humanize these heroes, these leaders, in order to shatter idolatrous illusions. All the Children of Israel have been charged with representing covenantal obligations — not just their leader Moses or Joshua or in the future Samuel, Saul, and David. This anti-idolatrous agenda is thus able to shed light on the mysteries of the red heifer and the brazen serpent.

It is not enough to characterize both objects — the heifer and the serpent — as vestiges of a more primitive period in the lives of this ancient people. One must appreciate that the idea of looking to external phenomena to effect purgation from sin or sickness is a powerful source of hope for anxious and insecure human beings. The Mishnah *Rosh Hashanah* brings the point home: "Does the brazen serpent really kill? Does it really bring life? Hardly, but when Israel looks heavenward and subjugates its heart to their Father in Heaven, then they will be cured. If not, i.e., if they don't look beyond the 'artifact,' then they will pine away in despair." But the Mishnah does not deny that people will somehow be determined to look to the artifact.

In worshiping the serpent or in placing one's faith in the efficaciousness of the red heifer to bring expurgation from sin, the Israelite is not so much rejecting God. What he is doing is avoiding taking the responsibility upon himself to deal with the sociomoral or medical problem. In looking for all kinds of secondary solutions one will often seek out a ritual which in essence helps one avoid the problem and the search for a resolution of the problem. The thought — as Milgrom suggests — that Moses is himself relying on an idolatrous incantation or is appearing to do so in surrendering to the people's needs is excessive, certainly where the great idol breaker Moses is concerned. Nevertheless, if Moses no longer has the spiritual, ethical, and psychological strength that he showed while coming down the mountain of Sinai and destroying the "golden calf," then he along with the Wilderness generation must be retired.

The Passing of the Old Leadership

In this Torah portion there are three deaths mentioned emphasizing the reality that the "Generation of the Wilderness," including its leadership, is to be replaced. Miriam dies unceremoniously with no public mourning recorded. Aaron dies very ceremoniously, having transferred his clothing and office to his son Eleazar. Moses doesn't physically expire in this portion; yet with God's awesome decree that he will not live to enter the Promised Land, in an acute personal sense he does "die." The fulfillment of his own personal redemptive dream will be denied him. Moreover, when he will actually go to his eternal rest — outside the Promised Land — all of Israel whom he has helped to redeem, present and future, will not even know where he is buried.

As Eldad has pointed out, there is a contrast in the people's reactions towards the deaths respectively of Miriam and Aaron. Miriam's reputation suffers in the last stages of her life. She is brought down from her initial pinnacle of "care-giving" when she had viewed from afar what fate lay before the infant Moses and had advised Pharaoh's daughter regarding the nursing of the child. She falls from the peak period of her own communal leadership exercised choreographically at the celebration of the victory at the Sea of Reeds. Towards the end she is described as gossiping behind the back of her beleaguered brother. She is punished with a leprous infection. This same brother will have to plead on her behalf in order to save her.

Aaron, on the other hand, has begun his career as Moses' confrere, assistant, spokesman before Pharaoh. He will be known in later talmudic discussions as the lover and pursuer of peace, the eternal compromiser. That he was instrumental in "cooperating" with a sinful Israel through the "golden calf" episode will elicit the wrath of Moses and God. But surprisingly, Aaron escapes punishment. He will be chosen to be high priest, a position which itself supervises the institution of general and individual atonement. The sacrificial system itself will be another mode of peaceful compromise in that the sinner is able to expiate his sin and achieve a peaceful resolution of previous guilt-informed behavior. When Aaron joins Miriam in her gossip about Moses, there is no record of him being punished. Perhaps it is because as priest representing at least the dream of peace and harmony he is to be treated as unblemished in any way. Perhaps God reciprocates Aaron's silence at the shocking execution of his sons Nadav and Abihu by being silent at Aaron's transgression.

As pointed out earlier, Moses has also begun a downward spiral which reaches its nadir at the "rock." Eldad reminds us that the "rock" speaks as well of the capital city of Edom — Petra — which will be conquered later in Jewish history by Amaziah, but which Moses at this stage of his career has not been up to conquering. Eldad says: "The nation is now at its full strength — a youthful army as thirsty for action as for water. God is now with them as is Moses the man of God. But Moses chooses to mount a long imploring address before Edom instead of taking action." In allowing himself to be rejected by this eternal enemy of Israel, Moses' leadership will be rejected by God. In Deuteronomy Moses will review the incident by claiming that God "commanded" him to bypass Edom; but the fact that such a command is omitted here in the immediate reportage indicates that Moses has been only too ready for such an "excuse."

Notwithstanding the somberness that the deaths of two of the venerable leaders of the people, Miriam and Aaron, represent, and the gradually deteriorating capacity of Moses to lead them politically and militarily, there is a bright side. It is represented by the fact that there is a new generation, a young mass of people who are not slaves and who have never been slaves. They have known the hardness of the Wilderness but have not been subjected to the spoliation and degradation of bondage in Egypt. They have the strength and energy of youth and can be inspired by the message of the covenant that has as its sine qua non the conquest and settlement of the Promised Land. It is the optimistic hope of this new generation of Israel which inspires the great Song of the Well.

The Song of the Well

Unlike the Song of the Sea of Reeds attributed to Moses and Israel, the Song of the Well is attributed exclusively to Israel. Israel could not have sung the Song of the Sea of Reeds without Moses. There he was the exclusive leader, visionary, redeemer of a slave population unsure of its next steps as it was dragged helter skelter into the Wilderness.

Here, it is a new Israel that sings a tribute to living water, confident that the sustenance will be there for them. The *Midrash Tanhuma* describes the structure and function of the Well: "It was made like a rock, like a beehive, like a turret, which would rotate as it was borne by Israel in its passages." When the ensigns camped and the Tabernacle was set up, the "rock" would be set down in the courtyard of the Tent of Meeting and the princes of the tribes would station themselves abreast of it. "They would call out: 'Spring up, O Well, sing to it.' And the Well would rise up, as it were, and give forth its water." Israel, this new generation of Israel, will carry with them, *within* them, the emerging living waters. Ultimately they will not need the red heifer, nor will they fall prey to the blandishments of the brazen serpent. They now have a goal, a realizable destiny.

As for Moses, his career will hardly be over. As stressed earlier, he is no longer needed to be the omniscient, omnipresent political leader. Joshua has always been the military chief of staff in any case. What the new generation will need, however, will be a teacher, an eloquent spokesman to remind them, to spell out for them in a constantly renewable rhetoric the terms of the covenant. Moses, the heavy of speech, the stammerer, he who has not been able to sustain a common vocabulary, let alone language, with the *dor ha-midbar*, will be charged with spending the last year of his life, teaching Israel, binding the new Israel to Torah.

He himself understands that personally he will not enjoy the fruits of his labor. He will not experience any part of the conquest and settlement except to see the Land from afar. He will be known forever after, however, as the most humble of men because he has sacrificed personal reward. Such reward could have been his as prince in Egypt, or as leader of a new people after the sin of the "golden calf" when God was considering choosing a new people with whom to partner the covenant. Moses chose Israel as his people after having had this people chosen for him. He would never abandon his flock. And now he will recover the common language. He will help this new generation — and indeed all later generations of the Jewish people — to understand the meaning of Torah, the meaning of building a society in the Land in the image of Torah. He will die with the "words" — *eileh ha-devarim* (these words)!

Balak בלק

We have faced the perennially puzzling question: "Why didn't Moses speak to the rock instead of striking it?" In response to the question we cited the thirty-eight years in the Wilderness with no record of significant conversations between Moses and Israel. For Moses had nothing significant to say! And so at the "rock" he could not as yet break out of his long silence. As "punishment" for this prolonged silence he will be "condemned" to speak and to speak and to speak to Israel in the last year of his life — words of sociomoral instruction, spiritual hope and challenge.

But now we read of Balaam who *is* ready to talk. He is a professional "talker" who can use words as a flaming curse. That God turns those curses into blessings does not deter the Jewish tradition from condemning Balaam as the *rasha*, the "wicked one." His intention after all was to do evil. In other words, a critical lesson to be learned from the story of Balaam is that there are words that can appear to be blessings when in fact they are a smoke screen for venom.

A summary lesson: There is a two-sided potential in words. Words are the blessings and curses inherent in human speech, language, expression, and communication. Because human beings have been granted the power of speech and the capacity to construct verbal modes of expression and communication, noble human beings will grace words by using them for benevolent purposes. At the same time, however, evil human beings will exploit words for malevolent purposes. In J.N. Findlay's *Values and Intentions* he underscores the "high-level moral depravity" which only a high level of articulateness can produce. But even ordinary men will use words with which to tell lies, to rationalize unethical behavior, to deceive others, and, most pathetically, themselves.

Balaam and the Ass

Words may embody a prescribed regimen for service to God and Man or may be used to constitute a contract with the devil. Whatever the purpose, words are indispensable as language — for language, as Leavis has put it, "is the heuristic conquest won out of representative experience." Language and experience operate reciprocally. Does experience give birth to language or does language define experience? With humankind it will be both. With Israel, emphatically so! For Torah is the language of Israel in that it defines its history, its collective experience. The history of Israel is made up of the adventures of the patriarchs, the Exodus, and the various exiles and redemptions experienced in the crucible of life. These experiences are then molded for Israel's understanding by the language of Torah.

The critical role that words play in the redemptive process as God has orchestrated it has begun with a private revelation to a man Moses who has described himself as heavy with speech, uncircumcised of lips. Yet God has given him the words as promised. In Balaam's case, the case of the professional "talker" who would deign to curse Israel, God puts words into his mouth as well. For even Balaam must serve as a pawn — even against his will — in the redemptive process. And the mockery of Balaam, the bringing to his knees of this would-be prophet, will be effected, to begin with, through the vehicle of his loyal ass.

Abrabanel questions the necessity of the miracle of the talking ass. Why, Abrabanel asks, do we need the miracle of the ass who talks if it is only a means for getting Balaam to see the angel of God who in turn will talk to him? Ramban's response to the question is that Balaam must learn in vivid personal terms that it is God who makes it possible for any creature — from human to ass — to speak or to be dumb. For God opens the mouth of the dumb; all the more so does He have the capacity — should He will it — to strike dumb those creatures who would imagine that their power of speech is an unconditional gift. Under certain circumstances God will place within the "mouth" of the speaker not only the power of speech but the specific content of the given utterances — prophecy!

Jewish tradition will maintain a complex attitude towards Balaam. He is obviously of sufficient imagination to communicate with God and of sufficient repute to be known as a reliable "curser-for-hire." At the same time he is held by Jews to be a *rasha* ("a wicked man"). Why wicked, if his words turn out to be blessings? The blessings are not his! He has intended to curse! What God brings home to Balaam is that whatever power of rhetoric he has, it is at best a derived rhetoric and therefore not at all to his credit. What credit, after all, should one grant to one's humanly exercised rhetoric, when even an ass can pontificate.

God's lesson to Balaam has been taught previously to Moses at the "burning bush" when the latter was protesting his own forensic inadequacies. God, as it were, had said to the future prophet Moses whose rhetoric would turn out to be singularly remarkable: "Don't worry, I can make the dumb talk! In any case, it's not what you're going to *say* to Pharaoh; it's what I shall *do* to Pharaoh! It's not just what you will say to Israel; it's whether or not you are ready to share their future, to help mold their destiny."

The Midrash goes beyond the lesson represented by the phenomenon of a talking ass. The content of the message that the ass shares with Balaam the prophet-turned-clown is pertinent, indeed crucial: "You are not capable of killing me — a single animal — except by means of a sword in your hand. Yet you would seek to uproot an entire nation with words!" The Midrash — elucidating the *peshat* as always — has underscored the juxtaposition of the stupidest of animals and the wisest of the wise. Once the ass has shown his own creaturely wisdom, the stupidity of the "wise" Balaam is too much for the latter to bear.

Even before the introduction of the ass, God's manipulation of Balaam raises a philosophical question with moral overtones: If God at first tells Balaam not to go with Balak's messengers, why then does God change His instruction when Balaam asks a second time? Why does God now tell him to go, but then gets angry enough with him to send an angelic messenger to serve as a lethal adversary, i.e., to kill him? Franz Rosenzweig points to the word *va-yosef* which means "again" or "repeats," that is, doing something a second time. It is Balak's *second* attempt to enlist Balaam in his ugly scheme that elicits Rosenzweig's attention. "Generally," Rosenzweig says, "einmal ist keinmal," that is, once does not count. In this story, a number of things happen more than once. Balak sends courtiers to convince Balaam a second time. Balaam wants to hear God's message a second time. Balaam beats the ass more than once. The adversary — the "satan" — keeps resuming his threatening pose before Balaam and the ass, a second and third time. Indeed, within the story, once does not seem to be enough!

Rosenzweig argues, however, that with respect to God — under certain portentous circumstances — once means once and for all. The first instruction that God gives Balaam is clear: "Do not go with Balak's messengers, do not curse this people *for it is blessed*." Rosenzweig concludes: "If we do not take God's first unequivocal word as being sufficient, but try that which God *resuming* speaks unto us, then God will without fail speak this time — the second time — the words of the demon that is within us." In other words, the human being is blessed with the power to understand an instruction, a proposition, a message. His power to see the reasonableness of the instruction, of the proposition, of the message, is abundant. There is a demonic force within him, however, which is the power to rationalize. And this power leads him not only to reject the patently clear and reasonable first instruction, but to build — out of his own stubborn determination to deceive himself in order to stray from the instruction — a "reasoned" or "rationalized" countermanding of the instruction.

In such cases, the instinctive or intuitive insight of an ass — a dumb animal — is more trustworthy than the satanic rationalizing "wisdom" of the human being. There is a pristine innocence associated with the dumb animal which unfortunately has been lost to the human being. The dumb animal in this episode is capable of employing or appreciating the phenomenon of irony in human expression and communication. For irony is that method of expression in which the ordinary meaning of the words is the opposite of the thought in the speaker's mind. The Midrash thereby summarizes Numbers 22:12 "Do not curse this nation" by having Balaam insist that he seeks only to bless them. But God then cuts Balaam short: "They don't need your blessing, for they are already blessed. Furthermore, in Israel's eyes, you Balaam are like the wasps: Israel doesn't want your honey, nor your sting."

The Honey and the Sting

On the *peshat* level, the Balaam story is straightforward. God uses Balaam as a mouthpiece with which to bless Israel. After all, two of the richest most fulsome praises of Israel come out of the mouth of Balaam: First, we have the exquisite "How goodly are your tents, Jacob, your dwelling places, Israel."

Then we have: "No harm is in sight for Jacob; no woe in view for Israel; the Lord their God is with them and their King's acclaim is in their midst." Why then would the later Sages of Israel still express their feelings towards Balaam in a mode of "thanks, but no thanks, neither your honey nor your sting"? The answer is as simple as the story: The Rabbis will see in anything an enemy of Israel says — even or especially in words which will sound like praise — curses!

A clearer evidence of irony may be seen in Balaam's proclamation, which climaxes the first poetic scene: *"Hen am le-vadad yishkon"* ("There is a people that dwells apart"); *"u-va-goyim lo yithashav"* ("which is not reckoned among the nations"). Such a description can be considered like honey, as the Ramban interprets it: "When I see this nation dwelling alone, so may it continue to dwell alone as it says in Deuteronomy 33:28 *'Va-yishkon Yisrael betah badad ein Yakov'* ('Israel will dwell in safety the fountain of Jacob alone'), untroubled shall be Jacob's abode; for no nation shall ever prevail over him, nor will he ever become assimilated to them."

But the sting lies embedded in these words when students of the reality of later Jewish history realize that Israel will not dwell with any kind of permanency in safety; that other nations will prevail over Israel; and that Israel — or large groups within Israel — will indeed become assimilated to these other nations.

Similarly, there is irony in Balaam's encomium "How goodly are your tents, Jacob." Against the perspective of later Jewish history, not to mention the brief period since the Exodus, has "goodness" pervaded the House of Israel? Certainly not in the eyes of the later prophets of Israel, highlighted in Micah's classic reminder to Israel through the ages: "It has been told to you, O Man, what is good, and what the Lord demands of you — do justly, love mercy, and walk humbly with your God." A sting in the "honeyed" phrase "how goodly are your tents, Jacob, your dwelling places, Israel" is that the tents and dwelling places of Israel will too often forget or pervert Micah's injunction.

Balaam's very name has an ironic tone for he has sought — notwithstanding his blessings — to *swallow* Israel up as a nation. Moses, on the other hand, is full of stinging criticism for his flock. Nevertheless he is called "Moshe" because just as he was *drawn up* out of the waters of extinction so he *drew* Israel out of the Sea of Extinction — the *Yam-Sof*!

The irony deepens when we consider that Balaam the wicked — whether he means it or not — is given to see the good. Moses, on the other hand, the *anav* (the humble) is given to see the bad in Israel, and notwithstanding all the good he has performed for Israel, Moses will be punished by God in not being able to enter the Promised Land. How is it possible? Eldad suggests the following as an answer to why Moses never says anything complimentary to the people: "Is there ever in the eyes of the prophet a stage on the ladder which may be considered 'complete,' 'perfect,' as it applies to his purpose in raising his people higher and higher? Isn't the constant demand for ascent upon that ladder the natural law of the prophet? Can the prophet ever free himself even for an instant from his preoccupation with the challenge to his people of 'if' and 'if not'? Can he ever allow himself to enjoy even for an instant the static state of happiness?"

The answers to these questions, of course, are in the negative. A prophet, as opposed to a poet or a painter, cannot tolerate a "still-life" — a situation frozen for aesthetic contemplation. Life is dynamic in the extreme. Moses the prophet stands inside the Israelite camp — unlike Balaam who views Israel from a distance. Moses — vis-à-vis his people Israel — feels the pulse and passion of his people's life. Balaam — vis-à-vis Israel — is like a poet who utters poetically pleasing praises from outside, as a spectator coolly photographing an experience frozen-in-stasis. But this very frozenness misses the reality of life being lived in dynamic tension every moment, every micro-moment. It is true that the prophet like Moses may go too far in his criticism of his people and as a consequence may get punished. But his punishment is inflicted on him *not* for being a prophet, but for being too human.

Balaam, on the other hand, in noting Israel's "goodness" is looking at the Jews from the outside and seeing them as good. But of what living value is a good which in its frozen preconceived goodness can be packaged, compartmentalized? Moses doesn't have to say *"ma tovu"* ("how goodly are you") from the outside. He knows the intrinsic goodness of his people. And he knows even better his own unconditional love for his people, proven unequivocally by his demand to be wiped out of God's book if God would ever seriously consider abandoning Israel. In short, Moses — from the inside — knows best the problems, the failures, the tragedies of this covenanted people. However sharp his criticisms, they will be aimed at enabling them to enter the Promised Land and surviving there socially, politically, ethically, and spiritually.

Israel the Unique

What Balaam does capture — if not in the *"ma tovu"* verse, then certainly in the *"am le-vadad yishkon u-va-goyim lo yithashav"* verse — is the dialectic which will characterize later Jewish history with regard to Israel's uniqueness. In the Talmud *Sanhedrin* (39a) a Gentile asks Rabbi Abina quoting II Samuel 7:23: "'And who is like Your people Israel a unique nation in the world,' where lies your superiority? After all, as a nation you are mingled with us among all the nations!" But Rabbi Abina reminds the Gentile that one of their very own Gentiles, Balaam, has said that Israel shall not be considered among the nations. It may be that to begin with, Israel is a nation among nations, sharing the basic trappings of material and cultural resources that all nations must have as minimal guarantees of survival. But to maintain its own special distinguishing ethos, Israel will also seek its own unique identity — that which spells out a covenantal reality and destiny.

To be a nation, Israel will discover and rediscover the painful truth that even with a desire for uniqueness — especially so — it will need sovereignty. Centuries upon centuries in exile will culminate in the proposed and well-nigh executed Shoah. Proposed as a "final solution" to the Jewish problem, the Shoah will be seen by Jewish activists following the Second World War as a "final endorsement" of the Zionist agenda. The building of this nation in its own land will require a special kind of statesmanship, moreover, which in biblical times will not have been reached until the chaotic period of the Judges will have given way to the period of the Kings.

In demanding a king — like the other nations — Israel will be attempting to convince God and his prophet Samuel that normal "raison d'état" sovereignty is necessary. But in order to establish the required sense of uniqueness, Israel will have to maintain in addition a sense of special destiny. A sense of unique destiny! For Israel, only the original covenant will have the power of originality, continuity, and revelatory authenticity to inspire and inform the national enterprise. Israel's own special attention and commitment to a transcendent, spiritual, ethical, and social purpose will make up the thrust towards this unique destiny.

Maintaining a national uniqueness will be extremely difficult in that a high degree of normalcy will have to characterize a sovereign state that seeks to interact with other nations. It will determine that it cannot survive without economic, cultural, political, and even military alliances. Moreover, the demand for *tikkun olam* (mending the world) will itself place a covenantal seal of approval upon Israel's mixing constructively with other nations. But how then will they be able to maintain their "tribal identity" if not by working at fulfilling their covenantal chosenness!

This tension within the dialectic of participation within the community of nations while maintaining a national uniqueness parallels what individuals go through in seeing themselves as members of a group like other members of the group on the one hand, but on the other hand — uniquely themselves! The individual will struggle to find out who he is against the background of whatever group, tribe, people, nation, religion he has been born into or put into or has put himself into. The Jew will have a particular propensity for asking the question: "Who am I?"

Franz Kafka, the ingenious but tortured twentieth-century Jewish writer, reflecting on his connection or non-connection with Judaism and the Jewish people will lament: "How can I have anything in common with Judaism? I hardly have anything in common with myself." In a sense, Balaam — while not an Israelite, while not a Jew — is a paradigm for the tortured Kafka. He is disturbed, torn, conflicted. He can't decide whether to curse or bless. Never mind the consequences for the recipient of the blessings or the victim of the curse! Balaam himself or Kafka or Spinoza or Elisha ben Abuya are split in their search for their own authentic selves.

Already quoted earlier, the Kotzker Rebbe will argue for a radically subjective — perhaps solipsistic — recognition of self in the search for authenticity: "If I am I because I am I and you are you because you are you, then I am I and you are you; but if I am I because you are you and you are you because I am I then I am not I and you are not you." As underscored earlier, this double proposition of the Kotzker may be true of the individual in his solitariness; but it cannot and does not characterize the individual who attempts to participate in a relationship, a friendship, or a marriage, in a community, within a people, within a nation. Here it is "I am I to a great extent because you are you. I am unique, it is true, but to build a community of souls seeking fulfillment as members of a community of souls, I am dependent for my fullest expression of identity upon you, as you are upon me."

The Jew will discover and maintain his identity only by seeing and actualizing his self as a member of his people. He will be his unique solitary self but in active social participation with others among his people. His people in turn, the Jewish people, will insist on its uniqueness, on its special character, while claiming its right and acknowledging its duty to meet and interact with other peoples in the collective task of mending the world.

Justice, Mercy, and Humility

Israel's tents and habitations then may be described as "how goodly" when the balance is maintained in good faith between Jewish exclusivity and ecumenicity. How is this "good" attained, retained, and maintained? Returning once again to the universal injunction of the prophet Micah who formulated the "good" which God requires of the human being — not just of Israel: "He has told you, O Man, what is good, and what the Lord requires of you: Only to do justice and to love mercy, and to walk humbly with your God."

There are three concepts and instructions based thereon in Micah's statement. Each of them — justice, mercy, humility — will call forth libraries of human concern and commentary. Justice and mercy are clearly the valuational pillars of any enlightened society. But even more fundamental to the long-term health and sociomoral vitality of a society is the third concept: humility. For humility is the Archimedes point from which the doing of justice and the granting of mercy emerge.

Justice and mercy are active manifestations of the "I" towards others. No one is just or merciful until put into a specific social position, an interactive position. Humility, on the other hand, is a character trait of the individual qua himself — an indispensable character trait — as he prepares to confront others justly and mercifully. God himself is described as humble in that He set aside all the great mountains in favor of the smaller Mount Sinai on which to reveal His Torah. Moreover, even before the great revelation at Sinai, He set aside all the good trees in order to let His indwelling Presence reveal itself to Moses in a lowly thorn bush.

If one takes the Latin root of humility — "humus" meaning "ground" —

one could make a case for Man ideally thinking of himself as *afar va-efer* (dirt) as with Abraham pleading before God on behalf of the condemned of Sodom. But the Abraham who calls out "Shall the judge of all the earth not rule justly" is far from a self-effacing cypher. And Moses described as the most humble of men is certainly not one who supinely obeys without question. Humility has nothing to do with cowardice or a lack of forthrightness. Abraham and Moses share a nobility of spirit and presence, but because of their fundamental humility, they do not allow their aristocratic character to breed and cultivate arrogance.

From the beginning the Bible is concerned with (1) the confrontation of the human being Adam/Eve with the Serpent, and (2) God's own confrontation respectively with Adam/Eve and the Serpent. Both confrontations underscore the tension between nobility and arrogance as the key crisis of the human ethical condition. To be truly human and to be truly covenanted is to appreciate the extremes of nobility and arrogance and to work at subduing the temptation to pervert the former into the latter. This is as true of nations as it is of individual human beings. Balaam as a tool of Nimrod/Balak becomes instead the staff of God's blessing over Israel. But because his intentions have been to curse, he is cast away as a "reject," unworthy to be in the company of even a dumb ass! Will Israel throughout its later political and cultural history prefer to rely on the Balaams of the world or on the intuitive wisdom of the ass? Will Israel be prepared to shoulder its Torah with nobility and humility, so that it will delight in looking to that Torah to provide the practical and prophetic wisdom demanded of its unique covenantal destiny?

Pinhas פנחס

A modern novelist will become enamored with the image of a long-distance runner and his loneliness as a paradigm for the human condition. In an entirely different context it is an image that ideally characterizes Moses who has been charged with going the distance with a stiff-necked people and doing it as every leader must do it, in utter loneliness.

Moses has borne the thickness of the burden. He has taken the advice of Yitro [Jethro] to decentralize the judiciary. He has accepted the parliamentary sharing of legislative and executive responsibility with the seventy elders. Nevertheless, Moses has always been alone in his vision and alone in carrying the weight of covenantal concern for his people.

He will not share the joy of entering the Promised Land. As a Levite he will not be able to leave a share of the Land to his children. Then again, the comforting thought is that the total inheritance for all of Israel will have been made possible by Moses' exemplary zeal — the singular zealot of the Lord, lonely and alone — but after all, alone with the One alone.

Shares in Settlement

The experience in the Wilderness has been a near-disaster. But the disaster has not deterred God, Moses, and collective Israel from moving forward to the Promised Land. A new generation will enter, conquer, and settle this Promised Land. And this Land will then have to be parceled out among the tribes. A census will have to be carried out; but this time not for military purposes but for equitable settlement of all the tribes.

There is an apparent confusion — reflected in biblical verses — as to how to parcel out the shares. From verse 26:53 we learn that "among these shall the Land be apportioned as shares, according to the listed names." In the Talmud this is interpreted to refer to those who will *enter the Land*. But verse

26:55 states that "the Land shall be divided by lot according to the names of the tribes of their fathers they shall inherit." This is interpreted to refer to those who *came out of Egypt*. The talmudic passage found in *Baba Batra* suggests a third opinion: that *both groups* are to be considered — those who began the national enterprise by escaping bondage in Egypt and those who will carry it forward by entering and building up the covenanted Land of Israel.

Rabbi Yoshia, Rabbi Yonatan, and Rabbi Shimon ben Elazar take up the legal discourse by considering the following cases:

(1) Among those who came out of Egypt was someone over twenty at the time of the Exodus. Falling victim to God's decree concerning the *dor ha-Midbar*, he died before Canaan was reached. His sons were born quite late during the period of the Wilderness and so were still minors at the time of the conquest of Canaan. According to Rabbi Yoshia, their father has earned a share in the Promised Land which in his death he has left to be divided by his sons.

(2) Rabbi Yonatan considers two other possible cases: (a) the father of sons has died in Egypt before the Exodus. His sons were minors at the Exodus and therefore not subject to God's decree concerning the *dor ha-Midbar*, but were over twenty by the time of the conquest; or (b) one could have left Egypt as a minor, died in the Wilderness, but had sons born in the Wilderness who would be over twenty by the time of the conquest. Rabbi Yonatan sees these cases as supporting the claim of the new living generation to be the designated heirs.

(3) Rabbi Shimon ben Elazar offers an all-inclusive interpretation. Halakhically speaking, one could have been over twenty at the Exodus, therefore condemned to die in the Wilderness. His sons who would have grown up in the Wilderness — having been under twenty when the decree was issued — would enter Canaan when of age. According to Rabbi Shimon ben Elazar they would be entitled to their share and their father's share.

This legal debate concerns not only the serious "business" of business, economics, and physical survival, for there is a theological and sociomoral dimension to the debate. Rabbi Yoshia's position does not relate to the early generation as the "Wilderness generation." In his eyes they are referred to as "*yotzei-Mizrayim*," a term lacking the contumely of the epitaph "*dor ha-midbar*." The slaves — whatever their shortcomings — had shown courage in leaving the known for the unknown. The prophet Jeremiah would look back upon the period in the Wilderness as one of innocent betrothal, the joy of early love. With all the vacillations of that generation, including their tragic rejection of the *aliyah* half of their emancipation from bondage, they *had, in fact, come out*. According to Rabbi Yoshia, therefore, they deserve a share in the present and future.

Rabbi Yonatan cannot see himself "rewarding" the slave generation. For him, only the *ba'ei ha'aretz*, those who actually will have shouldered the burden of conquest and settlement, have legitimate claims to patrimony. Jeremiah's longing for the pristine purity of the Wilderness cannot but be a therapeutic projection in the face of his own generation's civic and national failure. Rabbi Yonatan will argue that a Jeremiah knows and can appreciate the effort invested in building a society. He as a prophet has come to uproot what has become degenerate; but he knows that one must build again, plant again. And it is for *whosoever will bear this new responsibility* to share the Land.

Shimon ben Elazar's position acknowledges both claims. For him both generations make up the historic tribe and extended family that is the nation of Israel. Both generations — all generations of Israelites — share a collective life which reaches out beyond mortal life as lived by individuals and individual generations. *All* of Israel, in other words, will have been taken out of Egypt; and *all of Israel should be seen as full participants in the settlement of the Promised Land.*

Words and Deeds

If one adopts the attitude that "all of Israel is one," that in being responsible one for the other all of Israel share in the blessings, it may also be claimed that all of Israel suffer the curses imposed on any one of them or any group of them. All of Israel is thus perceived as guilty for having shown the hesitancy of the ten spies, the rebelliousness of Korah and his band, and the lusting after the harlots of Moab and Midian. At the same time, if such is the spiritual-moral calculus, then all of Israel through the ages will also be seen to have been hospitable to the unique religious and moral zeal of Pinhas.

Pinhas is the archetypal extra-legal agent of God's wrath in the face of a major threat to the norms which have had difficulty being accepted by a morally-weak populace. Rashi points out that the family background of Zimri — Pinhas' victim — is given. Who was Zimri? He was a prince of the tribe of Simon. And Rashi explains: "To make known the praise of Pinhas, that even though Zimri was a prince, Pinhas did not restrain himself from being zealous at Zimri's desecration of God's name." In Pinhas' judgment the crime of Zimri was serious enough to warrant capital punishment.

On the threshold of the Israelites' entrance into the Promised Land, the Moabites and Midianites have sent forth their harlots to lead Israel into wholesale lechery, which will lead inevitably to social disintegration. Among the women is no less than Cozbi the daughter of a leading Midianite. And she consorts with no less a public figure than the Israelite prince Zimri. The crime, in other words, is not just one of back-alley fornication. It is a publicly displayed political misalliance which proclaims to the Israelites: Forget Torah, morality, chastity, communal responsibility. Forget the purpose for which you were redeemed from Egypt. In the face of such a public desecration leading to a destructive plague, Pinhas acts. In the eyes of God, it is determined that Pinhas' act is the required act at *that* moment and *for that* moment.

We may contrast the character of Pinhas with that of Balaam, the evil Midianite prophet. It is a contrast between a Balaam, the man of words, who couldn't make up his mind whether to curse or to bless, and a Pinhas who not only makes up his mind but performs an act when needed — immediately and decisively.

In another context, one may recall the teaching of Shimon ben Gamliel in *Pirke Avot* (1:17): "All my life I was raised among scholars and I found that no virtue becomes a man more than silence; what is more essential is not words but practice; and in the wake of many words is sin." The usual interpretations of this passage point out that too much talk will lead to levity or gossip. Such interpretations do not quite suffice here, because the author is trying to contrast words — or verbal discussion and analysis — with deeds. He has stressed *"lo ha-midrash ikar ela ha-ma'aseh"* ("more essential than words is practice"). For Pinhas, the lethal consequences of Balaam's words leading to the appearance of the Moabite and Midianite harlots in the Israelite camp are much too dire for words to be considered at this crucial time — any kind of words.

Why could Balaam not be trusted, not by Balak, the man who hired him to curse the Israelites, nor by the Israelites, who felt that even his blessings were given insincerely? He could not be trusted because he was *just* a man of words. Appropriate deeds did not accompany his words. Pinhas, on the other hand, sees a situation in which his people, the Israelites, are worshiping the false Moabite gods, and, worse still, are consorting with Moabite and Midianite harlots. A leading Israelite prince is promoting — by example — the licentious activity in public, flaunting God and the very purpose for which God has taken Israel out of Egypt. All this is happening while a plague is decimating the camp. In such a situation Pinhas does not talk at all. He actualizes a sense of righteous outrage. He executes the prince and his consort — in public! And, thereby, as the Torah concludes, Pinhas brings peace to the camp.

Surely the Rabbis, along with Shimon ben Gamliel, are not adversaries of speech. Words are indispensable for prayer, for study, for reflection, for communication, for analysis. And words themselves, under certain circumstances, can be appropriately effective action. What the Rabbis fear is the substitution of words *for* action when action is needed and called for immediately. In this sense, the Rabbis and Pinhas himself understand that under certain circumstances, words can be the most insidious instruments available to the unique creature called "human being."

What was Pinhas to do in the face of a blatant public display on the part of a leader in Israel? Should he have discussed it, analyzed it, appraised it, evaluated it, called for a commission of enquiry? Under normal circumstances — yes! But action was needed now! Words and studies and analytical reports might have given the illusion that progress was being made in dealing with the problem of public fornication by high officials; but in fact nothing would have been accomplished. Worse, had Pinhas not acted, perhaps a worse disaster than the already catastrophic plague would have swept through the camp. Then no doubt a rationalization process would have begun, again based on verbal sophistry. The camp would have been filled with those who would have lamented "Oh what should have been done, what might have been done, what could have been done, etc."

Pinhas' act is, to say the least, not a gentle one. It is the antithesis of normal civilized behavior which would call for mediation or adjudication. Resh Lakish identifies Pinhas with Elijah, the Elijah who similarly steps into the breach on Mount Carmel when Israel is threatened with wholesale apostasy. The words of the later prophet Malachi characterizing the coming "great day" of Elijah are apt, if applied to Pinhas: "Behold, I send My messenger, And he shall clean the way before Me... And who may abide the day of his coming? And who shall stand when he appears? For he is like a refiner's fire and fuller's soap."

Pinhas' act will be considered — like Elijah's on Mount Carmel — as unique, as uniquely appropriate under the circumstances. It is clear that such an act would have to be condemned under ordinary circumstances. But the public fornication of Zimri the Israelite prince and Cozbi the Midianite princess with a lethal plague devastating the camp is not an ordinary circumstance. Pinhas must do something! And so he kills — is it murder? And so he executes — is it assassination?

Kana'ut, Pinhas, and the Rabbis

Later Jewish history will assuredly not endorse Pinhas' act as a precedent. One must not always act. Tradition will note the prophet Jeremiah's implacable urging of his compatriots *not* to act against triumphant Babylonian forces occupying Israel. Jeremiah certainly shares the agony of his people's defeat and subjugation under the yoke of an idolatrous Babylonian Empire. But to rebel against this Empire at this time is perceived by Jeremiah to be a contravening of God's decree. In Jeremiah's view — prophetically informed, as he is, by God — such a rebellion will compound the disaster. Jeremiah, like Pinhas, must act; but unlike Pinhas, Jeremiah's "action" is a passionate prophetic counsel to refrain from acting! Is Jeremiah then expressing dissent, or is it sedition? Does he have prophetic immunity — or is he guilty of treason?

Any such zealous action or inaction — as the case may warrant — must be the result of a totally disinterestedly pure motive. As the *Torah Temimah* will put it, a deed such as that of Pinhas must be animated by a genuine, unadulterated spirit of zeal to advance the glory of God. In such a case, however, who can tell whether the perpetrator has not really been prompted by some selfish motive, maintaining that he is doing it for the sake of God, when what he has done in fact is commit murder? It is for this reason that later sages in the Jerusalem Talmud consider excommunicating the likes of a Pinhas but reject the idea. For in this single unique situation it was the Holy Spirit and only the Holy Spirit which testified that Pinhas' zeal for God *in this* situation was genuine and that the resulting action *in this situation* was necessary.

A similar claim will be made by Rabbi A.I. Kook in explaining the authorship of the weekday petition in the liturgy to wipe out the slanderers, the heretics, and the traitors within the House of Israel. Shmuel ha-Katan is credited with the composition of this difficult petition precisely because no one will question his moral credentials. The assumption is that anyone can write a prayer pleading for mercy or expressing love. But if it is felt that in a pre-Messianic universe there is evil and that there are evildoers who should be hated and condemned, then a prayer that asks God to eliminate such evildoers is not out of place. But then who but a moral exemplar like Shmuel ha-Katan can be trusted with the formal composition of such a prayer!

Kana'ut (religious zeal) is a manifestation of *emunah* (faith) that is so strong that it enables one to stand fast against the tide of *shigratiyut* (dull-normal convention). Pinhas wants peace. At the same time, he judges that certain things are intolerable and he acts to correct the situation. His act is that exceptional act that can only be understood within an immediate existential crisis. It is beyond the purview of normative legal jurisdiction. After the fact it is "approved" as having brought peace. Lest his act be looked upon, however, as a recommended norm for the future, it is condemned by the Rabbis.

It is clear that the Rabbis are uncomfortable with Pinhas' act. In the Jerusalem Talmud, as already noted, some are ready to excommunicate him. Why? Because of the fact that Pinhas has slain a human being on the spur of the moment, without trial, without offering previous warning, without legal testimony having been heard, and in defiance of all the procedures of judicial examination prescribed by Torah legislation as it will evolve. In the Babylonian Talmud, a similar rabbinic discomfiture is expressed. By the time one arrives at the legal summaries of the medieval codifier Rambam, he has ruled in effect that an arbitrary act of such zealous passion is unacceptable and punishable.

The specific claims of the Rabbis, as summarized in the Maimonidean code, illuminate an evolving ethical refinement in Jewish law. The Rambam in the *Laws of Issurei Biah* 12:5 summarizes: (1) In a situation where it has previously been assumed that "zealots of the Lord" will attack a sinner, they are forbidden to do so except at the precise moment of the sin. For if the sinner should have ceased his disreputable act and then the zealot has attacked him, the zealot is then criminally guilty, open to being executed. (2) If the zealot appears before the authoritative court in order to seek permission to attack the sinner — even if the sinner is at such a time perpetrating his sin — the court does not give license to the zealot to act. (3) Moreover, if the sinner tries to protect and save himself from the onslaught of the zealot, and in the ensuing clash-of-arms the zealot himself is killed, the sinner is not subject to punishment.

Despite Rambam's summary codification, the talmudic debate has been "zealously" contested. In the tractate *Sanhedrin* (82a) Rav, Shmuel, and Rabbi Yitzhak offer their own analyses. Rav has Pinhas consulting Moses, reminding the latter of the recognized norm that zealots are permitted to strike down those who consort in public with heathens. Moses says, "He who reads the letter let him carry out its instructions." Moses, on the one hand, has clearly not instructed Pinhas directly as to what to do. At the same time, Moses is telling Pinhas that if that is the way he is reading the Torah let him act according to what he understands its provisions to be, but let him be prepared to accept full responsibility for his actions.

Shmuel appears to interpret Moses' comment to Pinhas differently. "He who reads the letter let him carry out its instructions" can be seen as an implied scolding on the part of Moses. If Pinhas would attend to the "letter," i.e., the Torah, he would have to acknowledge that the Torah cautions against the unilateral precipitous action contemplated by Pinhas. But Shmuel then defends Pinhas' position by citing the particular urgency of a situation in which there is a *hillul Hashem* (a desecration of God's Name). And where that occurs *"ein holkin kavod la-rav"* (the zealot does not consider the honor of his teacher) before he acts.

Rabbi Yitzhak speaking in the name of Rabbi Eliezer adopts a different perspective in pointing to the catastrophe taking place in the Israelite camp. It isn't "merely" a matter of public fornication in "high places." As serious as Zimri's crime is — he being a prince of a tribe in Israel — it is the crime of a single individual. Whatever punishment or amelioration of punishment is decided upon, it will directly affect only one individual. But the collective atmosphere of wholesale lechery that has infiltrated the entire people has led to the plague which is killing thousands. According to Rabbi Yitzhak, Pinhas has no time for consultation — even with his teacher Moses. In a situation where the nation is being decimated, he must decide quickly and must carry out his decision quickly.

Moses the Lonely Zealot

As to Moses, the question must be asked: "Why didn't Moses arrogate to himself the summary execution of Zimri? Or, at the very least, couldn't Moses or shouldn't Moses have done something to step into the breach at such a calamitous juncture in the Wilderness experience? Is this a further confirmation of Moses' gradual retreat from assertive leadership?

According to verses 25:4-6 Moses does act. He follows God's instruction to order the impalement of all those who are leading the public idolatry and accompanying lasciviousness. Nevertheless, according to the *peshat* it is only after Pinhas steps forward and makes a public example of Zimri, that the plague is stopped and *shalom* is restored to the camp.

It is clear that Moses' love and concern for the Children of Israel has in no way diminished. But it may be said that we have here further evidence that he is no longer in total command of events. For better and for worse, a new leadership must and will emerge. Moses will remain to teach Deuteronomy. He will give spiritual and sociomoral instruction, e.g., he will be careful to specify the appropriate worship sacrifices for the Holy days — the Shabbat, the Three Festivals, the first and tenth days of the seventh month. But as overall "chief executive" he is gradually moving off the scene.

Lest there be confusion as to Moses' future role, any special honor or consideration to be given to Moses' flesh and blood is rejected. Moses' sons will in no way inherit their father's exalted position, nor will they be granted any special appointment. Their names are not even referred to in the passage where consideration is given to the succession. Nor is there any trace of a suggestion by Moses to nominate his sons to succeed him. What finds expression in the text is Moses' concern for the welfare of Israel; therefore it will be Joshua, his long-term closest disciple, who will move into the leadership role. Moses' appeal to God, whom he addresses with the rare expression "Lord of the Spirits," confirms his acceptance of God's choice of leadership as the correct choice. The Lord of the *Spirits* will know how to measure the spiritual readiness of all men, all potential leaders.

The Midrash underscores the ongoing demand that leadership not be transferred by inheritance but by merit. Contrary to the *peshat*, the Midrash has Moses behaving at first like any ordinary father pleading with God on behalf of his sons. Moses mounts his appeal following the request of the daughters of Zelafhad for their father's inheritance: "May I now not attend to my own needs? If these daughters shall inherit, is it not right for my sons to inherit my glory?" But the Midrash has God respond with a proverb: "Whoso keeps the fig-tree will eat its fruit." And who is this to be but Moses' long-term disciple in tending to the needs of the "fig-tree" — Joshua.

Yet, one dare not turn away from the striking figure of Moses without fully appreciating his giant stature — not only as the archetypal teacher of Israel, Moshe Rabbenu, but as its model leader, emancipator, redeemer. Like all human beings, he will face eventual eclipse as leader. But such mortal necessity cannot diminish Moses' greatness. If Pinhas is described as *the* zealot, there are two other episodes where *kin'ah* (zeal) is referred to which lend a special insight into the necessary qualities that a leader must possess as part of his character if he is to lead. Moses has had these qualities in abundance.

We recall the first episode where Joshua — fiercely loyal to Moses — informs his master that Eldad and Medad are "prophesying" in the camp and that they should be imprisoned for such behavior. Moses reacts by saying: "Are you *zealous* for me?" Moses is scolding Joshua for his misplaced solicitousness on Moses' behalf. "Would that all the members of God's people were prophets." Rashi explains that the word *kin'ah* applies to a person who dedicates himself utterly to a task. He becomes *meshuga le-davar ehad* (maddeningly committed to that task). The activities which will elicit such zeal may stem from helping other human beings or avenging particular wrongs done to other human beings. But the primary quality of the zealot is his readiness to bear *be-ovi ha-masa* (the thickest part of the burden) of the given task. There is no question but that Moses has carried the thickest part of the burden of the redemption of Israel. He has been in the position of "*hineini*" — constant total readiness — from the personal revelation at the "burning bush" through the dangerous negotiations with Pharaoh, through the Exodus itself, through the shepherding of the people to Sinai, and through the tragically relentless sojourn in the Wilderness.

The second episode where the word *kin'ah* is used describes Elijah — associated by tradition with Pinhas — at a moment of utter loneliness in the prophet's mission to challenge the idolatrous rule of Ahab and Jezebel. Elijah has emerged triumphant at the do-or-die contest on Mount Carmel against the false prophets of Baal. He has supervised, moreover, the execution of these "prophets" at the river Kishon. But shortly thereafter, Jezebel's persecution of Elijah's prophetic colleagues has resumed with even greater ferocity. Elijah escapes, and in virtual despair flees to Horev-Sinai. It is there where he laments his sorry fate with the words: "It is enough, O Lord, now take away my life, for I am not better than my fathers…I have been very *zealous* for the Lord God of Hosts; for the Israelites have forsaken Your covenant, torn down Your altars, and put Your prophets to the sword. I alone am left, and they are out to take my life."

Elijah — not by coincidence — expresses his despair at being alone in his mission at Horev-Sinai. It is there, of course, where Moses will have experienced his own utter aloneness and loneliness in receiving God's revelation for his people. The idolatrous revelry around the "golden calf" may not have been as personally threatening to Moses as Jezebel's hordes are to Elijah. But the aloneness and loneliness which Elijah laments from time to time will *never* leave Moses. They haven't left him for an instant from the time he exited the Egyptian palace as a young prince in order to align his destiny with the Hebrew slaves. Now in the twilight of his unconditional commitment to God's covenant with Israel he will feel ever more lonely. But his unconditional *ahavat Yisrael* — his absolute love for the Children of Israel — will ameliorate the loneliness. For despite his personal disappointment in knowing that he himself will not be entering the Promised Land, his faith is steadfast that this new generation will enter and will make a genuine effort to fulfill the terms of the covenant.

Mattot מטות

Despite the tragic misadventures of the Children of Israel throughout the trek through the Wilderness, there has been movement — progress, as it were. A new generation has arisen, one which is preparing itself for the fulfillment of a covenantal destiny. Apparently gone is the heretical question "Shall we continue along the path laid out for us by the God of Israel and His messenger Moses." It appears that the new generation will not be deterred by internal doubts. It may be that they are far from "holy" in the Deuteronomic sense. But they will build towards the ideal once they are settled in the Land. And they do seem determined to conquer and to settle the Land.

In the meantime they will need to be given ways and means for testing their character, i.e., knowing themselves — truly knowing themselves as they are. Under the stubborn tutorship of their teacher Moses, who in his twilight years is determined to continue instructing them, if not leading them, they will be given modes for testing their resolve.

As one example, the Torah records specifications regarding vows and oaths and the fulfillment and canceling of vows and oaths. These specifications are to be treated by all Israelites as utterly serious modes for measuring individual accountability. "He who makes a vow to the Lord…he must carry out all that has crossed his lips." In the text, the Hebrew word for "all," however, is not *kol*, but *ke-khol*, that is, "like all." The extra "*k*" meaning "like" is intended to include homiletically, says a sage, not only the individual who mouths his vow publicly, but even the individual who does not mouth it but only *thinks* it in his mind-heart. The talmudic tractate *Shevu'ot* (Oaths) will state that the sin offering associated with the first day of each new month is to expiate those specific wrongdoings known only to God. This will include the sin committed by him who has vowed a vow in his mind-heart but has never fulfilled it.

Tradition will show compassion towards those who have vowed vows between themselves and God — whether declared or not — and failed to fulfill them. But it will insist that those vows taken in relation to other men must be fulfilled, i.e., full forgiveness can only be extended by the party who has been wronged. Still, the Torah recognizes that those vows taken within one's mind-heart and then broken are in the long run the most injurious to the development of the individual personality. Therefore, on the threshold of the Promised Land, each Israelite must truly be able to know himself and what he is capable of. He must be prepared to affirm by oath his *"hineini"* — what he swears himself to be and what he is prepared to do before God and his people.

God, in His turn, in relating to each individual personality within the House of Israel, will be known as *Elohei ha-Ruhot* (God of Individual Spirits). During the crisis of the Korah rebellion, as many of the confused Israelites had become fellow-travelers of the rebels, God had been ready to destroy one and all as a group. Moses had entreated the Lord addressing Him as he would in only one other place in the Bible — as *Elohei ha-Ruhot.* Rashi, fascinated by the strange appellation, sees Moses emphasizing God's capacity to know the thoughts, the spiritual true-sense-of-being, of each individual Israelite. Because God *knows* the psyche, the conscience, the soul of each individual Israelite, He knows that they are not all guilty. Would He, therefore, like a flesh-and-blood ruler destroy all members of a recalcitrant province because of the sins of the few?

A much later leader of Israel will see the Zionist revolution in similar personal terms. Ben-Gurion will encapsulate the Zionist aspiration in the following definition: "Zionism in its essence is a revolutionary movement. One could hardly find a revolution that goes deeper than what Zionism wants to do to the life of the Jewish people. (But) this is not merely a revolution against the political and economic structure — but a revolution undercutting the very foundations of the *personal lives of the members of the people*."

The only other place in the Bible where Moses has again addressed God as "Lord of the Spirits" has been following the zealous unilateral act of Pinhas. Moses is now entreating God to choose as his successor one who will be sensitive to the needs and aspirations of each individual personality within the camp — a task, of course, which is humanly impossible! But it is a consideration which a new leader needs to hear! He needs to be reminded that he is a shepherd of myriads of individual souls all looking for him to provide them with material sustenance and spiritual purpose. As individual souls they will need to be joined together, molded together in common covenantal purpose with very specific common goals to be attained.

The Readiness for War

All these individual souls will be asked to risk their lives and the lives of their loved ones in order to realize their covenantal goals. They will not be prepared to undertake such risks if as individuals they don't feel singularly inspired and motivated for sacrifice. They will, for example, have to wage war. There will be no doubt that they will have to be prepared for military action because the religion they will be embodying — Judaism — will recognize that human conflict is a fact of human existence. A later sage, Yeshayahu Leibowitz, will explain that human conflict exists "because humanity lives in a world which is not fully sound." And the scars of the world not fully sound are the marks of the cruelty which Man often manifests to his fellow man. War, in other words, is a multiplication of the cruelties of a world not yet redeemed.

In later Jewish history the question will be posed: Is there a Jewish attitude towards war? It will be fair and necessary to say that if there is a normatively Jewish attitude towards war, it is certainly not pacifist. The Rambam condemns those Jews who seek solutions to their geopolitical problems in the study of astrology and other false wisdom. Instead they should study how to conduct warfare in order to prevail when forced into a military conflict.

On the other hand, it will also be fair and necessary to say that a normatively Jewish attitude does not look upon war as providing a sought-for heroic mystique. A nation — if it is sane and humane — will not look to make war. Thus when Moses sends Israel out to make war on the Midianites, such a war is considered justifiable only within the historic value-framework of the Bible, i.e., within the framework of a revelatory command. Normative Judaism ever since will not approve such a command except in clear self-defense.

Not that the war against the Midianites cannot be construed as a war of long-term self-defense! The commentators have pointed out that in chapter 31 there are two contrasting phrases in verses 1 and 3: In verse 1 the justification of the war on Midian is the "vengeance of Israel"; in verse 3 it is the "vengeance of the Lord." Rashi seeks to resolve the contrast with what might seem at first glance to be an unabashedly prideful comment: "He who stands opposed to Israel is as if he stands opposed to the Holy One Blessed Be He." Rashi has aligned himself with the *midrash* that has Moses pleading before the Lord on behalf of Israel: "If we were idolators or deniers of the *mitzvot*, the other peoples would not hate us or pursue us. They hate us and pursue us only because of the *Torah* and the *mitzvot* which you gave us. Therefore the vengeance which we execute is Your vengeance."

It is true that Rashi's comment will be construed in a later period of Jewish history as dangerously chauvinistic. Apologists will overlook, however, what history will have often taught the Jewish people — that in order to maintain its integrity as a people they will have to stand alone against those who would deny them directly or indirectly their right to that integrity.

Moses — along with the Children of Israel — has had to suffer the well-nigh successful attempt of the Midianites and the Moabites to destroy the Israelite camp from within. The dramatic story of Pinhas' execution of Zimri and Cozbi has underscored the extremity of the threat. And with it, a plague has been decimating the camp. Normative Judaism will thus refer to the wars of destruction of the Midianites, along with those against the Amalekites and the seven Canaanite nations as *milhamot mitzvah* (wars commanded by God) — wars deemed necessary by God Himself to protect the covenant. At the same time, later rabbinic legislation will determine that such wars are not to be repeated in a post-biblical era. This will not gainsay the historic facts, however, that the House of Israel will encounter throughout their historic journeys threats to their existence as great or greater than that of the Midianites.

In other words, the ethnocentricism of Moses and of Rashi needs no apologies. In discussing in the Book of Shemot aspects of the "chosen people" concept, we focused on the teachings of the medieval philosopher and poet Yehudah Halevi. We pointed out that in the eleventh century Yehudah Halevi offers comfort to his generation of the House of Israel caught politically, militarily, and religiously between two titanic masses of people fighting for hegemony in Spain and other parts of the world. Christianity and Islam will each have claimed ultimate truth and have arrogated to itself the exclusive right to offer salvation. Each will have amassed sufficient worldly power to offer empirical proof for its claim of suzerainty. Yehudah Halevi is faced with the basic motivational problem of how to maintain the morale of his quantitatively weak and beleaguered people. His *Kuzari* attempts through clearly ethnocentric means to focus on the spiritual and ethical superiority of Judaism and Jewish peoplehood. He cannot use any other nationalistically inspired therapeutic means except to see his people as the truly chosen by God.

Caught in the religio-ethnic "sandwich" between the giant "loaves" of Christianity and Islam, Israel will find its peculiar vulnerability tested again and again throughout its history. It will be trapped between accusations of being capitalists and communists, particularists and universalists, nationalists and cosmopolitans. Israel will at one time or another be despised by everyone. It will regularly conclude that if everyone stands against the people of Israel, Israel must be very "bad" — or very "good." But if Israel is very "bad," then its enemies throughout the ages must have been very "good." Yet the list of such "good" enemies would have to include the likes of Haman, Caligula, Nero, Torquemada, Stalin, and Hitler. Confronting such a list, greater credence would have to be given to the thought that indeed the enemies of Israel must perforce be the enemies of God!

The Lesson of the Two and One-Half Tribes

Indeed it would be Judaism and Jewish peoplehood that would insist on asserting its own unique identity and destiny in the face of the Pax Romana, the Pax Catholica, the Pax Fascistica, and the Pax Communistica, and any latter day attempt of international Islam to claim exclusive rights to dominate the world in the name of its Allah. Many of these battles would be waged by the Jews in exile, in positions of particular national weakness.

From Israel's biblical beginnings, sovereignty bespeaking national independence would be considered the sine qua non for national survival. It had been perceived as necessary in order to blunt the sharpness of the various imperialist attempts to submerge if not swallow up Judaism and Jewish separateness. Israel would be forced to surrender its sovereignty twice; yet through its prayers and dogged perseverance to survive as a corporate entity in whatever "exile" situation it found itself, it would continue to manifest its yearnings to be given another opportunity for sovereignty.

Because of its historic yearnings for sovereignty, Israel would look back to pre-sovereignty days in the Wilderness and note certain recalcitrant patterns of behavior even among those of the new generation as they stood on the verge of entering the Promised Land. The Torah would condemn any compromise with the idea that sovereignty on Israel's chosen Land had to be the goal. And it had to bind all the tribes to its implementation.

The *dor ha-midbar* (the Wilderness generation) has in its entirety virtually expired. The members of that generation will not enter, will not settle the Land. But their children will. Yet, even among these new Israelites, these who were not emancipated from slavery but were born in freedom, there seems to be some hesitancy. The tribes of Reuben and Gad announce their preference to remain in Transjordan where there appears to be greater material opportunity. Moses reacts by recalling the other great refusal — the refusal of the *meraglim* (spies). Moses addresses them with contempt: "And now you rise in order to take the place of the other refusers, you breed of sinful men; you've replaced your fathers and added still further to the Lord's wrath against Israel."

In a much later period reminiscent of the Wilderness — the early twentieth century — leading rabbis will hesitate to endorse the Zionist resurrection of the Land of Israel as a place for Jewish settlement. The then Lubavitcher Rebbe Yosef Yitzhak will visit the Ashkenazic chief rabbi of Eretz Yisrael in those pre-State days Avraham Yitzhak Hakohen Kook. The latter sage will ask the Lubavitcher directly whether or not he has been pushing his disciples to make *aliyah*. The Rebbe will not be able to say "yes" because he has been among those who are concerned *"shema yaldeihem yitkalkelu"* ("lest their disciples will become contaminated") here in the inchoate settlement of a newly reborn Israel.

Rav Kook then gives the following homily: "God forbid you to speak in such a manner. The Sages have said that because Moses and Aaron called the Israelites *'morim'* ('rebels') they were punished by not being permitted to bring Israel into the Promised Land. And furthermore the Rambam confirms this reason as does Isaiah who similarly denounced Israel by describing them as a people of impure lips. But now one should refer to Moses' use of the phrase *'tarbut anashim hata'im'* (breed of evil men) with which to describe the Reubenites and Gadites. Despite using such abusive words Moses was nevertheless *not* punished (even though he had been punished for a similar damnatory expression at the 'rock'). Why was he not punished here for his anger? Because here he was manifesting a righteous anger in thinking that the attitude of Reuben and Gad would impact on the other tribes and deter them from going up to Eretz Yisrael. For such anger, for such a 'sin' the scolder is not to be punished."

The word *tarbut*, which is appropriately translated "breed" as it introduces the phrase "evil men," appears only this one time in the Bible. Yet this word *tarbut* serves in modern Jewish history as the word for "culture." It is used at the onset of the modern enlightenment as a signal to Jews to open themselves up to a "breed" or "mixture" of other cultural influences. But here the one subject upon which Moses must have a unanimity of views, aspirations, and goals is settling the Promised Land. He will brook no excuses, no rationalizations, no further delays.

It is not just the reluctance of Reuben and Gad along with half the tribe of Menashe which is disconcerting. Moses feels that any hesitation on the part of any of the tribes at this time must be considered seditious. Moses pleads with these tribes not to take an action which will "turn the mind-hearts of the Children of Israel from crossing into the Land that the Lord has given..."

Because the threat to the morale of the people is so imminent, these two and a half tribes must be and will be forced into becoming "shock-troops at the instance of the Lord." They are to be *halutzim* (pioneers). Moses insists that any right of these two-and-a-half tribes to remain on the "wrong" side of the Jordan must be based on their readiness to go before their brethren in the fight for the Promised Land until they have done their share in assuring the victory. The word "pioneer" comes from the French, meaning foot soldier, usher, chess-pawn. The derivation of *halutz* in Hebrew, on the other hand, is from *haletz* meaning to remove oneself. In the case of the two and one half tribes, to be *halutz* is to step out ahead of everyone else, to lead the way, to be ready to face any dark eventuality in order to bring the new light and to inspire others to follow that light.

The two and one half tribes agree to serve as the pioneer shock-troops after building in Transjordan sheepfolds for their flocks and towns for their families. But they will not settle down in Transjordan until they have fought with their brethren to conquer the Promised Land to the west of the Jordan. In this mode Eldad defines a *halutz* as someone who leaves behind an inheritance and the quiet of established residence. He removes himself from a situation of relative security to one of relative danger. A *halutz* is not someone who has nothing, i.e., nothing to lose. He is one who does have what to lose, but he leaves it in order to perform a necessary function for his people. He returns to his home only when performing the function is no longer needed.

Nevertheless, despite the readiness of the two and one half tribes to serve as the vanguard of the conquest, the tradition will follow Moses in essentially condemning their separation from their brethren. The Rabbis will speak in the *Midrash Tanhuma* of three gifts which God in His creation has given the world: wisdom (*hokhmah*), strength (*gevurah*), and wealth (*osher*). If a human being has merited any one of them, let alone all of them, he has in effect merited everything — provided they are genuinely perceived as gifts from Heaven! The wisdom, strength, and wealth granted to the two and a half tribes are judged not to have been from Heaven, because had they been, the tribes would not have separated themselves from their brethren because of their flocks, etc., i.e., their wealth, their strength, their "wisdom."

The Rabbis' antipathy to the strategy of the two and a half tribes is underscored in the following homily: "There were two wise men in the world, an Israelite and a Gentile, Ahitophel and Balaam. Both were destroyed. There were two strong men in the world, an Israelite and a Gentile, Samson and Goliath. Both were destroyed. There were two wealthy men in the world, an Israelite and a Gentile, Korah and Haman. Both were destroyed. Why? Because the gifts which they took pride in, they had not 'received' from the Holy One Blessed Be He. They had seized these gifts for themselves. Similarly the two and a half tribes were wealthy, in possession of great flocks. They loved their money and their power. Their 'wisdom' recommended that they remain outside the Land. Such 'wisdom' proved that their gifts had not been given to them by God. Therefore it was they who were exiled first from among all the tribes, as it is written in I Chronicles 5:26: 'And the God of Israel stirred up the spirit of Pul king of Assyria, and the spirit of Tillagath-pilneser king of Assyria, and he carried them away, even the Reubenites, and the Gadites, and the half-tribe of Menashe…' And what brought this catastrophe about? Because they had separated themselves from the camp."

The prophet Jeremiah will summarize the biblical attitude towards wisdom, strength, and wealth gotten through exclusively human initiative (9:22): "Thus said the Lord: 'Let not the wise man glory in his wisdom; let not the strong man glory in his strength; let not the rich man glory in his riches. But only in this should one glory: in his earnest devotion to Me. For I the Lord act with kindness, justice, and equity in the Land; for in these I delight.'"

To please the Lord, in short, one must reach the Land, conquer it from its dissolute idolatrous inhabitants, settle it, and begin to build a society based on kindness, justice, and equity. To resist this agenda by remaining geographically close but as spectators from the wrong side of the border will incur the severest of punishments: exile!

Again — the Vows

Thus the bitterness of the Wilderness has not been completely exorcised from the collective consciousness of the new generation of Israelites, those who will have the merit of entering and inheriting the Land. Even at this threshold juncture, not all the tribes are truly ready. Not every individual is ready — certainly not individuals among the two and one-half tribes. The vows of such individuals are suspect; for having come so far, they still prefer *galut*, even if it is a geographically close *galut*.

The significance of these individual vows will become the focal point of Jewish liturgical concern henceforth throughout later Jewish history. As indicated earlier, on the night of the solemn holy Yom Kippur (Day of Atonement), each Jew will re-enact his own association with the Wilderness experience — whether he will know it or not. The folk-spirit of the House of Israel will set aside at the beginning of this Yom Kippur a legal formula that will serve as a *hattarat nedarim* (a dispensation of vows). It will be preceded by a legal invocation bringing together, as it were, the heavenly court and the earthly court. In other words, at such a moment of high solemnity each member of the House of Israel will be praying (1) with faith in God's "heavenly" empathy for His covenanted partner Israel, and (2) with joy in the presence of the "earthly" community of fellow Jews. Concluding the invocation will be a declaration made by every worshiper that he is hereby permitted to pray among those who have sinned.

Which vows are being spoken about? They are utterly serious vows because the biblical quotations accompanying the legal formulas are from the most critical episodes in the Wilderness. In particular they refer to the decisive sin of the spies who led their people into questioning the entire destiny of this covenantal enterprise that was to take a slave rabble out of Egypt into the Promised Land. In this Yom Kippur liturgy, the legal formula — the *Kol Nidre* — the dispensation of vows serves as an expression of God's mercy. Within such a liturgical moment, however, quoting for all later generations passages from the Wilderness episode is sobering because that generation will have always been given the less than flattering epithet *dor ha-midbar* (Wilderness generation).

Yet, the purpose of this liturgical moment is to focus precisely on each member of the House of Israel. It is to probe each member's soul and psyche as if he is still a member of the *dor ha-midbar*, whether of those who came out of Egypt or of those who would enter Canaan or of those like the two and a half tribes who would come close but would desist. Standing with the sinners, who is the individual if not himself a sinner? For on Yom Kippur, the night of vow-dispensation, each one has to question his own pretence at righteousness, let alone his own awareness of his sins. And each one in the presence of celestial and terrestrial judges, as it were, is in essence judging himself. If he is destined in the coming year to break a vow of a trivial nature before God, then he knows that there is merciful dispensation, forgiveness. But if, God forbid, the individual member of the House of Israel, the latter day member of the *dor ha-midbar* should break the all-important vow, the oath given through the covenant at Sinai, then there can be no dispensation, no forgiveness.

The Eternal Zionist Vow

Historically, there is added weight given by the House of Israel to the original covenantal vow made at Sinai by means of the agreement sworn to at the first *Shivat Tziyon* (Return to Zion) by the Babylonian exiles under Ezra and Nehemiah. As has been stressed before, the new agreement promulgated by the first *Shavei Tziyon* (returnees to Zion) is the *amanah* (the affirmation) called for in chapter 10 verse 1 of the Book of Nehemiah: "Despite everything we — Israel — a new generation — have returned to take up again our covenantal destiny." This renewal made at a time when unlike Sinai, God is in eclipse, becomes a paradigm for all later commitments made by Jews throughout the generations. In essence, the Jew is stating that if in any way he weakens in his contemporary resolve to fulfill the vows, the oaths, the promises, the commitments, which he has made to the God of Israel and to the People of Israel concerning the covenant — including fundamentally the attachment to the Land of Israel — there can be no dispensation; there will be no forgiveness.

Throughout the ages the Jew will stand in prayer on the most awesome night of the year with a stark sense of the Wilderness surrounding him if the Land of Israel is distant from his consciousness. He reviews his status, his determination to commit himself to the well-being of the Land of Israel. He is like a latter-day soldier in the army of Israel who at a swearing-in ceremony marking the end of his training period will be asked to shout to the court-on-high and to the world below *"Ani nishba"* ("I swear")! That oath forces the Wilderness to recede in the face of a new Godly-human encounter rendered possible by a land of Canaan ready after the long exile to be subdued and rebuilt as the Land of Israel and the modern State of Israel.

Mas'ei מסעי

The Book of Numbers is a severe book. It is a frightening book. Among the five books of the Torah it is the most frightening. The principal reason for its severe and frightening quality is that it is a book full of crushing disappointment. God is disappointed in His people whom He has chosen for greatness. He will have to wait for the new generation. Moses as God's deputy is disappointed in having failed to anticipate or forestall the catastrophe of the spies' mission and its adverse consequences. The full weight of the disappointment falls on the Children of Israel themselves who have permitted the spies to lead them astray in rejecting their destiny as God has projected it for them. And so they have been sentenced to death in the Wilderness. Such an eventuality has condemned them to an unrelieved despair.

As we read this concluding portion of the Book of Numbers — the Book of Disappointment — is there nothing positive which can be said of the *dor ha-midbar* (the Wilderness generation)? After all, can it not be granted that despite its failures, the generation of the Wilderness did bring the new generation to the threshold of redemption. And this is hardly a small matter! The commentator Sforno on the opening words of the portion "These were the stations of the Children of Israel..." says: "The Lord wanted to have all the stations of Israel recorded in order to make known the virtue of that Wilderness generation which had followed Him through that unseeded land in a way that should have made them worthy to enter the Promised Land."

In other words, as guilty as they were, there is a virtue to be found in the generation of the Wilderness. They did prepare the way. It may be said that one way or other, good or bad, one generation always prepares the way for the next generation. It reminds one again of Bialik's epic poem *"Metei Midbar"* ("The Dead of the Wilderness"). As we've indicated earlier, the poem is based on the legend that this original stiff-necked generation may have perished in the Wilderness by the decree of God; but they lie petrified in a secret nook somewhere in the Sinai Peninsula ready to be restored to life and to full vigor. Bialik (Maurice Samuel's translation) describes them as an army in deep deep slumber. Yet "Strong are their faces and burnished and darkened to bronze are their eyelids.... Yet though the hammer of time beats long and unceasing upon them; Like to the stone that enfolds it, the strength of their hearts sleeps forever."

The hammer of history that will see the Children of Israel hobble through a "wilderness" of endless exile will strike once too often, however. It will thereupon awaken the hearts of these *Metei Midbar* from their "eternal" slumber to a new possibility, to a new opportunity...

Passages and Stations

In the earlier discussion on the portion of *Shelah Lekha*, I asked: "Why is Bialik interested in the Dead of the Wilderness?" I stated there: "These 'Metei Midbar' had a certain strength, call it pride, which was aroused upon hearing God's devastating decree. They *had* escaped from Egypt, they *had* defeated Amalek." Then, granted, they had hesitated, they had reconsidered, they had resisted, they let themselves be talked into denying their destiny, and were condemned. But according to Bialik they were not totally defeated! The Torah text itself has them defying the decree by going up "presumptuously" (*ha'apalah*) to fight the Amalekites and the Canaanites — and losing. But Bialik in 1902 sees the "Dead of the Wilderness," this Jewish people asleep in stony silent exile for 1,800 years, coming alive someday soon!

In his epic poem Bialik resurrects the dead army of the House of Israel and has them proclaim to the universe: "We are the mighty, the last generation of enslaved, the first to be redeemed!"

Bialik presents us with an ambivalent picture of a great people asleep, but with tremendous power ready to explode with the creative energy of revolution. Sforno has sensed this energy in his comment on the words "These were the stations of Israel..." This in fact will be the twentieth-century story — "the last generation of enslaved, the first to be redeemed."

Enslavement and redemption will have been the fundamental national-tribal myth of the Children of Israel ever since Joseph's rise to power in Egypt. His story and the story of his brothers served to bring to a close the period of the patriarchs and their individual conflicts, failures, and successes. But

Jacob's insistence upon Joseph taking an oath to bring his father's remains back to the Promised Land for burial was more than a hint that Abraham's original "Covenant of the Pieces" was to be realized: enslavement for a lengthy period followed by redemption.

A larger myth is being played out as well. It is the primordial myth of God's creation and the Garden of Eden. The American writer Stephen Crane will describe a Godless morally neutral universe: "A man said to the universe, 'Sir, I exist!' The universe replied: 'Well, well, the fact that you exist has not created in me a sense of obligation.'" The primordial biblical myth comes along to argue that the universe and human life within that universe would be *tohu va-vohu* (chaos) if not for God's singular illumination: *"yehi or"* (let there be light). The myth insists that there be in this morally-neutral, seemingly anti-human universe an explanation for living as a human being. There must be a purpose, a destiny, a meaning to existence. And so the Bible tells a story from *"yehi or"* until *"eilei mas'ei benei Yisrael"* (these are the stations at which the Children of Israel have stopped). This story reflects the comprehensive Jewish vision, a vision that begins with Eden, continues with the journey, circuitous as it may be, arriving at settlement of the Promised Land and culminating in a Messianic era at the end of time.

This concluding portion of the Book of Ba-Midbar is appropriately entitled *"Mas'ei"* meaning "stations" or "passages." There is a long list of stations which the Children of Israel have passed through during the forty years in the Wilderness on their way to the Promised Land. Rashi asks: "Why are all these stations mentioned?" He answers: "To make known the kind acts of the Lord, that although He had decreed that they were condemned to wander in the Wilderness for forty years one should not conclude that they had no points of rest." And these points of rest, these stations, make up the foci of the ongoing story of Israel — even in the "wilderness" beyond the Wilderness. This ongoing story of Israel — this history of the people enables them to keep striving within what otherwise would be a cold and indifferent universe.

The Midrash provides an analogy in which a king has a son who has been ill. The king has taken him to a distant place to find a cure. Presumably the cure is found; but on the way back the father counts all the stations at which they had stopped and recounts the conditions of the illness prevailing at each station, e.g., here we caught cold, here your head ached, etc. The analogy may not be perfect in that the Israelites are not physically going back to their original starting point, which would be Egypt. They are reviewing in their collective mind-heart the places in the Wilderness at which they have camped. But the analogy does recognize enslavement as the sickness and recalls all the stations at which the patient Israel endured, suffered, found relief, and ultimately would be freed from the sickness. For Israel would eventually find its way to the health-giving borders of its home. And it would be a home with specified borders so that it would be clear where exile ended and where home began.

Rashi and the Midrash are saying in simple terms what the entire Torah says with the broadest possible strokes: there is a story full of passages, the Israelite-Jewish story, with passages leading to stations for rest. And the stations for rest provide the opportunity for reflection. The reflection chiefly entails the review of one's story, one's history. Lionel Trilling, speaking of the revolutionary mode of reflection in the Bible, has said: "In the beginning... a beginning implies an end, with something in the middle to connect them. The beginning is not merely the first of a series of events; it is the event that originates those that follow. And the end is not merely the ultimate event, the cessation of happening; it is a significance or at least the promise, dark or bright of a significance. The task is not told by an idiot but by a rational consciousness which perceives in things the processes that are their reason and which derives from this perception a principle of conduct, a way of living among things." Israel's review of its passages and stations lends the very Wilderness of their forty-year wandering a significance!

A Sacred Story

Rashi and the Midrash are saying something in addition which is clearly reflected in the midrashic analogy of the king and his son the prince. The parent and child go through life. They meet trials and sickness in their search for a *refu'ah* (cure). God is the *rofei* (physician) who will accompany Israel the child and patient through a history of external threats which turn into afflictions as well as internal tumult that tear down resolve, motivation, determination to carry on with covenantal concern.

Jeremiah will diagnose the internal affliction within his people as he lives and prophesies at a time when the story is on the brink of a tragic dénouement — one of several in Jewish history. In chapter 2:13 he agonizes over his people's shortcomings: "For my people have done a twofold wrong: they have forsaken Me, the fountain of living waters, and hewed them out cisterns, broken cisterns, which cannot even hold water." According to the commentator Radak, a fountain of living waters has two advantages over a cistern, especially a broken one. First, the fountain doesn't need to be replenished with water from other sources; secondly, the very image of the fountain giving forth a constant stream of water is an image of unbroken continuity.

Because an essential part of the redemptive process has been the telling and retelling of the Israelite story, God has assumed that the "fountain of living waters" that is their story will not need any other external stimuli to motivate them to continue. Even the tragedy of the enslavement has been made part of a story which ends in redemption. It had been predicted to Abraham that there would be a part of the story which would be subsumed in darkness. But as early as Abraham the darkness was shown to be part of a story of ultimate illumination.

In the Book of Job (3:20–26) there is an image of unbearable suffering which leaves no room for redemptive light: "Why is light given to the sufferer and life to embittered souls who long for death — but it comes not. For the fear I had has come upon me, and what I dreaded has overtaken me. I have no ease, no peace, no rest. What has come is agony!" But unlike this image from the life of Job, the suffering and fear and denial of ease, peace, and rest which has characterized the enslavement of Israel will have ended. Redemption is at hand! The story, therefore, underscores again and again the reality of redemption, the neutralizing of the bitterness of the enslavement.

And so the stations in the Wilderness, even and especially the ones that recall collective pain, suffering, defeat, disappointment, and frustration will also be listed within a context of redemptive advance — forty years of it. And, in keeping with the story, Israel will be rewarded, as Isaiah will prophesy: "The arid desert shall be glad, the wilderness shall rejoice and shall blossom like a rose. It shall blossom abundantly, and rejoice, even with joy and singing."

To speak of a story should not be misconstrued as the telling of a story with the same dimensions as any other story. The story of Israel — at least as far as the Bible's view considers it — is to be a sacred story. The Rambam says: "...for the sake of future generations. At the time, it was obvious that Israel's existence for forty years in a Wilderness which was infested with wild beasts and lacked natural resources was a miracle by God. But in the course of time, people might be led to believe that the places in which Israel dwelt in the Wilderness were either near to inhabited regions — such as are now inhabited by Bedouins — or that the places themselves contained food and water sufficient for the maintenance of Israel's population. It was necessary to name all these places for later generations to know they were not inhabited and did not contain natural resources."

The thrust of Rambam's comment is to assert the "reality" of God's miracles. But the more profound underlying message is that the Children of Israel are bidden to discover a new way of looking at all of reality. The instruction in the *Ethics of the Fathers* that one is to know whence he has come and to where he is going and before Whom he will have to give a reckoning is a positing of a sacred reality as the existential substructure of one's view of the universe.

The very idea of history is a biblical idea. Time is to be defined in terms of mutability. The world as reality is not to be seen as an infinitely repeating mechanism but as an unfolding process. And the process offers a concept of destiny. Life has meaning for it has direction. But the idea of sacred history adds to the idea of history and its ramifications the concepts of responsibility and accountability. The Vilna Gaon will answer the question: Why a *din veheshbon* (an account and a reckoning)? When a man sins he has done two terrible things: the commission of the sin itself and his failure instead to utilize that moment for doing good. He therefore has to give account for the commission of the crime and a reckoning for failing to do good.

Israel will see itself as surviving with a special sense of dignity precisely because of its sense of history modified to become sacred history. And the sacred history entails God's supervising that history only to the extent that Israel accepts its responsibility and accountability as partners in that history.

Moses has been able to generate among the people a sense of sacred history which their ancestors had had, but which the enslavement in Egypt had caused the Children of Israel to forget. We may picture Moses upon his return to Egypt from Midian after many years of living out a bucolic existence as a shepherd. He has been inspired to action by the revelation at the "burning bush." He gathers the Israelite elders about him in order to share with them a message of redemption. We may surmise that he reviews with them the material of the saga which today make up the contents of the Book of Genesis. He speaks of the creation of the world and the deluge and Noah and the selection of Abram and the passing of the covenantal blessing to Isaac and then to Jacob. He recalls for them undoubtedly the events that led to the descent of the Children of Israel into Egypt. He describes the career of Joseph, the economic success of Joseph's brothers and their descendants in Goshen. And then he reminds them of the new king who arose "who did not know Joseph…." Moses is reminding them that they are an integral part of a sacred history.

Moses is the ideal person to teach them about their sacred history. For, whereas in slavery they were incapable of imagining a narrative progression leading to their current plight, Moses, on the other hand, had always been a free man. And, as a free man, he had had a narrative — an Egyptian narrative.

From the outset, Moses had been a free man, having grown up as a prince in a sovereign Egyptian empire. Having experienced freedom, he would never allow himself to become a slave. He would not be able to tolerate others being enslaved. Once he realized that he was a Hebrew, an Israelite, even though these Hebrews, these Israelites, were slaves, he would not allow himself to become a slave when he joined them — certainly not in his own mind. But moreover, whatever Egyptian narrative, story, history he had digested as a youth in Pharaoh's palace, at the "burning bush" he had summarized for him another narrative — the story or history of his Hebrew-Israelite ancestors. As a free Hebrew-Israelite he would now be ready, able, and willing to inspire within the Israelite slave community this new/old story, a new/old story *for them* with its central illuminating theme a vision of freedom — a sacred vision of freedom.

Learning the National Story

But what is a sacred vision of freedom if not an autobiographical story written with sacred dimensions. The slaves have forgotten their story and have certainly lost touch with the sacred. Moses restores their story, but can only do it as part of a process of emancipation. The content of their emancipation is the sacred story and the sacred promise within the story. Without their story, the reminder of their history, their freedom would be mute.

The slaves would certainly not have understood what freedom might be without their story. After the Exodus, whenever Moses to his consternation sees the Children of Israel backsliding into despair, yearning to escape their destiny, what does he do — what can he do — but repeat the story, their sacred story. When they have conquered the Promised Land and Joshua seeks to renew the covenant with Israel at Shekhem, he similarly inserts as a haunting preamble to the ceremony a review of the sacred story.

Later students of comparative religion, mythology, literature, and cultural anthropology will understand what Moses and Israel have undertaken to create as they have moved from a situation of enslavement to redemption. They will understand that a story provides meaning to the human condition. Without the story, there would be fantasmagoric illusion or lifeless abstraction, but no living, pulsating, human striving. Man must have a story. For this reason Man is a myth-making animal and a myth-sharing animal. He invents stories because he refuses to live with and accept the possible incomprehensibility of his own existence. His imagination thereupon structures amenable or idealized relationships between himself and God, between himself and members of his family and tribe, between his tribe or nation and other nations.

To speak in terms of "invention" should not suggest that the myth-maker or author or storyteller is not using the stuff of reality. He is, wherever possible, subjugating that stuff of reality — names, places, events, memories, dreams, ideas — to a form which will have aesthetic delight and moral inference. The myth or story or saga becomes familiar to a given myth-sharing community. Its familiarity not only speaks *to* them but more and more speaks *for* them. It identifies them as a distinct community. And the more familiar, the more definitive of the community the myth or story becomes, the more critical a role it plays in building the social, psychological, and meta-ethical substructure upon which each individual person within the community stands.

Moses reminds the Children of Israel that they are connected to the very creation of the universe; that all humanity is so connected. Yet somehow the revelation of God to their patriarchs, Abraham, Isaac, and Jacob serves the Children of Israel in particular as a center-point of a circle. It is a circle of imaginatively structured sacred experiences whirling back in time to the creation of Eden and expulsion from it, and thrusting forward to enslavement on the way to a new humanly cultivated "Eden" called the Promised Land.

Moses has hoped that all the slaves will become so imbued with the story at its beginning — that beginning which has God creating a single human being in His image — that each single human descendant of the first human being will experience the built-in majesty of creation. The entire House of Israel will have by this time appropriated the story of the Patriarchs and the Exodus and the Sinai revelation so that each newborn will be initiated into the common fellowship of the story. Because of God's decree forbidding everyone except Joshua and Caleb of the slave generation from entering the Promised Land, no one of the new generation will have participated in the Exodus; yet everyone of this new generation will feel *as if* he indeed was there and *as if* he himself came out. The ritual *seder* of *Pesah* will place within the consciousness of every later Jew that sublimely transporting *as if.*

Similarly, all the stations in Jewish history will serve as permanent guideposts for the integration of later Jews into the sacred story of Israel. The sacred story — with each enforcing station, be it triumphal or tragic — develops a mythic power. For myths are the abstracted residue of all the happenings which the House of Israel will have sensed as recurrent in different guises. The rabbinic idea of *ma'aseh avot siman la-banim* (that which happens to one generation is a sign for the next or later generation) places in axiomatic form the idea that actual happenings may never occur the same way twice, but a pattern repeats itself often enough for it to become part of the group subconscious. An overriding pattern of enslavement, emancipation, empowerment through a covenant of redemption will seize the mind and collective psyche of all future descendants of the Israelites.

The covenantal story which will reinvent or recycle or reinterpret the given events of a particular era will enable the community or nation of Israel to survive with a sense of proud continuity. An Ezekiel will sustain the collective mythic truth of Jewish history by refusing to accept the death of his people following the destruction of the First Temple and the loss of sovereignty. The "dry bones" dare not mean that all hope is lost. Even exile, i.e., a new enslavement, following upon the loss of sovereignty cannot be the end of the story of the Jewish people. There will be, if necessary, a resurrection from the dead in order to restore hope and will lead to the realization of that hope in the first *Shivat Tziyon* ("return to Zion").

Always "Shivat Tziyon"

But Ezra and Nehemiah, who follow upon Ezekiel's and Jeremiah's and Second Isaiah's comforting forecasts, will not be able to sustain the mythic truth that is the repeatable saga if not for the fact that the group of Israelites who before them have made up the community, the tribe, the nation, have developed a tradition which now has its own pedagogic momentum. In the exile they may find themselves discouraged, despondent, and even depressed. But there are enough of the faithful who will never lose the vision by which they live and work and pray. They will pass on the tradition by which even during the long exile leading up to modern times the House of Israel will sustain its hope that a second *Shivat Tziyon* is possible.

It will not only be possible but it will happen. And it will happen after a cataclysm which even the starkest predictions of the Torah and the Prophets will have been incapable of imagining. The depth of the cataclysm, however, will be matched by the height of apocalyptic joy when the second *Shivat Tziyon* comes to pass. The story of Israel will always feature as both background and foreground the threshold of Eretz Yisrael waiting to be crossed, insisting that it can be crossed and will be crossed! And it will be crossed with covenantal expectations! The words of Torah insist upon it…

DEVARIM

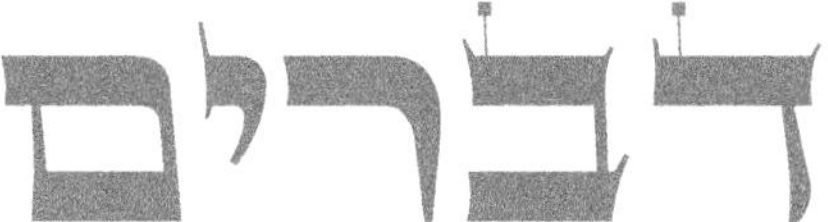

Commitment to Mending Reality

Arnold Schoenberg's tragic opera *Moses und Aron* ends with Moses lamenting his apparent failure to communicate. For his last words in the opera are "das Wort, das Wort, das Wort," as if anticipating the Christian scriptural verse "In the beginning was the word." What words can Moses find? And does he need words, new words? He may have once characterized himself as *lo ish devarim anokhi* ("I am not a man of words"). But he has since received the words of the Torah. He *has* the words: *"Eileh ha-devarim"* ("These are the words"). And they are matchless words.

It is said that Schoenberg had another act to compose; that the second act dominated by the "Golden Calf" apostasy was not meant to be the end with Moses searching for "the word." Had Schoenberg's artistic sensibility been more attuned to the Torah he might have had Moses not just looking for "the word," but for "the deed." The Book of Bamidbar dominated by another even greater apostasy — the sin of the spies — does have another "act" with which to neutralize the shadows cast by the dire events surrounding the fate of the *dor ha-midbar* (the Wilderness generation). It is the Book of Devarim — the Book of Word-Deeds.

The Ramban offers a preface to his commentary on Deuteronomy: "Before embarking on his final review of the Torah, Moses begins by scolding them and reminding them of their sins — how they rebelled in the Wilderness. Yet also of how the Holy One Blessed Be He behaved towards them according to His attribute of mercy. And this to inform them of His eternal grace towards them lest any one among them might feel that because the Book of Kohelet states that there is no human being who doesn't sin — and they have sinned — none of them will be able to enter and possess the Land. For God's attribute of justice will condemn them to perdition!" But no, contends the Ramban: "Moses our teacher informs them that the Holy One Blessed Be He is full of compassion for them because pardon and forgiveness come from Him just as assistance and support will be given to all human beings who worship Him."

The Book of Devarim thus serves a tri-partite purpose. It insists first of all on a review of all the wrongdoings of the Children of Israel. This anticipates a teaching of Martin Buber who will say: "Man is the being who is capable of becoming guilty and is capable of illuminating his guilt." The people must appreciate the indispensable therapeutic function of the statement: "We were wrong, we erred, we sinned." The people must feel the responsibility of looking into its own collective soul or psyche in order to expose the evil there and then to expunge it. How? By remembering their sinful deeds, reviewing them, examining them, and then condemning them. *Eileh ha-devarim* (These are the word-deeds) which Moses will use to elicit the collective confession.

Secondly, therefore, the Children of Israel must not lose faith in themselves that they will be deserving of the appropriate words of comfort. God is, before all and after all, merciful. He recognizes that Man is only Man. In plain terms it means that the people of Israel have the opportunity to turn — to start again, to try again. This will become the very essence and meaning of the collective Jewish refusal to die in the face of exile, to refuse to die, as it were, in the face of death itself.

Finally, and in as much detail as possible, Moses will attempt to sketch for his people a sociomoral program — not just of words but of deeds — which will actualize what the experience at Sinai has postulated as a covenantal relationship between God as Creator-Revealer-Redeemer and the people of Israel. *Eileh ha-devarim* (These are the word-deeds) refer to the laws, the statutes, the normative acts by which the Children of Israel are to build their society in the Promised Land. If they mean to worship God sincerely, committedly, then they will understand the necessity of legislating a sociomoral order for every aspect of what is intended to be a collective organic life-experience.

Devarim

Jewish liturgical history will determine that one of the bitterest rebukes given by a prophet to his own people is chapter one of the Book of Isaiah. This chapter is read on the Shabbat before Tisha B'Av (the day set aside as Israel's day of national mourning) which is also the Shabbat on which the portion of *Devarim* is read. It is a brutal self-criticism; its self-flagellation is withering. Is there another people which will expose itself to such an annual orgy of self-incrimination? This notorious first chapter of Isaiah sees Israelite society — of a later period, of course — entirely sick, "from head to foot, no spot is sound, all bruises and welts, and festering sores..." And God — as reported by Isaiah — is offended especially by the hypocrisy of so-called "religious behavior" as a mask for social degeneracy.

But before this *haftarah* portion of Isaiah is read on *Shabbat Hazon Yeshayahu*, Moses' testimony in the Torah portion of *Devarim* is heard. And Moses is teaching Torah! The absorption of this Torah of Moses will enable Israel to endure the later critiques of Isaiah, Hosea, Amos, and the other prophets. Israel will even "welcome" the prophetic rebukes as a necessary therapeutic tool for correcting its sociomoral failures as a people. Moses is now reviewing Israel's history, Israel's story — and glory — because it is *their* story. And even though Moses — as Isaiah and the other prophets — will be "cruel" in their relentless scolding, their love for their people will never be in doubt. For the Children of Israel will hold to the proposition that a people that is sensitive to its own prophetic voices will be worthy of carrying God's ensign to mend the world.

Moses' Summary Teaching

With the opening of the Book of Deuteronomy, Moses is using the opportunity to recall the sins of the people. He chooses this opportunity as the

Israelites stand on the threshold of the Promised Land. He is speaking to the few remaining members of the old generation that had sinned; but he is addressing principally the new, bronzed, eager, younger generation. And he is saying to them: People, you stand on the threshold of a new situation. You are being given the opportunity to build a new society. You have been given a Godly task. As Jews, God has selected you to be a model of ethical sanctity for the rest of the world. This task is as momentously serious a task as any group has ever been given. Whether or not you will be able to fulfill this task will depend not only upon your ability to remember and appreciate the significance of certain achievements in your past. It will also depend upon your capacity to acknowledge and to learn from your mistakes of that past.

Undergirding Moses' admonitions — as the Ramban has noted — is God's basic readiness to forgive Israel's mistakes, to show eternal grace to a people when it errs. God's attribute of mercy is the necessary correlate of His attribute of justice. Mercy is necessary because ever since Eden God knows that the human being whom He has created is not only physically vulnerable but morally fragile. It may be said that God's understanding of humanity requires that He have an utterly serious *sense of humor.*

It is that serious sense of humor which lies behind the piquant talmudic tale of Elijah appearing to a rabbi in the market place. The rabbi asks Elijah: "Who among the men now present in the market place are destined for Paradise?" Elijah points to two jesters, two clowns, men of no learning and small piety, whose great claim to immortality is that in difficult days they bring a smile to the faces of the distressed. Moreover, it is said that when they see two people quarrelling they strive hard to make peace between them.

Why jesters and clowns should be considered worthy of nothing less than immortality can be found in their capacity to make people laugh at human frailties, fallibilities, and pretentiousness. The particular trait of pretentiousness shows itself in sundry forms of idolatry, of which the most treacherous is self-idolatry. The Book of Devarim consisting of Moses' concluding addresses to his people is hardly a humorous book. But buttressing the high seriousness of purpose is the mocking polemic against any form of idolatry. The idea of a covenant between God and a particular people which will be the eternal iconoclast, the persistent jester poking fun at other peoples' vanities, places a burden of self-criticism upon Israel which Moses can only pray that the people will fully fathom.

The idea that covenantal legislation will have to pervade every aspect of individual, social, civic, and national life will demand constant vigilance to assure renewable application of spiritual and moral standards. The tension produced by such a demand will be reminiscent of the ancient Greek philosopher Heraclitus' bon mot: "One cannot pass twice through the same stream." One of the philosopher's disciples then sharpens the thrust of the bon mot: "One cannot do it even once." The disciple is surely not trying to outwit his teacher. What both the master and the disciple are emphasizing, however, is the "mad rush" of life. One who thinks he can easily duplicate an act of commitment in a new situation which may call for a revised application of a standard must remember that it is indeed like passing through a stream. To commit oneself to God's commands requires enormous strength of will to examine and re-examine every new situation. For, like flowing water, every situation is indeed new and demands renewed examination.

Moses' Deuteronomic addresses are the message of a leader who has in effect already passed the scepter of executive leadership to another. The Midrash gives a vivid description of Moses and Joshua the chosen successor arriving at the *Ohel Mo'ed* (the Tent of Meeting). The pillar of cloud descends and separates Moses from Joshua, so that only the latter can enter and receive God's word. When the pillar of cloud is dissipated, Moses questions Joshua: "What did God say to you?" Joshua's curt answer is the appropriate answer under the new circumstances: "When God's word was revealed to you, was I apprised of it?" At this point Moses cries out: "O one hundred deaths rather than let me show any envy!"

Nevertheless, Moses is still the teacher. In Judaism he is Moshe Rabbenu, the archetypal teacher, the supreme religio-moral authority and inspiration. He is lecturing before the House of Israel — the *entire* House of Israel, those who are with him on the Plains of Moab, and all the generations that will follow. He is talking to the Children of Israel as a collective and at the same time he is reaching out to each individual Israelite.

He begins his "*Eileh ha-devarim*" with a lament — the traditional interjection of woe: "Eikha!" (How!) "How can I bear unaided the trouble of you, the burden, and the bickering!" This traditional *eikha* will be repeated by Isaiah in his later castigation of Jerusalem: "*Eikha*, she has become a harlot, the faithful city, that was filled with justice, where righteousness dwelt — but now murderers." It will be repeated by Jeremiah in his later elegy over the destruction of Jerusalem and Judah: "*Eikha*, lonely sits the city once great with people! She that was great among nations is become like a widow; the princess among states is become a thrall."

But grounding the three *eikha*'s of Moses, Isaiah, and Jeremiah is a fourth *eikha*. This fourth *eikha* is, in biblical fact, the original *eikha* which was God's poignant call to Adam: "*Ayeka!*" For if Israel is destined to fall short and as a result to degenerate into corruption with exile the disastrous climax, does its predicament not extend back to the original *ayeka* — that which calls out to the guilt-ridden individual sinner and which portends the sinner's exile from his primordial Garden of blessedness?

Moses' *eikha*, emerging as it does from the depths of his own depression with the Wilderness generation, is an anticipatory *eikha* for the later ones of Isaiah and Jeremiah. If Israel means to settle a land and to build it according to terms mandated by the covenant, of necessity it will have to develop the art and discipline of self-criticism. This self-criticism will be in the name of sociomoral exemplariness. This process can only take place collectively if each individual Israelite considers himself permanently addressed by the covenant and therefore permanently response-able to its terms. Each individual Israelite, vigilant in the name of the covenant, will be called upon to exert more than normal effort in building the requisite society.

Should the individual fail in his effort — or worse, avoid making the effort — then that which Isaiah will lament will certainly befall the Land of Israel and the people of Israel. For the internal quality of life will have imitated Sodom; and the fate of Sodom is a universal by-word for darkness, destruction — and extinction. Isaiah may be indulging in prophetic hyperbole when he accuses the Israelites of being no better than "officers of Sodom and Gemorrah." But such hyperbole will always be the underside of the later teaching that it is not enough for this covenanted people to apply merely normal modes of conduct in society. Where possible, behavior must aim at *lifnim mi-shurat ha-din* (beyond the strict line of the law). In other words, supererogatory behavior by definition may be considered above what normal human beings should be expected to do. Nevertheless, the terms of the covenant insist that supererogatory behavior should be the goal wherever possible.

The result of the failure of God's *ayeka* to break through the corrosive wall of stiff-neckedness will be the destruction of the First Temple and the loss of the covenanted First Commonwealth. Jeremiah's *"eikha"* will then become the millennial dirge of the Jewish people over their loss of "Eden." Not that Jerusalem or the First Commonwealth was ever expected to be Eden. Ever since Eden and the later Deluge God was willing to compromise with humankind. He would narrow His concerns. He would lower His expectations. And so He had arrived at His choice of Abraham and Abraham's future descendants. He would establish a covenant with them, a covenant which, it is true, would make demands. But these demands, spiritual, moral, social, and political, would take cognizance of the unredeemed world in which this covenanted people would have to maneuver. For this reason, the prescribed legislative constitution for this people, the Torah, would of necessity be *lo bashamayim* (not in Heaven) but on earth, i.e., an achievable mode of living on earth with spiritual and moral dignity.

The Ultimate Threat: Exile

As Moses stands before his people in what he knows is his last opportunity to influence them, the four *eikha*s are very much a part of his pedagogic agenda. Like any parent he is anxious about his children's future. He dreads the results of possible covenantal failure — what Isaiah and Jeremiah will witness. Yet he knows how stubborn and recalcitrant this people can be. They have already shown it. They have been rebellious from the beginning. Even unparalleled glories such as the victory at the Sea of Reeds and the revelation at Mount Sinai — *the* Revelation — will not have precluded an immediate round of murmuring and complaining. Moses had even been subjected to their absurd yearnings to return to what was certainly an impossible alternative — the imagined womb of Egypt, a womb of bondage and national demise. Moses had had to endure the sacrilege of their accusing God of hating them and showing his hatred by taking them out of Egypt!

Previous blasphemies and other errors aside, however, a new generation of Israelites — unlike the *dor ha-midbar* — has been charged with moving ahead to the Promised Land. This new generation is primed for it, is enthusiastic for it. But Moses has no illusions that human nature allows for a total alteration of tribal, national, and individual character. Moses is deeply concerned that unless there is a true awakening to the *ayeka* which Sinai — not Eden — has proclaimed, even this generation and their descendants will fall short of carrying the covenantal burden successfully. As will become apparent in Moses' prophetically prescient addresses, he will anticipate possible exile for his people should they fail in their mission. And should that happen, it will require all of God's unconditional love to allow Israel to repent and to begin the long road back to redemption.

Will Moses anticipate both exiles? Certainly the first — the short one of Jeremiah and Ezekiel — which will end in fifty to seventy years culminating in the first *Shivat Tziyon* (return to Zion) of Zerubabel and Ezra and Nehemiah. But will Moses dare to imagine the long exile, an exile of unrelieved vulnerability, victimization, displacement, expulsion, pogrom — in which God's love will appear suspended, distressingly absent?

A much later poet-prophet Bialik will cry out to Heaven following a pogrom in Kishinev, Bessarabia — with forty-five Jews murdered, eighty-six Jews wounded, and fifteen hundred Jewish homes and shops destroyed. As pogroms go, historically speaking, Kishenev will not be the worst. But following the European Emancipation Kishenev will serve as a crushing blow to Jewish naïve optimism regarding the benevolence of exile. Bialik's poem *"Al ha-Shehitah"* ("Concerning the Slaughter") will seek to unmask the protective shield of faith which the long exile will have cultivated among Jews who persist in praying for God's mercy and finding no relief: "O Heavens, seek mercy for me! If there is a God among you, and a path to that God among you which I have not found, pray for me! As for me, my heart is dead, there are no more prayers on my lips, I am helpless, I've lost all hope. How long, how long, how long!"

The year of the Kishinev pogrom will be 1903. A year later Bialik's tirade will break through all traditional barriers of human protest in the face of God's apparent eclipse or worse: His own helplessness in the face of the slaughter of His covenanted people! Bialik publishes his *"Be'Ir ha-Hareigah"* ("In the City of Slaughter"). In this poem, God pleads pathetically: "Forgive Me, O Miserable Ones, I, Your God, am as poor and as helpless as you, poor and helpless in your lifetimes am I, and all the more so in your deaths. You will approach me tomorrow seeking the reward for your suffering; you will knock on My door. I will open it for you and invite you to see for yourselves how I have become bankrupt! And I am sorry for you, My children; My heart goes out to you, but as victims, you are victims for nothing. For neither I nor you know why you have died, for whom and for what you have died. There is no reason for your deaths, just as there has been no reason for your lives."

It may be argued that Bialik's rage follows in a direct line from some of Moses' grievances before God on behalf of his people. Hannah's prayer for a child is transformed by the Rabbis of the Talmud into a lengthy rebuke on Hannah's part of God's ways. Elijah, the Book of Psalms, and the Book of Job all reflect the need of believing Jews to pour out their authentic feelings of despair before a God apparently in eclipse or worse — insensitive to the pain and suffering of His people. But Bialik goes beyond the others. It is the sheer length of the exile. It is the temper of the secular mood "afflicting" all believers in a post-Enlightenment age. The cord of faith in an active Providence will have snapped for Bialik's poetic conscience as it will for myriads of Jews who will reject the idea of a covenant with God, though not necessarily rejecting their people.

And worse will come! A crime of genocide will be perpetrated on the Children of Israel by the most enlightened people in Western Civilization. The Shoah will send a shock-wave to a people who have already had thinkers and artists like Bialik warning them of the "fires" of exile. These thinkers and artists, along with some rabbis and plain-speaking Jews, will admonish the God of Israel Himself with the outcry that the punishment must come to an end; that if exile has been the logical conclusion of Israel's having violated the principles of the covenant, the people have long since paid for their violation. And if the God of Israel persists in delaying the sending of His Messiah, then the Children of Israel will have to initiate by themselves an active reassertion of their national will-to-live.

A Re-grounding in Faith

Franz Kafka will summarize the collective disenchantment with the long-term policy of waiting for messianic deliverance: "The Messiah will come only when he is no longer necessary; he will come only on the day after his arrival; he will come — not on the last day, but on the very last day."

In order to grasp Kafka's ironic rejection of the literalist position vis-à-vis the Messiah's coming one must review the Midrash which seeks to explain the reason for the destruction of the Second Temple: "Why was the First Temple destroyed? Because of three sins: idolatry, sexual perversity, and homicide.

But why was the Second Temple destroyed since the Sages at that time were occupied with the Torah, with *mitzvot*, and with charitable deeds? Because in that period there was a pervasive feeling among the people — including the Sages apparently — of gratuitous hatred. This teaches that *sinat hinam* ('gratuitous hatred') is considered equivalent to the three cardinal sins of idolatry, sexual perversity, and homicide."

But how is it possible that the Sages — and let us presume the people — could be genuinely occupied with Torah, *mitzvot*, and charitable deeds and still be guilty of gratuitous hatred? The answer given within the Midrash itself — that gratuitous hatred is tantamount to idolatry, sexual perversity, and homicide — doesn't answer the puzzlement. Unless an agonized hyperbole is intended!

The Midrash seems to be saying that gratuitous hatred of the sort which tears asunder the social fabric of a society cancels out whatever Torah and *mitzvot* and charitable deeds may be practiced. To consider fighting off the Roman legions even in a situation of national unity is an awesome proposition. To do it with the inner social cohesion in disarray is lunacy. In other words, whatever good efforts may be expended in the constituent areas of Torah, *mitzvot*, and charitable deeds, overall social and national unity is the indispensable cementing medium for survival as a sovereign unity. Such unity cannot come from God. It never could. It would have to come from a supreme effort among the people.

When Kafka, therefore, says that the Messiah will come only when he is no longer necessary, he means that a this-worldly effort on the part of the people united in a commitment to their own survival and revival will bring *by themselves* a "Messianic era." Moreover, the redemptive spark with which the Messiah would be expected to ignite the revival will have already been there among the people or among some of the people who will then have inspired the others. This is what Kafka means when he says that the Messiah will come only on the day after his arrival. As to the concluding conundrum: "he will come — not on the last day, but on the very last day," the group that is Israel will dare not assume — ever — that the day is here, that the Messianic era is here, that no further human effort is needed. For there is always another day and more investment to be made in order to make possible a mending of messianic proportions.

Moses anticipates all of this later Jewish history of catastrophe in his

Deuteronomic lectures. This new generation of Israelites will listen to these lectures and will then leave him on the plains of Moab as they move on. Moses has difficulty concealing his own personal remorse at not being able to continue with them into the Promised Land. He cannot stifle his charge that it was because of them that he was punished — not because of his alleged misdemeanor at the "rock" recorded in the relevant passage in the Book of Bamidbar. But the greatness of this teacher Moses is manifested in his acceptance of his fate and, notwithstanding his personal future, he is unwavering in his commitment to preparing this people, this same people — the descendants of the Wilderness generation — for their redemptive task.

That later Jewish history will be scarred by a number of national catastrophes will be implicit in Moses' overarching message. Israel as a nation like other nations will participate in a normal, historic, political, moral process in which they will be forced to learn and to suffer from the confirmation of a true proposition regarding national survivability: a nation inadequately prepared economically, socially, militarily, *and spiritually* can and will be defeated and exiled by stronger foes. Furthermore, for Israel to have achieved the fulfillment of a dream and promise — emancipation from slavery, revelation at Sinai, and settlement and sovereignty in the Promised Land will assure nothing permanent. There must be an ongoing strengthening of the spiritual and sociomoral fiber of society or else the insides of that society will become rotten. Defeat — *and exile* — will surely follow.

Moses' exhortations will seek to inspire within his people — this new generation of his people — an *emunah* ("faith") which had served Moses and the first ancestor of this people Abraham. It was Abraham — the first *ba'al-emunah* (possessor of faith) — who was taken out by God to view the stars in the heavens and told that even at his advanced age he and his aged wife Sarah would give birth to a son from whom myriads of descendants would come forth. And Abraham had a faith firm enough to believe it. He believed it because he believed in God's overall justice which was promising him a leading role in seeing such justice rule the universe which God had created. Abraham's sense of the reasonableness, meaningfulness, and ultimate rightness of the enterprise made the birth of the future Yitzhak not a laughable phenomenon but an eminently just endorsement of an overall just creation.

Emunah would undergird Moses' own mission as he had been commissioned by God to lead Israel out of slavery. Hadn't the Children of Israel been described at the Sea of Reeds as *"va-ya'aminu be-Adonai u-ve-Moshe avdo"* ("they had faith in God and in Moses His servant"). And even though this faith experienced by Israel at the Sea would from time to time be tarnished, assailed, and otherwise weakened, it would be strong enough to carry them forward — at least into a Wilderness beyond the Sea of Extinction. And thus this people — the Wilderness generation — would prepare the way to a long and enduring history of faith.

The Linkage-in-Faith to Zionism

Israel's history of faith would be required in order to respond to all the formidable attacks on its faith through the ages. Israel would be attacked ideationally and physically for being covenanted. These enemies of the covenant would justify their anti-Semitism by referring to the "Jewish scandal" of exclusivity. But there would always be a significant few among the surviving Jews who would live their lives *be-emunah shleimah* ("in complete faith"). They would understand Isaiah's exhortation (7:9), "If you will not believe, you will not be affirmed." The faith would be strong enough to lay the foundation of a Third Jewish Commonwealth in the Promised Land, *initiated, promulgated, and actualized by the people themselves*. The work of Yitzhak Lamdan would call to the faithful: "Bear it — bear it, my aching back! A man of Israel. Too proud am I to go and seek another refuge and salvation! Beneath this orphaned shrub in the desert of refuge. This is not the cast-off son of the Egyptian. Here faints from thirst Isaac, seed of Abraham and Sarah!"

Isaac (Yitzhak), son of Abraham and Sarah, had been the patriarch who had never left the Land. It was right for the latter-day Zionist to identify with Isaac because of his landedness. Moses now has the task of educating a people which has never been in that Land to be so thirsty for it that their faith will propel them into the tasks required for conquering and settling that Land. They will need to move forward without hesitation, without an enervating skepticism regarding purpose. Moses must find the words, the words, *the* words, which will inspire the deeds.

Va-Ethanan 

The Kotzker Rebbe once put into the mouth of Moses the prayer that not only did he hope to enter the Promised Land but that he would merit seeing the "good" in the Land. With such a prayer Moses was clearly separating himself from the derogatory view of the spies. But Moses would be doubly disappointed. He did not get to enter Israel, nor did he get to see the goodness that would "grow" there, that would emanate from there. Yet if Moses could be comforted, it was in the knowledge that the generation which he was now instructing as well as later generations of Israelites *would* have the merit of entering the Land and seeing the goodness therein. In this sense he would be doubly comforted, as would those privileged generations.

God through His prophet Deutero-Isaiah — the prophet of the first exile and first return — would exhort all the prophets to offer double comfort to Israel: "Comfort, oh comfort My people. Speak tenderly to Jerusalem, and declare to her that her term of service is over, that her iniquity is expiated. For she has received at the hand of the Lord double for all her sins." The exhortation would be calling on all those of the first *Shivat Tziyon* (Return to Zion) to appreciate the double comfort and to rededicate themselves to the covenant in the light of the double comfort. As for Moses, how does he deal actively and constructively with his double disappointment? He sublimates his feelings of personal regret into a matchlessly eloquent agenda of detailed instructions as to how the people are to build a spiritually secure and socially responsible society based on a coherent system of spiritual and ethical values. In building such a society the children of Israel will earn their double comfort.

Ahavat Yisrael as the Comfort

Sustaining the agenda is the eternal comforting knowledge that the covenant's chief purpose is to bind Israel to God. The Children of Israel in their later history will have to live through a series of Tisha B'Av catastrophes. But following the Tisha B'Av reality there will always be, so to speak, a *Shabbat Nahamu* (A Shabbat of Comfort). And this *Shabbat Nahamu* will mitigate the pain of Tisha B'Av. It will mitigate it; it won't expunge it. For Tisha B'Av will remind Israel of its doubts, of its apprehensions, and of its fears induced by its knowledge that the world has real and present dangers. Prominent among these dangers are enemies who are relentless in their hatred of Israel and its purposes.

How can Moses prepare Israel to combat in its own collective mind and psyche and soul the withering distress of feeling *hated*? Fundamentally Moses will have to convince Israel that it is also *loved* with great abundance. Not by any of the nations, but by the source of all being, the God of Israel!

Moses will anticipate the *Sefer ha-Ikkarim* of Joseph Albo in which the latter will underscore that God has not chosen to love Israel because of its great numbers. In Deuteronomy 7:7–8 it is written: "The Lord did not set His love upon you, nor choose you, because you were more in number than any people — for you were the fewest of all peoples; but because the Lord loved you, and because He would keep the oath which He swore unto your fathers, the Lord brought you out with a mighty hand, and redeemed you out of the house of bondage, from the hand of Pharaoh King of Egypt." Furthermore Albo will note that in Deuteronomy 9:5 Israel has not been chosen because of any intrinsic qualitative moral superiority: "Not for your righteousness, or for the uprightness of your heart do you go in to possess their land; but for the wickedness of these nations the Lord your God drives them out from before you, and that He may establish the work which the Lord swore unto our Fathers."

Albo will go on to emphasize that God has chosen Israel and given Israel the Land because of His love for them. "And this love is an unconditionally committed love which continues because of the sheer will of the lover." This love is the eternal comfort during the days when the Children of Israel are most vulnerable to the dangers of creaturely realities. Israel neutralizes any hatred that its enemies may bear it by knowing with the certainty of faith that it is loved by the omnipotent omniscient "Presence" that is truly important in this world.

Jewish liturgical practice will formulate an expression of comfort which one Jew will extend to another in a situation of personal mourning: "May the Place (the Lord) comfort you among all mourners in Zion and in Jerusalem." There is comfort in that God is *the* "Place," the ground of all being. He will give the ultimate comfort as His covenantal commitment to Israel will give Israel a sense of ultimate personal and national dignity and majesty.

But what of Israel's love for one another? Shouldn't fraternal love within the House of Israel be a quid pro quo condition for deserving God's love? Moses has witnessed personally from the beginning of his ministry what fraternal enmity can perpetrate. Attempting to separate two belligerent Hebrews from one another in Egypt — perhaps trying to adjudicate between them — Moses is accused of "lording" it over them. He is forced thereby to flee from Pharaoh's wrath. But worse is to follow, once Moses accepts the full charge and responsibility for leading Israel out of Egypt and shepherding it through its wanderings in the Wilderness. Later Jewish history will place an onus of guilt upon the Children of Israel themselves for the loss of sovereignty. The guilt will be fostered by the division of David and Solomon's kingdom which will lead eventually to the loss of the First Commonwealth. The guilt will be aggravated by the loss of the Second Commonwealth and its accompanying explanation that *sinat hinam* ("gratuitous internal hatred") would be the principle cause for the catastrophe.

The Jewish calendar will seek to remind Israel of the virtues of fraternal love by inserting a celebration of Jewish comfort on the fifteenth day of the month of Av. Placed appropriately within the week following Tisha B'Av, Tu B'Av will be a day for focusing on love for one another. Among the historical associations which will be attached to the day will be (1) the recalling of the elimination of the ancient ban on intermarriage between the tribes of Israel; (2) the canceling of the excommunication of the tribe of Benjamin from the national polity following the Gibeah atrocity and subsequent civil war; and (3) the removal of the orchards obstructing the roads leading to Jerusalem that had been put up originally by Jeroboam I who had instigated the tragic division of the Davidic kingdom of Israel.

Each of these annulments of previous obstructions to fraternal love will represent Israel's renewed appreciation of the necessity for a national imitatio Dei in demanding loving relationships. Moses will stress over and over again the indispensability of the covenant in underscoring the relationship of love between the God of Israel and the people of Israel on the one hand, but on the other hand among the people of Israel themselves. Israel is enjoined to hold fast to the Lord; for that is why they are "alive today." But their holding fast must equally be to one another in order to guarantee a national life today and tomorrow.

Moses' preachment in favor of cleaving to God and to one's fellow Israelite is summarized in the call to Israel in Deuteronomy 4:4: "*Ve-atem ha-deveikim be-Adonai Eloheikhem hayyim kulkhem ha-yom*" ("You who hold fast to the Lord your God, are all alive today"). The love manifested between God and Israel — their *ahavat olam* (eternal love) — can only come through the study and application of Torah in the lives of the people. Such holding fast to the pillars of Torah and its loving application in day-to-day life is to be understood and accepted by Israel as its special *hokhmah* (wisdom).

Rabbi A.I. Kook will comment: "The uniqueness of the House of Israel lies in the fact that it senses, with all the strength of its being, that life only possesses value to the extent that it is Godly, and that life which is not Godly is not to be termed life at all." The connection of the verse from Deuteronomy with Torah study and its application in daily life is that once the House of Israel has accepted the Torah as "God's Word," then the Torah itself, the study of it and its application becomes in essence an ongoing loving attachment to the Lord Himself — and from such attachment comes authentic "life."

But this love and this "life" lived between the Lord Himself and Israel is only validated by the love and "life" lived with other Jews — as it must be, for where else can it be lived? Only then will the tri-partite covenant of God, oneself, and the other human being closest to oneself, i.e. one's fellow Jew, be made possible.

Love of the Land

Moses himself will not participate in the application of the Torah covenant. For that participation can only take place fully in the Land and Moses will not be there. It is for him personally an emotional blow. The "human" part of him feels it as a crushing end to his life. He reminds his flock that he knows his fate has been decided in that he is to die in exile along with the *dor ha-midbar* (the Wilderness generation).

The *Midrash Tanhuma* reflects his recurring despondency, his frustration at having come so far personally and yet to have fallen short. The Midrash has Moses complaining to God:

> Lord of the Universe, everyone seems to be equal before you; You destroy equally the blameless and the wicked (Job 9:22). The spies angered You by slandering the Land. I, on the other hand, who served Your children for forty years in the Wilderness, are my fate and the fate of the spies to be the same? To take an example: A king seeks to marry a particular woman; he sends his emissaries to see if she is beautiful or not. They go and see her. They then return to the king and report to him that they have indeed seen her and that there is no one as ugly and forlorn as she.
>
> At the same time, however, the king's confidant — who has not seen her — insists to the contrary: there is no more beautiful woman than she in the whole world. On the basis of the confidant's appraisal the king decides to wed her. He comes to the bridal home accompanied by his entire entourage including the emissaries and the confidant. But the father of the girl says to the emissaries of the king: "I swear by the life of the king that not one of you may enter here, because you have despised my daughter and slandered her before the king." At that point, the confidant seeks to enter. But the father forbids him to enter as well. The confidant protests that even without ever having seen her, he had told the king that she is the most beautiful woman in the world while the emissaries were insisting that she was the ugliest. On that account, shouldn't he, the confidant, be especially welcome at the wedding festivities?
>
> Thus said Moses to the Holy One Blessed Be He: "Lord of the Universe, the spies slandered the Land by saying it is a land which devours its inhabitants. I, on the other hand, have never seen the Land, and yet I have praised it before Your children in telling them that their God is bringing them to a good Land. And now all I ask is to be able to pass over and see the good Land on the other side of the Jordan." But God refuses to give him permission. Moses says to Him: "If such is the case, then indeed everything is equal before You; You destroy the blameless with the wicked."

In other words, from time to time Moses' personal disappointment clouds his ability to see that he has already been comforted in knowing that he has brought a tough mixed multitude out of slavery into a Wilderness of expectation and opportunity. And now he has brought them to the gateway of their personal and national fulfillment — if not his. Is that not a comfort? Moreover, his entreaty "to pass over and see the good Land" will be partially answered. The Hatam Sofer will note that God will allow him to at least *see* the Land from afar if not enter it. Thus like future generations of Israelites, Moses will be doubly comforted — primarily by means of the vehicle of *ahavat ha-aretz* (love of the Land) — whether from near or far.

Following the initial entrance of Israel into the Land under Joshua, there will be two further collective actualizations of Israel's love of the Land: the first *Shivat Tziyon* after the short exile and the second *Shivat Tziyon* after the long exile. The first *Shivat Tziyon* will have the clear sanction of the revelatory spirit of the Bible endorsed by prophetic prescience and promise. The second *Shivat Tziyon* will be a self-propelled protest against any further religiously endorsed extensions of a seemingly endless exile. After almost two millenia of exile, the House of Israel will have been lulled into national torpor by the repetitiveness of wandering and the religiously sanctioned acceptance of the permanency of exile. Virtually forgotten will have been the mandate of the Torah covenant to inhabit the Land and make of it a place hospitable to the love of God for Israel and the love of Israel for God.

On the threshold of this first entrance into the Promised Land, however, Israel in its own eyes is more than ready. And Moses is too great a personality to allow his own visceral need to enjoy personally the fruits of his labor to get in the way of his instructions to them. If his speeches reflect anxiety — and they do — it comes from the fact that he knows how difficult it is going to be for them to build a society which attempts to be holy in the sight of God and ethical in the sight of God and men. And yet that is precisely what the covenant demands. Moses' concluding addresses to his people do not hide the challenge: "See, I have imparted to you laws and rules, as the Lord my God has commanded me, for you to abide by in the Land that you are about to enter and occupy. Observe them faithfully, for that will be proof of your wisdom and discernment to other peoples."

Moses keeps stressing this challenge when he says to the Children of Israel that their wisdom, their skill is being ethical. Other peoples may have other skills and abilities. Other nations may have particular national cultural characteristics which stamp them as strong physically or ingenious artistically or clever commercially. Israel has been chosen to serve as an example of ethical nationhood. And no matter what other success Jews may have, if as Jews they are not clearly distinguishable wherever they live — *especially in their own land* — as practitioners of the wisdom and skill of being kind, merciful, honest, and loving, then the other nations will look upon them as fools. For they will have tossed away the most blessed mission any nation can be given — to walk with God.

Moses, therefore, arrogates to himself the responsibility of reviewing for this new generation what its Torah is. A great Russian writer of a later millenium will talk of a nation's literature as "the living memory of a nation. It preserves and kindles within itself the flame of a country's spent history, in a form that is safe from distortion and slander. In this way, literature, together with language, protects the soul of a nation." Moses has well anticipated Solzhenitsyn but has gone further. Torah protects the soul of the Jewish nation — because it defines who the Jews are, where they come from, and where they hope to go. But Moses projects one additional category indispensable to the people beyond literature and language and that is the category of law, that which is concerned with behavioral actualization of values promulgated by the nation's literature and language.

"Ahavat Torah"

Moses wants to pave as clear and as firm a road as possible for this covenanted people. What must covenantal teaching do? The introduction to Moses' review in Deuteronomy of the Ten Commandments says: "The Lord our God made a covenant with us at Horeb. It was not with our fathers exclusively that the Lord made this covenant, but with us, the living, everyone of us who is here today." This will be emphasized further towards the end of Deuteronomy 29: "You stand this day, all of you, before the Lord your God.... I make this covenant, with its sanctions, not with you alone, but both with those who are standing here with us this day before the Lord our God and with those who are not here with us this day."

This statement serves as a classic summary statement of what is entailed in receiving and obligating oneself to Torah. It is the product of revelation: its rhetoric is unambiguously covenantal; it bespeaks the indispensability of continuity vis-à-vis family, tribe, and nation; it calls for a distinctive way of life; it prescribes a special destiny. All this will be spelled out again and again, if not already spelled out in the Written Torah, but also in the ongoing Oral Torah.

There will have to be an ongoing Oral Torah. For even though the Written Torah will declare that nothing shall be added nor subtracted from the Torah which God has commanded, it will become clear that there is no possible way of anticipating what new issues will arise in the future that will test the creativity of Jewish law. In anticipation of the unknown future there will be a number of principles based on Torah itself that will serve as guidelines for changing, suspending, neutralizing, and even uprooting laws when necessary.

A verse from Psalm 119 will be translated either as "It is time to act for the Lord; for they are violating Your Torah," or "You may even violate the Torah if it is time to act for the Lord." When? When it is perceived that Torah itself is being violated. There will be times when in the name of Torah, the true intentions of Torah are being perverted. At such times radical non-normative acts may need to be performed in order to maintain the long-term validity and vitality of the Torah. The tractate *Temurah* will state that "it is better that some Torah be uprooted in order that true Torah — the comprehensively valid Torah in its entirety — not be forgotten." Similarly, the tractate *Menahot* will state that on occasion the canceling of Torah affirms its foundation. A comprehensive summary statement of the purpose of Torah legislation will be the short phrase in verse Leviticus 18:5: "*Va-hai bahem*" ("You shall live by the commandments") expanded to mean, "you are not meant to die by them."

The Written Torah and the Oral Torah taken together will become the bedrock of Jewish covenantal existence in the Land. "See, I have imparted to you laws and rules for you to abide by in the Land that you are about to enter and occupy. Observe them faithfully, for that will be proof of your wisdom and discernment to other peoples, who on hearing of all these laws will say, 'Surely, that great nation is a wise and discerning people!'" Moses wants the individual Jew to understand very clearly that the covenant demands ethical attention to all areas of human life; that the covenant demands a positive attitude towards the worship of God along with sufficient personal intellectual growth at all ages and stages in life so that there is a never-ending cultivation of sensitivity to ongoing opportunities for ethical mending in the world.

The allusion to the questioning child here in Deuteronomy will become the paradigm for the brightest, the most interested child of the four children at the *Pesah Seder.* The allusions to children's learning about the Exodus in the Book of Shemot will have been simple and general. Here in Deuteronomy, however, the child wants to know the "meaning of the decrees, the laws, and the rules which the Lord has enjoined upon us." In Deuteronomy, Moses is anticipating the growing legislative complexity which will henceforth occupy Israelite leadership.

To achieve the constant application of Torah to the world, the Israelites will need to be alert to the demands of change along with the fixed commitment that will transcend change. And should they fail, he will educate them not to blame their earthly enemies no matter how overwhelmingly powerful these enemies will be. They will blame themselves and their violation of Torah. The later legend will relate that when Jerusalem and the Temple(s) will be burning, groups of young priests will gather on the roof of the burning Temple(s) with the keys in their hands. They will call out to God saying: "Lord of the Universe, since we were unworthy and did not merit the ministry of serving as faithful treasurers of Your house, here are the keys." And they will thereupon hurl the keys upward. A heavenly hand will catch the keys, at which point the young priests will jump into the fire.

Moses understands that the interpretation of Torah will demand constant creative applications of Torah according to the given contemporary situation. As revelatory and as comprehensive as the listing of the Ten Commandments will be for any generation, it will not be detailed enough to serve as anything more than an inspirational document. Considering the ten statements seriatim:

(1) What will the opening statement concerning God as the Emancipator of Israel mean for a generation bent on conquest under Joshua as opposed to a generation subjugated to Rome, ghettoized by the Pope, selected for extermination by a Hitler?

(2) Will idolatry always mean the worship of idols in the literal sense? Or will the incarnation of Satan in men like Hitler worshiped by the intellectual leadership of Europe — Germany — provide the horrifyingly vivid realization of idolatry at its most destructive?

(3) Will taking God's Name in vain always be associated with theurgic

consequences? Or will it caution in particular all religious institutions against moral corruption in the Name of God?

(4) Will definitions of work prohibited by Shabbat injunctions be immutable, notwithstanding future advances in technological knowledge and applications of that knowledge?

(5) How shall honoring parents be concretized — in an absolute sense under all conceivable circumstances?

And as for the remaining apodictic negative commands — condemning murder, adultery, theft or kidnapping, swearing falsely, envy — surely, they will have to be applied according to sundry individual circumstances. And so the Oral Torah will represent the eternal demand to legislate relevantly, creatively, and ethically — in order to insure, indeed, that Israel is enabled to *live* by the Torah, not *die* from it.

Against the Torah for the Sake of Torah

The passion for Torah and its application will increase following the demise of the First Commonwealth and the rise and fall of the Second Commonwealth. Guilt over having failed to fulfill the covenant will exacerbate the tendencies to build defensive ramparts around the Torah, protecting Torah, as it were, against outside influences. Torah as an elixir of life will be perceived in such therapeutic fashion that, as cited earlier in the portion of Toldot, a Sage will state: "He who while walking along the way and contemplating a passage of Torah pauses from his study in order to admire a tree, a meadow, will be considered as one who has forfeited his life."

But the demands on the reinvigoration of Torah will be such that the long exile followed by the Enlightenment and Emancipation will call not only for a revolution within the ranks of the traditional Jewish community but for an attack on traditional Torah as well. As mentioned earlier, one such revolutionary, Micah Berdichevski, will reflect on the rabbinic proposition quoted above: "I recall from the teaching of the sages: 'Whoever walks by the way and interrupts his study to remark, "How fine is that tree, how fine is that field" — forfeits his life!' But I assert that then alone will Judah and Israel be saved, when another teaching is given unto us, namely: Whoever walks by the way and sees a fine tree and a fine field and a fine sky and leaves them to think on other thoughts — that man is like one who forfeits his life! Give us back our fine trees and fine fields! Give us back the Universe."

Berdichevski will represent a secular revolution against a Torah which will have been perceived as stultified and petrified. The House of Israel of that future time will need to be reminded to listen as Moses calls upon his people: "*Shema Yisrael* — Listen O Israel." Moses is imploring his people not just to attend physiologically, but to listen in order to learn: "*Shema Yisrael*, the Lord who is our God is the Lord who bestows unity of purpose to our being alive in this world as a people." We are to learn that His "oneness" and "uniqueness" bespeak a collectivity of power drawing us to Him inspiring our own sense of "oneness" and "uniqueness" expressed in the thought "Who is like the people Israel, a one and unique people on earth." And that the desideratum is for all generations of Israel — through Torah as reinterpreted for its day — to pull all its own powers and propensities together for unified purpose: His service.

Ekev עקב

As theological and psychological concepts the two Hebrew words *emunah* and *bitahon* are related. They refer respectively to "faith" and to "confidence" or "trust." Yet, they are different, and the difference is significant. *Emunah* is a theological and psychological value that is held to override everything including death as it gives life meaning, purpose, and hope. "God loves me no matter what...," so to speak; or as Job says it according to the way the Masoretic authorities read verse 13:15: "Even if He slay me, I will hope in Him." Even if one reads the text as it is *written* — not according to the Masoretes — it can be interpreted with the same theological and psychological depth: "He may well slay me; I may appear to have no hope; yet I will argue my case before him. In this too is my salvation." *Emunah* then is a stance in which one's entire existence rests on one's hope in God's salvation — and the salvation comes from one's very connection to Him *in* life as well as *beyond* life.

Bitahon, on the other hand, is confidence or trust in oneself and one's fellow human beings and the hidden blessings of God's creation which have been bestowed upon human beings. For example, as important a gift as bread is, more important is the gift humanity has been given to "find" bread, to uncover and discover new sources of sustenance. *Bitahon* is the confidence or trust we have in ourselves and in others and in our capacities to secure the blessings we need in order to survive on earth.

Two anecdotes illustrating respectively *bitahon* and *emunah*: In the days of sailing ships a young inexperienced sailor is sent aloft in a storm to disentangle a broken sail. In spite of the raging wind, the young man climbs up swiftly and does the job. When it is time to descend, he looks down and sees the vessel tossing and rolling in the angry sea. Suddenly he loses his "nerve" or *bitahon*. He feels dizzy and faint. Looking down to the mate below he yells: "I'm going to fall!" The mate who has spent many years at sea, yells above the storm: "Don't look down, boy! Look up!" The young sailor does just that, and with renewed *bitahon* comes down safely. God hasn't directly brought him down any more than God has disentangled the sail. The young sailor has done it. The blessing of *bitahon* within him has given him the capacity to climb up, to do the required task, and to come down safely.

In another tale of the treacherous sea, a storm has raged and sunk many ships. One ship has made it safely to shore. Relieved, the captain and his chief petty officer look out gratefully to the wrathful waves battering the reefs. But, lo and behold, another ship is seen to be trapped on one of the reefs with passengers screaming for help. The captain orders his chief petty officer to join him in going out to try to save these helpless human beings. The sailor pleads with his captain: "But sir, we may not come back!" The captain responds: "We don't have to come back; but we must go out!" The captain is not looking to commit suicide. He has enough *bitahon* to believe that he and his mate have enough know-how to have a chance at saving the people. But he clearly also has *emunah* — that *emunah* which leaves the ultimate fate of his sacrificial efforts — life or death — to the Almighty.

Testing

Whether one is focusing on the need for *emunah* or the need for *bitahon*, one is always being tested. In these Deuteronomic addresses Israel is reminded by Moses of the constant testing which God has been imposing upon them (8:2). The Malbim points out that there are two words in Hebrew for "test": *behinah* and *nisayon*. The word *behinah* applies to situations in which we test a substance to see, for example, whether gold is really gold; that is, to test whether we are what we claim to be. The word *nisayon* refers to situations in which we are put to the test to see not what we are but whether or not we have capacities we did not know we had.

Another way of putting it is that if *behinah* tests what we claim to be, *nisayon* tests what we may yet become if we are ready to push ourselves to grow beyond our present capacities. On a number of occasions prominent figures in the Torah respond to God's call with the word *hineini*. The word *hineini* is not a response to a call for attendance. It refers to situations when the given individual knows that he is being tested to see if he is ready to become more than he ever thought possible. In such situations, the given individual grounds his *hineini* in a full measure of both *bitahon* and *emunah*.

There is a tradition which says that God gave three special gifts to the Jewish people that would test their capacity to endure hardship (Sifre Deuteronomy 32). The gifts are Torah, Eretz Yisrael, and *Olam ha-Ba*. In each case Israel is being tested. And the test is not a *behinah*. It is a *nisayon*. In order to stand up to the test and to prevail in it, Israel will have to call at various times on its *bitahon* or its *emunah*, or both.

In the case of Torah, the cultural struggle of the Jewish people over the centuries to retain their special view of what it means to build a spiritual/moral universe will require them to embody Torah under all kinds of difficult conditions. They will find that the Torah is a great source of *bitahon*. And under extreme conditions the Torah is the ultimate source of *emunah*. The same strivings will be required from the Jewish people collectively and individually as they will struggle for Eretz Yisrael. That struggle will entail a constant exercising of skills in survival — physical, economic, political, and spiritual. Finally, every human being — Jew and Gentile alike — will learn what it means to live in a world of challenge, pain, illness, disappointment, frustration, and tragedy. The concept of *olam ha-ba* will provide the Jewish people and Gentiles through the ages with the long-term optimism necessary to re-energize their *bitahon* and to re-enforce their *emunah*.

Moses has the task of convincing Israel that the gifts which Israel has already received and will continue to receive are a vehicle for testing both their *bitahon* in themselves and their fellow Jews as well as their *emunah*, their "faith" in their God, the God of Israel. Moses is explicit: "You shall faithfully observe all the instruction that I enjoin upon you today, that you may thrive and increase and be able to possess the Land that the Lord promised on oath to your fathers. Remember the long way that the Lord your God has made you travel in the Wilderness these past forty years, that He might *test* you by hardships to learn what was in your hearts, whether you would keep His commandments or not. He subjected you to the hardship of hunger and then gave you manna to eat, which neither you nor your fathers had ever known, in order to teach you that Man does not live on bread alone, but that Man may live on anything that the Lord decrees."

Using the precedent of God's test of Abraham at Mount Moriah, the Ramban explains the purpose of a test: It is to put into the hands of Man an opportunity to exercise his absolutely free will. If he truly wishes to perform the given act, he will do it; if not, he won't do it, because this kind of extreme test will not brook an indecisive or half-way response. God the tester is not giving Abraham the tested a hypothetical test, i.e., "What would you do if I commanded you to do…" It is a categorical test, i.e., "Do it!" As such, the reward which the tested will receive under such categorical circumstances will be of infinitely more worth than if the test had been hypothetical. The reward will not be merely for a "good heart," i.e., a good thought, a noble intention, etc. It will be for a good act, realized, done! And because in having *done* what he never thought he could do, he will have truly passed a test which was a *nisayon*!

The *akeidah* test of Abraham and Isaac serves Moses as a pedagogic model. Abraham's test was clearly a test of his will — his absolute free will. His absolute readiness to act — for after all he was stopped in the very process of physically acting — reaps a categorical reward, not a hypothetical one. His reward is the blessed anti-thesis of what he was prepared to do. He was prepared to slay his precious beloved son out of his own understanding, albeit mistaken, of God's command. Prevented just in time, he is now to be blessed with myriads of descendants from this very son who was always meant to remain alive. Moreover, this son Isaac — the son of this model man of faith who had been told at the very beginning that he would be a blessing to all the families of the earth — this son himself will be the living link to Jacob-Israel whose Children of Israel will indeed bring blessings to all the nations of the world.

Moses now applies the characteristics of the test of Abraham to Israel in the Wilderness and beyond. With all the traditional sources referring to God's unilateral redemption of Israel from slavery in Egypt, there is still a strong degree of autonomous free will which must be exercised by the people. Without it, the fulfillment of the enterprise of redemption cannot and will not take place. The stiff-neckedness, the stubbornness, the rebelliousness of Israel in the Wilderness have all been signs of a free will in conflict with impulses of fear, panic, ignorance, and the untold insecurities which plague an erstwhile servile rabble upon being taken into the unknown. In the final analysis, however, the Children of Israel — like Abraham, Isaac, and Jacob — will go on to meet their covenanted destiny with that same free will.

Meeting their destiny will entail committing themselves — as Moses emphasizes over and over again — to an ongoing series of spiritual and ethical refinements in day-to-day living. The test is a test of action leading to concretization of ideological theory. Spiritual and ethical refinement must be actualized in a sociopolitical sense. And as in Abraham's case, the reward will be growth. History will testify to the survival and revival of a people who will find the world less than hospitable to their Torah as a mechanism for mending the world. The future historic reality of the descendants of the Wilderness generation will record both successes and failures, successes in standing up to the test and failures in not standing up to it. There will be personal and collective failures; but there will also be personal and collective redemptive achievements.

Among the tests in the Wilderness which Moses keeps reviewing is the manna, the heavenly all-purpose food. Simply stated, it has been given in order to test Israel's loyalty and appreciation to God. God has explained that Israel is to "remember that it is the Lord your God who gives you the power to get wealth, in fulfillment of the covenant that He made by means of an oath with your fathers — as is still the case." The nineteenth-century commentator *Ha-Ketav ve-ha-Kabbalah* stresses that the test has certainly not been to test the Lord; for with the Lord there has been no doubt as to His purposes, intentions, or expectations from Self. But Israel the tested, the recipient of the "manna-gift," is to be judged — by God and by themselves — as to their capacity to abide by the terms of the "manna-gift." Their test is a *nisayon*, all the way into the Promised Land when the manna will stop.

In the Wilderness the manna has been sent from Heaven every day. It has provided them with what they need for that day. It has tested, therefore, their ultimate *emunah*. As said earlier, *emunah* is a stance — immovable and immutable — in which one's entire sense-of-being rests on one's hope in God's salvation — and the salvation comes from one's attachment to Him and His purposes. The half-verse in Psalm 27 will express the quintessential stance of the believer: "If I had not believed (*lulei he'emanti*) that I would see God's ultimate good in the universe..." There is no need to add the obvious conclusion to the verse. For the believer, that is, for the *ba'al-emunah* or *ma'amin*, there is no conceivable alternative. *Bitahon* then follows.

As stressed earlier, *bitahon* is the confidence in oneself and one's fellow human beings to discover in themselves, despite mortal limitations, the blessings in God's creation. The test of the manna, therefore, has not been a test of *bitahon*. That will come when they have entered the Land of Israel and will need to use all their human resources of inventiveness to sustain themselves. But here in the Wilderness the terms of the "manna-gift," i.e., renewing their faith every day that every day God will provide — has been a vivid daily test of *emunah*.

The Fear of Stiff-Neckedness

Moses — the captain of Israel's "ship-of-state" — wants every individual Israelite and Israel as a whole to perform a regular *heshbon ha-nefesh* (examination of soul) in order to reassert his and their *emunah*. This *emunah* is indispensable to Israel's long-term survivability. For it will bestow upon Israel a transcendent certainty which will translate itself into hope even beyond death.

But then *bitahon* must also be cultivated. This entails the confidence that Israel as a nation and each individual Israelite within the nation can succeed in their earthly steering. Milan Kundera's important post-modern novel entitled *The Unbearable Lightness of Being* will represent in despairing terms a cynical antithesis of what Torah preaches. It will argue against Torah's search for meaning. It will insist that living is light, trivial, fickle, and inexorably tragic. From its revelatory origin Torah will stand firmly against the challenges of the Kunderas of every generation in claiming that with *emunah* and *bitahon* living is serious but purposeful, burdensome but bearable. On the contrary, Israel's covenant will demand that it shoulder "the bearable heaviness of being," as it climbs — often ploddingly — Jacob-Israel's ladder of redemption.

Moses is arguing the case for describing Israel as not only a chosen people but as a tested people. Out of the test, however, and the *heshbon ha-nefesh* which must accompany meeting the test will come the *bitahon* based on *emunah* that will bring Israel to whatever redemption can be achieved on earth with the hope that the ultimate redemption awaits all who "believe"!

Often Moses puts his argument in such simple terms as to arouse in commentators an ironic astonishment based on later events in Jewish history. For example, on Moses' statement to the people: "What does God seek from you except to fear Him," the Talmud says: "Is the fear of Heaven such a simple thing? Perhaps for Moses it is, as the teaching of Rabbi Haninah who will say that it is analogous to one who is asked for a large vessel which he possesses as opposed to one who is asked even for a small vessel which he does not possess." To the one who does not have even a small vessel, that sought-for small vessel will seem awfully large. In other words, how can Moses assume that the common people of his flock will be on a sufficiently high spiritual, moral, and intellectual plane to truly fear God. Surely he can't compare them to himself!

Does Moses assume that because he has been blessed with a perception of certain truths that others will see them too? Are they as spiritually endowed as Abraham who receives God's encomium: "Now I know that you fear the Lord"? Surely not! And Moses cannot be that naïve as to say to his people "Be like Abraham." Instead he spells out for them the elements necessary for being God-fearing even on their level. They are not to be stiff-necked before God. They are to be just to the orphan and the widow. They are to love or at least to befriend the stranger. These are the requisite elements for the fear of Heaven. Moses is convinced and must convince his people that to build a healthy society over the long haul the basic elements of an open, welcoming, and supportive polity must be accessible to all. One doesn't have to be the spiritual, moral, intellectual equal of an Abraham or a Moses in order to understand the fundamental lesson of "treating others fairly."

Such will be the mandate for Jewish survival with spiritual and moral distinction throughout the ages. It will enable a beleaguered Jewish minority in country after country throughout the long exile to maintain its pride as a special people. Following the modern Emancipation this humane mandate will claim a special place for Jews within various enlightened societies. There will be no greater claim than that made by Samson Raphael Hirsch in post-enlightened post-emancipated nineteenth century Germany where he will lament the opportunity lost to the Jews before the Enlightenment-Emancipation to be a visible example for good before the Gentiles. These European Gentiles, Hirsch will claim, could have been exposed to a model sociomoral Jewish community and learned from it how to mend its world. And now in a new civic setting how wonderful it could be with a new vital emancipated Jewish community serving the larger German community.

All the sociomoral political optimism associated with the European Emancipation in general and with Germany in particular will be shattered, of course, with the Shoah. Issues of basic survival will totally dominate the

Jewish agenda as the Zionist program for establishing a sovereign Jewish state will dominate Jewish concerns. But never so much as to erase completely sociomoral considerations! On the contrary, from before its inception, not to mention afterward, the young State of Israel will be tested not just externally by political enemies dedicated to its destruction but will be challenged internally by the relentless stresses and strains of religious, moral, social, and cultural writhings and turbulence, ignorance and exploitation, tearing at the fabric of what will otherwise be a wondrous Zionist achievement.

Moses is in no way naïve as to the prospects of his people vis-à-vis their capacity to fulfill consistently all the terms of the covenant. He has reproached the people in the severest terms. He has reminded them that it is not because of any intrinsic righteousness on their part that God has chosen to bestow upon them the gift of this wonderful Land. If anything, they are indeed a stiff-necked people. Their record thus far has been a litany of rebelliousness from the day God took them out of Egypt. There is obviously nothing complimentary in Moses' use of the term *am keshei oref*. But his criticism has a noble purpose.

The phrase has been used in a similar context surrounding the sin of the "Golden Calf." But here Moses, knowing that this particular form of stubbornness is unacceptable, implores: "it was to your fathers that the Lord was drawn in His love for them, so that He chose you, their lineal descendants, from among all peoples — as is now the case. Cut away, therefore, the thickening about your hearts and stiffen your necks no more." Moses and his people know what a stiff neck is. One cannot move it without experiencing pain. To look to be stiff-necked, therefore, is to voluntarily invite restrictive views, limited perspectives, debilitating pain and suffering. Only when one can turn his neck from side to side, up and down, with ease, is one able to see the world from different angles sufficient to maneuver successfully within that world. If one cannot loosen his neck then he is destined to become the abject figure described in Proverbs 29:1: *"Ish tokhahot makshei oref"* ("He that no matter how often he is corrected, stiffens his neck more and more"). What will happen to him? *"Peta yishaveir ve-en marpei"* ("He shall suddenly be broken, broken without remedy").

Compassion in Rebuke

The tone and content of Moses' instruction, spiced as it is with rebuke, has a noble purpose: it is before all and after all cushioned in a larger framework of compassion. Granted, the compassion is not easily "audible" or "visible." The remonstrance, the often vitriolic rebuke is cutting, grating, even at times savage. How can Israel not appreciate all that God has done and will continue to do for them, e.g., destroying the enemy nations before them, providing them with food and water, sustaining them through natural upheavals, etc. Do they not realize that the ground of their existence must be the faith, the *emunah*, that as Bnei Israel, the Children of Israel, they are God's chosen people to be brought into God's chosen Land? Does Israel not understand that it has been chosen to receive the greatest of rewards: to be God's own laboratory for working out a model spiritual and ethical nationalism. Isn't that enough for them!

Moses' pedagogic style may appear strange. His mode of address to a chosen people is reminiscent of a contest winner being told that he has won not because he is especially noteworthy. For in truth, the winner is told, he does not deserve any largesse; it is that the other contestants are complete nonentities; and the reason the winner has been chosen is due to the merit of the winner's ancestors. Yet it is precisely this pedagogic style of Moses which will become the collective historical educational style of the later Jewish people. That style will scold ruthlessly and relentlessly. Its purpose will be to expose the stiff-neckedness and self-deceptions of this chosen Jewish people.

When the later Rabbis will want to lament the sad state of their generation they will carry on in the spirit of their teacher Moshe Rabbenu. They will go beyond Moses in their sarcasm as they will debate the condition of criticism or lack of it in their own society. As cited previously in the discussion on *Parshat Kedoshim* in Leviticus, they will comment on the verse: "*hokhe'ah tokhi'ah et amitekha*" ("reprove, scold, criticize your neighbor when he does wrong"). Rabbi Tarfon will begin by saying that he would be astonished to find in his generation someone capable of giving criticism. For to be capable of being such a critic, one would have to have objective standards. The critic himself would have to be a paragon of virtue based on those standards.

Rabbi Elazar Ben Azariah responds in the same rhetorical style but switches the focus. He would be astonished, he argues, to find in his generation someone capable of *accepting* criticism. In effect he is asking whether there is anyone secure enough in his own self-esteem that he is capable of receiving negative criticism. Such a one would have to be capable of living with the fact that he is less than perfect; and yet he must be sufficiently motivated by a compelling desire for self-improvement so as to welcome criticism.

The preoccupation with the importance of criticism will allow even a student to criticize his master if the situation calls for it. In the modern era, S. R. Hirsch will summarize the communal and national purpose of such criticism: "A society in which every member can call the conduct of every other member to account presupposes that every one is equally prepared to accept admonition on his own behavior."

As a rejoinder to the discussion between Rabbi Tarfon and Rabbi Elazar ben Azariah, Rabbi Akiva adds that he would be astonished if there were anyone in his generation who knew *how* to criticize. He is asserting that there is a way to give reproof! Is such a way the way of Moses' addresses in Deuteronomy? Where is the alleged compassion? Is this the way? Yes and no! The Ramban and other commentators will be disturbed at the degree of vilification in Moses' words: "stiff-necked, rebellious, reprehensible!" And Moses does speak at times with anger, even with resentment: "Forty days and forty nights; I did neither eat bread nor drink water; because of all your sins which ye sinned." The Ramban cannot fail to note, however, that Moses has insisted all along that God loves Israel — and that that love must include all of Israel, not just the righteous among them, but the sinners as well. The Ramban's conclusion is that the rebuke is properly meant for that Wilderness generation which has in fact rebelled against their covenantal destiny. The rebuke — as sharp and as stark as it is — does not mar or in any way compromise God's love for Israel as a whole.

The Ramban is interpreting Rabbi Akiva's insight as suggesting that rebuke which has a constructive purpose must be within a context of an overall atmosphere of approval, i.e., a permanent covenant of unbreakable love. Here is the compassion! Israel through the ages, filled with the intense self-criticism associated with Tisha B'Av, will reflect a secure sense of love emanating from God. And this love will cushion justifiable guilt which Israel must feel and must try not to mitigate.

Israel will accept the punishment as deserved, because it will have faith that the overall permanency of the covenant will guarantee that there will never be Godly rejection or abandonment. And should there be occasions in the future when Israel will feel temporary rejection or abandonment, it will hurl its own criticism at the Almighty. The Psalmist will cry out (44:23–27): "It is for Your sake that we are slain all day long, that we are regarded as sheep to be slaughtered. Rouse Yourself, why do You sleep, O Lord? Awaken, do not reject us forever! Why do You hide Your face, ignoring our affliction and distress? We lie prostrate in the dust; our body clings to the ground. Arise and help us, redeem us, as befits Your faithfulness."

The "*Berakhah*"

The compassion which undergirds Moses' rebuke in the Wilderness is as real and as present as the basic day-to-day nourishment which Israel has been receiving from the moment of its exodus from slavery. True, how Israel receives the manna — whether it fully understands that it is a test of their faith — is critical to its understanding of the conditions which permeate the covenant. But more basic as a sign of God's compassion and unbreakable love is the *fact* of the daily manna, the reliable daily sustenance. And this fact, Moses insists must be digested, understood, and fully appreciated. Thus will be established the liturgical core of appreciation in Jewish traditional prayer — the *berakhah*.

Why *berakhah?* A piece of the dialogue between Yehudah Halevi's "*haver*-teacher" in the *Kuzari* and the King of the Khazars brings out the essence of the function of a *berakhah*. The King acknowledges: "If a drunken person were given all he desires, while being completely intoxicated, he would eat and drink, hear songs, meet his friends and embrace his beloved. But if told of his drunken stupor when he has now become sober, he would regret that he had been drunk and would regard it as a loss rather than a gain since he had had all these enjoyments while he was incapable of appreciating them." The *haver* then says: "Preparing for a pleasure, looking forward to it, then experiencing it, doubles the pleasure. One must have in other words *kavanah ve-havanah* — attention/intention and understanding." What is being spoken of, of course, is not merely pleasure, but life itself. A transcendent sobriety is what Moses wants Israel to condition itself for as he defines through Torah the parameters of a way of life for them — for them especially as a covenanted people.

The *berakhah* is an appreciation in transcendentally sober terms of what the God of Israel has given to the people of Israel. The traditional *Birkat ha-Mazon* (The Blessing after Meals) will be derived halakhically from the verse in Deuteronomy 8:10, "*Ve-akhalta ve-savata u-veirakhta et Adonai Elohekha al ha-aretz ha-tovah asher natan lakh*" ("when you shall eat and have been satisfied you will give thanks to the Lord your God for the good Land which He has given you"). The expanded prayer will first contain an appreciation of the Lord's gift of universal sustenance to all humankind. It will then focus Israel's attention on the unique Land of Israel as the place for economic growth and social well-being and on Jerusalem as the central source for combined political sovereignty and spiritual aspiration. It will add a further *berakhah* as a prayer for ultimate Messianic deliverance into a world of total goodness. The *berakhah* will thus redeem the rebuked. It will be the cathartic acknowledgment of God's compassion. The compassion may not cancel the rebuke; but it will effectively neutralize it in order for Israel to renew daily with confidence and trust its faith in the covenant.

Re'eh ראה

Moses knows that he is nearing the end of his *shelihut*, his ministry. He has much to say to his people. He is seeking desperately to review all of the *mitzvah* responsibilities which the Children of Israel will have to assume as partners to the covenant. He moves frenetically from topic to topic, from concern to concern: proper worship, prohibition of blood, suspicion of religious seducers and false prophets, idolatrous cities, dietary laws, sabbatical years, holidays, and so on. What unify the sundry elements in his discussions are verses such as Deuteronomy 14:2: "For you are a people consecrated to the Lord your God: the Lord your God chose you from all other peoples on earth to be His treasured people."

Free Will?

At the same time that Moses is reminding his people of God's choice of them as a covenanted partner, he reminds Israel of its own choices. God has gifted humanity with free will. "This day, see that I have set before you a blessing and curse..." Finding it difficult to accept the proposition that God is the source of the curse along with the blessing, the Midrash quotes Rabbi Elazar: "From the time when God uttered this on Sinai it has been laid down that *'Mi-pi Elyon lo tetze ha-ra'ot ve-ha-tov'* ('Evil and good do not proceed out of the mouth of the Most High,' Lamentations 3:38); but evil and good come on account of those who do evil and good." The Midrash then quotes Rabbi Haggai who says that God may have indeed given humankind a choice between two paths — one bringing blessings and life, the other curses and death — but in a special entreaty appearing in Deut. 30:19, God pleads with humankind to choose life! Rabbi Haggai puts it in these terms: "I have not merely placed before you two paths; but I am hereby going beyond the letter of the law or the strict conventional law in imploring you to choose life."

The Torah and Midrash are not philosophical treatises. They are works expressing the interface between God and humanity and between God and Israel. Yet serious thinkers have looked upon the above teachings as concerned with the question of the human being's free will — specifically the Israelite's free will. Certainly Rabbi Elazar's teaching seems to be talking about the issue of free will. It will be expanded by the Rambam in his *Mishne Torah* in the section on Repentance (Laws of Teshuvah 3:4): "A person should consider himself all year long as if he were half innocent and half guilty. Similarly he should view the whole world as if it were half innocent and half guilty. Should he, therefore, at any given point commit one sin, he will tilt himself and the whole world towards guilt with the concomitant condemnation bringing on summary destruction. On the other hand should he perform one *mitzvah* he will tilt himself and the whole world towards innocence with the concomitant merit which will bring on himself and itself ultimate salvation."

Religionists and atheists alike will recognize the ethical power, the absolute necessity of free will serving as a ground for moral responsibility. For the religionists — with the exception of some theological determinists — free will will be axiomatic in any consideration of moral education and moral action. But even and especially for atheistic thinkers who struggle to establish a basis for moral theory, free will is the sine qua non for any concept of moral responsibility and decision-making. Sartre, for example, will argue that an individual is in a situation of choosing at every moment of his life. He is thereby fashioning and refashioning himself at every moment. When each of us as an individual makes his choices, he in essence is choosing for all human beings. In creating the human being that we want to be, there is not a single one of our acts which does not at the same time create an image of the human being as we think he ought to be. Thus, our responsibility is limitless. It is much greater than we might have supposed, because it involves the destiny of all humankind.

As we have pointed out before, the moral aspiration reflected in the position of the atheistic existentialist is dangerously naïve. It appears prodigiously courageous in its exclusive reliance upon Man to begin with nothing and to be expected to make life-giving choices at every turn. In contrast Moses is highly skeptical of Man's pristine moral propensities. The position of Rabbi Haggai reflects this skepticism. The supererogatory necessity of God's entreaty to "choose life" comes out of a concerned awareness that the human being is torn evenly — as Rambam notes — between eros and thanatos, between a life-wish and a death-wish. And Moses and Rabbi Haggai do not consider Man, if left to himself, reliable enough to make the choice consistently of eros over thanatos.

In fact, God's statement to "choose life" is not an entreaty at all. It is a command! It cannot be anything but a command, because His overwhelming Presence makes of any utterance of His a prescription — an absolute command!

Put another way, the Torah states that God has built into His creation blessings, good, and life. He has also built into creation curses, evil, and death. His bias, however, is in favor of life! Both Rabbi Elazar and Rabbi Haggai see much evil and death in the world. Rabbi Elazar is ready to relegate God to a deistic position, i.e., respectfully removed from the crucible of humanity-on-earth, leaving all the evil and all the good in the world to come from Man. Pedagogically speaking, such a position may have merit from a moral point of view. But existentially and theologically it is highly unsatisfying. It does not and cannot relate to the reality of disease and pain and natural disasters and their impact upon Man. The evils of war in general and of the particular type of war of which the Shoah will serve as its most infernal example — war and murder for its own sake — cannot be placed in an isolated morally neutral cell of human existence removed from the struggle of Man's free will and God's free concern. The deistic position is spiritually disastrous for the human being looking to find transcendent meaning in his daily moral struggles.

Rabbi Haggai at least accepts the Torah text as it is: reality-as-created has blessings of good and of life; and curses of evil and of death. But God *is* concerned. He is concerned enough to insist — to command — that Man choose life, good, and blessings, for Man has been given the capacity — by God — to create on this earth occasions for life, for good, and for blessings. He has been given the capacity to confront and to ameliorate the effects of disease, pain, and natural disaster — and to discover the means with which to eliminate or minimize violence and war. He is being given a Torah intended to legislate for the betterment of Man's sociomoral, economic, and political condition.

Moses, of course, is not merely relating to the Israelites on an individual universalist basis. He is projecting a vision of covenantal choice for Israel as a nation. He is addressing both the individual and the nation at the same time. He is saying that the God of Israel is a God who is biased in favor of life. Whatever the Israelites do as individuals or as a people which promotes life and human well-being is good and is a blessing; whatever Israelites do as individuals or as a people which does not promote life and human well-being is evil and a curse. The rest is detailed commentary which Moses explicates throughout the Deuteronomic addresses. Commentary, application, and specification!

Is Moses offering a reward to the Israelites for choosing the good? To choose life bears with it an *intrinsic* good. But Moses knows that covenantal responsibility entails sacrifices which in an immediate, middle-term, and long-term sense may not be "good." Moses is aware of the example of the self-righteous man who goes to see his master. "I was taught once," the man complains, "that they who learned to do the right things are happy. I have not found it so. I am tired of doing the right things when I do not get rewarded for my sacrifices." "I see your difficulty," replies the master. "There is something yet for you to learn. It is not enough just to do the right things. If you would be happy, you must learn to enjoy doing them."

What Moses is stressing, in effect, is the fruitlessness of the pursuit of happiness-for-itself. One never finds it as a result of pursuit — ruthless or conscientious. One does what one does — the *mitzvot* — because it is right and the doing itself bestows the happiness. For the Jew whose identity is defined by the covenant, this idea is translatable into wanting to be committed to the covenant, appreciating the opportunity, loving it, and in the love of it finding reward. Nothing else is needed. No matter what sacrifices may be called for, they are to be looked at as situations in which one is called upon to offer oneself up for making God's creation better. And the "something" better is part of a means-end continuum that is already good!

Children of God Forever

Moses refers to Israel as *banim atem la-Shem* (you are the Children of God). He is echoing a much earlier appellation bestowed upon Israel by God Himself — that Israel is to be referred to as "My firstborn son." That Pharaoh would have dared to attempt to exterminate God's "firstborn" son — Israel —

begged for a grimly appropriate measure-for-measure punishment: the final plague!

To be referred to as *banim la-Shem* (children of God) is a wondrous appellation. Is Israel worthy of it? Are they truly dedicated to the betterment of God's world? Are they sufficiently sensitive to the privilege they have been given to partner the ongoing molding of God's creation? As the Children of God — His first born — they should never be discouraged or misled into believing that powerful forces "out there" in the world, alternative to God, will or can provide ultimate meaning to human effort. Only God's teachings can provide that meaning. They should never be disappointed or disillusioned in leaders who err. Such leaders are human, and they are never to be idolized so as to be viewed as sitting in the place of God. Isaiah will caution Israel *"Im lo ta'aminu ki lo te'amenu"* ("if you don't believe, you won't be firm enough to survive"). Isaiah will be stressing the importance of uncovering one's inner *emunah* and building together with others one's true community of *emunah*, so that authentic Godly integrity will determine one's staying power, not various idolatries based on the worship of human pretense.

In a debate in the talmudic tractate *Kiddushin*, Rabbi Yehudah and Rabbi Meir argue over the citation by Moses that the Children of Israel are the *children of God*. Rabbi Yehudah says that when they behave like children should, they are then considered the children of God. When they do not, they lose the designation. Rabbi Meir insists that no matter how much they fall short, no matter how much they violate the covenant, they continue to be referred to as God's children. And Rabbi Meir brings four verses as proof texts. The Children of Israel are described as foolish children — but still children; as children with no faith — but still children; as corrupt children — but still children. And even where they will be described as "no longer God's nation," they will continue to be called "the Children of the Living God." The perennially relevant lesson in the citation of these verses by Rabbi Meir is that no matter how "down" Israel may feel about themselves as a people, they dare not forget for a moment who they have been and who they are — the Children of their Creator, Revealer, and Redeemer, the God of Israel.

The essence of the debate between Rabbi Yehudah and Rabbi Meir is over the question of the survivability of the Jewish people. The destruction of the First Temple and the concomitant loss of sovereignty have been catastrophic; but with the inspiration of prophets like Ezekiel, the exiled Jews have recovered enough to send a contingent back to resettle the Land and to begin a reconstruction which will lead eventually to sovereignty under the Maccabees. From a historic perspective, however, this sovereignty will be short-lived. And the debate between Rabbi Yehudah and Rabbi Meir will come in the wake of the second destruction and the second loss of sovereignty that will be accompanied by a profound national depression. Rabbi Yehudah is echoing the judgmental side of God's attributes. When Israel violates their filial responsibility they forfeit the filial relationship and become at best mere servants. Rabbi Meir insists that the filial relationship is never broken — despite this nation's foolishness, its lack of faith, its moral corruption, and even its seeming rejection of the covenant itself.

The unconditional quality of God's love for Israel will be asserted by many throughout later Jewish history. In the Middle Ages Rabbi Yitzhak Arama will comment on the eternal nature of the covenant: "Its continuity into eternity as a covenant bespeaks God's love; for His people is not dependant on any material aspect of mundane reality, but on an attachment to a compelling supernatural force. The covenant can never be cancelled by any worldly phenomenon." Thus the religion, the history, the civilization of Israel is meant to be a living out of the covenant — for better and for worse. In other words, even if as a nation, they behave foolishly, faithlessly, corruptly, in a way begging for rejection, the Children of Israel are before all and after all the Children of the Living God!

It is understandable that later generations of Israelite Jews from Rabbi Meir to Yitzhak Arama will seek to build a faith that won't allow for any questioning of the solidity of the covenant relationship. Moses is not in the same situation. He is at the helm of a ship-of-state in the making, at the beginning of its voyage in fulfilling the terms of the covenant. And Moses wants to confront the Children of Israel at the outset of their adventure with a clear enunciation of terms. There should be no misunderstanding of what is demanded of them and what will be the consequences of their disobedience. Not that Rabbi Meir and Arama are ready to relieve Israel of its spiritual and sociomoral responsibilities. Regardless of how firm and unbreakable the covenant may be in the eyes of these later teachers, the threatened punishments will nevertheless be severe enough to hold the people to attention and to commitment.

Moses never ceases to press Israel to learn to fear God, to revere Him.

What is this fear, this reverence, this *yirah*? Again, Moses must relate to the perennial question "Why should one do spiritual acts or moral deeds?" The normal answer is "reward." But *yirah* doesn't have a reward attached to it that is easily defined. In Isaiah 40:10 there is the phrase "*hinei sekharo ito*" ("behold the reward is with Him"). Feeling close to God is the reward, especially when one feels himself in a state of reverence. Who are described as *yerei Elohim* if not Abraham during the *akeidah* episode and Job before and during his severe trials. What they have in common in being "reverent" is an attachment to the Almighty — no matter what the situation. As a covenanted people, Moses will remind them time and time again that the task is to want life with high purpose — not reward per se. The high purpose will itself be enough of a reward.

Authentic *yirah* will not only strengthen the filial relationship with God in a normative sense. It will serve to strengthen the immunity of the people to idolatry, to idolatrous people, and to idolatrous forces in the world looking to infiltrate their midst. These idolatrous forces will always be seeking to lead them to ruin. These forces have already shown themselves capable of atrocities such as the sacrifice of children in the name of religion. Israel in its Land will have to extirpate these forces without compromise. This kind of idolatry will not be tolerated. It is this extreme kind of idolatry which will be exemplified in the legislation to destroy completely the "*ir ha-nidahat*" ("that city — under Israelite sovereignty — condemned to destruction because of wholesale idolatry"). All evidences of such heinous practices must be wiped out — totally.

Moses knows that the common people will often be tempted to turn for relief and healing to false prophets, soothsayers, demi-gods, and gods, thus relieving them of their own responsibilities and necessary self-criticism that goes along with making and applying their own decisions. And so Moses warns his people to be particularly wary of a "prophet" who may come along and who will offer all kinds of signs and wonders in order to influence the people to follow him and to pay allegiance to him. Rabbi Yose ha-Gelili will warn the people that even should idolaters achieve mastery over the sun and the moon, the stars and other celestial bodies, these idolaters are not to be followed, let alone worshiped. Human power is never to be worshiped. It is to be used; it is to be dedicated to worthy purpose.

Rabbi Akiva will offer a more daring interpretation in disagreement with

Rabbi Yose ha-Gelili: "Perish the thought that the Lord would intentionally bestow upon idolaters as gifts, so to speak, control of the sun and the moon, the stars and other celestial beings." Thus would He not be giving even minor justification to idolatrous worship and false prophecy? "The text," says Rabbi Akiva, "is referring to true prophets who become false prophets — such as Jeremiah's adversary, Hananiah ben Azur." In other words, even if a man has been as close to God as a prophet, and thus has been "right" in a given situation, there is no assurance that he will be able to arrogate to himself a certainty that he is "right" under all circumstances. He must constantly be alert to God's current message.

The Rabbis in their expansion of Moses' prophetic instruction are offering a doubly powerful repudiation of idolatry. The world as it is seems to be hospitable to powerful forces, natural and human, which at various times seem to be in effective control. They are from Israel's point of view destructive forces, evil forces. Moses, and Rabbi Yose ha-Gelili, are urging Israel to be prepared and strong enough in its knowledge and commitment to God, truth, justice, mercy, and human betterment to persist in fighting for *tikkun olam* ("mending such a world"). In the battle against idolatry, there can be no shoddy, superficial moral equivalences. Israel will always have to fight the war against idolatries of all kinds. The Land of Israel and any future State of Israel will always be on the cutting edge of the battle against idolatry — geographically, culturally, religiously, socially, and morally. It will be "sentenced" to stand up for God and Torah indefinitely.

But Moses — reinforced by Rabbi Akiva — is saying even more. In the world as it is, there will be individuals who will be in positions of leadership, who will at given times appear to be "close to God" in their perceptions of truth, of the given situation, of the correct path under the circumstances, etc. It is necessary to remember, however, that even these individuals may err. In their error they must receive the required corrective criticism. If and when necessary, they must be removed. Such ongoing critical appraisal demands of all Israelites individually and collectively a special alertness as well as a persistent faith in the source of all ultimate power and truth. Isaiah's caution "If you don't have faith, you won't be firm enough to survive" is a summary injunction to be constantly vigilant enough to impose a Godly critique on all human action, especially that of mortal leaders.

Rabbi Akiva refers to Hananiah ben Azur as his example of a false prophet who misleads Israel at a particularly critical moment in its history. His confrontation with Jeremiah has been discussed earlier. Shall the Children of Israel rebel against their Babylonian occupiers and oppressors? Jeremiah the true prophet of the God of Israel proclaims an emphatic "No!" Hananiah ben Azur presents himself as Jeremiah's adversary. In the eyes of the people Hananiah is a prophetic patriot, for he supports the rebellion against Israel's evil oppressor. But in this case, Hananiah turns out to be wrong. And his error will be fatal for him personally and disastrous for Israel. Jeremiah is the true prophet, because notwithstanding his "jeremiads," the prophetic insight lighting his way is his genuine love for Israel and his unswerving faith in the God of Israel who even as He is punishing His children continues to love them.

Dietary Holiness

The idea that Israel remains God's children, God's first born, is correlative to the idea that Israel is an especially endowed people, separated for holy purposes. Listed among the miscellany of *mitzvot* are those that are there to promote Israel's distinctiveness. Among the most prominent of these *mitzvot* are those dealing with *kashrut* (dietary laws).

One may go back to the very beginning of the Torah and review the very first dietary norm given to humanity. The image in the Garden of Eden is that there is to be virtual equality among the animal creatures: "God said, See, I give you every seed-bearing plant that is upon all the earth, and every tree that has seed-bearing fruit; they shall be yours for food. And to all the animals on land, to all the birds of the sky, and to everything that creeps on earth, in which there is the breath of life, I give all the green plants for food."

It has been noted by many that God compromises on his original herbivorous intention for Man, because God's primary creature as the Torah tells it — Man — shows himself to be potentially violent. Rabbi A.I. Kook will ascribe Man's descent from his lofty rung of the ladder of God's preferred creatures to his inability to bear the splendor of the supernal light of creation. As a creature of flesh and blood, Man will inevitably fall short of God's loftiest expectations. And yet, the hope that Man can achieve a sense of purity and beauty despite his animal habits must never be abandoned. And so the aim of realizing a pristine form of justice and righteousness on earth to include even animals may not be achievable. That is, to argue that animals shall be maintained on the same preferred level as humankind and therefore off-limits to Man's diet will be seen to be impossible. The Torah concludes, therefore, that it will be enough to impose moral restrictions on Man's behavior to his fellow men.

In Torah legislation this will not countenance torture of animals. But under meticulously careful conditions, the Torah will allow for the killing of animals for food. Man will be permitted to kill in order to eat and only to eat. Let him at least not be a cannibal who will eat his own species. But let him train himself to rise ultimately to the stage in some future era of not having to kill animals. Or, if he must kill them, let him so control the act of killing — of ritual slaughter — and the succeeding preparations for food, that the entire process will be an opportunity for refining human behavior — even sanctifying it.

Moses is charged with educating his people to relate to the subject of sanctification as both a method of assuring distinctiveness and as a means of lifting otherwise animal acts to the level of aesthetic transport. In other words, Israel will be taught not to glorify the act of killing for food and certainly not to justify the act of killing for sport. Early in the Torah Nimrod's hunting and Esau's hunting have not been viewed sympathetically. Neither will later generations be encouraged to indulge in festal orgies of food preparation and consumption. At the same time, Judaism will not opt for the ascetic extreme as an alternative. It will not impose a burden of guilt upon the nobility among God's creatures — humankind — provided that human beings are clearly doing what they are doing in order to help their own physical survival.

And so Judaism sets a four-stage control: (1) Israelites will not be permitted to eat all kinds of meat (and all kinds of fish). (2) The meat which they are permitted to eat will have to be slaughtered mercifully. (3) The most vivid symbol and symptom of life, and loss of life — blood — will have to be completely removed before the meat is to be permitted to be eaten. And finally, (4) the entire act of preparing to eat, the eating, and concluding the eating are to be transformed, sublimated by the accompaniment verbally of various rituals into the hoped-for process of sanctification.

The Terrain of Sanctification

The covenant cannot have meaning and relevancy if it is couched exclusively in lofty propositions meant to inspire intellectual and emotional commitments, yet stopping short of directed behavior. The intellectual and emotional dimensions of the covenantal commitment are necessary — indispensable for motivational purposes. But the *mitzvot*, the behavior, must be directed to the most mundane aspects of being a creature. Those aspects are sufficiently dominant in the human being's daily routine of living that to avoid the attempt to sanctify precisely the most creaturely acts of daily life is to relegate holiness and distinctiveness to a segregated negligibility. Moses — and God — will not accept such a limiting.

Everything associated with life must be turned into a blessing. Israel is being enjoined to choose life — not to give into the blandishments of idolatry which can only lead to evil and death. Choosing life and the process of opening up all the sundry details of living to legislated sanctity is the ultimate blessing.

Shoftim   שופטים

Moses continues sweeping across a vast legislative range: the establishment of judicial and executive institutions; laws of warfare including grounds for exemption from military service; concern for homicide and other crimes and misdemeanors plaguing the social fabric. Two declamatory high points in this Torah portion are the injunctions: *"tzedek tzedek tirdof"* ("Justice, justice shall you pursue") and *"tamim tihye im Adonai Elohekha"* ("Be wholehearted with the Lord your God"). Taken together these injunctions are intended to impress upon Israel that pursuing justice is arriving at the most reasonably justifiable position under given circumstances, and this entails building a comprehensive legal system reflecting an overall value complex which is spiritually uplifting and socially fair. Such a system will be fragile if there is no individual, familial, social, and national "wholeheartedness" dedicated to the overall enterprise.

Torah under the Circumstances

The Torah pronounces in grand fashion *"tzedek, tzedek tirdof"* ("justice, justice shall you pursue"). Why the need for the double-word *tzedek tzedek*? Ramban says: The first *tzedek* refers to the heavenly state achieved only as part of God's ultimate reward. The second *tzedek* is that which is demanded of all human beings — the justice that they are mandated to achieve in their society on earth, through their effort. Should they fail in their effort at striving for human justice they will not be worthy of the justice reserved in "heaven." In other words, there is a justice that is *absolute*, found only in the glory of God's Presence and which no human being possesses while on earth. In one's striving for human "justice-on-earth," one hopes to be somehow worthy of the reward of God's absolute "justice-in-heaven."

There is a *relative* justice to be striven for on earth. It is often so elusive that it is a challenge to every Israelite to achieve it, including those who think of themselves as just but who are only human — and thereby fallible. When the Ramban adds the other injunction "be wholehearted with the Lord your God," he is conditioning the entire enterprise of establishing justice in a society of human beings upon the capacity of each individual within that society to respond to the questions: "What are the values one really holds to? Are they worthy of being valued? Do the laws one promulgates, legislates, obeys in the name of justice reflect these values?"

We used the phrase above "under given circumstances" to qualify the pursuit of justice on earth. What is meant by this phrase? Moses and the Torah of Israel are sensitive to the fact that the world is not utopian. For that very reason the education of a people and the preparation of that people to build an ethically viable society must be based on laws — and laws must be workable and enforceable "under the circumstances." With such a mandate the latter day philosopher of law Chaim Perelman will reject various mathematical models of justice espoused by thinkers as distinguished as Pascal, Descartes, and Spinoza.

Perelman criticizes Pascal who decries the problem of the changeability of laws and legal systems due to different historic circumstances, geographical and cultural factors, etc. For Pascal such "chaos" and unpredictability make it impossible to build a society that will conform to a vision of absolute justice. But it is on this point where Perelman takes issue with Pascal and with others like Descartes and Spinoza for having attempted to build models of justice and truth on *mathematical* models in the first place. From an intellectual point of view such mathematical models are off the mark as they relate to fallible human beings. From a social and ethical point of view such models are entirely mistaken, dangerously so.

What Perelman refers to as "classical rationalism" — the rationalism of Descartes and Spinoza — errs on two counts respectively: (1) Descartes' postulate of God's perfect will *determining all other truths* and (2) Spinoza's postulate of God's perfect intelligence *dominating all other wills*. Under both these postulates, according to Perelman, there is no possibility for Man to make a less-than-perfect decision and have it be a wise decision. For the only wisdom, the only rationality for Descartes and Spinoza, is perfect. In weighing a decision, therefore, a human being, ideally speaking, has committed himself to discovering the rationally best decision as a manifestation of the absolute truth of God or the absolute will of God. Once he finds that rationally best decision, how can he be wrong? He must be right absolutely; but if he is right absolutely, then his adversary must be wrong absolutely. But what if he and his adversary are both right? Is that possible?

Perelman cites the talmudic axiom which characterizes wise and humane societies as those in which debates between different schools of legal and moral concern prove that there are times when *"Elu ve-elu divrei Elohim hayyim"* ("Both schools of thought are expressing the words of the Living God"). The human being in his decision-making for society cannot find the *perfectly* just truth and certainly not the *perfect* will of God. What Man does pursue, however, is wisdom *under the circumstances.* For human beings do have wisdom, and their wisdom may lead to decisions which are not unanimously agreed to, yet are wise.

There is no doubt that the pursuit of wisdom leading to justice under the circumstances is difficult because by definition perfect "justice" is never achieved. Nevertheless one never stops pursuing it. And the effort is not to be perceived as being expended in an ambience of chaos. As long as one is wholehearted, he should believe that he is standing before the God of wisdom, justice, and truth. He, along with all of Israel, should pursue earthly *tzedek* and he will be properly rewarded, as the Ramban sees it, with the emanation of the ultimate *tzedek* in the *Shekhinah* (God's Indwelling Presence).

Because of the difficulty in legislating for specific norms of justice within a pulsating newly developing society, Moses knows that he needs to cultivate within Israel as mature an attitude as possible towards God, to the demands of the covenant, and to the understanding and application of Torah under all circumstances. Israel's overall attitude towards God and Torah must never be a mask for idolatry, superstition, psychological and intellectual infantilism. Moses has been stressing and will continue to stress that the fundamental initial doctrine which must be digested by the people is that God is the source of good, blessing, and life — but that the world surrounding Israel, a world which God has created, also has evil in it, curses, and death. In other words, the world with which humankind has been gifted is host in its totality to a mysterious congeries of blessings and curses, forces for good and for evil, for life and for death.

But the Children of Israel are charged to believe that God wishes them, commands them, to choose the blessings of life and the goodness thereof in this world. They are to understand that the covenant of Torah is a mandate for partnership with God in moving this world towards the good, towards life-giving purpose. How? Through the reasonable application of Torah and its search for truth and justice — under all circumstances.

A Mutable Torah

The Torah expects that adjudication which purports to find just decisions under all circumstances will need an elastic clause within itself to free Torah for renewal through reinterpretation when necessary. Such is the injunction in Deut. 17:8–9: "If a case is too baffling for you to decide, be it a controversy over homicide, civil law, or assault — matters of dispute in your courts — you shall promptly repair to the place that the Lord your God will have chosen and appear before the levitical priests, or the magistrate in charge at the time...." Whoever, in other words, is in charge *at the time* weighing the *circumstances at the time* will determine the just verdict.

The application of Torah will not only have the burden of a maximalist detailing of legislation for each emerging generation and its specific problems, it will have to endure the apocalyptic changes wrought by radical historical upheavals in the condition of the Jewish people. With such upheavals, will the Torah of Moses be the same Torah as that of Shimon bar Yohai? That of the Netziv of Volozhin? Of Ahad Ha'am, Jabotinsky, and Ben Gurion?

Moses is legislating for a people that is headed towards establishing an independent, sovereign state. God will be worshiped as the Ultimate Ruler; but human kingship will eventually assume executive responsibility for running the state. Joshua's autocratic rule will give way before the instabilities of the period of the Judges. And Samuel will be instrumental in establishing human kingship as the mode of rule for the duration of the First Commonwealth. But one underlying premise of Torah application from the period of Moses through the period of the later kings of Israel and Judah will be that it is meant for this world, for the mending of this world, today, tomorrow, and the days after tomorrow. The struggle for Torah application in this world is intended to be an immediate and comprehensive one — on all fronts concerned about all issues related to the well-being of Man as he makes his way in this world.

Is this Torah the same Torah which will be taught by Rabbi Shimon bar Yohai? Moses' Torah is, as mentioned, the Deuteronomic series of codes dealing with the building of a society in which every aspect of that society is to be the concern of Torah — conquest, settlement, legislation for humaneness and sanctification, all under Israelite or Jewish sovereignty. Shimon bar Yohai's Torah, on the other hand, will reflect the rabbinic struggle a millenium and a half later to keep the Jewish people alive in a hostile, dependent, *galut* situation. His generation and the generations following will be forced to survive in the twilight zone of a day-to-day struggle to reject evil, curses, and death without surrendering the covenantal mandate to strive for *tikkun olam* — at least internally. Without sovereignty, trying to endure in a threatening environment, they will seek to build an internal spiritual citadel in order to protect their Jewish way of life from outside contamination.

Shimon bar Yohai's Torah will despise the non-Jewish world. For as long as the evil empire of the idolatrous Rome of his day will rule the world, how can Judaism not sequester itself into a cave, removed from the world, in order to wait for an apocalyptic change. The legend will have Bar Yohai and his son emerging from the cave to face a Jewish people that is planting and harvesting, notwithstanding Roman domination of the world. In Bar Yohai's eyes such a world cannot and must not survive. And so the legend has Shimon and/or his son incinerating the crops. The continuation of the legend has Bar-Yohai at a later stage tolerating such a world when he sees that Jews are keeping Shabbat even under Roman domination. Again, is Bar-Yohai's Torah the same as Moses' Torah? In most details it is. But in its basic political grounding — national dependency versus national sovereignty — it is not. And Bar-Yohai's view of Torah vis-à-vis the world will color Jewish thinking and behavior for many centuries.

The Emancipation will pull Bar Yohai's Torah abruptly and violently out of the cave. An otherwise otherworldly figure like the late nineteenth century Netziv of Volozhin who will oppose the teaching of secular subjects at his Torah institution will nevertheless recognize that some halakhic applications of Torahitic *mitzvot* will have to change. He will allude, for example, to the positive Torahitic *mitzvah* of electing a king to rule: "It appears that modes of governmental rule are changing from autocratic monarchy to representative democracy. There are states which cannot tolerate monarchy and other states which without a king would be like a ship without a captain. And so this issue cannot be decided on the basis of the positive *mitzvah* of the Torah, i.e., preferring monarchy. Because governing a society is an issue of life-and-death, the 'command' to elect a king must be suspended as long as the people will no longer accept a monarchy. The prevailing custom in the surrounding areas will determine the practice of choosing the governing power."

The Netziv will have been of the traditional school of Torah learning; but he will support the Hibbat Zion Movement even with its secular pioneers. Will then his Torah be a literal parroting of Bar-Yohai's Torah? Will its grounding be more akin to the Torah of Moses? A major question will then be how much of the Torah of Moses, of Bar-Yohai, or of the Netziv will be considered the heritage of emerging "free-thinking secularists" such as Ahad Ha'am, Jabotinsky, and Ben Gurion.

With various interpretations and modifications these "secularists" will accept the Torah as *moreshet Yisrael* (the heritage of Israel). They will consider the Torah to be an integral part of Jewish culture. But in this process of integration or acculturation, they and others like them will insist on a new readiness for radical interpretations of major parts of the heritage. They will be calling for an openness to the world and its values. These values will have to be examined, weighed, measured to see if they are welcome in a new Jewish society on its land — the reborn Land of Israel.

The precedent of a changing Torah will have been established long before in Ezra's day with the concept of the *Torah she-Be'al Peh* (the Oral Torah). This Oral Torah will have recognized the necessity of reinterpretation of legislation in order to constantly see God's will as a supervening ethical will. Two examples will underscore the necessity for such reinterpretation — one example from a previous discussion and the other from this portion, but both interconnected within talmudic thought.

As we've seen earlier, in the *Torah she-bi-Khetav* (the Written Torah), the wife accused by her husband of adultery is subjected to a trial by ordeal which is blatantly unfair to the hapless and helpless woman. The Rabbis of the *Torah she-Be'al Peh* (the Oral Torah) will insist that the testing of the wife by the "bitter waters" can only be valid if the husband is himself innocent of sin. It is clear that the Rabbis' moral sensibility will not allow an idea such as the "trial-by-ordeal" to reflect *forever* the will of God. It can't have been the will of God unconditioned by further detailed provisions. This is no criticism of Moses who has had the daunting task of legislating for all aspects of life for a generation living under different circumstances over a millenium before the Rabbis. Again, the Rabbis living much later with their own evolving sociomoral sensibility will find that they must reinterpret the Torah in order to do legislatively whatever they have to do — considering *their* circumstances.

The second example: The ceremony of the breaking of the neck of the heifer is intended to bring expiation to the community for an untraced murder. The elders of the community nearest to the corpse announce that "our hands have not shed this blood and our eyes did not see who did; forgive your people Israel whom you have redeemed and don't permit innocent blood to be shed amidst your people Israel." In the *Torah she-bi-Khetav* Moses juxtaposes to this ritual atonement for an untraced homicide the laws of warfare. And they will similarly be juxtaposed in the Oral Torah, noting that in warfare there will be many corpses; and that the warfare itself may have come because of Israel's sins — the kinds of sins exemplified by the *sotah* (the suspected wife).

Returning, therefore, for a moment to the *sotah*: there is an entire talmudic tractate devoted to it — to this wife suspected of infidelity. At the same time that the Rabbis are liberalizing the terms for dealing with the *sotah*, they can't help noting the metaphorical appropriateness of the image of the *sotah* in describing their sinful people Israel. The tractate *Sotah* will end with a merciless description of the disintegration of an immoral Israelite society leading to its destruction. Adultery will be so rampant that the bitter waters of the trial of the *sotah* will be considered ludicrous. *And murders will have so increased that a ceremony for public atonement will seem a mockery!*

In other words, the *sotah*, that is, collective Israel, despite its legitimate concern for warfare against external enemies, must attend with equal concern to the state of morality and immorality within its own community. Moses in his legislation has known that Israel must build a strong society internally as a bulwark for facing external problems. The Rabbis will know it as well — to their sorrow. But the Rabbis will sense that Torahitic legislation concerning the *sotah* and the *eglah arufah* (the expiating heifer) are just not relevant any longer. These examples are extreme. But the principle is clear. Given certain mutations in life, the Torah must show its own mutability.

War, Murder, and Life

Moses cannot emphasize enough that it is absurd for Israel to expect to be victorious in war against external enemies when internally they will have been violating the covenant. Moses encourages the people that should they be confronted by war, they are not to fear, not to panic, not to be in dread of their enemies. "For it is the Lord your God who marches with you to do battle for you against your enemy, to bring you victory." The Ramban asks "What does it mean to say that God will bring you victory?" Is it that Israel's active role is unnecessary? On the contrary, the Ramban explains that the spiritual leadership of the people is charged with lifting the morale of the people while the "secular" officials of the people will have the "down-to-earth" task of guiding the people in their day-to-day struggle for achieving the victory. In other words, God's victory is contingent upon Israel's readiness to deal with those mundane challenges which humanity must confront — with or without God's "help." Yet the most fundamentally "mundane" challenge will always be the maintenance of spiritual morale. And spiritual morale is contingent upon the sociomoral health of the community.

War is the starkest of the situations to be faced by a nation seeking to build a secure environment for its people. Required, therefore, is the two-sided strategy of fearing God enough to make certain that His covenant is being kept while at the same time learning the tactics of battle with enemies of this covenant. "God goes forth to fight for you with your enemies in order to save you." Is there not an embarrassing arrogance to Israel's confidence that God is on its side? The conditions for such confidence will exist only if Israel has been sufficiently critical of itself in building an exemplary humane society. Only then can it compare its worthiness favorably with their enemies who have shown themselves, presumably, to be not only anti-Semitic but anti-human. Israel must then accompany its inspired élan with a full awareness that war demands material, physical, economic, and military readiness buttressed by worldly wisdom, diplomatic cleverness, and strategic ingenuity. The world of men is to be seen as a world of conflict where survival dictates the terms by which Israel must confront those forces bent on its destruction.

When Israel will need to fight a war, it will only come following unsuccessful attempts to negotiate peace. If the Written Torah includes instructions for punishing idolatrous enemies with total destruction, the Oral Toral will reinterpret the terms presented to enemies before the recourse to war in accordance with its modified understanding and compassion for other human beings. The Rabbis and their later descendants will institute appropriate checks and balances so as to avoid total indiscriminate war. They will look to Torah to mandate "turning swords into plowshares and spears into pruning hooks" — *wherever possible* under *the circumstances.*

When it will not be possible to achieve the necessary compromises to avoid war, then the Torah will have directed Israel to recognize that it lives in a world of ravenous nations. As it struggles, therefore, to survive among these nations it must remember the lesson from the Midrash on Koheleth: "He who is merciful to the cruel will eventually become cruel to the merciful." In other words, Israel will under certain circumstances have to fight for its collective life. At such times the nation will have to be absolutely clear and unified about its moral purposes, motivated sufficiently to fight to defend these purposes, and determined enough to prevail against its enemies whatever the cost.

At the same time, the Children of Israel will have learned from the Torah of Moses never to lose sight of the horrors of war and blood lust. The *Torah she-bi-Khetav* will have been sensitive enough to the personal psychological emotional needs of these Children of Israel to provide, for example, exemptions from battle for those who are marrying, who are dedicating a new home, who are planting a vineyard; and for those too psychologically terrified to fight.

In addition, because the world will be understood to be what it is — *olam ke-minhago noheig* — with its constant potential for destructiveness, it will be essential for Moses to caution his people against giving in to their predatory instincts. In the same breath, as it were, that Moses is explaining the rules of warfare, he emphasizes the Torah's agenda for bringing blessings of love and well-being into the world — not the curse of destructiveness. Moses introduces the principle of *bal-tashhit,* meant to prohibit gratuitous waste and destruction — even of "unimportant" inanimate objects. In turn the Torah will forbid the mistreatment of animals. And this in turn is expected to lay the ideational groundwork for prohibiting the killing of human beings. The Rambam will codify the law of *bal-tashhit*: "We don't cut down trees which provide food for purposes of destruction. Not only trees, but all who break vessels and tear clothing and demolish buildings and block-up wells and waste food are guilty of violating the law against gratuitous destruction."

Neither Moses nor the Rambam will address directly, however, the lurking question: "Why does God destroy? Why death — is death not the greatest waste?" Moses and the Rambam do provide a powerful indirect answer to these questions in all that they teach and preach about the insidious attraction of idolatry — idolatry which is essentially self-idolatry. The Talmud will explain: "He who tears his clothing in anger or breaks his vessels in anger or wastes his money in anger is like an idolater. For such is the art of the evil impulse. Today it tells you to do such and such and tomorrow this and that until someday it tells you to worship idols and you do it." In other words, the human being for the most part knows what is right when he is calm and cool enough to listen to his *sekhel* (common sense).

But the human being's evil impulse clouds over his common sense with anger. Anger in turn brings on intellectual and moral confusion which opens the door to idolatry. When the human being — basing his decisions on his impulses and unbridled passions — considers himself the exclusive yardstick for determining right and wrong, then he is guilty of self-worship! Death is the only ultimate antidote to the hubris of the idolatrous human being. Death is the final incontrovertible proof that human beings are before all and after all only creatures.

In the midst of these stark discussions concerning war, destruction and murder, Judaism's Torah will be committed to teaching its primary lesson — the thirst for life. For the human being to turn his life into an engine for the destruction of life — even the "life" of an inanimate object, not to mention animals, and certainly not to mention human beings — is the ultimate blasphemy, the utter desecration of God's creation. A human creature may lust for life, but at the same time may harbor a "death-wish." Such a human creature will lack a sincere appreciation for the gift of life which he has been granted, and which has been granted equally to fellow human beings. He is capable of descending to the level of Raskolnikov in *Crime and Punishment* who certainly yearns for life, but at the same time commits murder:

> where is it I've read that someone condemned to death says or thinks, an hour before his death, that if he had to live on some high rock, or such a narrow ledge that he had only room to stand, and the ocean,

> everlasting darkness, everlasting solitude, everlasting tempest around him, if he had to remain standing on a square yard of space all his life, a thousand years, eternity, it were better to live so than to die at once! Only to live, to live and live! Life, whatever it may be!

Raskolnikov — the latter-day Cain — is eloquent enough in his invocation to life to elicit a modicum of empathy from the reader who — if a normal human being — has a similar passion for life. Raskolnikov's passion for life, "whatever that life may be," as he puts it, is a passion, however, which has not prevented his taking another's life. And so Raskolnikov's soliloquy is a testimony to moral and spiritual hypocrisy! Indeed, from the vantage point of the earliest sections of the Torah, a passion for life such as Raskolnikov's can in no way make a case for warranting immortality! On the contrary, the price of such immortality would be the utter self-idolatry of the murderer!

The Torah — Judaism — will argue that the body must be returned to the dust from which it came. Certainly the Cains, the Nimrods, the Raskolnikovs, and the Hitlers! But all human beings! Mortality will be one of the essential conditions of being human, of being alive. The comfort for those human beings who will have chosen a way of life which has rejected the curse of evil — the curse of Nimrod and Hitler — will be the knowledge that the most blessed gift within the gift of life is the soul of the human being. That humane soul will have been described in the Bible as the candle of God. That humane soul — *just and wholehearted as it has been under the circumstances* during its sojourn on earth — will endure.

Torah and the Wholehearted

And so Moses prods, cajoles, entreats, and exhorts his people, resolutely moving from instruction to instruction, injunction to injunction. His summary statement "*Tamim tihye im Adonai Elohekha*" ("Be wholehearted with your God") is fleshed out by the Ramban: "We are enjoined to integrate our mind/hearts to Him exclusively...as Abraham when the covenant was sealed with him and his descendants was told by God 'walk before Me and be wholehearted....' It was his faith (Abraham's) which enabled him to stand fast against the Chaldean idolaters of his day..." Moses knows the difficulties that Abraham faced being one against the many. Moses' entire life and mission has been a singular faith-posture which has shepherded a slave-people into freedom. Joshua will challenge his people in Shekhem as will Elijah on Mount Carmel to choose between the path of the covenant and the tempting alternatives.

This watchword, this slogan "be wholehearted before Me" parallels the quintessential declaration of Jewish faith announced early in the Deuteronomic addresses — the all-inclusive *Shema*: "Hear O Israel, the Lord our God, the Lord is One!" On the basis of this momentous comprehensive call, Moses is seeking to build a series of value-concepts and *halakhot* or behavioral patterns which are to make up the way a Jew walks in the world. Abraham knew how. And Isaac and Jacob and the following generations would produce those Israelites, those Jews, who would know how to be wholehearted, unified in one's understanding and purpose.

Such wholeheartedness would not necessarily require intellectual acumen of an exceptional sort. To be *tamim* would certainly relate to "the *hakham*" ("the wise one") of the *Pesah Seder*. But it could just as readily relate to "the *tam*" ("the simple one"), the intuitively sensitive Jew who would develop a visceral single-mindedness of purpose, dedicated unswervingly to fulfilling the covenantal destiny. Such wholeheartedness would then welcome the teachings of the Torah with all its potential for making life-on-earth a *tamim* blessing — a blessing of wholeheartedness. What would the Torah be for such a *tam* along with the *hakham*?

The Jerusalem Talmud in the tractate *Rosh Hashanah* would use various loving metaphors with which to describe Torah, its study, and its application: In the name of Rabbi Levi a comparison would be made with a king who had a clock which he turned over eventually to his son. Or with a king who had a guardhouse to be transferred eventually to his son. Or with a king who had a ring of authority, or tools, or treasures or a bag of medicines, all to be given for safekeeping to his son. How would all these metaphors relate to the learning and application of Torah? The Torah as clock would give coherence to human life and its existence in the world. The Torah as guardhouse would distinguish between the forces for creativity and destruction in the world. The Torah as ring of authority would render Israel as participant in the creative governing of the world. The Torah would suggest the tools for governing and mending that world. The Torah would provide the keys to uncover further joys and beauty among the resources of the world.

And finally, the Torah would offer a mode of human healing when necessary — and it would be necessary. For notwithstanding progress and growth and expansion, there would be failure and sin, illness and mortality. But the Torah — and Moses couldn't stress it enough — was joined in a covenantal union with the God of Israel and the people of Israel. Such a union was the essential wholeness of heart which would make the pursuit of justice-on-earth curative and redemptive — under all circumstances.

Ki Tetze כי תצא

The Rambam will note that there are no less than seventy-two *mitzvot* in the portion of *Ki Tetze*. But the *Midrash Devarim Rabbah* expands the number "infinitely" by quoting Proverbs 1:8–9: "My child, heed the discipline of your father and do not forsake the instruction of your mother, for they are a graceful wreath upon your head." The word for "wreath" in the passage is *leviah*, but the Midrash sees in the word the root *lavah*, meaning "accompany." In the name of Rabbi Pinhas ben Hama the instruction is given to remember that wherever Israel goes, the *mitzvot* will *accompany* them — providing that Israel permits the *mitzvot* to accompany them. In other words, the tradition, i.e., the teachings of parents and ancestors, has given Israel 72 *mitzvot* (in this portion alone) and many more up to 613. But the thrust of Rabbi Pinhas' instruction is that there are an infinite number of opportunities in life with which to sanctify or at least to dignify human behavior. These opportunities call out to Israel to wear the "wreath" of *mitzvah* proudly.

The Midrash summarizes the purpose of all these *mitzvot*: "The Lord created this Torah in order to grant Israel eternal life. He left no area of human experience and endeavor empty of *mitzvah*." Put another way, God has planted within Israel the legal statutes that will bestow upon Israel eternal values, and through the embodiment of these values in every area of life, it gives all of life the glow of eternity. The Midrash gives examples. A man thinks of plowing a field: the Torah specifies, "Do not plow with an ox and donkey pulling together." A man mourns his dead: "Do not mourn by cutting yourselves so that you bleed." A man builds a house: "Build a parapet on the roof" so that adequate protection is given to all inhabitants and guests. A woman is left a widow: society must provide her with protection. A man eats: there is a proper way to eat. A man marries: there is a proper way to marry and there is a proper mode of behavior for all of marital life.

The *Tzipor* of Torah

Moses anticipates the perennial attempt of later competing views of reality to think of Godliness as an illusion — along with religion in general. If it is — if it is only a "grand illusion" — it is at least an indispensable illusion if for no other reason but its capacity to criticize human conceit, puffery, arrogance, and vanity. But the tradition of *mitzvot* goes beyond this "negative" description of the importance of Godliness and religion. It stresses the affirmative. It argues for the sanctification of all of life in deed and thereby in personal and collective testimony to the essential goodness of the *mitzvot*.

The positive inspiration for the system of *mitzvot* may be summarized in the verse from Psalms 97: *"Or zaru'a la-tzaddik, u-le-yishrei lev simha"* ("Light is sown for the righteous and joy for the straight of heart"). The system provides the life of the individual Israelite with a sanctified and ethically inspired order and motivation to his life. He is like a man who has fallen into the sea and is in danger of drowning. A ship appears before him, and the ship's captain tosses him a rope and shouts to him: "Grab the rope and never let go, for if you let go, you will lose your life." Thus says God to Israel: "As long as you hold on tightly to the order of *mitzvot*, by studying them, by adopting them, and by living with them and through them, you will be redeemed. For you will be cleaving to God and to God's life-giving spiritual and ethical nourishment."

The Talmud will summarize the conflict going on in the human being as he struggles to survive with purpose in life: *"Oy li mi-yotzri, oy li mi-yitzri"* ("Woe is me in the presence of my Creator and woe is me in the face of my hedonistic Drive"). The Creator and the Drive are in perpetual conflict over the soul of the Israelite. Neither side ever wins a decisive victory. For he who would think that because he stands with God, he has vanquished or suppressed the Drive, needs to remember how deceptively agile the Drive is. And he who is constantly given to surrendering to the Drive also needs to remember that repentance is available and accessible. There is no righteous person who doesn't sin, the Bible says. The system of *mitzvot*, therefore, may not be an automatically assured cure-all for the ills and anxieties of life. What it has promised, however, is to refine human beings, to make them better than they would ordinarily be. And along with that refinement, that betterment, the Psalmist promises, will come light and joy for the "righteous and straight of heart."

This attempt at refinement and betterment is to be applied to all situations, in a world which is hardly a paradise. Moses has begun this portion by referring to conditions associated with going out to war. He concludes the portion by reminding Israel of the decree which the God of Israel has issued against war-intoxicated Amalek. The world in short is a world of wolves and to survive in such a world requires wisdom, cleverness, and courage. But Israel must never lose its yearning to refine itself spiritually and to better itself ethically along with the rest of humankind. Torah as lived by Israel can contribute to the refinement and the betterment of all of humanity. But Israel must then make certain that it survives as a Torah-inspired nation.

In this world of wolves, Moses has already noted that there have been and will continue to be challenges to Israel's chosen role. There is a strange *halakhah* which permits the taking of birds from their nest, provided the mother sitting over the fledglings or the eggs is first permitted to fly away. As a reward for letting the mother go, the Israelite will fare well and have a long life. The commentators will have much to say about this *halakhah* taken literally. Metaphorically, the image of the bird, the *"tzipor,"* being let go, conjures up another place in the Book of Genesis where the *tzipor* is mentioned. In the portentous "Covenant of the Pieces" which God and Abraham agreed to before the descent into Egypt and before the subsequent ascent from Egyptian bondage, there appears a *tzipor.* Abraham is instructed to bring a three-year-old heifer, a three-year-old she-goat and a three-year-old ram, a turtledove, and a pigeon in order to represent in cut pieces the sharing of covenantal responsibility between God and Abraham. The heifer, the she-goat, and the ram are cut. But the birds are not, as it is written: *"ve-et ha-tzipor lo vatar."* Abraham desists from cutting the *tzipor.*

David Kimhi, one of the great post-Maimonidean commentators, points out that Abraham cut in half the other animals: "because all the nations (represented by the animals) behaved badly towards Israel. Therefore, they will all be severed and divided, warring with each other until destruction. They will similarly be divided in their faiths and teachings resulting in mutual confrontation and hatred. But Israel will be different. Its faith as expressed in its Torah will not be divided — just as the *tzipor* will not be divided. It may be that Israel is currently scattered to the four winds in exile;

but they are nevertheless one nation cleaving to its faith and to its Torah. Whether they be in the East or in the West they have one Torah."

Letting the uncut *tzipor* fly away from the captive nest is a sign of Jewish survival. How? By means of one Torah undivided. How will Kimhi be able to write such an optimistic scenario for his people at a time when Jews will be persecuted all over the world and when there will be internal Jewish strife over the writings of someone as distinguished as Maimonides? Yet Kimhi is undaunted in his determination to stress the unifying necessity of one Torat Yisrael giving life to one unique nation — Am Yisrael.

Following the Emancipation, the idea of one Torah for one unique people will suffer severe modification. Not that the idea of the *tzipor* will have become "dismembered." After a long period in exile in which Shimon bar Yohai's Torah will have eclipsed Moses' Land-of-Israel-centered Torah, the *tzipor* will seek to redirect its flight to Eretz Yisrael as a focus for revitalizing the Jewish people as a nation. In so doing there will be a chance to reinvigorate the idea of Torah with purposes closer to Moses' initial visions.

Bialik's poem *"El ha-Tzipor"* will see the fabled bird as a symbol of freedom and renewal. The *tzipor* returns to the poet who is trapped in the cold, in the darkness of a doomed exile: "Shall I tell my tale of sorrows / now well known in all the places / Near and far alike, / Those innumerable sorrows / Of the present, or the others / that are yet to strike… / All is gone but pain / Yet I bid you, birdling welcome / From the warmer climes returning / Sing your song again."

In its day, Bialik's vision, emerging out of an entirely different historical situation than that of Moses, will pierce through the harrowingly lengthy exile. This exile will have been recalled in every prayer as having been brought on by the degeneration of an Israelite Jewish commonwealth which failed to apply Torah to its own internal sociopolitical situation! For Moses and his generation, there is no focus on exile. Not when these children of the "Wilderness generation" are preparing themselves for entry into the Promised Land.

Bialik's *tzipor* will be deriving its freshness of spirit from its renewed promise, inspired by Moses' original vision. This vision will be based on expectation of success in settling the Land. Not that Moses doesn't have concerns about Israel's readiness to fulfill the terms of the covenant as it moves into the Land. He doesn't hide his fears of impending suffering should

Israel fail in its mandate. But it hasn't happened yet. Now is the time for this new generation to rise from slumber and to move eagerly to an acceptance of the challenge of living in the Presence of the Divine. And so Moses pushes and pushes his covenantal agenda.

"Mitzvot" and *"Mitzvot"*

The *mitzvot* are listed one after the other in order to refine, to sanctify each member of the Jewish community along with the community as a whole. It dare not be merely a collectivity. It must be a community of caring, each Israelite for the other. The range of *mitzvot* which are meant to reflect communal concern and responsibility is unlimited: paying workers on time; protecting the disenfranchised, e.g., the widows, the orphans, and the strangers; maintaining honest weights and measures in business dealings; discretion in receiving and returning pledges for loans.

The *Torah she-bi-Khetav* reinforced by a vital *Torah she-Be'al Peh* will relate to every conceivable human issue from every conceivable human angle. What will appear at first as clear and straightforward in Deuteronomy will be opened up for further discussion under rabbinic scrutiny later. The commentaries on all the *mitzvot* will be extensive because life's conditions will be seen for what they are — a "blooming, buzzing" confusion.

To take one example, the *mitzvah* of returning "your fellow's ox or sheep which has gone astray." Rashi will underline the word *ve-hit'alamta* (and you hide yourself), lest the finder feigns not seeing the lost object in order to avoid his responsibility of returning it to its owner. Basing his own addenda on the "halakhic *midrashim*" and the Talmud, Rashi cautions the finder against such temptations. At the same time, all the commentators argue that there can be extenuating circumstances which the finder can claim have prevented him legitimately from performing the *mitzvah*. For example, the financial loss which the finder may suffer in taking the time to return the lost object may be too great. The *halakhah* is not insensitive to such real and legitimate considerations.

Nehama Leibowitz notes the insight of the sixteenth-century commentator Alshikh in his discussion of "you hide yourself" regarding the obligation to return lost objects: "*Mitzvot* train and discipline the doer. At first he fulfills a religious obligation in response to the imperative of the Torah.

Subsequently the *mitzvah*, as a result of constant practice, endears itself to him so that he performs it willingly and spontaneously…the *mitzvah* is, once and for all, firmly implanted within you, so that whatever the circumstances, you cannot hide yourself."

Not hiding oneself from doing the right thing whatever one's mixed or conflicting intentions may be becomes a byword for the religious and ethical agenda. In another example Moses cautions his people regarding vows. Koheleth will reinforce the caution before those individuals who vow — undoubtedly with good intention — but then fail to fulfill their vows. "It is better not to vow at all than to vow and not fulfill. Don't let your mouth bring you into disfavor, and then don't plead before God that it was an error." Thus there is a line of consistency leading from Moses to Koheleth to the Alshikh on the question of the primacy of doing — doing not only for the accomplishment of that particular *mitzvah*; but doing for the purpose of educating oneself towards the performance of other *mitzvot*. This is even more highlighted by the *mitzvah* of *shikhhah* (forgetting).

One of the strangest *mitzvot* of all is that found in Deut. 24:19: "When you reap the harvest in your field and overlook a sheaf in the field, do not turn back to get it; it shall go to the stranger, the fatherless, and the widow." It is strange because one would think that doing a *mitzvah* and receiving "credit" for it ought to involve intention. Yet how can intention be involved when one didn't "intend" to overlook a sheaf in the field? By definition, overlooking or forgetting is the very antithesis of intending. Why then should it be called a *mitzvah*? Is it because in any case the unfortunate in society are benefiting? Does this mean that the system of *mitzvot* is basically behavioristic, that is, interested exclusively in *acts* of kindness — never mind whether or not they are intended as such?

In the *Tosefta Peah* (3:8) the story is told of a pious man who forgot a sheaf of barley in his field and in a joyous spirit said to his son: "Go and offer up for me a bull as a whole-offering and a bull as a peace offering." The son said to him: "Father, why do you look with greater joy upon this *mitzvah* than upon all the other *mitzvot* in the Torah?" The father answered: "All the *mitzvot* in the Torah God gave us to do consciously; this one he gave us to do unconsciously. For if we were to do this one, so to speak, willingly, the *mitzvah* could not be performed, that is, could not be performed in conformity with the command in the Torah that when we are harvesting our crop and we perchance forget a sheaf in the field..." Furthermore, the conclusion must be that if a person who did not intend to do the *mitzvah*, yet does it, and receives merit for doing it, how much more so would he who with full intention does a *mitzvah* warrant being merited for doing so.

In other words, while the whole idea in the *Tosefta* seems to be an emphasis on proper behavior, the importance of *kavanah* (intention) is not denied. Especially urged would be creative intention and implementation in order to discover new ways of applying *hithalekh le-fanai* ("walk before Me"). But clearly, Moses is insisting, there has to be *doing*, not just intentions, promises, vows.

Nevertheless, the problem with the *mitzvah* of *shikhhah* lingers on. Granted, the widow, the orphan, and the stranger benefit from the unconscious behavior. That it is, therefore, a source of blessing for the widow, the orphan and the stranger is understandable and acceptable. Yet, it is odd that, spiritually speaking, one who forgets still receives "credit" for forgetting.

In Jewish tradition, there will be another concept which will be the obverse side of *shikhhah: "mitzvah ha-ba'ah ba-averah"* ("a *mitzvah* which comes from a transgression"). Some might say it is like making the "wrong" move at the "right" time. But ethically speaking such concepts become acceptable because the doer's overall intention is to do a *mitzvah*. There is the example of Yael who as a woman sacrifices her chastity with full intention so as to save Israel. The *averah* which she commits by seducing and then killing Sisera the enemy general makes possible the greater *mitzvah* of assuring Israel's triumph. The milieu in which "credit" is earned even when one does a *mitzvah* unintentionally (*shikhhah*) or when one does an *averah* intentionally in order to lead to a *mitzvah* is a milieu of *shemirat mitzvot* (keeping *mitzvot*). It is the *mitzvah* milieu which legitimizes these odd cases.

Amalek and the *Tzipor*

Can war be considered a blessing? Hardly — even when commanded by God! At the same time, as long as war or the circumstances leading to war persist as part of the nature of human efforts to live and maneuver within complex competitive environments, the Torah seeks to establish certain norms — or *mitzvot* — to be observed even in times of war. Going out to fight enemies does not exempt the Israelites from keeping themselves from wrongdoing.

The Ramban explains: "Scripture warns us particularly in situations where sin is an intrinsic part of the general situation. It is known as customary within the military fighting a war that every abominable food will be devoured, theft and violence of a personal nature and even adultery and every other kind of perversion will be tolerated. Even the otherwise honest person under normal circumstances will in wartime dress himself in cruelty and rage when going out to war."

In other words, even in the midst of war, the Torah insists that ethical standards must be maintained. At no time does a human being have a right to say. "What does it matter now? What does anything matter? I can throw off all restraints. I have no obligations, no values by which to test and control my impulses. Nothing matters anymore, no rules bind me, anything goes!"

The Talmud will speak of the criminal who is hanged, but whose corpse according to the Torah must be taken down the same day. People must not be permitted to stare — perhaps gloat — over the criminal who, after all, was still a human being. The story is told of twins who grew up to become respectively a king and a thief. When the thief was caught and hanged, the people looked upon the figure and thought it was the king! The tale does not just offer a conventional moralistic "prince and pauper" message. The king may be seen as God and it needs to be remembered that the thief has been created in the image of God. When the thief hangs in disgrace, it is the image of God who hangs in disgrace. In war no matter the rightness of the cause, the defeated are to be treated as creatures of God.

Moses and the Torah are prescribing a regimen by which it may be said that when conditions conspire to make us less than human, we must strive to be more than human. But there seems to be an anomaly within this regimen for humaneness. Moses is listing all the *mitzvot* for building a society which as a result will be firmly established and purposeful, even righteous, even holy. Included in the list, however, is the jarring command to remember Amalek in order to wipe it out, erase it totally from existence. Israel has been enjoined not to forget any of the commands which she has received. Through these commands, these *mitzvot*, Moses is attempting to instill in his people a basic attitude of benevolence. Yet in Amalek's case, there must be an unremitting compassionless sentence of death. Moses has the prodigious task of transmitting to his people an appreciation of God's loving attributes while at the same time coming to grips with the reality of Man's potential for evil in the world — a potential actualized in the bloodlust of Amalek and his descendants.

Moses is charged to teach a theology which recognizes God as All-Powerful while All-Merciful. At the same time, he must also teach an anthropology which acknowledges that the world hosts good, but also evil. In a later liturgical poem God will be described as "guided with justice and equity.... He lives, but He is awesome and fearsome. He suspends the earth in space." The last phrase may be translated from Man's point of view as "the earth hangs on nothing." Because of the existence of human evil on earth, Man constantly prays for God's mercy. But with the kind of evil — Nazi-like evil — represented by the likes of Amalek there can be no mercy. There can be no fudging over of wickedness in the name of forgiveness. God's uncompromised moral justice must prevail and must be seen to prevail.

It will not always be simple to preach this theology and this anthropology. On an individual level as well as on a communal and national level, both the theology and anthropology will have to be internalized as personal lives are affected by injustice and the national life of the Jewish people is overturned by enemies as ruthless as Amalek. No matter what the threats facing the Jewish people, the individual Jew and the nation are mandated in any and every way possible to carry on with their faith in the indestructibility of the *tzipor.* This cannot be done in an environment where Amalek is granted moral "asylum" in order to do the work of the Serpent. No superficial "moral equivalences"! The absolute evil represented by Amalek must be eradicated!

Neutralizing an Inside-Out Theology

For Abraham, for Moses — and for Bialik — the *tzipor* will serve as the symbol of Jewish hope, a hope nurtured by a Torah charting a humane and sanctified national life for the nation of Israel in the Land of Israel. When Bialik, reflecting on the long exile, welcomes the *tzipor* who is heralding a new return to the Land of Israel, he is reaching back to Moses and to the people in the Wilderness who are on the verge of taking up the covenant in the Promised Land. His poetic imagination buttressed by a Zionist longing arches itself backwards over almost two millennia of Jewish *galut* suffering.

Bialik and other Zionist contemporaries will note the irony that the Deuteronomic law of sending the mother-*tzipor* of the fledglings away will have become the focus of a revolutionary theological interpretation by the rabbis of the talmudic era and the era of *galut*. This revolutionary interpretation will have turned Moses' covenantal theology inside out. It will have replaced a theology based on landedness in Israel with a theology conditioned by *galut* homelessness. It may be that this "inside-out" theology had helped to maintain Jewish theological sanity through the long night of *galut*. Would such a theology, however, serve a national reawakening of the House of Israel following the Emancipation?

What was this *galut* theology? In the talmudic tractate *Kiddushin* (39b) Rabbi Jacob teaches that in connection with honoring parents it is written "that your days may be prolonged, and that it may go well with you" (Deut. 5:16). In reference to the dismissal of the nest (Deut. 22:6–7) it is similarly written, that it may be well with you, and that you may prolong your days. (In its entirety this *mitzvah* reads: If along the road, you chance upon a bird's nest, in any tree or on the ground, with fledglings or eggs and the mother sitting over the fledglings or on the eggs, do not take the mother together with her young. Let the mother go and take only the young, in order that it may be well with you and that you may prolong your days.) Rabbi Jacob continues:

> Now, if one's father said to him, Ascend to the loft and bring me young birds, and he ascends to the loft, dismisses the dam and takes the young, and on his return falls and is killed — where is this man's happiness (literally the goodness of his days) and where is this man's prolonging of days? But 'in order that it may be well with you' means on the day that is wholly good; and 'in order that your days may be long' means on the day that is wholly long.

For Rabbi Jacob and this "exile" theology both these phrases refer to the next world, not to this one, and thereby emphasize that reward comes only then — in *olam ha-ba* ("the next world") — not in *olam ha-zeh* ("this world").

The entire context of this passage discusses the absence of reward for the righteous in this world placed alongside the apparent happiness of the wicked in this world. "How can that be?" the rabbinic mind protests. By the principle of *middah ke-neged middah* (measure for measure) such a situation according to God and His Torah would be a perversion of justice, a mockery of the meaning of a moral destiny for this world. The Rabbis' response is to see the suffering of the righteous in this world as a full atonement for any sins committed by the righteous in this world, so that in the future world all that will shine forth will be their good deeds and therefore they will receive their full reward. The wicked, on the other hand, having enjoyed the full delight of their evil deeds in this world will not have the opportunity through lack of suffering in this world to atone for these evil deeds. The full suffering, therefore, will await them in the future world.

The logic of this "inside-out" theology is incontrovertible, assuming that one has faith in God's justice and the reality of the "future world." This logic of the Rabbis and their commitment to the Torah and to the Jewish people will have saved the concept of a moral purpose for Jewish destiny — even in *galut*. It will inspire the Jewish people while in *galut* to keep faith with the system of *mitzvot*, regardless of whether or not there are imminent rewards. The "inside-out" theology will have supported the embodying of as much of Torah legislation as possible in *galut* — certainly laws related to personal chastity, integrity, familial trust, and loyalty.

With Moses and the generation looking forward to establishing sovereignty in the Promised Land, however, is this "inside-out" theology appropriate? It cannot be! If left by itself to serve as an a priori normative theology for the Children of Israel, it would divert the entire purpose of a theological-anthropological covenant intended by God to mend the world — *olam ha-zeh* ("this world") — at this time! The Torah of Moses is arguing that Israel is entering the Promised Land in order to help mend the world. If the mending cannot be completed at this time, then Israel is charged to look for the opportunity for further mending "tomorrow," i.e., in the accessible future, or, if need be, in the distant future following *galut*. The covenant will call for the constant effort to be expended in *olam ha-zeh*. Ultimate reward may have to wait for *olam ha-ba*, but the mending — the *tikkun* — will require in basic covenantal terms a return to the Land — always to the Land — in order to try and try again. Bialik will realize this. The modern Zionist Movement will have awakened from its *galut* slumber because of such a realization.

Ki Tavo 

Moses must share with his people the frightening consequences of their possible failure to fulfill the terms of the covenant. There is no way he can avoid it and feel that he has fulfilled his function as their leader, as their teacher. And this *tokhehah* (admonition) and its dramatic prelude of curses is indeed frightening. It is a harrowing description of all conceivable horrors that will follow the destruction of the Jewish commonwealth should Israel surrender its covenantal mandate.

At the same time, Moses will also remind his people that there are blessings the foundation of which is the covenantal relationship between God and Israel: "You have *affirmed* this day that the Lord is your God, that you will walk in His ways, that you will observe His laws and commandments and rules, and that you will obey Him. And the Lord has *affirmed* this day that you are, as He promised you, His treasured people who shall observe all His commandments, and that He will set you, in fame and renown and glory, high above all the nations that He has made." The key to this double "affirmation" is its reciprocity. God and Israel each gives the other — reputation! And it is a reputation redolent with blessings.

Later liturgical tradition will have honorees reciting blessings to God as the Torah is being read aloud in the synagogue. Custom will dictate, however, that the long *tokhehah* is not to be divided among several honorees, but that it is to be read in a hushed undertone by the Reader. God Himself will be imagined lamenting: "It is not right that I be praised while My children are being cursed." As Psalm 91 will note: *"imo Anokhi be-tzarah"* ("I [the Lord] am with them in their trouble"). From the choice of the lowly burning bush in which God had first made Himself known to Moses, God has always sought to impress upon His chosen people the importance of empathy. Empathy serves as the indispensable condition for covenantal loyalty and commitment. If

Israel is to be condemned to adversity, then God Himself will "suffer" along with them.

The Two Covenants

The search for such empathy must characterize the attempt to find one's authentic self whether the covenant is between God and self or between self and another human being. The indispensable condition for covenantal loyalty and commitment cannot be mere reciprocity. Reciprocity reflects the *terms* of the covenant. Any thought of establishing a covenant must be built on a prior empathy.

From the Ramban to Erich Fromm there will be those who will argue that one begins by loving oneself. For without a sufficiently high self-esteem one cannot extend his caring to anyone else. But Emanuel Levinas will reject the egoistic approach. As opposed to my deriving my caring for the other from my love for myself, Levinas will argue, I must seek to derive my own value, my own self-esteem, by my readiness to sacrifice for the other. Cain, therefore, dare not protest: "Am I my brother's keeper?" He should rather glory in an empathetic readiness to be his brother's keeper, his protector, his guardian. In drastic circumstances God may punish Israel in sending her into exile. But he has punished Himself as well by going into exile with them.

In other words, the covenant established with Abraham — sealed by God's oath *"Bi nishbati"* ("I have sworn by My Essence") at the *akeidah* — is one of eternal unconditional empathy. Moses, on the other hand, at this juncture on the Plains of Moab before entering the Promised Land, is promulgating another kind of covenant or contract. It is still between God and Israel; but it is built on a number of conditions.

A contract of the Mosaic type — as opposed to the covenant with Abraham — will have five essentials: (1) it will be promulgated between two or more parties; (2) there will be a common intention in effecting the contract; (3) the contract must be possible to execute, that is, within a commonly accepted valuational framework, it must be legally reasonable; (4) the agreement must be "written," i.e., expressed in some evidential manner by all sides; and (5) the agreement must be solemnized by some formal public act.

Moses in Deuteronomy is covering all the essentials of the contract which had been agreed to at Sinai. The first essential is recognizing that the two parties to the contract are respectively a people that was enslaved in Egypt and God who is the redeemer of this people and who has promised to bring them to a new land. The second essential — common intention — has the descendants of this slave people wanting redemption. Evidence supporting their intention is their readiness upon hearing Moses' instructions to bring *bikkurim* (first fruits) as a thanksgiving offering when they will be settled in the Promised Land. God's own intention has been apparent from the earliest period of Creation. Ever since the expulsion from Eden and the later Deluge, God has planned to redeem this people in order to initiate the fulfillment of His large plan for humanity.

The third essential — that the fulfillment of the contract must be possible — is honored by the high motivation which both Moses and now the new generation of Israelites are manifesting as they ready themselves for entrance into the Promised Land. These Israelites have been preparing themselves as they have been maturing in the Wilderness. They have been attending to Moses' weighty words and are showing no hesitation before the coming challenge of conquest and settlement, and the subsequent concretization of the sociomoral terms of the covenant.

The fourth essential will be fulfilled as soon as the people will enter the Land. They will engrave the essence of the covenant in stone as a memorial and as a permanent reminder. They will then fulfill the fifth essential in a solemnly appropriate chorus when they reach Shekhem. Antiphonal choirs on Mount Gerizim and Mount Ebal will chant the black-and-white either-or alternatives of blessings and curses. The choices will be alternatingly glorious and ominous — but above all, clear!

In truth the covenant with Abraham had not been a contract. It had been a promise, an oath on the part of God to fulfill His plan through Abraham's descendants. Whatever bad choices Israel might make in their future attempt to embody the terms of the Mosaic contract, God's promise to Abraham would never be abrogated. The promise would enable an exiled people to endure persecution, expulsion, partial annihilation. But the agenda which Moses is now presenting to his people is not intended to have them luxuriate in the unconditional promise to Abraham. The recollection of such a promise might do well as a spur to future action and as an after-the-fact strategy for survival following catastrophe. But now Israel under Moses — and Joshua — is not facing catastrophe, but an opportunity. Here the blessings and the warnings are meant to motivate Israel to take proper advantage of the opportunity.

Moses' pedagogic task is to bind up together the four components which are to be considered integral to any coherent understanding of Israelite purpose and destiny. These make up an integrated relationship of *the God of Israel and the People of Israel through the Torah-covenant of Israel within the Land of Israel.* The Land must be considered as indispensable a component as the other three regarding the question of the spiritual, ethical, and social relevancy of Judaism. Eldad will quote Moses' instruction to his people: "When you enter the Land that the Lord your God is giving you as a heritage and you possess it and settle in it..." And then he will add:

> It means that it is not enough to enter the Land but you must *possess* it; and the way to possess it is to *settle* it; for God has given you this Land only on condition that you make it your property. Only when you've done that, you may deign to offer up the first fruit of the Land; for only when you truly own the Land, will the Land offer up to you its fruit. Moreover, remember to say about yourself that your ancestor was a wandering Aramean. Remember where you came from, what you possessed before you came here. Remember your ancestors' wanderings in exile. Remember Amalek and Pharaoh. And contrast the memories with the good which you have now.

The Land and *Bikkurim*

Later Jewish history will confirm in the starkest terms what the lack of a sovereign piece of land will cost the Jewish people. The long *galut* will contribute to what will seem like a permanent state of political vulnerability, chronic political disenfranchisement, penury for most, assimilation for many, as anti-Semitism and self-hatred will combine to make Jewish existence as fickle as a driven leaf. The Shoah will prove unequivocally that without at least some measure of sovereignty over some piece of land, a people like the Jewish people invites catastrophe leading to extinction! The culminating threat in the *tokhehah* ending a long list of horrors is *galut*!

Modern Zionism will emphasize anew what Moses is projecting as the basis for any hope of covenantal effort. Even in its secular incarnation —

especially in its secular incarnation — there can be no hope for Jewish survival without land. Jacob Klatzkin will proclaim: "The *galut* has a right to life for the sake of liberation from the *galut*." And a later Zionist, Hillel Halkin, reflecting on the reality of a new State of Israel and its melange of internal socioethical and cultural-religious conflicts, will declare: "All hybrid Zionisms, e.g., prophetic morality Zionism, social revolutionary Zionism, asylum for the persecuted Zionism, messianic God-in-history Zionism, will sooner or later fly apart into its originally discrete and possibly antagonistic elements. The only lasting Zionism is the unhyphenated kind that believes in a Jewish land for the Jewish people as an end in itself and not as a means to anything else."

Moses, of course, is not recommending the pursuit of a secular embodiment of the covenant. Theologically and epistemologically such an idea is utterly foreign to him. But later Jewish history which will have Jews sitting at a *galut Pesah Seder* year after year and reciting the eloquent Deuteronomic statement intended for the Israelite bringing *bikkurim* (first fruits) to the Temple *in the Land* will confirm the ease with which people can become accustomed to a land-less religion despite its accompanying disabilities.

Moses is preparing his people for his long rebuke. And a blood-curdling rebuke it will be! Yet, he begins on a promising note with the *mitzvah* of the bringing of the *bikkurim*. The declaration to be recited at the ceremony of the *bikkurim* reflects a health-giving optimism based on a rich historic consciousness. By way of the *bikkurim* Moses urges the people never to forget their history. In the rabbinic period the Sages will take this declaration of the *bikkurim* and make it a centerpiece of the *Haggadah*.

What gives the *bikkurim* declaration its optimistic thrust is its comprehensive attention to the total personal-national existential posture of the Israelite Jew. The traditional commentators will all be attracted to the mysterious opening of the declaration *"arami oved avi."* What does the phrase mean? Whom is it referring to? The continuation states: "And he went down to Egypt and dwelt there with very few, but became there a great and powerful nation." But again what is the meaning of *"arami oved avi"*?

Rashi sees the *arami* as the Aramean Laban who was *oved avi* (the destroyer of my father). Laban is recalled as having attempted to uproot everything which Jacob had built. And Rashi recalls others who have tried to put an end to Israel, all leading to Jacob's family descending into Egypt.

Rashi's interpretation glides over a non-grammatical use of the word *oved* which is not an active verb. But Rashi is particularly sensitive to the ongoing attempt among many nations to destroy Israel. The *Haggadah* will feature the Rashi interpretation of Laban as the treacherous "white" sinner. Until Laban (the white one) everyone surmised that sin was black and dirty. Laban, however, dressed sin up to appear white and clean. He knew how to make evil look respectable. And the *Haggadah* points to every generation which threatens Jews with potential and actual liquidators — "white" and "black."

Ibn Ezra argues that if the Torah wanted to have the verb of the phrase express an *act* of attempted destruction, it should have been in the *pi'el* or *hiph'il* form, i.e., *me'abbed* or *ma'avid.* It must refer, therefore, to someone who is in a state of being abandoned or lost. Ibn Ezra sees the Aramean as the Israelites' father Jacob who while in Aram was poor and who while later in Egypt was an alien. A *midrash* in tune with this interpretation sees Jacob's flight to Aram as nothing else but for the purpose of disappearing. This image will characterize Diaspora Jewish history particularly on the threshold and heels of the Emancipation. Jews will have come out of a poverty-ridden past hungry for freedom and opportunity. Jews will eagerly seize whatever economic, social, and cultural opportunities become available. They will join a variety of political movements to the neglect of their own people's national aspirations — and they will in huge numbers become lost to their own people's history and destiny.

The Rashbam has the phrase *"arami oved avi"* referring to the Israelites' father Abraham who was commanded to "wander into exile" from his birthplace in Aram, from his family, from his "homeland," so to speak. At a later date Abraham will even acknowledge that God "led me astray" from my father's house. Abraham is willing to admit that God's *"lekh lekha"* demanded a personal price to be paid by him. There is no evidence that Abraham had been in conflict with his father Terah. According to the text, the entire family left Ur together. Abraham received the special call, however, and had to journey on — no matter what the personal cost — alone! But because Abraham had to transcend his natural personal familial feelings, he had to have the confidence of true self-knowledge. The covenantal demand would be too great for Abraham to be anything less than wholehearted — *tamim* — in his life-journey.

All these interpretations point to a comprehensive collective self-understanding which Moses is demanding from his people. They dare not enter the Promised Land and begin to settle it successfully enough to offer fruits of thanksgiving without fully appreciating the terms and conditions of their having gotten to the Land and the requirements for their holding on to the Land. They will have to know their enemies; they will have to be sensitive to their own weaknesses; and they will have to be absolutely wholehearted in their resolve to build their Land according to the full detailed terms of the covenant — or else!

The Agony of Covenantal Testing

Having bestowed upon his people the gift of *bikkurim* to be celebrated in the future with joy and thanksgiving, Moses now bludgeons them into catatonia with his long rebuke. There is a remarkable rabbinic tradition which attributes the words of the "long rebuke" to Moses *himself* as opposed to the "short rebuke" found in Leviticus which the Rabbis attribute directly to *God*. The nineteenth-century commentator Shadal will say: "We may learn how liberal was the commentary of our ancient sages. The authorities of the Talmud referred the verse 'because he has spurned the word of the Lord' (Numbers 15:31) to one who claims that the Torah is not from Heaven, even if he claims that the entire Torah is from heaven except one verse. In other words, one could say that when Moses articulated the 'long rebuke' *himself* instead of it coming from *God*, he is to be considered the presumptuous one 'spurning the word of the Lord.' Yet the authorities of the Talmud didn't hesitate to state that the curses mentioned in Deuteronomy were the statements of Moses — implying that he is nevertheless *not* to be condemned for them. They obviously didn't think of Moses as having 'spurned the word of the Lord.'"

What will motivate the rabbinic tradition that will not feel that it is committing a heresy by attributing the rebuke to Moses and not to God? Simply put, they will not want to entertain the notion that such horrendous curses could come from God. Better to have them associated with Man! Not that Moses is cursing Israel, God forbid! But in having a human being like Moses stating and reporting the threats, the maledictions, the possible horrors, the association will be made with human error and humanly practiced evil as the cause of the apocalyptic destruction. God will not bring the destruction! It will be human misbehavior! At times Israel will be guilty; at times, many times, Israel's enemies will be guilty.

Focusing on Man's behavior — and misbehavior — will lend "some" comfort to Israel as they will try in some way to comprehend their relentlessly oppressive *galut* history, the nadir being the Shoah. Believing that the Shoah will not have come from God, but will have been brought about by Man will indeed serve as a "comfort" — if one will believe in God as God. Granted, for the victims and the survivors any "comfort" will be inadequate in the face of the unparalleled horror. But for those who despite the Shoah will insist on "believing," traditional theology alluding to God's attributes of justice and mercy will remain intact — scarred, but intact. At the same time, if as a result of naïve expectations nurtured by the promise of human enlightenment one has put his "faith" in Man as God, then the Shoah becomes a fatal blow to any redemptive promises of such a God-less and groundless humanism.

For the Torah and the Bible will ask: Did human beings ever have the right to believe in Man? To trust in Man? To put blind faith in Man? In Judaism's "aggadic" view of Man, the Bible looks upon Man as little lower than the angels, but at the same time declares "What is Man that You have been mindful of him, mortal Man that You have taken note of him." The Torah itself acknowledges that the "devisings of Man's mind are evil from his youth." And Jeremiah reminds us that "cursed be the man who trusts his fellow man!" Moreover Judaism's "halakhic" view of Man is highly conservative regarding the granting to the State or other humanly governed institutions ultimate authority over the lives and destinies of human beings without some sort of counterbalance usually provided by religion at its prophetic best — uncompromisingly critical of human vanity.

The Torah will never despair of Man. It will always believe that Man has the capacity to reach for the good. But it also understands that Man can be a pernicious and lethal animal; that Man has been prone to idolizing Man; and that this idolizing of Man — from Nimrod to Pharaoh to Hitler — inevitably brings on enslavement of human beings by human beings and murder of human beings by human beings.

Moses and the Prophets never leave Israel without hope, however. Similarly the later Elie Wiesel will emerge with hope even out of the Shoah. Wiesel will often speak of despair and the obligation of coping with it: "Faced with despair, the Jew has three options. He can choose resignation, total resignation. Or he can seek refuge in self-delusion. But then there is a third option — the most difficult but the most beautiful of all. To face the human condition — and to do so as a Jew. Voltaire said, 'When all hope is gone, death becomes a duty.' Not so for Jews. When all hope is gone, Jews invent new hopes."

These new hopes, Moses insists, can only come from a unique ultimate source: God! The ultimate comfort is that God does not bring the curses, the evil. God brings life. God brings hope. God brings the light of redemption.

Moses anticipates a *midrash* which offers an inspiring dream: God has said to Israel that in this world there are blessings and curses, good and evil: but in the future He will remove the curses and the evil and there will only be blessings and good. A simple, fundamental gift of religion — the dream of blessings and ultimate good! Without it humankind cannot survive with any sense of hope and purpose. With the gift — the gift of ultimate justice and mercy bound together — humankind in general and Israel in particular can look forward to a future, can survive with sanity on the way to a hope-filled future. It has started with Abraham who was "to be a blessing" in a world which God created as good.

For Israel in particular the dream promises a future in which they will be so recognized as blessed to the point that all the nations will recognize that they are a seed blessed by God. In order to contribute to this future, Israel will have to have gone through a history of constant covenantal testing. The testing will hold out blessings or curses as consequential to all acts — personally and collectively. But as dominant in Moses' rhetoric as the listing of curses and series of rebukes often seem to be, the covenant with its clearly balanced reciprocity gives the dream of blessings pre-eminence. God has affirmed the blessedness of Israel as Israel has affirmed the blessedness of God! God and Israel have indeed given each other a reputation for promised blessings for all humankind!

The Dream of Total Blessedness

"Reputation" means that God and Israel will be spoken about in blessed terms. Blessings will emanate from the covenant: *"Barukh ata be-vo'ekha u-barukh ata be-tzeitekha"* ("Blessed are you in your coming and blessed are you in your going"). The dream promises that ultimately being a Jew especially in

Israel will evoke thoughts and feelings of blessedness. The fulfillment of such a dream will not be simple and therefore in no way can it be sudden or immediate. The Serpent operating as an adversary to the efforts of humankind in general and the Jew in particular will make it difficult. The Serpent's machinations are relentless!

In other words, the idolatrous inclination of humankind in general and the Jew in particular will forestall the coming of the era of blessedness. In the tractate *Sotah* the primordial Serpent will be described as not being content with what he has been given: "God had intended for the Serpent to be the King of the animal world; but since the Serpent was not content with the gift, but sought to challenge God's very own Kingship, he lost even what he had been given. He would be the most cursed within the animal world. He had been granted erect posture; he would now crawl on his belly. He had been given human food to eat; he would now eat dust."

Like the Serpent, Adam and Eve representing humankind would suffer from the same hubris. They and their descendants might have ruled the universe in harmony as deputies of God. Instead these descendants would show themselves capable of more bestiality than beasts. They could have represented dignity and majesty; instead they would degrade not only the image of God, but the image of Man. And so they — as humankind — will have elicited the curses of pain and suffering, war and affliction.

But then came Abraham accompanied by God's reconsideration of His discouragement with humankind. And the charge to Abraham to be a blessing would be the invocation to the covenant which God would contract with Israel. And Israel — despite the machinations of the Serpent — would carry the blessing, would become blessed in a Land which would be blessed — or God help them! Thus, the terms of the Mosaic covenant having been fulfilled in all its details would evoke the blessed state of total empathy promised and assured by the original covenant with Abraham.

Nitzavim נצבים

There is certainly justification for a somber reaction on the part of Israel to the curses which Moses has hurled at them. But worse! Later Jewish history will testify that all the curses will have come true!

Here Israel stands, however, being told that they must walk *with* God, that they must walk *before* God. Yet after such a cosmic rebuke who of them would have the courage to dare to walk with God, to dare to walk before God? But Moses will call out to them: "*U-baharta be-hayyim*" ("You shall choose life")! These words will bring home the message that Moses has been preaching throughout Deuteronomy: to reject idolatry utterly and finally — that idolatry which turns a people into a "stock sprouting poison weed and wormwood." Life is being given to Israel, a life guaranteed to be fruitful as long as the covenant is secured. Thus, Rashi finds comfort and instruction in the *aggadah* which interprets Moses' opening words "you are standing this day" as purposely juxtaposed to the curses in the previous chapter. "Because when Israel heard all these curses," notes Rashi, "their faces turned pale and they exclaimed, 'Who can possibly stand against these?' Therefore Moses began to calm them: 'See, you are *standing* today before the Lord! Many a time you have provoked the Lord to anger and yet He has not made an end of you, but you will continue to *stand* and *live* in His presence."

Obligatory Choice

When Moses exhorts Israel to choose life he is continuing the overall theme that he has presented earlier — contrasting blessings and curses, good and evil, life and death. Previously he had given them a short pungent, "See I have set before you this day blessing and curse." Now he presents a fuller contraposition adding the parallels of good and evil, life and death. He not only adds them — at first look in perfect rhetorical symmetry — he then has

God tilting the listeners towards the good, towards the blessing, urging Israel, commanding Israel, to choose life!

Rabbi Haggai — as noted earlier — has God saying "I didn't just offer you two paths from which to choose — with a mild curiosity, so to speak — as to your decision. I am impressing upon you My preferred choice: 'Choose life.'" Rabbi Haggai describes God as performing therein a supererogatory act, going beyond what He needs to do. In other words, God's setting up of the tripartite parallels appears to be giving Israel a free choice of whether to represent blessings, good, and life in the world or their negations. But when God — the vividly present God in all His glory — adds "Choose life!" how can a mortal people deny the clarity of instruction, the passion of the exhortation, the command! It is a command given by the Almighty! How can mortal men equivocate in the face of the command, deny the command! Israel must obey!

Indeed they will struggle to fulfill the command throughout their later history as a nation — even in *galut*, dreaming of a time when their choice of life-as-a-nation will bring them back to the Land. Nehemiah will return from the first exile to find a tiny group of Judeans who had come earlier to resettle the Land. And — we've discussed earlier — Nehemiah will call out: "*U-ve-khol zot anahnu kortim amanah*" ("Despite everything we are re-establishing a covenant"). This time the covenant will not be called a *brit*, for God at this stage of Jewish history is in relative eclipse. But the *amanah* will be an affirmation of Israel's refusal to disappear as a national entity — a resounding *amen* to national resurrection! Precisely because God is no longer the initiator as he had been earlier in Egypt, Israel's achievement under Nehemiah may even be greater than the first entrance into the Promised Land. It will write its own covenantal page as a self-dedicating people to God's creative work of mending the world.

Following the Shoah an even greater determination to express the national will-to-live will be required. Emil Fackenheim's 614th commandment will give a precise formulation to the national commitment of the Jewish people to survive as a people just because of the Shoah. Many a broken survivor will identify himself with Job seeking God in the maelstrom of human despair. And he will find the God of Israel calling to him out of Job's whirlwind. It will be the old/new whirlwind not really explaining the why of the curses, the evil, the humanly produced engines of mass murder. But he will sense God peering through the whirlwind waiting for Israel to rise again and proclaim *"u-ve-khol zot"* (despite everything) we *shall* choose life!

Moses has set the tone for the continuity of commitment to the covenant throughout the generations. For he will state clearly that the covenant includes "him that stands here with us this day and also him that is not here with us this day." The commentator Abrabanel will emphasize this to mean that from the moment at Sinai when Israel binds itself to serve God, all later generations are similarly bound. What does it mean to say all Jews are eternally bound? Surely history will show that through the ages many Jews will have unbound themselves, will have ostensibly "freed" themselves. But the message asserts that no man can be utterly free. That's impossible. It depends on whom one chooses to be one's master. When one rebels against God, he does nothing else but accept a new master! In leaving Egypt one doesn't "go free," one becomes a servant of God. In leaving God, one doesn't go free, one becomes a slave to Egypt again. In this light Jews will understand the liturgical conclusion of *Ne'ilah* on Yom Kippur: the Shema, followed by "Praised Be His Kingship Forever," and then seven times, "Adonai *Hu Ha'Elohim*" ("*God* is the God")!

And yet Abrabanel does raise a critical theological and moral question. Who has given the generation of the Wilderness, the generation which stood at the foot of Mount Sinai, the right to obligate all those who would come after them to accept the implications of their statement *"na'aseh ve-nishma"* ("we will do and we will listen")? In effect they have bound them to all the words of the Torah and the covenant and the penalties for violating their contents. Does this mean, Abrabanel's question suggests, that the individual who will come later has no choice? He has the same choice which his ancestors at Sinai had! But did his ancestors really have a choice at Sinai? Did Isaac have a choice to go or not to go with Abraham to the *akeidah*? Abraham may have had a choice; Isaac did not. Do children have untrammeled choices?

The story is told of the woman who has given birth to her firstborn, a boy. And both she and her husband wrangle about what to name him. The husband wants the newborn boy named after *his* father. She wants the boy named after *her* father. Coincidently, the names of both grandparents are the same: Nathan. They come before a wise man who is going to settle the issue. "You see," claims the wife, "my father was a pious man, a great scholar, but my husband's father was a thief. How can I name my son after a thief?" After serious contemplation the wise man responds: "My decision is to name the boy Nathan. If he turns out to be a scholar, then you'll know that he was named after his mother's father. If he turns out to be a thief, you'll know that he was named after his father's father."

The most significant note in this enigmatic tale is that the name itself means "given." The child, to begin with, is the result of his parents' choice, not his. He has been *given* the gift of life by them (and by God). If he is a Jew, he has been given tribal or ethnic or national life by being born into the House of Israel. The only positive choice he has is whether to become a pious scholar or a thief. But the basic "given" — the life he was given represented by his name "Nathan" — is to affirm and constantly reaffirm his acceptance of his fate-destiny which as a Jew means joining the covenant. He also has the negative option of denying or rejecting the choice which has been made for him. Choosing this option — rejecting the covenant — becomes then rebellion, heresy, treason.

Granted, the ability to rebel is the ability to express one's free will. It certainly manifests a proclamation of one's individuality. But at the same time, one's endorsement of the covenant, one's agreement not to rebel is also a manifestation of one's individuality. It has been argued that Moses' opening remarks are therefore directed to each individual qua individual even though it is obvious that Moses is addressing the entire collectivity of Israel: "See, I have given you today — 'you' in the singular — life and good, death and evil, choose life!"

Ongoing Historic Choice

The Shoah and its aftermath will demand from its individual survivors extreme acts of individual choice and commitment to remain Jews. It will not be the same as the House of Israel under Moses and Joshua standing on the border of the Promised Land bringing every individual Israelite under its wing, lending of its collective strength and élan to the individual who may be uncertain of his allegiances. The Shoah will have left survivors whose connections to life itself will be tenuous, let alone to the idea of a living aggregate of people joined together by covenant. The readiness of the survivor to announce himself anew as a member of the House of Israel will be tested individually.

A modern Israeli author, Aaron Appelfeld, will exemplify in his own life-story a series of renewed existential acts announcing to himself his agreement to join his people in facing their destiny. He describes his family before the Shoah as having been totally assimilated, ashamed of being Jewish, wanting passionately to be German, speaking German. But then the Holocaust! It destroys his family. It leaves him a young adolescent alone at the end of the war on the Italian beaches — alone, that is, with other abandoned adolescents, devoid of connections, loyalties, commitments. He has before him a choice, a clean choice of whether to go to Israel and rejoin his people — for better and for worse — or to move on in other directions away from the people which, in his case, he has never known in any other way but as hapless victims of evil. He chooses Israel. He will later on choose to become a writer. He will reject out of hand his native German tongue. Hebrew will become his freely chosen adopted tongue. He will think of himself literally reborn as a Jew.

Another example among the thousands of individual stories of covenantal renewal following the Shoah: A refugee couple from Hitler's Europe reach a "safe" haven and seek to rebuild their lives. They want children but are diagnosed as unable to have children of their own. They are given the opportunity, however, to adopt a non-Jewish infant. In the joy of the moment, they plan to convert her to Judaism. But they pause and reflect as to the advisability of burdening this innocent child with the fate of being a Jewess. They struggle with the question and decide "Yes"! They *will* bring her into the covenant. They as individuals are recommitting themselves. And, as if they were with Moses on the Plains of Moab, they commit to the covenant a child of the next generation. Without asking her they bring her to the altar and the thicket of covenantal Jewish destiny!

Moses throughout his mission has been struggling to mold a slave rabble into a self-consciously reborn people. He knows that he must convince each Israelite, to sense his own indispensability before God as a witness to the covenantal mission. This will continue to be the burden of every future Israelite, every future member of the Jewish people.

Two distinguished teachers of the Mishnah Rabbi Eliezer and Rabbi Yehoshua will bear in their own difficult historic period the burden of having to inspire their downtrodden people to feel born again to Jewish destiny, for better and for worse. They will debate a theoretically playful question: In which month of the Jewish calendar year was the world created and similarly in which month were the patriarchs born? Rabbi Eliezer points to Tishre as the month of creation and birth. For Rabbi Yehoshua it is Nisan.

Rabbi Moshe Munk notes that Nisan is the month of spring, the month of the renewal of nature, the month of fertility and growth. Tishre is the month of ingathering of the crops, the month of benefiting from the fruits of nature, the month in which the process which began in Nisan now reaches its fulfillment. It may be said that Rabbi Eliezer sees the world-as-created and Abraham (and the Patriarchal period) serving as the *climax* of a chaotic period which has preceded and led up to it. He therefore chooses Tishre as the month of creation and birth. Rabbi Yehoshua sees creation and the coming of the Patriarchs as the *very beginning* of a new era in spiritual and moral development. For Rabbi Yehoshua, therefore, Nisan has to have been the month of creation and birth.

Moses anticipates what Rabbi Eliezer and Rabbi Yehoshua are both expressing: a metaphorical description of a recommended historic appreciation of the creation and birth of covenanted individuals and then a covenanted people. Israel must be made to appreciate this gift of memory — at least incipiently — and then it must nourish it. Moses has announced clearly that the covenant is intended for both "those who are here today and those who are not yet here today." Any generation starts at the intersection of past and future. The present must be a fully conscious and committed present. It can only be so if an appreciation of the past and an awe-filled expectation of a fulfilling future can come together in Israel's collective mind-soul prehension.

This collective mind-soul prehension needs to be sufficiently optimistic about the future in order to be able to continue with maximum energy dedicated to the task. Retaining and sustaining the energy will not be easy. Bialik will describe the poignant effort of the determinately optimistic poet to express the joy of the experience of life in the world. He sends out every morning the innocent dove to seek life and to bring back in the evening fragrant fruits of that life. But alas, when evening comes, the dove has given way to the raven who has spent the day pecking "ravenously" through the offal, the garbage of life.

Moses knows from his own early life about the opposition of blessings and curses, good and evil, life and death in the real world. He orders that the ceremony of the proclamation of the blessings and curses shall be given on the juxtaposed mountains of Gerizim and Ebal. The Israelites will see these two mountains when they move into the heartland of Canaan and come to the city of Shekhem. As they look at Mount Gerizim they will see a mountain that looks green and healthy, a mountain which has the look of blessedness. When they look at Mount Ebal, on the other hand, they will see aridness, a bald mountain, a cursed mountain.

When Israel will enter the Promised Land under Joshua they will conduct the contractual ceremony at these two mountains. Furthermore at the end of Joshua's career he will call his people together again at Shekhem in order to remind them of the terms of the covenant. He will emphasize particularly that they are to fear God and to worship Him *"be-tamim u-be-emet"* ("in sincerity and in truth"). In later Jewish history at the annual *Pesah Seder* Jews all over the world will begin the telling of the story of their people with this same passage from the book of Joshua. In a sense, every year Jews will consider themselves as standing facing the blessing of life represented by Mount Gerizim and the cursed threats of Mount Ebal. And each Jew will ask himself the question: "Am I relating to the covenant that we established with the God of Israel at Mount Sinai in sincerity and in truth?"

The ongoing symbolic meaningfulness of Gerizim and Ebal will plague all of later Jewish history. Assumptions by eager optimists that a messianic era will have arrived following the Emancipation will be shattered by the Shoah. And even after the State of Israel will be born again, it will be stalked by the shadows of Ebal. The naïve optimists will believe that anti-Semitism will now be a disease of the past and that the State of Israel will henceforth have an unquestioned legitimacy in the eyes of all peoples. But war and terror and a Nazi-like recrudescence of hate-filled incitement by a new Islamic-inspired anti-Semitism will continue to mar the blessedness of a Jewish return to the Israelite homeland. There will continue to be a Mount Ebal out there with its curses for evil and death confronting Mount Gerizim and its blessings for good and life. Both mountains in a seemingly eternal counterbalance in the battle for the spirit of Israel — and through Israel humankind!

Standing

"Atem nitzavim hayom..." Moses' call to Israel of all generations to "stand" has a force which goes much beyond taking up a given space or assuming a particular posture, i.e., standing as opposed to sitting. When God is described in Psalm 82 as *"nitzav ba-adat El"* ("standing in the Divine Assembly"), He is not merely there as an inert "presence," but as an "Overwhelming Presence." When Abraham sits in front of his tent and suddenly sees three men *nitzavim* (standing) in front of him, their presence is a portent. They are there for a purpose. They are there to promise the blessing of a son to Abraham and Sarah and at the same time to serve as heralds of the coming destruction of Sodom. Their "standing," in other words, has a significance which is awesome.

The best example of the implications of the word *nitzav* is its appearance in immediate association with the similar word *omed* in I Samuel 19:20. King Saul has sent deputies to arrest David. They arrive at a place where they see a chorus of prophets in an ecstatic attitude with Samuel described as *omed nitzav* among them, i.e., *omed* and *nitzav*. It is clear that Samuel is *omed* — physically standing there with the chorus; but he is also *nitzav* — emphatically *standing* among them so that Saul's deputies are swept up by the scene and the general mood into joining in with the prophets and thereby abandoning their sinister mission.

In short, *nitzavim* means to arouse oneself and one's affiliated group to heightened attention. Not to merely stand, but to stand for, to stand up to — if and when necessary! If in the world which Israel faces there is evil, then Israel's *nitzavim* will have to be a consciously active "presence," a collective emphatic *"hineini"* involving a readiness to resist and to endure to victory. Moses knows that future generations will have to resist in the name of *life* those enemies of Israel who will represent "death-on-earth." He knows that Israel will have to see itself as representing vividly the force for good against this evil. And that in fighting this evil, Israel will at times have to be ruthless and cruel. As has been mentioned earlier, it will need to have internalized the teaching of Koheleth Rabbah 7: "Should one become merciful when he should be cruel, he will eventually become cruel when he should be merciful." In other words, Israel — in the face of utter evil — will not be able to afford itself moralistic rationalizations and vacillations, fudginess and fuzziness when decisiveness is required.

The latter-day Israel will be subject to the ultimate incarnation of evil in the Shoah. It will learn from the fact of the Shoah that every humanly perpetrated evil is not only possible but actual. The covenantal demand will have to be seen, therefore, as a commission to destroy evil, to endure beyond the period of conflict with evil in order to make possible the establishment of God's Kingship on earth. Knowing that the confrontation with evil will require a full commitment of physical and moral energy, later Israel will realize the indispensability of sovereignty in its Promised Land. Moses will have always known and understood God's plan — that the return to the Land was itself a form of redemption. For the biblical injunction to choose life was articulated in a rhetoric which set the survivability of Israel on the Land as the goal. The price for such survivability was detailed commitment to the covenant.

A triad of short prayers within the later High Holy Day worship of the House of Israel will become a fulcrum of liturgical faith and hope for all humankind. In "*u-ve-khein tein pahdekha...*" the Jewish people will be praying that the fear of God will cast its enchanted spell over all creatures. In "*u-ve-khein tein kavod le-amekha*" they will be praying that in so doing Israel's covenantal glory will be recognized. And in "*u-ve-khein tzaddikim yir'u ve-yismahu,*" they will be hoping that the false kingdom of evil will be expunged permanently from the face of the earth.

Moses knows that Israel's confrontation with evil may itself be destructive even when the good which Israel represents emerges victorious. But for Moses there is no alternative but to fight evil; and even should Israel at various junctures in its history suffer defeat at its hands they will dare not lose hope. They will dare not react to the "bad news" of defeat as the messenger to Job reacts. The messenger describes to Job how the latter's servants have been killed, how his flock has been taken away, nay, how his flock has been destroyed, and worse, how Job's children have been slain.

And when the messenger's final statement to Job is "And only I have escaped in order to tell you," Rashi sees in the statement an overeagerness to run away from situations which are fraught with danger and trouble, sorrow and catastrophe. Rashi translates the Hebrew word *melitah* — escape — as *hashmatah* — desertion. There is, in other words, an escape from trouble which Rashi cannot excuse. He therefore describes it as desertion, as abandonment. And Rashi adds that because the servant has been found wanting, as soon as he reports the baleful news to Job, he himself dies. Moses cannot afford for Israel to run away, to desert, to abandon the field in its campaign to have good conquer evil, blessings neuteralizing curses, and life prevailing over death.

Moses knows that the ideal mode of behavior in the face of danger, trouble, sorrow, and catastrophe is to go back spiritually to the metaphorical significance of Moses' initial revelation at the Burning Bush. Why is God seen in the lowly *sneh*, if not to remind the beleaguered, enslaved people that *"imo Anokhi be-tzarah"* ("I am with them in their trouble").

And just as Israel was brought out of the "burning bush" of Egypt, all future generations, no matter what the given "trouble," must persist in hoping. Psalm 27 will be evoked as the inspirational slogan: "Had I not the assurance that I would enjoy the goodness of the Lord in the land of the living..." The verse in the psalm does not have to be concluded, as it is indeed not concluded in the text. For the Psalmist won't entertain an alternative notion. The concluding verse says: *"Kaveh el Adonai, hazak ve-ya'amietz libekha, ve-kaveh el Adonai"* ("Hope in the Lord, be strong and of good courage, and hope in the Lord"), One has to hope in the Lord, and when it is particularly difficult to hope, one girds one's strength more aggressively, one digs deeper inside himself in order to recharge his courage, and then, more affirmatively, one hopes in the Lord.

The Individual Choice to Stand

Moses' urgent Deuteronomic messages will serve as the model for later homiletical exhortation. The Jewish people throughout the ages will look to hear particularly strong words as the old year is waning and the new year beginning. An old tradition will have the sermon followed by the *kaddish d'rabbanan*. It will be held that when the congregation recites the words *"Yehei Shmei Rabbah Mevarakh"* ("May His Great Name Be Blessed") the Lord will immediately tear up any adverse decree which He might have issued regarding the Jewish people. It will also be believed that the very readiness of a congregation to listen to spiritual and moral exhortation is a merit or credit to them. And even if most of the congregation are not ready to listen, as long as one person present listens and takes what he hears "to heart" it is worth giving the sermon as Moses is saying in his own "Days of Awe" homily portion: "See I set before you this day, life and prosperity, death and adversity... choose life!" And "you" as already stressed, is written in the singular!!

Moses must be addressing the Jew in the singular along with his constant exhortations to the collective. The covenant from its beginning has been promulgated with an individual Abraham who will have to pass it on only to that individual who is deemed worthy, to Isaac and not to Ishmael. Similar is the case with Isaac and Rebecca who, unlike Abraham and Sarah, are parents of each of their sons, Jacob and Esau. Nevertheless, Jacob the individual is chosen while Esau the individual is rejected. Only when Jacob has been brought to an understanding of the dimensions of the covenantal struggle which he and his children will have to sustain throughout human history, will the covenant come to envelop more than single individuals, but rather an entire family, tribe, nation. But each collective unit will be dependent upon the individuals making up the unit.

Moses reminds his flock that they dare not ever allow themselves to degenerate to the status of Sodom. The implication is that if there had been even ten individuals worthy of being saved, Abraham's appeal before God would have been successful. For Israel, therefore, multiple *minyanim* ("quorums") of individuals will be the prerequisite for life — life for the nation, and through the nation all the nations of God's universe.

Va-Yelekh וילך

Moses' career and life are coming to an end. Considered by the Rabbis a *tzaddik* ("a righteous one"), he is afforded the reward of the righteous — to live out his full portion of years, 120! As the Talmud puts it, the day of his death will be the same as the day of his birth — a full 120 years. The Torah will comment that when he died "his eyes were undimmed and his vigor unabated." Moreover, he will be described as having recited all the words which he intended to recite to the people *"ad tumam"* ("until the very end"). All the words! All his life!

Yet the *Midrash Tanhuma* has Moses fighting for more life. Early in Deuteronomy, Moses recalls that God has informed him that his days are numbered and that just as Adam had to die so must every man. Moses protests that Adam had to die because he had sinned, whereas he — Moses — had not sinned. He had been God's obedient representative to the people. Unlike Adam who had rebelled at the first opportunity, Moses was unreservedly faithful to God's purposes. Besides, in the special case of Moses couldn't God's attribute of mercy be appealed to? If a special grant of mercy was deserved by anyone, it was certainly Moses! But God rejects Moses' plea. He reminds Moses of two oaths which He, the Almighty, had once taken: one, that He would destroy Israel because of the sin of the spies; and the second, that Moses like all human beings without exception must die. God reminds Moses that He cancelled His first oath regarding the destruction of Israel because of Moses' own plea-bargain at that time. It was Moses himself who stood in the breach and saved Israel — reminding God of His prior oath to Abraham *"Bi nishbati,"* that God's covenant with Israel would be eternal.

But shall God now cancel the second oath as well — the oath that Moses shall not die? God ponders: "Shall oaths be treated so casually?" He then rules: "To cancel both oaths is impossible." He gives Moses the choice: "Either you or Israel!" Moses has emancipated, nurtured, and shepherded this people through a "wilderness" of trial and ordeal. He cannot countenance the thought of Israel disappearing while he would continue living. He has already shown his supreme love for this people when offered the opportunity to become the head of a new people after the episode of the "golden calf." At that time he had protested to God that he preferred being wiped out of the Book of Life rather than seeing his people Israel abandoned. In this case, therefore, Moses cannot but surrender — eloquently: "May Moses die and a thousand like me, but let not one from among Israel die!"

The "Joy" of Covenantal Living

Moses has invested his total self in this people. *"Ad tumam"* ("Until the very end"), his words are intended to criticize them, to warn them, yet at the same time to uplift them and to bless them. As their involved teacher, he fears for them; for he knows their weaknesses, their stubbornness. He has also lived the life of a human being and as such knows of the disappointments — often tragic — of being just a human being, let alone a covenanted one. And therefore can he really condemn the Children of Israel for being no more than human, notwithstanding their privileged status as "chosen."

There is a lengthy discussion in the *Midrash Tanhuma* based on the injunction in Psalm 75:5: *"La-holelim al taholu"* ("Do not be overly cheerful, do not be wantonly cheerful")! And the examples to be learned from are not the wicked who may indeed be overly and wantonly cheerful. The patriarchs are the illustrative models to be studied.

Abraham, the Midrash reminds us, was full of joy. He felt blessed, he had grown in wealth; he had defeated kings in battle; he had been given progeny in his old age. But all his joy was neutralized when he was told to offer up his beloved son. Even though he was excused from slaying Isaac, he nevertheless had to bury Sarah as a result of the test. And finally, as all human beings, he was confronted with old age which was not, could not consist of untrammeled joy — even if Abraham was described in the text as having reached "a good old age." Would it be, could it be an old age with the unlimited prospects and expectations of youth? Where then, the Midrash asks, is the enduring joy in life?

Isaac's life, it is assumed, was full of joy in that he was spared the sword throughout most of his life. The text gives limited space to Isaac in contrast to the other patriarchs. His conflict with the Philistines of Gerar ends with an agreement of sorts. It is recorded that the Gerarites were impressed with Isaac's good fortune and therefore sought peace and reconciliation with him. These Gerarites were prepared to testify that God must truly be with this man Isaac. Yet Isaac's old age was fraught with blindness bringing on consequences which were plagued by filial and fraternal strife. How long-term then was Isaac's joy?

What greater joy could Jacob have had than to be known forever after as Israel, and as Israel, to be called by God "my firstborn son"! Jacob had the privilege of experiencing God's vivid Presence in his vision of the ladder. He had the virtue of escaping Esau and finding relative safety with Laban and raising a family there. He was even able to reconcile with his brother upon his return to Canaan. But the rape of Dinah and the tragic events surrounding the disappearance of Joseph had to have destroyed Jacob's joy, as he would later admit to Pharaoh. Rediscovering his beloved Joseph after many years in Egypt could not have been an unqualified joy — not when Jacob and his entire family were now in *galut*!

Even God Himself — the ultimate model — should have had unlimited joy in His creation. He saw everything that He had made and it was "very good." The Midrash underscores that God could take overwhelming pride in everything He had done — until, that is, the failure of the jewel of His creation Adam to live up to the Creator's expectations. The consequence was that the jewel was turned into dust. And God laments: "I created everything for Adam. Now that he is dead, what joy and satisfaction is left to me?" According to the Midrash, God's "case" is the most tragic of all because it touches the raw nerve of creation itself.

The case of Moses is not included in this particular *midrash*. Yet one dare not argue that because Moses' end showed "no waning of insight and physical vigor," he experienced more "joy" than the Patriarchs. It is clear that once Moses was charged with his life's mission at the Burning Bush, his life would be filled with frustration and dread.

Moses and the Patriarchs have learned that life is determined by *din*, and *din* does not mean exclusively "justice." It also means "decree" — and decrees may bring sorrow as well as joy. The blessing to be recited when hearing bad news will be "*Barukh Dayan Emet*" ("Praised be the True Judge"). Yet the truth is too often burdensome. Apparently there is meant to be joy in life and those who will have been blessed with joy ought not to feel guilty over their good fortune. But the human being must also be aware and must have the strength to face life not only when it is "velvet" but when it is "raw."

In Moses' case, there had been three periods of joy — or, more accurately, two periods of tranquility and one event so colossal as to bring forth from him and his people a song of victory. His youth as a prince in Pharaoh's palace in Egypt, we may assume, had been a time of growth filled with the pleasures of pomp and royal comfort. Nevertheless, some force within him compelled him to witness with horror and then with empathy the plight and suffering of the Hebrew slaves. His escape to Midian would lead to a marriage and a situation of tranquility as a shepherd. But again, something would pull him towards an alternative way of life — a life of rare joy and much anguish.

It is inappropriate to juxtapose against Moses' anguish an *ecstasy* in his achievement. There has been nobility in his leadership. His stewardship of his people and his advocacy of his people before God have been exemplary. But if there is a dimension of joy in the expression of ecstasy, then Moses has not been an ecstatic leader, steward, or advocate. More importantly and more critically, he has been the paradigmatic redeemer of the Jewish people. But he has never cast a messianic shadow. He is the deliverer from bondage, the lawgiver to a newly born people that is charged with building a covenanted society. He will be forever known and esteemed as *the* teacher of Israel — Moshe Rabbenu. As Moshe Rabbenu he will be seen as the incomparable model for directing human beings to a way of life which is spiritually and morally achievable in a world of tension, conflict, and marred visions. But Moshe Rabbenu in his oft repeated exhortation *"hazak ve-ematz"* ("be strong and of good courage") is not promising *joy* as such. More critically, he is encouraging hope and ultimate peace-of-soul!

The Loneliness of Leadership

Now as Moses stands on the threshold of death, he is restive, even irascible in his concern for his people's future. It is not a reflection of an egotistical "après-moi la deluge" attitude. But Moses, who has seen God face to-face, as it were, and has experienced fully the relentless demands of day to-day covenanted living made upon a people which is "only" human, is genuinely fearful of the future. "For I know your rebellion and your stiff neck; behold, while I am yet alive with you this day, you have been rebellious against the Lord, and how much more after my death."

Moses is described as walking singularly alone, utterly alone, towards his retirement and disappearance from the scene. He will be replaced by Joshua who will be fully aware of the responsibility of leading this rebellious, stiff-necked people. But what has deepened Moses' apprehension is his overly extended solitude. He has been in a process of *va-yelekh* — walking alone as leader — for the full extent of his stewardship. He has never been in a position of an Abraham who ultimately walks together with his son and successor Isaac (*"va-yelkhu shneihem yahdav"*).

It is true that Abraham began by walking alone before God. But Abraham felt secure even in his loneliness because he was *tamim* (wholehearted). He had had to be in order to break away from family, birthplace, and land. But the weight of loneliness began to affect even Abraham when he stood alone before God arguing on behalf of Sodom and failing. Moreover, what shocked Abraham in his failure to save Sodom was his realization that there were pockets of evil in this world of individuals, peoples, and nations that were unredeemable. That Abraham had had his name changed with the added Hebrew letter *he* to represent his destiny as a father of *hamon goyim* (a multitude of nations) was of little comfort when here — with Sodom and the other four "nations" of the plain being destroyed — he was being deprived of some of what had been promised to him. And his sense of loneliness in the face of an increasingly complex destiny was becoming more and more discomforting.

If Abraham needed to find a remedy for his loneliness, someone to "walk with" towards his destiny, there followed the ordered expulsion of his first son Ishmael. He learned thereby a tragic lesson concerning the frustrating human endeavor to establish constructive relationships, to find the appropriate someone to "walk with." Ishmael would not be the one to walk with Abraham. He would certainly not be in a position of *"va-yelkhu shneihem yahdav"* with Isaac. He would threaten the entire covenant. Ishmael did not represent the evil incarnate Sodom that would have to be destroyed. But he did represent a clear and present danger to Isaac and therefore would have to be separated from him.

Abraham was being taught the necessity of solitude. But did this mean that this new faith was so severe that Abraham the individual "knight" of that faith would be compelled to walk utterly alone with God? Could it be that the reason that Abraham responded positively to God's test of the *akeidah* was because with his first *"hineini"* he had lost all awareness that there was a significant *human other* in his life — his other son Isaac? And that the real test which God was placing before Abraham was to see whether Abraham — after the necessary destruction of Sodom and equally necessary expulsion of Ishmael — could still be ready to try walking together into the future with someone — with an Isaac.

At first Abraham hadn't permitted the call of Isaac, *"avi"* ("my father"), to pierce his solitude. But Abraham's total commitment to the test as he perceived it would be brought short abruptly. For Abraham's faith was in danger of degenerating into a spiritual narcissism lethal to the possibilities of a future human covenant of any kind. The emphatic call from Heaven not to slay Isaac, the other human being, was a call of *"va-yelkhu shneihem yahdav."*

It will be the same call which Ruth will answer much later as she — unlike "Orpah" (a name derived from the Hebrew word *oref* meaning "back of the neck") — will not turn her neck away from her currently relevant "other" — Naomi. She will plead with Naomi not to reject her offer of *"va-yelkhu shneihem yaldav."* In the case of Naomi and Ruth the exercise will involve a re-commitment to the covenant by returning to the Land which was earlier rejected in the *yeridah* of Elimelekh. The outsider Ruth in this case will intrude herself, but in so doing will energize the formerly embittered "pleasant one" Naomi to look forward to rebuilding, replanting, and giving birth to a future messianic hope for Israel and for all of humankind.

The *"va-yelkhu shneihem yahdav"* of Abraham/Isaac and Naomi/Ruth are life-giving for them as individuals trying to shoulder the burden respectively of a new covenant (Abraham and Isaac) and a renewal of that covenant (Naomi and Ruth).

Moses has been in an entirely different situation. From the beginning, his burden has been to shepherd an entire people into the undertaking of covenantal living. Moses' Children of Israel, like Ruth, have not been born into the covenant. They have — at Sinai — signed on to the covenant whether out of choice or partial coercion. That they have often behaved like Orpah does not gainsay their having made of their Sinai experience their defining moment as a people. Could Moses consider himself as "walking with them"? Is *leading* them *walking* with them?

Who better than Moses has been witness to their rebelliousness? Because of it, along with their stiff-neckedness, Moses has had to walk alone. And his alonenesss — and loneliness — has been increasingly more difficult to sustain. He has been *with* them but not *of* them. He has walked ahead of them — at times too far ahead of them.

Joshua will be different. As a leader he will walk with them. He will be with them and of them. At times his faith will be less firm than that of his master. He will panic after the defeat at Ai, for example; but he will serve as the appropriate leader for his time — as others will do later.

Moses himself will encourage Joshua to be with the people — certainly with the elders in bringing the people into the Promised Land. Rashi notes the discrepancy between two instructions given to Joshua. Moses sees Joshua as *going along with* the people whereas God has Joshua *bringing* in the people himself: "Moses said to Joshua," according to Rashi, "The elders of the generation will be with you; act entirely in accordance with their understanding and their counsel." "But The Holy One Blessed Be He said to Joshua," according to Rashi, "Bring them in even against their will, for everything depends upon you. If need be, take a rod and smite their heads, for one leader should there be for a generation, not more."

Moses' instruction to Joshua has as much psychological projection as practical political insight. Most of Moses' career has been the antithesis of what he is suggesting to Joshua. Moses has stood alone — before God, before Pharaoh, before the people. When he returned to Egypt from Midian in order to begin his great mission before Pharaoh, the Israelite elders began by accompanying him but ended by abandoning him. Aaron was at his side for the most part; but the debacle of the "golden calf" episode proved Aaron to be less than totally reliable. When out of genuine distress, Moses pleaded with God for help in the Wilderness he was granted his wish. But one suspects that the seventy elders never served as more than an adjunct to the necessary judicial and legislative processes which the Wilderness situation required. They never shared fully Moses' lonely ultimate responsibility.

Because he knows the cost of loneliness, Moses' best wishes for his long-time disciple are to share the burden. But in God's eyes, Moses ought to know better. True, judicial and legislative processes may be — have to be — shared. But executive decisions and subsequent actions based on these decisions can only be made by leadership, i.e., ultimately and essentially one leader who represents in himself the collective will of the people. In the case of Israel, of course, the leader is representing as well the will of God, which may at times be at odds with the will of the people. God's edicts cannot be allowed to be neutralized by a backsliding majority of the people. It will be Joshua's task — and Moses knows this better than anyone — to lead Israel, even and especially when they do not wish it. And so Moses encourages Joshua with "*hazak ve-ematz*" — *hazak*, to be strong and solidly convinced of his own right and capacity to lead, and *ve'ematz* to have the tactical ingenuity and dogged determination to carry the people with him.

Moses' Fears

The Torah's ideal vision for leadership appears to be the single prophetic servant of God who leads and instructs the people. But the people's role can never be underestimated. There are too many aspects to building a covenantal community that require the full creative commitments of individual members of society — men, women, children, all classes. The instruction to gather all the people at least once every seven years in order to "hear" the Torah underscores the democratic underpinning of the envisioned community. True, it will be the king or high priest of that time, i.e., the ruler, the respected ruler, who will be doing the public reading. But it will nevertheless be a joint recognition of the entire community's attachment to common purpose.

When the Talmud wishes to emphasize by illustration the importance of seeking originality or novelty in learning, it refers to Rabbi Elazar ben Azariah's teaching of the *hakhel* (assemble) passage which Moses is citing especially at the end of his career. The Talmud asks for Rabbi Elazar ben Azariah's exposition of the specific reference: "Assemble the people, the men and the women and the little ones." Rabbi Elazar responds: "If the men come to learn, the women come to at least hear; and why must the little ones come? In order to grant reward to those who bring them." But surely the reward is not merely a ritualistic bonding of the children to a public reading of that which is incomprehensible to them! It is an essential bonding, a pre-literate allegiance to community which will become articulate later but which at the virtual beginning of consciousness is to stamp every member of the people as participant.

The necessity to bind the people individually and collectively to the covenant is intended to prevent them from ever deteriorating into the situation which Moses has feared from the time he delivered the short *tokhehah* (rebuke) in Leviticus. Should Israel ever divorce itself from the covenant, they will suffer an ignominious scattering *ke-aleh nidaf* (like a driven leaf). Indeed, when Israel does find itself exiled to the four winds, it will include in its prayers a pathetic allusion to the image: "Bring healing to one who is as helpless as a wind-driven leaf. Have compassion upon us who are merely dust and ashes. Cast our sins away in pity for us your handiwork. For see, there is no man to intercede for us." Alas, God will have warned them of the possibility that He will hide His face from them, even if they found an intercessor.

The image of the driven leaf will come to represent the condition of the Jews in exile who are wafted here and there and everywhere as they will move through history. The direful *tokhehah* as God's admonition of His people — the short one in Leviticus and now the long one in Deuteronomy — will predict as a law of nature that should the Jewish people not be faithful to its mandate, it will be driven all over the world to face horrific persecution. The surviving remnant, remaining in an exile of total vulnerability, will be so afraid that even the sound of a driven leaf will terrify them into falling. Indeed "*ve-naflu ve-ein rodef*" ("they will fall even when none pursue them"). And by a not unusual association, the Jews in the exile will habituate themselves to referring to themselves as a "driven leaf."

That Jews-in-exile will conclude their plea to God with a clear allusion to Moses is ironic: "See (O Lord), there is no man to intercede for us." At the very beginning of Moses' career as potential redeemer of an enslaved people, he had gone out of his sheltered palace in order to share the plight of this people. He had been witness to the reality in totalitarian Egypt that "there is no man to intercede." There was no Egyptian defender of the disenfranchised. There was no Hebrew slave self-possessed enough to rise up against the oppressor. The irony within the prayer-in-exile will be that God is implored to intercede when the original inspiration for the prayer was an act of human initiative and daring.

And so Moses is deeply concerned about the future of his people. As noted earlier, it isn't a personal matter of "après-moi la deluge." There has been sufficient evidence heretofore that the Children of Israel may forfeit their opportunities. The "driven leaf" metaphor joined to the image of

Israelites "falling when none pursue them" conjures up the picture of "falling leaves" in which the great danger of dropping out of a noble enterprise dominates. Will the average Israelite or later Jew be able to sustain the effort to build a covenanted society? Will later generations in exile be stubborn enough to remain Jews in the face of oppression, assimilation, expulsion, Shoah? Will post-emancipation Zionists have the long-term strength and will to further the upbuilding of a new State of Israel?

The *mitzvah* of *hakhel* will only be a ceremonial reminder every seven years of what is to be a necessary ongoing educational program. The collective and individual memories of the Children of Israel will dare not risk forgetting the saga of their coming into being as a people. Moses is afraid that as new generations of Jews will be further and further removed from the memory of Egypt and Sinai there will be a double-edged atrophy setting in: passive loss of memory and active de-mythologization of the past. The first will be natural and inevitable unless a conscious programmatic effort will be made to remember everything from the past. Ritual observance of prayer and Holy Days will have to integrate the key seminal moments of the past into a permanent agenda of remembering with accompanying appreciation and awe.

The second more insidious danger to memory — demythologization of the past — will characterize a post-Spinoza critical sensibility. In the name of "historic truth," transcendent dimensions of aspects of the saga which make the Torah a sacred scripture for the House of Israel will be stripped away by "enlightened scholars." It may be that "new-historians" in any age looking to claim greater truthfulness for their revisionist theories of "what really happened" will fail to dislodge the deeper religious truths from the collective consciousness of the people. But Moses fears that the cumulative impact of a certain kind of unengaged "knowledge" will undermine covenantal faith and loyalty.

Moses to the End

It is this fear which will inspire in Moses the compulsion to leave with his people a concluding song and a concluding blessing for each of the tribes. The song will not only allude to their own past. It will anticipate the future history of a people that has not entered its Promised Land as yet. But it will bespeak a vision of future history which Moses wishes to impose upon them even at this juncture. He will be forecasting situations in which Israel will feel itself "a driven leaf," helpless before the stratagems of evil nations. He will even envision an eclipse of God's Presence as Israel will suffer through its epochs of disarray and suffering.

But Moses will also anticipate the future blessings. They are perceived by him to be as certain as the very grounding of his entire long life of service to this God of Israel on behalf of the Children of Israel. The future may see individual Jews who, like falling leaves, will abandon their story, their ongoing historic destiny. But there will remain the collective, the people, those steadfast people who — despite the threats associated with their being who they are — will maintain a commitment to their covenanted destiny, and will by their very endurance represent a blessedness.

Moses walks alone to join his ancestors. He leaves his people a message, a text, a life. As the ages will now define him, i.e., Moshe Rabbenu — Moses our teacher, he will indeed have left the message of the text which will now not be left to exist alone. But like the covenanted life which Moses has lived, the people will now assume a life, a Torah-endowed life, *"ad tumam"* ("to the end").

Ha'azinu האזינו

In defining the word "coda" the average dictionary limits itself to a general description of the conclusion of a musical or poetic composition in which the ending is to be energetic, perhaps accelerated, in order to bring final exuberant satisfaction. True enough! But the genius of a punctuating coda is that it brings to a brilliant summarizing statement all that has come before. It compresses all the themes or the major theme — or it puts forward a new statement which nevertheless comes naturally as a consequence of all the material which has come before. And all of this rushes to a thunderous climax! The key then to a successful coda for Moses' Deuteronomic speeches is its compression leading to the climax. For in its review of what has come before it contains a latent energy ready to explode into a thousand prophetic flashes of covenantal memory and prescience.

For all his early limitations as an "orator" who was heavy-of-speech, Moses knows very well the principles of a good coda. He has made of the Book of Deuteronomy itself a long summary-coda of the first four books of the Torah. And now he compresses further into this electrifying "Song of Moses" all that he has wanted to say and in fact has said. But it will be ever so much more powerful for its concise self-contained focus. The *Sifre* will describe the coda as follows: "Great is the Song, as it embraces the present, the past and the future, this life and the hereafter." The Song, in short, "says it all!"

The Netziv of Volozhin quotes the talmudic tractate *Nedarim* which attributes the term "song" to the whole Torah. "But surely the whole Torah was not written in the form of poetry. Nevertheless, we must conclude that it possesses the nature and essential character of poetry." The entire Torah, in other words, is to be seen as a compressed corpus of images, promptings, stories, ideas, instructions, laws, admonitions, and promised blessings, all meant to affirm the identity and destiny of this emerging new nation.

Song of the Covenant

The covenantal structure of the coda is true to the covenantal nature of the whole Torah relationship. After God has despaired of his original Garden of Eden model for creation, He has remodeled His vision for humankind by focusing on a single family-tribe-nation which will henceforth serve as His cohort in building, mending, and rebuilding His world. From the vantage-point of the "Song" — whether it be this portion of *Ha'azinu* as the coda or it be the whole Torah — there are, of course, other peoples in the world besides Israel. But the Torah of Israel is a record of the covenant which has been sealed between the *God of Israel* and the *People of Israel*. Even when there is rancor between the principal "signatories" of the covenant, i.e., between the God of Israel and the People of Israel, there is no thought of other nations playing a central role in the scenario of the story of Israel.

Other nations may serve as instruments of God's wrath visited upon Israel — but that's all. The Song will attest: "I thought I would make an end of them (Israel), I would make their memory cease from among men. Were it not that I dreaded the enemy's provocation, lest Israel's adversaries should misjudge and say, 'Our own hand has prevailed; none of this was wrought by the Lord!'" There is no way the Lord God of Israel will permit such arrogance. The nations are spectators of the principal drama taking place at the center-stage of human history as interpreted by the Torah. They may be brought up on stage as occasional props or background "choruses" to serve or to witness the action. They may be brought to the foreground — principally when they are presented as idolatrous models deserving contempt, "no-nations" like Sodom and Gemorrah. Therefore, they dare not arrogate to themselves any other autonomous role.

From Israel's point of view, there is a cathartic satisfaction in believing that — for better and for worse — Israel is center-stage. To even suffer punishment at the hands of God is to maintain one's relevancy in God's scheme; how much more so when Israel feels rewarded by God's largesse.

This is the position taken by Rabbi Nehemiah in his debate with Rabbi Yehudah recorded in the *Sifre*. On the verses "for they are a nation void of counsel" and "for their vine is of the vine of Sodom," Rabbi Nehemiah has the Babylonians in mind whereas Rabbi Yehudah sees them as referring to Israel. The grounds of the debate are reminiscent of the ambiguous phrase in the

Deuteronomic description of the sins of Amalek. Following upon the review of Amalek's treachery in attacking the weak and the weary, the phrase *"ve-lo yerei Elohim"* ("they didn't fear God") appears. Who didn't fear God? Amalek? Or was it Israel who was therefore punished with God's rod of anger Amalek!

The logic of the entire section would argue strongly for Rabbi Nehemiah's position. The obtuseness of the enemies of Israel in assuming that their success had anything to do with their worthiness! Would that they understood God's ways, the Song cries out. On the other hand, there is enough prior support in the Book of Deuteronomy and the entire Torah for Rabbi Yehudah's claim. Would that Israel had the wisdom to understand that the covenant demanded faithfulness, that when Israel declines to exercise its elementary wisdom it defies its covenantal partner and is only begging for punishment.

God through his prophetic poet Moses laments Israel's lack of gratitude: "a generation crooked and perverse...." Hadn't God created and fashioned Israel? Hadn't He set it firmly on earth as His chosen one, blessed it with the richness and abundance of fruit and oil and honey and milk and wheat and wine? But Israel became fat and thick and gross and went after "no-gods." How could Israel forget! The punishment *had* to come and *would* come with fiery bolts of destruction for young and old.

But then no matter how much punishment Israel would suffer, it would endure and would receive ultimate compassion from its loving covenantal partner. The enemy nations, on the other hand, in defying God, the God of Israel, would not be so fortunate. They would be destroyed by a God who would exact his vengeance upon the idolatrous pretenders who thought that they were acting independently of Him and His will. The nations would have been guilty of "original sin," the sin of the Serpent in the Garden who insisted on his own independence and thereby condemned himself to being brought down literally to eat the dust.

As tough-minded as the Song is to Israel, there is, in other words, an undergirding of love that pervades this coda to the Book of Deuteronomy. "He found him in a desert land and in the waste, a howling wilderness; He compassed him about, He cared for him, He guarded him as the apple of His eye. As an eagle that stirreth up her nest, hovereth over her young, spreadeth abroad her wings, taketh them, beareth them on her pinions..."

Abrabanel has raised the question as to why God doesn't refer nostalgically to His discovery of Israel in Egypt prior to the Wilderness experience, to which Rashi responds: "God found them loyal in the desert land in that they accepted His law, kingdom and yoke, which Ishmael and Esau did not do." Rashi is noting and crediting Israel with their acceptance of the Torah — the detailed embodiment of the covenant — which took place not in Egypt but in the Wilderness. In Egypt, the Children of Israel had been mired in a slavery that had deprived them of the capacity to exercise any free will. It was only at Sinai, where the reciprocal aspects of the entire redemptive enterprise became vivid, that Israel had the opportunity to show those qualities which would make it worthy of God's ongoing eagle-like concern.

There is an additional feature characterizing the unique sojourn in the Wilderness. God and Israel have for the most part been alone in the Wilderness. Not only has Israel been described by Balaam as *"am le-vadad yishkon"* ("a nation dwelling alone"), but in Moses' song, God Himself is *badad* (alone) as he betroths Israel to Him. Indeed the Wilderness has been the place and opportunity for genuine betrothal, for "getting acquainted," for cultivating a special intimacy. In the future prophecy of a Jeremiah, it will be the betrothal period in the Wilderness that will be recalled with nostalgic yearning by God. Despite the many disappointments experienced by God and Moses in the Wilderness, Jeremiah will romanticize that time and that place as the time and place of purity and innocence.

A Life of Blessings and Curses

To reminisce about a past which one sees as a place of purity and innocence is to program into one's collective personality as a people an ideational strategy for coping with a world which not only seems but is in actuality often hostile. God Himself can be construed as having created a world which from the point of view of human sensibilities is the antithesis of purity and innocence. Following the twentieth century, can anyone describe the world as pure and innocent? One comment of one survivor, Aharon Appelfeld, will suffice: "After the experience of the Shoah, there are no surprises. The thought of harmony is ludicrous. Reality is a cluster of clichés. The psychological explanation of human evil is flaky thin. Social remedies are a mockery of the downtrodden. In other words, all aesthetic, moral, and religious conventions have expired. And any reliance on them is anachronistic."

God Himself in His attribute of justice seems so often cruel and uncaring. The Zohar will dare to ask God — as He sits on His seat of judgment — to remember Isaac's ram's horn in order for Him to embody fully the attribute of mercy. When Israel will blow the *shofar*, the Zohar promises, "Happy will they be because they know how to remove the potentially severe judgment in favor of the merciful exercise of that judgment."

Moses as Israel's pre-eminent teacher knows of the complexities, ambiguities, and general vicissitudes of life. He yearns to share with his people whatever intuitive understanding he has always had about life along with the unparalleled practical experience he has had as a prince in Egypt, as a shepherd in Midian, and as a spiritual and political leader of Israel in the Wilderness. He knows what the later Jewish liturgy will underscore with incomparable poignancy in the High Holy Day *"U-Netaneh Tokef"* prayer. Each Jew as an individual will reflect on the questions: "How many will pass on, how many will be created, who will live, who will die, who will be at rest, who will wander, who will be tranquil, who will be tormented, who will be brought low, and who will be exalted." All these alternatives lying in wait for the simple Israelite Jew! But then, the recommended path as the antidote to despair will be paved with values taught by the Rabbis but intuited from Moses throughout his ministry: "Repentance, prayer, and righteousness will avert the severity of the decree."

No sooner will the liturgy of *"U-Netaneh Tokef"* give a redemptive direction, however, when a more depressing litany of certainties — not possibilities — is announced. Beginning with the sorrowful awareness that the human being's beginning is dust as his end is dust, he is analogous to a "broken clay vessel, withering grass, a fading flower, a passing shadow, a fugitive cloud, a fleeting breeze, scattered dust, a dream that vanishes." What follows differs from the short-term redemptive verse arguing for repentance, prayer, and righteousness that in any case cannot save the human being from inevitable dust. Only God Himself the Creator and Revealer and Redeemer can validate the human being for eternity, when the latter acknowledges the Former as "You who are the truly living and eternally existing King!"

In what way is this latter statement of faith relevant to the total picture that Moses wishes to leave to his people? And how will such a statement of faith verify the Zohar's proud boast that Israel can influence God's attribute of justice to give way before His attribute of mercy? Moses is intent upon leaving

Israel with an earnest view of life — not somber, but hardly lighthearted. The later Midrash will recommend a vision of *olam ha-ba* (the future world) as an ultimate comfort to a people which will have suffered from the curses and evils of *olam ha-zeh* (this world). But the prophet Isaiah, taking his cue from Moses, will envision a time *in this world* when Israel will only have blessings and the good. Moreover, such a future will see all the nations recognizing that Israel is a seed truly blessed by God.

In the meantime, and Moses has been preaching the message throughout Deuteronomy, there is an active volatile mixture of blessings and curses characterizing *olam ha-zeh*. And the Children of Israel as a nation and as individuals will have to realize that life-on-earth testifies to an up-side and down-side to all human experience, predictable and unpredictable.

Moses has been instructing his people "halakhically" and "aggadically" on the up-side of being a creature, the glory of being a covenanted human being. At the same time, he has from the beginnings of Eden underscored the down-side of creatureliness wedded to hubris aiming to stifle moral conscience and spiritual humility. The Torah has already anticipated what hubris can evoke and then actualize to the shock, chagrin, and dread of humanity-in-general and Israel in particular. Cultures of hate and oppression and genocide will walk the earth, forces blaspheming God and humanity-as-created-by-God in one. And Israel will find itself too often at the epicenter of sociomoral earthquakes ignited by the Serpent and its historic incarnations.

Israel collectively and individually will learn new suffering along with achievement, frustration along with success, sorrow mixing itself with joy. It will experience wars without end even after expecting that atonement will have long been achieved. In short, Israel will endure the active exercise of God's attribute of "*din*-justice" not only with understanding, but often, limited by its human creatureliness, *without* understanding.

Israel will learn to conclude that there is a *din* in life, but, as noted earlier, that *din* doesn't always mean justice. It means "decree." When a Jew will recite a blessing upon hearing bad news, he will be saying: "Praised be God whose decrees are true, real, ever present." There are, of course, blessings in life as well. But again, the blessings will always come out of shadowy backgrounds with hints, omens, threats, reminders of the possibilities and realities of danger.

How then are the Children of Israel as individuals and as members of a collective to cope with life when it is bleak and exposed? With the disappointments, the frustrations, the pain, the anxieties, the agonies of life lived in an unredeemed world? Again, by adhering to the profound truth inherent in the conclusion of the liturgical excerpt quoted above: "*Ve-Ata Hu Melekh El Hai Ve-Kayam*" ("You are the true eternally living King") who has created us and revealed Your pattern of human legislation to us, and who redeems us by means of an eternal covenant.

Torah, *Teshuvah*, and the Land

Each member of the Children of Israel will learn to cope with the decrees he faces in life in unique ways. Each will bear testimony to the possibilities of faith in a covenant, no matter what the severities of the decrees one has experienced. In this sense, these will be the Jews who will have in their pattern of living and coping solved the Rosenzweig enigma. For Rosenzweig will have argued that those Jews who constantly pray for the coming of the Messiah and anticipate his appearance at every turn are the more *faithful* Jews. But those Jews, Rosenzweig will continue, who reject out of an eternal skepticism every would-be Messiah are the *stronger* Jews. The integration of both characteristics in one's person, and by extension, in the people as a whole would be vital to any hope of survival — in a pre-Messianic world.

In order to cultivate such an integration of characteristics Israel will need to look even more creatively at Torah and its curative potential for treating faithlessness and moral weakness. Moses, therefore, looks to Israel to be in a permanent state of *teshuvah*, that is, in a constantly attentive "response-mode." Israel is to be at all times in a state of existential readiness for responsive and responsible activity. Soloveitchik will interpret the Rambam on *teshuvah*: "The essence of this *mitzvah* is not in deeds and activities; it is rather in an ongoing process, throughout one's life. The process begins with regret, with feelings of guilt, with Man's own recognition that purpose has been taken from his life, with feelings of solitude, of error, of shock by the sense of vacuum, a sense of bankruptcy, of frustration and failure. And the path of this process is a long one, long to the goal which is the actual *teshuvah* itself." In other words, *teshuvah* is not connected to one decisive act; it rather grows slowly and methodically until it brings Man to a metamorphosis in his personhood.

Moses knows what Koheleth will state later that there is no human being on earth, no matter how righteous, who doesn't sin. Israel, therefore, will be prone to sinning, to rebelling against their destiny. And Moses in these final teachings is determined to transmit to their collective conscience the idea of eternal process in achieving *teshuvah*. The Torah will have to be the marker bringing Israel into the process. Moses will try to impress upon his people the difficulties of learning, teaching, and applying Torah. He has described before — according to the Midrash — his own travails while on Mount Sinai: "You don't know how much I suffered, how much I labored, how I worried myself during those forty days and nights with God. I came among the angels, among the living beings, among the fiery creatures, anyone of whom could have burned up the world and all its inhabitants. I gave my flesh and blood to the effort. Just as I learned it in suffering so shall you; or, just as you will learn it in suffering so shall you teach it in suffering."

Moses anticipates what Israel will have to endure in surviving with understanding and with unbroken faith in the covenant. How will Israel continue to "believe" when God is hidden? How will God continue to believe when He knows that there have been times when He has characterized the Children of Israel as *"lo emun bam"* ("they are not trustworthy in their belief")? It will be a difficult, complex struggle to build, to resurrect faith and its actualization in Torah in each new age, for each new situation. Yet authentic ongoing *teshuvah* will require precisely such constant and concerted innovation. Israel will be compelled to recognize that within the Torah there are values whose legislative concretizations may be obsolete and therefore change is necessary. But the change will require imagination, a sense of communal and national responsibility — and courage! Such was Moses' struggle on Mount Sinai and throughout his life. Such will be Israel's.

Will Israel be wise enough to know the parameters of the struggle? Moses laments: *"Yisrael lo yada, ami lo hitbonan"* ("Israel doesn't know, my people does not discern"). The Midrash will add that Israel doesn't know — doesn't really understand — what has transpired in its past; and that Israel will disenfranchise itself from discerning the future. What is it that Israel doesn't know? What is it that Israel will not discern? Israel will easily wax fat and thick spiritually, morally, and socially. It will kick itself loose of its covenantal obligations as if the Exodus and Sinai had never happened.

It will be infinitely more problematic to reconstruct for the future because the challenges of the future cannot be entirely anticipated. But Israel will need to realize that it has initiated and embarked upon a spiritual, moral, social, cultural, political, and intellectual revolution. Change will characterize this revolution as it will have — by definition — characterized every revolution in the history of humankind. It may be that in general, the human psyche does everything it can to avoid coping with change. Institutions, establishments become so convinced of their immutable correctness that they often deliberately deceive themselves. A challenge may be coming their way, and yet they are so frozen in their organizational pattern that they are unable to come to grips with it.

Israel will not have the luxury of stasis. It will be entering a land by conquest and settlement. It will need to measure every step it takes with wisdom, cleverness, and a sense of transcendent purpose. It will need to dedicate itself and rededicate itself to an appreciation of the indispensability of the foundation stone of the covenant.

The *Midrash Tanhuma* will summarize:

> The Land of Israel is beloved since the Holy One Blessed be He chose it. You find that when God created the world He distributed the various lands to the heavenly ministers and chose the Land of Israel for Himself. How do we know this? Moshe said; when the Supreme One apportioned to the nations their inheritance, when He separated the children of Man, He set the boundaries of the people according to the number of the Children of Israel. He also chose the people of Israel as His portion, as it is written, "for the Lord's portion is His people; Ya'akov is the lot of His inheritance." Said the Holy One Blessed be He: Let Israel who became My portion, inherit the Land which became My portion.

Its Torah, therefore, will have to be tuned in to the future; and the future will be one of living-in-the-world. It will be a humane Torah — for everyone; where justice and mercy and redemptive beauty and sanctity will be applied to all, to the Israelite and to the stranger who chooses to sojourn among them.

Preparing for the Final Blessing

It is this message which at the end of his life and at the prophetic peak of his mission Moses insists on imparting to his people. The song, Moses' song, serves as a *shofar* call urging the people to attend with particular vigilance. Like the *shofar* call, it pleads with God Himself to attend to the situation of His people Israel. Will Israel have the faith to believe that it is truly *"helek* Adonai *amo,"* the *Lord's* portion? The Zohar will take this phrase from Moses' song, will focus on the Name of God in the phrase — the Tetragrammaton — and then quote for itself the verse from earlier in Deuteronomy (4:4) *"Ve-atem ha-devekim be-*Adonai" ("And you will cleave to *Adonai"*). Israel, in other words, will be bound to God's Presence. It will thereby be in a position to remind God as He sits on His throne of judgment on Rosh Hashanah that the *shofar* is in memory of the ram of Isaac and that the *shofar* pleads for mercy to be shown to the descendants of Isaac, *God's portion Israel!*

Moses has already spoken in Deuteronomy of the struggle of humanity to choose between curses and blessings, evil and good, death and life. Dickens will say it for the Gentiles: "It was the best of times; it was the worst of times." Rabbi Abraham Yitzhak Hacohen Kook will say it for the Jews: "Our generation is a wonderful generation, an astonishing one. It is made up of opposites. Darkness and light are mixed up in interlocking confusion. It is entirely depraved; it is entirely full of majesty. It is entirely guilty; it is entirely innocent." Long before Dickens and Kook, the Rambam will have seen the world as evenly balanced, left to Man, left to Israel, to tilt the balance in the direction of the blessing and the good — to life.

Moses' song of Torah is his legacy to his people and through his people to the world. It is a legacy meant to unscramble the mixture of good and evil in order to assure the coming of the blessing. Indeed, Moses' very last words will begin with *"ve-zot* ha'berakha" ("this is the *blessing*").

Ve-Zot ha-Berakhah וזאת הברכה

The rabbinic sensibility will echo Moses' last words *"ve-zot ha-berakhah"* by considering in depth the subject of *berakhot* (blessings) in the first tractate of the Talmud. From that tractate a particularly exotic image is presented in the comment of Rabbi Abin the son of Ada in the name of Rabbi Isaac:

> How do we know that the Holy One, blessed be He, puts on *tefillin*? For it is said: "The Lord has sworn by His right hand, and by the arm of His strength." "By His right hand": this is the Torah; for it is said "At His right hand was a fiery law unto them." "And by the arm of His strength": this is the *tefillin*; as it is said: "The Lord will give strength unto His people." And how do you know that the *tefillin* are a strength to Israel? For it is written: "And all the peoples of the earth shall see that the name of the Lord is called upon you, and they shall be afraid of you..."

Objectively speaking, later history will not necessarily bear out this talmudic "prediction." The purpose of the talmudic "prediction," however, is not to forecast empirical certainties as much as it is to maintain Jewish morale in the face of national trial and peril.

The Rabbis continue in this mode:

> What is written in the *tefillin* of the Lord of the Universe? "And who is like Your people Israel, a nation unique in the earth." Does, then the Holy One, blessed be He, sing the praises of Israel? Yes, for it is written: "You have affirmed the Lord this day....and the Lord has affirmed you this day." The Holy One, blessed be He, said to Israel:

> "You have made Me a unique entity in the world, and I shall make you a unique entity in the world." "You have made Me a unique entity in the world by proclaiming within your *tefillin* '*Shema Yisrael Adonai Elohenu Adonai Ehad*' ('Hear O Israel, the Lord our God, the Lord is One'). Therefore I shall make you a unique entity in the world by proclaiming within My *tefillin* '*Umi ke-amkha Yisrael goy ehad ba-aretz*' ('And who is like your people Israel a nation one in the earth')."

Israel, Torah, and the Land

It is clear, as it has been from the beginning, that God's Torah is meant for Israel. It might have been intended initially to be shared with all the nations; but another well-known *midrash* records:

> When the Omnipotent revealed Himself in giving the Torah to Israel, He not only revealed Himself to Israel but to all the nations. First He repaired to the sons of Esau and said to them, "Will you accept the Torah?" They answered him: "What is written therein?" Said He to them: "you shall not kill." Whereupon they answered: "Lord of the universe, the basic commitment of our ancestor was to be a slayer, as it is written: 'And the hands are the hands of Esau'; and regarding that, his father promised him: 'By thc sword you shall live.'" He repaired to the sons of Ammon and Moab and said to them: "Will you accept the Torah?"
>
> They replied: "What is written therein?" Said He to them: "You shall not commit adultery." Whereupon they exclaimed before Him: "Lord of the universe, our whole essence is committed to immorality, as it is written: 'And the two daughters of Lot conceived from their father.'" The Almighty then went and found the sons of Ishmael and said unto them, "Will you accept the Torah?" Said they to him: "What is written therein?" Said He to them: "You shall not steal." Whereupon they exclaimed before Him: "Lord of the universe, the basic commitment of our father lay in brigandage, as it is written: 'And he will be a wild man.'" There was no nation He did not go to and speak to and knock at their door to see whether they would be willing to accept the Torah. You might have thought that as soon as they

> actually heard the Torah that they would have accepted it? It is therefore stated: "They hear Your words but they will not do them" (Ezek. 33:31). They could not even abide by the Seven Noahide Laws, i.e., the seven laws of nature that according to Judaism consist of the prohibition of murder, idolatry, incest, blasphemy, robbery, meat cut from a living creature, and a prescription for establishing courts of justice.

Such *midrashim* reflect an animus which is aimed at idolatries of all kinds. It comes out of a defensive reflex against the anti-Semitism of the nations who are thereby considered hopelessly immoral. Even the Seven Noahide Laws without which no human society is possible are seen to be irrelevant to the visionless enemies of Israel. But there is a message in the Midrash directed at Israel as well. The basic moral values represented in the Ten Commandments and the Seven Noahide Laws will not be concretized easily, even in the emerging Israelite-Jewish society. Moses' constant scolding, reminding the Children of Israel of their stiff-neckedness underscores in uncompromising tones the difficulty of living out these values in community. Why? Because of basic human nature that is caught in the thicket of an ongoing struggle between blessings and curses, good and evil, life and death.

At the same time, Moses' determination, desperate at times, won't permit him to surrender his confidence that the eternal will of Israel is dedicated to living out in community these values — the values of life and good and blessings. The necessary determination and commitment will be burnt into Jewish souls by the *esh-dat* of the Torah — the "burning bush" of the Torah. It will be bound upon their Jewish arms and Jewish heads by the *tefillin* which they will wear. Here and there these Children of Israel will fall short, at times even greatly — enough to be punished with exile. But they will never be totally rejected because they will never totally reject God and His Torah. Moses' teaching legacy to his people is embodied in the verse "*Torah tzivah lanu Moshe, morashah kehilat Ya'akov*" ("Moses has commanded us the Torah, an inheritance to the community of Jacob-Israel").

Issachar Shlomo Teichtal of the martyrs of the Shoah will underscore the word *morashah* as "inheritance," in that the Torah has not just been earned by Moses' generation and the generations immediately following. The Torah has been transmitted after interpretive legislation to all succeeding generations. It shall always be thus. Finding himself trapped by the Shoah, Rabbi Teichtal will call out to his people to recognize that this inherited Torah is further legitimated by its relation to Eretz Yisrael:

> Torah and Eretz Yisrael were said in a single utterance. They are two inseparable companions. Concerning the Torah it says: "Moses has commanded us a Torah, an *inheritance* to the community of Jacob!" Concerning Eretz Yisrael it says: "And I will give it to you as an *inheritance*!" Thus Torah and Eretz Yisrael are set apart and designated by the same expression, "*morashah*" as a "*gezerah shavah,*" (a hermeneutical principle in which a word common to two different passages is seen to connect the two passages analogously) demonstrating that for us they are equal and inseparable.

Only within the community of Jacob-Israel on its Land can the fullness of Torah be practiced. Only in community in general can covenantal human living take place. For members of the House of Israel, life is never lived merely for one's singular self. Life must be dedicated to the organic community into which one has been born or which one has chosen to join.

Liturgically speaking the House of Israel will "canonize" the bedrock indispensability of community as the laboratory of Torah living. For example, the Talmud records the teaching of Rabbi Yehudah who said:

> A person should never petition God for his personal needs during the first three blessings of the *Amidah* (*the* Prayer), nor during the last three blessings of the *Amidah*, but he may during the middle blessings. For Rabbi Haninah has said that the first blessings are to be like those of a servant who is addressing words of praise to his master; in the middle blessings the worshiper resembles a servant who is asking for largesse, for special gifts and favors from his master; the final three blessings are like those of a servant who has received benefit from his master and is now taking his leave.

The question is compounded in that Rabbi Yehudah and Rabbi Haninah are talking of the weekday *Amidah* where there is room *prescribed* for *bakashot* (petitions). But on Shabbat and Holidays, *bakashot* are prohibited. And yet on the *Yamim Nora'im*, the Days of Awe, we have in fact petitions "intruding" within the first and last series of blessings. They are "remember us for life, inscribe us for a good life, may we be remembered in the Book of Life...."

Why this liturgical "violation"? The answer is twofold: The *Tosafot* commentary on the Talmud summarizes the geonic view: "It may be that one shouldn't ask to have his needs fulfilled in the first three and last three blessings. But that only regards his *personal* needs. Petitioning to have the *community's* needs fulfilled is entirely different — and permitted." The thirteenth-century sage Menahem Meiri will add a second dimension to the issue. These "intrusive" petitions don't ask for material goods but for life itself. As such, it must be permitted! And the full life to be experienced by the individual can only be experienced in community.

Continuity of Blessings

Moses is to bless the people — all of the people as divided into the tribal groupings. Moses, like Jacob, seeks to leave an ethical will to the tribes who are the expansion of the families of the sons blessed by Jacob. The Midrash finds a continuity between Jacob's blessings and those of Moses:

> And this — *ve-zot* — is that which their father spoke unto them (Gen. 49:28) — it is not stated "their father Jacob" but just "their father." This is in order to point to another man of similar stature who is destined to bless you and where I, Jacob, have left off he shall begin, as it is stated "And this — *ve-zot* — is that which he spoke." As soon as Moses stood forth he opened with the phrase "and this" — "*ve-zot*" — as it is stated "And this is the blessing." And with what did Moses conclude? "Happy — *ashrei* — art thou, O Israel" (Deut. 33:29). David as well, when he began to sing praises to the Almighty, began where Moses left off: "Happy — *ashrei* — is the man..." (Psalms 1:1).

It is this continuity that is to contribute to the salvational power of the covenant. In a world of hellish uncertainty, a world in which God Himself may occasionally or often be in eclipse, the continuity of generations is itself a guarantor of the happiness that is apposite to the serenity of knowing that what one is committed to is right. The continuity of blessing begins with the individual patriarch Jacob-Israel blessing his individual children. But this blessing of individuals must be connected to the later emerging House of

Israel. Jacob's blessing is to anticipate the larger blessing of Moses which is to acknowledge how "happy" the House of Israel is to be once it believes it is "redeemed by God." In turn, such collective happiness will revert back to the happiness of the individual as represented by David's Psalm 1, provided the individual keeps himself removed from the wicked, from the sinners and scoffers.

The blessings of Moses are redolent with joy in anticipation of material well being for Joseph — favored as always — but not only for Joseph. The tribes of Gad and Dan, Naftali, and Asher are all promised the fruits of *osher* ("happiness") as all of Israel will dwell securely in its Land with abundant grain and wine. Even the heavens will bestow their dew generously. Later tradition will interpret Moses' words as anticipating the specific future of tribes like Benjamin as host to the Temple, Issachar and Zebulun as partners in learning and commerce, and Judah — especially Judah — as the resource for help in days of trouble. The Midrash will cite Judah as the first, always the first. It was the example of Nahshon ben Aminadav of the tribe of Judah showing the way at the Sea of Reeds and being among the princes in offering sacrifices of dedication. It will be the initiative of the tribe of Judah "going up" first to fight the Canaanites in the settling of the Promised Land. It will be Judah showing leadership from the days of Joseph through the blessings of Jacob-Israel the father and, as the Rabbis will interpret it, through the last words of Moses.

Not that there aren't differences between the blessings of Jacob and Moses, most notably those extended to the tribe of Levi! In Jacob's "blessing," all that the patriarch can bring himself to say alludes to their conspiracy with Simon against Shekhem in defense of their sister Dinah's honor. It was this episode that had embarrassed and angered Jacob at the time, even though Simon and Levi had a succinct and powerful counterargument: "Shall our sister be treated as a harlot!" Nevertheless, Jacob issued to Levi — and Simon — the following "blessing": "Simon and Levi are brethren; weapons of violence their kinship. Let my soul not come into their council; unto their assembly let my glory not be united; for in their anger they slew men, and in their self-will they houghed oxen. Cursed be their anger, for it was fierce, and their wrath for it was cruel; I will divide them in Jacob and scatter them in Israel."

Moses' blessing will reflect Jacob's "division and scattering" — but ironically. For Simon isn't mentioned at all. Later Jewish history will see the tribe of Simon absorbed into the tribe of Judah. But Levi will be "divided and scattered" not because of their anger, wrath, and violence, but for constructive reasons. It was the tribe of Levi which had aligned itself with Moses in confronting the rebellion surrounding the "Golden Calf." When Moses needed loyalty in the face of wholesale communal chaos, it was Levi who joined with him in the fight to preserve the covenant. It is they therefore who in Moses' blessing will protect the Urim and Thumim. It is they "who shall teach Jacob these ordinances, and Israel the law." In other words, they will be "scattered" throughout Israel in order to teach the Torah!

And what is to be the long-term purpose of teaching Israel the Torah? It is to recognize that God is the Creator, Revealer, and the Redeemer of Israel and through Israel the world of humankind. Through the Torah Moses has been reviewing for Israel God's history as legislator beginning with Adam and Eve in which these archetypal human figures struggled to develop their basic human self-awareness and awareness of the other. In the struggle they failed. They hid from themselves, they blamed each other. The Torah then indicates that the pristine human condition degenerated further to a situation of fraternal murder and societal license to wholesale wickedness. This could only bring on apocalyptic destruction.

When humankind was given another chance, the building of the Tower of Babel would reflect a new totalitarian challenge to God and to Man. Meanwhile, the Torah took up the saga of Abraham, Isaac, and Jacob and their families. They emerged and struggled through a variety of adventures underscoring function and dysfunction in family life, all in preparation for assuming a long-term covenantal relationship with God, the Creator, Revealer, and Redeemer. Before taking up this responsibility, this family growing into a nation became enslaved to a genocidal totalitarian regime. Eventually Israel was taken out of slavery, would reach the Promised Land, and would succeed in building a commonwealth. The commonwealth would endure through the vicissitudes of material expansion and contraction, social welfare and degeneration, spiritual celebration and moral decay. The end of the commonwealth would signal the first national exile — all predicted not only by the later prophets but by Moses himself.

Is this all that Moses wishes to say — that the history of Israel confirms that God's *middat ha-din* ("attribute of justice") hangs over humankind's head and especially Israel's head like a cleaver?

Or is there along with God's condemning *middat ha-din* an enduring manifestation of God's *middat ha-rahamim* ("attribute of mercy")? True, Eden had been lost; but there had been the exchange of the utopian boredom of Eden for the real world of vigorous growth. Seth and the opportunity for creative rebuilding had succeeded the destructiveness of Cain and Abel. Along with the wickedness of the Flood generation there had been the righteous exception of Noah. Through the vehicle of family growth, the patriarchs Abraham, Isaac, and Jacob had inspired the building of a nation — and it would be a unique covenanted nation. The totalitarian enslavement of Egypt had brought on the Exodus to freedom and the giving of the Torah to the covenanted Israel. And even Israel's spiritual and sociomoral failure after building its commonwealth would bring in its wake the first *Shivat Tziyon*, the first return to Zion.

What then does Moses hope to teach Israel in this chronicle of negative and positive events? That individual Israelite Jews and Israel as a collective representing humanity are intended to live according to legislated standards by which whatever is done will be judged. There will be descent and ascent of Man as there will be the working of God's attributes of justice and mercy in reaction to Man's descent and ascent. There is no escape within the human condition from this dialectic. There is no escape unless one seeks to abort authentic human living!

Covenantal Direction through Liturgy

In Israel's future, as the Jewish people struggle to formulate and live out a theology which is mature in its understanding of reality, they will create a classical liturgy for the Day of Judgment which will speak to the human predicament of escape, descent, and ascent. In the *Malkhuyot* section of the *Mussaf* prayer on Rosh Hashanah all the verses will be dedicated to proclaiming God as ruler of the universe — a universe which is meant to have a moral order and will therefore invite moral judgment. Man, the Jew, Israel, will from time to time rebel against God's moral order. Idolatry reflecting the perversion of moral standards will be the principal sin of Man through the ages. Man is to learn — and he won't — that neither he nor any other human being is King. Not in one's private domain nor in one's public domain! The task as Moses has understood it long before is to mend the world towards recognizing the kingship of the Almighty.

The sin of idolatry will project itself in its starkest form when the future emancipated Western World will countenance nothing less than a Shoah intended to totally liquidate God's "firstborn," the Children of Israel. And the Shoah will come on the heels of a philosophical evolution to an alleged ideal of human rationality that will nevertheless be overwhelmed by a moral nihilism orchestrated in the most dehumanizing terms by the most culturally advanced nation on earth. The multifaceted irony of an efflorescence of technological achievement being hospitable to the demonically fixated organizational power of Nazism will sear the collective conscience of "civilized" humankind. Will Man — following the Shoah — absorb finally the truth that he is not and cannot be King; that he is at best a *servant* to an ultimate moral judge? That moral judge is the King of Kings, the Creator of the universe — and the God of Israel!

Because of the horrendous technological potential of idolatry in an amoral world, the *Zikhronot* section of the Rosh Hashanah liturgy will dedicate all its verses to acknowledging God as a mysterious force operating throughout the history of nations, hovering over the interaction among nations in peace and in war with a special role reserved for Israel, God's tortured but "chosen" people. The history of the world will need to be perceived as reflecting a legislative plan with judgments accruing. It will need to be understood that somehow there is a "providence" that plays a mysterious role in determining national destinies. Nations as aggregates of individuals who have free will will also contribute to the determination of their own destinies. But Moses' Torah will have been proclaiming that God, i.e., "Providence," must not be perceived as deistically unengaged. Albeit mysteriously, God remembers everything, records everything, and judges everything.

The "end of history" of which post-modernists will speak will not have arrived — especially when neither horrific wars on the one hand nor unimaginable scientific achievements on the other hand will have changed Man's idolatrous "nature." Moses' prophetic prescience will have long intuited that as long as nations will continue striving to fulfill their "manifest destinies," there will be conflict. The conflicts may be hot or cold. But they will preclude the possibility of individuals escaping in wholesale fashion to their own private hiding places. It may be possible for the few to succeed in building for themselves solipsistic "sanctuaries" — but not for too many and not for too long. Israel will thus never be relieved of its responsibility to serve as the model foundation stone for the upbuilding of a purposeful humanity. And Moses' Torah will have to be there to provide the pattern for building that foundation.

Therefore, the *Shofarot* section of the Rosh Hashanah liturgy will focus on God as Revealer and Redeemer. For God and His Torah will have to be seen as giving meaning to life beyond creatureliness and creaturely comfort. Escape to oneself will never become an acceptable norm for Israel. Moses had learned this lesson in Midian long before when he was called from his contented solitude to national service. In going out — again — to his brothers, Moses had found his true calling. In participating in their emancipation, calling it forth and effecting it along with God, he would merit the singular opportunity of participating in the revealing of God's Torah to His people — the covenanted Israel. Following Moshe Rabbenu each member of the future Children of Israel would similarly be charged with carrying on the revealed mission of the covenant.

The Mission

In reviewing his own life as he prepares for his own death, Moses sees it all as an opportunity that he was granted to bestow upon his people a blessing — *the* blessing. The blessing for his people is the unique blessing of insight into their *destiny as a covenanted partner with God in mending the world*. Moses-in-himself as Israel-in-itself have committed themselves to the values of Torah. Again, the liturgy of the Days of Awe will lend focus to the efforts of the Israelite Jew as an individual, and to the whole House of Israel as well, to understand and to appreciate these values. "*Teshuvah, Tefillah*, and *Tzedakkah*" are meant indeed to avert the severity of life's decrees, or at least to mitigate them — whatever these decrees may be.

Teshuvah will mean not merely repentance from wrongdoing or returning to a pristine purer time in an idealized past. Its ongoing meaning will focus on *responding*, responding to life totally, authentically in full actualization of one's covenanted self. Israel's commitment to Torah would be ideally exemplified in the martyred life of Akiva. In the story of Akiva's explanation to

Pappus of what living for Torah means, there would be captured the essence of Israel's authentic self. The Torah, as Akiva would explain it, is what would stamp Israel as Israel. For Israel ever to abandon Torah would be to deny itself and to deny thereby its own role in mending the world. A Pappus would be envious of Akiva because, unlike Pappus, Akiva knew who he was and why he was put on earth. He was a covenanted servant of God, of God who wants a world of blessings and goodness and life! And Akiva would know that he has the resources to respond to the vicissitudes, the dangers, the upheavals in life, because he would be secure in his own identity, in his own personhood, in his conviction of attachment to peoplehood.

Tefillah will mean a conscious standing before God and thereby a constant attempt to validate oneself and one's people for high purpose. Standing before God spiritually, morally, socially, politically, will lift Israel and all humanity above God's other non-human creatures. Once the people will allow themselves to stand before God, secure in the knowledge that they have been committed to the "mending process," they will grant themselves the right to question Him, to complain to Him, to argue with Him, as a Hannah or as a Levi Yitzhak of Berditchev. Hannah will represent the individual Jew questioning God's power and justice in having created her but limiting her creative capacity to serve Him — in her case by leaving her barren. Levi Yitzhak will speak for the Jewish people challenging God to explain how the only nation loyal to Him, Israel, is nevertheless tormented! Is it not enough! Yet, in both cases, as with Rabbi Akiva, God's decree will be accepted — but only because Akiva and Hannah and Levi Yitzhak will be certain as to who they are and what the ultimate Godly largesse must be — ultimate redemption somehow!

Tzedakkah will mean a vision of justice and the application of justice to the world of human beings. Israel's struggle as a nation encompassing each Israelite's individual struggle as a Jew will be a struggle to actualize in the world a dream of universal blessing, love, and justice that will be intended to bring life to all. It will be a battle against evil and any human pretence at assuming God's power. Any ideology — even and especially a religious one — which would pretend to assume God's power will be by definition false. An individual or an institution which would seek absolute control over human beings would be insisting in vain on its own omniscience and omnipotence. It would know that the more omniscience and omnipotence it insisted upon, the lonelier it would become and the more false-hearted it would become. Like Pharaoh, trapped in his refusal to accept the fact of his ignorance and impotence, the latter-day individual or institution would be doomed to perdition. An Akiva would never hope nor seek to rule the world. At the same time he would not permit the ruling pretenders, in his day the Romans, to rule him and his people. He would want nothing from the Romans except to be left to his own sense-of-presence in his own Land with his own way of looking at the world. And he would know that *tzedakkah*, true justice, insisted on the inevitable coming of a pluralistic world serving only the true King!

Moses' blessing which will produce Jews like an Akiva is a blessing offered by an acknowledged servant of God and servant of his people, God's covenanted people. As the crowning concerns of his blessing, he hopes for two things: (1) the welfare and safety of his people; and (2) the reward of serving as a witness to God's Unique Oneness.

Regarding Moses' first wish, Sforno studies the conclusion of the blessing: "And Israel shall dwell in safety, the fountain of Jacob alone, in a land of corn and wine; yea, his heavens shall drop down dew." And the commentator adds:

> O Yeshurun (Israel), be different from other kingdoms, on two counts: First, that no other nations should enter your land to fight, and that no man should covet your land for fear of you, as it was all the days of Joshua and the elders, as if the land was locked with bars of iron and brass. Second, that your kingdom should not rise and fall (fluctuating like other kingdoms) "and as thy days," referring to the days of youth and the beginning of your entry into the Holy Land, "so shall thy strength be," referring to the days of your old age when you beget children and children's children and become old in the Land. This blessing of mine shall come to pass, since there is none like unto God who is your Provider, "who rideth upon the heaven as thy help" — since the God who is your Helper "rideth upon the heaven and is supreme."

Moses' second and final wish is to have his monotheistic faith truly affirmed: "I ask of You one favor before I die, that as I enter the Hereafter, all the gates of Heaven and the deep be opened for all to see that there is none beside You. Whence this? For it is said: 'Know this day and lay it to your heart, that the

Lord he is God...there is none else' (Deuteronomy 4:39). Whereupon God replied: You declare: 'There is none else (*od*).' I too say: 'And no one else (*od*) has arisen in Israel like Moses...'" (Deuteronomy 34:10).

In finding and affirming God's uniqueness, Moses the human being has found and affirmed his own. His supreme teaching to his people the House of Israel will be to impress upon them similarly *their* uniqueness as a "*goy ehad ba-aretz*," a uniquely gifted people in its own Land. Happy indeed is such a people, Israel, a people redeemed by its God — the God of Israel who is the Lord of the Universe.

POSTLUDE

A Jew alive at the beginning of this new century and new millennium looks at the world — at his Jewish world. He can summarize his impressions cynically or hopefully: either with the bon mot "plus ca change, plus la meme chose" ("the more things change, the more they remain the same") — anti-Semitism, assimilation, apathy; or, he can invoke the Psalmist's ecstatic *"zeh ha-yom asa Adonai, nagillah ve-nismeha vo"* ("this is the day that God has made; let us exult and rejoice on it"). We have an Israel! And the Israel we have offers us as a people another chance — another chance to work at fulfilling a covenant we agreed to eons ago. Do we have a Torah adequate to the task and are *we* adequate to the task? Our answers to these questions should be in the affirmative. The long exile culminating in the Shoah insists that our answers be in the affirmative. But are we certain?

Hayyim Nahman Bialik, the national poet of the Jewish people and the Zionist awakening, wrote: "After I am dead / say this at my funeral: / There was a man who exists no more. / That man died before his time, / And his life's song was broken off halfway. / He had one more poem, / And that poem has been lost / Forever." Bialik felt this personally, like any artist, like any scientist, like any businessman who hopes for "one more season." But as the national poet of the Jewish people a hundred years ago, his words continue to apply to the state of Judaism, Jewishness, and the Jewish people today: that the Torah has one more message that may die before it is ever heard.

Fifty years ago and fifty years after Bialik, Akiva Ernst Simon said it another way in recognizing that the old organic Jewish Torah community has been shattered; that the post-emancipated Jewish individual is going to have to forge a new way with Torah, a new way to get to Torah in order to wed

Torah to life. He talked about a new Israeli, a new Jew looking for values based on tradition but not ready to mimic blindly the old: "These Jews are in the situation of Abraham our father but *after* the giving of the Torah." Simon was arguing that for many Jews the Torah is known; yet for too many other Jews it is not known, it has been lost. Therefore, the Torah "has ceased to be given; instead it has turned into a task.... Just as Abraham (who did not have the Torah) chose God, we must choose Him and His Torah, entirely or partly, all according to our personal capacities."

Simon saw this new Torah — a creative interpretation of the original — as having something meaningful to say about everything in life: family, society, work, love, affairs-of-state, and culture. Simon was hoping for a new "Abraham" model who would free himself from his pagan civilization in order to walk a new road, to rediscover the new/old God of ethical monotheism and to be ready to commit to a new/old covenant with this God. Each of us as individuals would aim to be like Abraham; but unlike Abraham, we were fortunate to have a rich Torah civilization which has existed for 3,500 years; and we could build on that civilization. It would not be a simple task because there had been an Emancipation and many of us didn't know whether we wanted Torah any longer, and if we did want it — and one hoped that we did — we weren't sure which Torah it would be.

There has been a cultural battle going on in the Jewish world for the last two to three hundred years. Ahad Ha'am in an essay which he called "Torah in the Heart," written ten years before Bialik's poem, criticized the phrase which ostensibly described the Jewish people as the "people of the book": He said: "a 'people of the book,' unlike a normal people, is a slave to the book. It has surrendered its whole soul to the written word. The book ceases to be what it should be, a source of ever-new inspiration and moral strength; on the contrary, its function in life is to weaken and finally to crush all spontaneity of action and emotion, till men become wholly dependent on the written word and incapable of responding to any stimulus in nature or in human life without its permission and approval."

Ahad Ha'am along with other cultural Zionists wanted a Torah of life. Instead they saw stagnation: "The people stagnates because heart and mind do not react directly and immediately to external events; the book stagnates because, as a result of this absence of direct reaction, heart and mind do not rise in revolt against the written word where it has ceased to be in harmony with current needs."

In other words, a Torah of life would give Torah to life and a new life to Torah. And Israel was to be the fountainhead of such a new Torah of life. One hundred years after Ahad Ha'am and Bialik and fifty years after Simon, has this happened? Sociologists and educationists claim that there is more "Torah" being studied in Israel and Diaspora today, more traditional Torah material being published today than ever before in history. There appears to be a resurrection of the old yeshiva-world of the past.

In his essay "Rupture and Reconstruction" Hayyim Soloveitchik describes the phenomenon with mixed feelings. He argues that this resurrection is no longer a reflection of the old "mimetic" community developing Jewish identity, i.e., learning by imitating family and community. We have instead new Jews needing to look elsewhere for this elusive identity: "There is a shift of authority to texts and their enshrinement as the sole source of authenticity." Are we then back to being the "people of the book"? Is this irremediably bad? Perhaps not! And yet is it a Torah of Life? Certainly not for those who are alienated totally from any aspect of the Torah heritage! But even for "Torah" Jews — however one defines the word "Torah" — is the idea of Torah-as-covenant motivating and mobilizing the contemporary Jewish people to a full Zionist *tikkun* in the State of Israel and in the Diaspora?

Bialik and Ahad Ha'am's deep concern along with Simon's vision and Soloveitchik's reflection have a relevancy anticipated seventeen hundred years ago in the Talmud. In *Eruvin* (55a) Rava and Rabbi Yohanan each comment on the phrase *"Lo ba-shamayim hi"* ("It is not in Heaven") referring to the Torah: "Raba expounded 'it is not in heaven' to mean that it is not to be found with him who, because he possesses some knowledge of it, towers in his pride as high as the heavens.... Rabbi Yohanan expounded 'it is not in heaven' to mean that it is not to be found among the arrogant...merchants or dealers."

I suggest the following homiletical interpretation: Rava was worried about traditional Torah learning in that he was concerned that achievement in traditional Torah learning would create an arrogance based on alleged "heavenly" insight. Torah would then be in danger of serving as a force that would excuse non-participation in the earthly world. Applied to our contemporary situation, such arrogance would extort for an education that would border on "art-for-art's-sake," being parasitic on the backs of the secular community. Rabbi Yohanan, on the other hand, was worried about those who would be thrilled to leave Torah "in heaven" so that their lust for earthiness would not have to be concerned with it. In contemporary terms, these would be the vulgarly smug who in their anti-spiritual posture would delight in a this-worldly conceit — all the while refusing to admit to their ignorance of the potential vitality of Torah if properly respected and applied.

To both groups, therefore, it was and is necessary to assert in the strongest terms: *"Lo ba-shamayim hi"* ("It is not in Heaven")! The question is whether or not there will be enough lovers and students of Torah to respond to the concerns of both Rava and Rabbi Yohanan — and Bialik, Ahad Ha'am, Simon, and Soloveitchik.

In short, are we ready to assume the proud burden of the covenant?

Is each of us sufficiently sensitive to the questions that are being asked of us since the Emancipation, since the Shoah, since the establishment of the State of Israel? Are we truly *engaged* with the Torah if and when we study it, if and when we listen to it? There is a teaching: *"Im ani kan, ha-kol kan, ve-im eineni kan, mi kan"* ("If I am here, then all is here, but if I am not here, then who is here")? With this statement Hillel the Elder epitomizes the joyousness of *Sukkot* in the Holy Temple. Rashi sees the "I" who is "here" as representing God's conditional Presence. Without God's Presence in the Temple what other possible source of joy can matter? The *Tosafot* identifies the "I" with Israel itself. The Temple on *Sukkot* without the people "being here" cannot be a tabernacle; it would be a desolate sarcophagus.

The Temple is no longer "here" or "there" or anywhere-on-earth. Hillel's *"im ani kan"* ("if I am here") should be looked upon as referring to each of us. Where may "I" — today's Jew living in Israel or in the Diaspora — share the joy of God's Presence or at least the semblance of it? The answer is in the *mikdash me'at* — the miniature movable sanctuary which is the historic synagogue. Assuming that I am "there" in the synagogue, wholly "there," given over intensively to "being there" — particularly alert to the Torah being read aloud, calling to me, invoking *my* presence, *my* absorbed attention, then everything *is* there! For if I am not vehemently "there" — attending, hearing, listening, then what does it matter whether or not others are there or whether or not God is there...

Is God there? Or is it the unrealizable void into which I project an imagined Creator, Revealer, Redeemer? The Bible says that "no man shall look upon Me and live." Bialik has said that the human creature cannot avoid looking into the void; but in concealing his dismay and dread of the void he structures words, concepts, ideas by which to protect himself from his sense of creatureliness, his felt vulnerability, his aloneness. In being a creature, in feeling myself a mere creature, a mere human being, I hope to experience God's Presence in the synagogue when I find there a *minyan* ("a quorum"), a group of ten other Jewish human beings. But can there be a more ironic derivation for this *minyan* than the Wilderness *edah* — the *minyan* of ten who couldn't decide whether to "go up" to the Promised Land in the Presence of God or to "go down" in retreat to the *meitzarim* ("the straits") of Mitzrayim, Egyptian bondage!

Nevertheless, I join myself to this *minyan*, this cluster of other Jewish human beings in the synagogue who have wagered their "Jewishness" on "being here." They are present — even if as an *edah* they struggle today to reveal to themselves whether or not they are prepared to risk "going up." In the *minyan* of the synagogue I feel God's Presence as the Torah is being read and as I am being reminded again and again of the demands of the covenant. And in my prayers with that *minyan* I feel within me an anticipation that there is a post-Wilderness generation which *may* "go up," which *will* "go up." What will inspire them to go up if not the words of the Torah, engaging them, pulling them into maximal attention to the call of the moment, this moment.

A Zionist song sung during the Second World War yearned for "*shalom*, *berakhah*, and Torah" ("peace, blessings, and a renewed Torah"). To actualize this yearning in today's Israel as well as in the Zionist Diaspora has been a glorious but excruciatingly painful effort. Yet, for committed Zionist Jews all three goals must be pursued today, thankfully, vigorously, and joyfully. And the prayer must continue...the prayer which yearns for peace, for the blessings of spiritual and sociomoral fulfillment and for the renewed illumination of Torah. The prayer must continue for the benefit of our people wherever they find themselves, as they strive to reaffirm their commitment to Israel, to the Torah, and to the Land.

www.ingramcontent.com/pod-product-compliance
Lightning Source LLC
LaVergne TN
LVHW081250100826
845148LV00009B/1182